Lecture Notes in Computer Science 10364

Commenced Publication in 1973
Founding and Former Series Editors:
Gerhard Goos, Juris Hartmanis, and Jan van Leeuwen

More information about this series at http://www.springer.com/series/7408

Stefania Costantini · Enrico Franconi
William Van Woensel · Roman Kontchakov
Fariba Sadri · Dumitru Roman (Eds.)

Rules and Reasoning

International Joint Conference, RuleML+RR 2017
London, UK, July 12–15, 2017
Proceedings

 Springer

Editors

Stefania Costantini
University of L'Aquila
L'Aquila
Italy

Roman Kontchakov
Birkbeck, University of London
London
UK

Enrico Franconi
Free University of Bozen-Bolzano
Bolzano
Italy

Fariba Sadri
Imperial College London
London
UK

William Van Woensel
Dalhousie University
Halifax, NS
Canada

Dumitru Roman
SINTEF/University of Oslo
Oslo
Norway

ISSN 0302-9743   ISSN 1611-3349   (electronic)
Lecture Notes in Computer Science
ISBN 978-3-319-61251-5   ISBN 978-3-319-61252-2   (eBook)
DOI 10.1007/978-3-319-61252-2

Library of Congress Control Number: 2017943851

LNCS Sublibrary: SL2 – Programming and Software Engineering

Printed on acid-free paper

This Springer imprint is published by Springer Nature
The registered company is Springer International Publishing AG
The registered company address is: Gewerbestrasse 11, 6330 Cham, Switzerland

Preface

The International Joint Conference on Rules and Reasoning (RuleML+RR 2017) is the first conference of a new series of conferences, joining the efforts of two existing conference series, namely, RuleML (International Web Rule Symposium) and RR (Web Reasoning and Rule Systems). The ten conferences of the RR series have been a forum for discussion and dissemination of new results on all topics concerning Web reasoning and rule systems, with an emphasis on rule-based approaches and languages. The RuleML series of conferences has been held since 2002, being devoted to disseminating research, applications, languages, and standards for rule technologies, with attention to both theoretical and practical developments, to challenging new ideas, and industrial applications. Both series of conferences aimed at building bridges between academia and industry in the field of rules and their applications. Therefore, RuleML+RR is expected to become a leading conference for all subjects concerning theoretical advances, novel technologies, and innovative applications about knowledge representation and reasoning with rules.

This new joint conference provides a valuable forum for stimulating cooperation and cross-fertilization between the many different communities focused on the research, development, and applications of rule-based systems. It provides the possibility to present and discuss applications of rules and reasoning in academia, industry, engineering, business, finance, health care, and other application areas.

RuleML+RR 2017 was hosted by Birkbeck, University of London, UK. The conference was co-located with the following events: the 13th Reasoning Web Summer School, which is a high-level educational initiative devoted to reasoning techniques related to the Semantic Web, Linked Data and Knowledge Graph application scenarios; DecisionCAMP, a renowned event in the field of Business Rules and Decision Management Technology; and BICOD, the 31st British International Conference on Databases, a venue for research papers in the broad area of data management. BICOD and RuleML+RR shared a session that included a keynote talk and presentations of two research papers. The conference also included a Doctoral Consortium, an initiative to attract and promote student research in rules and reasoning, with the opportunity for students to present and discuss their ideas and benefit from close contact with leading experts in the field. RuleML+RR 2017 also included: an Industry Track as a forum for all sectors of industry and business (as well as public sectors) to present, discuss, and propose existing or potential rule-based applications; and the 11th International Rule Challenge, prividing competition among work in progress and new visionary ideas concerning innovative rule-oriented applications, aimed at both research and industry.

The technical program of RuleML+RR 2017 included the presentation of 14 research papers, carefully selected by the Program Committee among 38 high-quality submissions, with an acceptance rate of 37%. The review process included the possibility for authors to respond to initial reviews. These responses were thoroughly discussed by the reviewers and the Program Committee chairs before finalizing the reviews. All submissions received four reviews, with only one exception receiving three. Presentations of accepted papers were divided into sessions on Rules and Databases, Rules and Description Logics, Applications of Rules, and Rules and Logic Programming. The best Doctoral Consortium paper was presented as a full paper, accompanied by short presentations of the other five accepted Doctoral Consortium papers.

RuleML+RR 2017 offered successful Invited and Keynote Talks and Tutorials by experts in the field, as listed here.

The following keynote talks were given:

- Robert A. Kowalski, Imperial College London, presenting "Logic and AI – The Last 50 Years" (Social Dinner talk)
- Elena Baralis, Politecnico di Torino, presenting "Opening the Black Box: Deriving Rules from Data" (BICOD joint talk)
- Jordi Cabot, Internet Interdisciplinary Institute, Open University of Catalonia, Barcelona, presenting "The Secret Life of Rules in Software Engineering"
- Stephen Muggleton, Imperial College London, presenting "Meta-Interpretive Learning: Achievements and Challenges"

An industry talk was also given (joint with DecisionCAMP):

- Jean-Francois Puget, IBM, presenting "Business Analytics and Decision Optimization"

Four tutorials:

- "Decision Modeling with DMN and OpenRules" by Jacob Feldman (Open Rules, Inc.)
- "How to do it with LPS (Logic-Based Production System)" by Robert Kowalski, Fariba Sadri (Imperial College London), and Miguel Calejo (InterProlog Consulting)
- "Logic-Based Rule Learning for the Web of Data" by Francesca A. Lisi (University of Bari, Italy)
- "Rulelog: Highly Expressive Semantic Rules with Scalable Deep Reasoning" by Benjamin Grosof (Accenture), Michael Kifer, and Paul Fodor (Stony Brook University, NY)

The Chairs sincerely thank the Invited and Keynote Speakers for accepting to contribute to the event, and all those who submitted tutorial proposals and presented tutorials for their excellent proposals. The chairs wish to recognize the hard work of the Program Committee members and of the additional reviewers for the revision and careful selection of submitted papers. The reviews were balanced, provided constructive criticisms and useful comments and suggestions for improving the papers, and resulted in high-quality publications. The chairs are also grateful to all authors for their interest in the conference and for the efforts devoted to preparing their submissions and camera-ready version within the established schedule. Sincere thanks are due to the chairs of the co-located events and to the chairs of the additional tracks, namely, the Doctoral Consortium, Rule Challenge and Industry Track, for the excellent cooperation; thanks are due to the publicity, sponsorship, financial, and proceedings chairs, who actively contributed to the organization and the success of the enterprise; thanks also to the sponsors, including EurAI, ALP, Oxygen, and Binary Park, who provided vital contributions that helped us organize a high-standard event for the participants; and to the publisher, Springer, for their cooperation in editing this volume and publication of the proceedings.

July 2017

Stefania Costantini
Enrico Franconi
William Van Woensel
Roman Kontchakov
Fariba Sadri
Dumitru Roman

Organization

General Chairs

Roman Kontchakov   Birkbeck, University of London, UK
Fariba Sadri   Imperial College London, UK

Scientific Program Chairs

Stefania Costantini   University of L'Aquila, Italy
Enrico Franconi   Free University of Bozen-Bolzano, Italy
William Van Woensel   Dalhousie University, Canada

Industry Track Chairs

Paul Fodor   Coherent Knowledge Systems, USA
Mark Proctor   Red Hat, UK
Leora Morgenstern   Leidos Corporation, USA

Doctoral Consortium Chairs

Antonis Bikakis   University College London, UK
Theodore Patkos   Institute of Computer Science, FORTH, Greece

DecisionCAMP

Jacob Feldman   OpenRules, USA

International Rule Challenge Chairs

Nick Bassiliades   Aristotle University of Thessaloniki, Greece
Marcello Ceci   University College Cork, Ireland
Adrian Giurca   Brandenburg University of Technology,
                                 Cottbus–Senftenberg, Germany
Firas al Khalil   University College Cork, Ireland

Sponsorship Chair

Nick Bassiliades   Aristotle University of Thessaloniki, Greece

Publicity Chairs

Giovanni De Gasperis	University of L'Aquila, Italy
Konstantinos Gkoutzis	Imperial College London, UK
Mark Proctor	Red Hat, UK
Frank Olken	Frank Olken Consulting, USA

Proceedings Chair

Dumitru Roman	SINTEF/University of Oslo, Norway

Financial Chair

Tara Orlanes-Angelopoulou	Birkbeck, University of London, UK

Poster Chairs

Stefania Costantini	University of L'Aquila, Italy
Enrico Franconi	Free University of Bozen-Bolzano, Italy
William Van Woensel	Dalhousie University, Canada

Web Chair

William Van Woensel	Dalhousie University, Canada

Program Committee

Mario Alviano	University of Calabria, Italy
Nick Bassiliades	Aristotle University of Thessaloniki, Thessaloniki, Greece
Leopoldo Bertossi	Carleton University, Canada
Pedro Cabalar Fernández	Corunna University, Spain
Diego Calvanese	Free University of Bozen-Bolzano, Italy
Wolfgang Faber	University of Huddersfield, UK
Sergio Flesca	University of Calabria, Italy
Thom Frühwirth	University of Ulm, Germany
Giancarlo Guizzardi	Free University of Bozen-Bolzano, Italy
Michael Kifer	Stony Brook University, USA
Markus Krötzsch	Technische Universität Dresden, Germany
Evelina Lamma	ENDIF, University of Ferrara, Italy
Domenico Lembo	Sapienza Università di Roma, Italy
Maurizio Lenzerini	Sapienza Università di Roma, Italy
Francesca Lisi	Università degli Studi di Bari Aldo Moro, Italy
Thomas Lukasiewicz	University of Oxford, UK
Viviana Mascardi	University of Genoa, Italy

Alessandra Mileo	INSIGHT Centre for Data Analytics, Dublin City University, Ireland
Marco Montali	Free University of Bozen-Bolzano, Italy
Marie-Laure Mugnier	LIRMM/Inria, Montpellier, France
Adrian Paschke	Freie Universität Berlin, Germany
Andreas Pieris	Vienna University of Technology, Austria
Alessandro Provetti	Birkbeck, University of London, UK
Francesco Ricca	University of Calabria, Italy
Fabrizio Riguzzi	University of Ferrara, Italy
Riccardo Rosati	Sapienza Università di Roma, Italy
Rolf Schwitter	Macquarie University, Australia
Mantas Simkus	Vienna University of Technology, Austria
Giorgos Stoilos	National Technical University of Athens, Greece
Umberto Straccia	ISTI-CNR, Pisa, Italy
Anni-Yasmin Turhan	Technische Universität Dresden, Germany
Leon van der Torre	University of Luxembourg, Luxembourg

Additional Reviewers

Marco Alberti	Tiantian Gao
Alessandro Artale	Elem Güzel Kalaycı
Jean-François Baget	Nikos Katzouris
Elena Bellodi	Magdalena Ortiz
Julien Corman	Luigi Pontieri
Giuseppe Cota	Despoina Trivela
Giorgos Flouris	Federico Ulliana
Daniel Gall	Riccardo Zese

RuleML+RR 2017 Sponsors

XML Editor

**Association for Logic
Programming**

Keynote Talks

Opening the Black Box: Deriving Rules from Data

Elena Baralis

Politecnico di Torino, Turin, Italy
elena.baralis@polito.it

Abstract. A huge amount of data is currently being made available for exploration and analysis in many application domains. Patterns and models are extracted from data to describe their characteristics and predict variable values. Unfortunately, many high quality models are characterized by being hardly interpretable.

Rules mined from data may provide easily interpretable knowledge, both for exploration and classification (or prediction) purposes. In this talk I will introduce different types of rules (e.g., several variations on association rules, classification rules) and will discuss their capability of describing phenomena and highlighting interesting correlations in data.

Keywords: Rules • Data exploration • Model interpretability

The Secret Life of Rules
in Software Engineering

Jordi Cabot[1,2]

[1] ICREA, Barcelona, Spain
jordi.cabot@icrea.cat
[2] Universitat Oberta de Catalunya, Barcelona, Spain

Abstract. Explicit definition and management of rules is largely ignored in most software development projects. If the most "popular" software modeling language (UML) has already limited success, its companion, the Object Constraint Language (the OMG standard to complement UML models with textual constraints and derivation rules) is simply laughed at. As a result, rules live hidden in the code, implemented in an adhoc manner. This somehow worked when data was mostly stored in relational databases and DBAs could at least enforce some checks on that data. But now, data lives in the open (e.g. data as a service, big data) accessible in a variety of formats (NoSQL, APIs, CSVs,...). This facilitates the consumption and production of data but puts at risk any piece of software accessing it when no proper knowledge of the structure, quality and content of that data is available. And with the emergence of open data, it's not only the software who accesses the data but people.

In this talk, I will argue that rules must become first-class citizens in any software development project and describe our initiatives in discovering, representing and enforcing rules on (open and/or semi-structured) data.

Contents

Meta-Interpretive Learning: Achievements and Challenges (Invited Paper) . . .   1
Stephen H. Muggleton

Dischargeable Obligations in Abductive Logic Programming   7
Marco Alberti, Marco Gavanelli, Evelina Lamma, Fabrizio Riguzzi,
and Riccardo Zese

Using Rule-Based Reasoning for RDF Validation   22
Dörthe Arndt, Ben De Meester, Anastasia Dimou, Ruben Verborgh,
and Erik Mannens

Three Methods for Revising Hybrid Knowledge Bases   37
Sebastian Binnewies, Zhiqiang Zhuang, and Kewen Wang

Can My Test Case Run on Your Test Plant? A Logic-Based Compliance
Check and Its Evaluation on Real Data   53
Daniela Briola and Viviana Mascardi

Semantic DMN: Formalizing Decision Models with Domain Knowledge   70
Diego Calvanese, Marlon Dumas, Fabrizio M. Maggi,
and Marco Montali

A Set-Theoretic Approach to ABox Reasoning Services.   87
Domenico Cantone, Marianna Nicolosi-Asmundo,
and Daniele Francesco Santamaria

Verifying Controllability of Time-Aware Business Processes   103
Emanuele De Angelis, Fabio Fioravanti, Maria Chiara Meo,
Alberto Pettorossi, and Maurizio Proietti

A Decidable Confluence Test for Cognitive Models in ACT-R   119
Daniel Gall and Thom Frühwirth

On the Chase for All Provenance Paths with Existential Rules   135
Abdelraouf Hecham, Pierre Bisquert, and Madalina Croitoru

Rewriting Queries with Negated Atoms   151
Enrique Matos Alfonso and Giorgos Stamou

Fast ABox Consistency Checking Using Incomplete Reasoning
and Caching.   168
Christian Meilicke, Daniel Ruffinelli, Andreas Nolle, Heiko Paulheim,
and Heiner Stuckenschmidt

An Online Tool for Tuning Fuzzy Logic Programs   184
  Ginés Moreno and José A. Riaza

Hybrid ASP-Based Approach to Pattern Mining   199
  Sergey Paramonov, Daria Stepanova, and Pauli Miettinen

Inconsistency-Tolerant Instance Checking in Tractable Description Logics . . .   215
  Rafael Peñaloza

ArgQL: A Declarative Language for Querying Argumentative Dialogues   230
  Dimitra Zografistou, Giorgos Flouris, and Dimitris Plexousakis

Author Index   239

Meta-Interpretive Learning: Achievements and Challenges (Invited Paper)

Stephen H. Muggleton$^{(\boxtimes)}$

Imperial College London, London, UK
s.muggleton@imperial.ac.uk

Abstract. This invited talk provides an overview of ongoing work in a new sub-area of Inductive Logic Programming known as Meta-Interpretive Learning.

1 Introduction

Meta-Interpretive Learning (MIL) [12] is a recent Inductive Logic Programming [7,13,14] technique aimed at supporting learning of recursive definitions. A powerful and novel aspect of MIL is that when learning a predicate definition it automatically introduces sub-definitions, allowing decomposition into a hierarchy of reusable parts. MIL is based on an adapted version of a Prolog meta-interpreter. Normally such a meta-interpreter derives a proof by repeatedly fetching first-order Prolog clauses whose heads unify with a given goal. By contrast, a meta-interpretive learner additionally fetches higher-order meta-rules whose heads unify with the goal, and saves the resulting meta-substitutions to form a program. This talk will overview theoretical and implementational advances in this new area including the ability to learn Turing computable functions within a constrained subset of logic programs, the use of probabilistic representations within Bayesian meta-interpretive and techniques for minimising the number of meta-rules employed. The talk will also summarise applications of MIL including the learning of regular and context-free grammars, [11], learning from visual representations [3] with repeated patterns, learning string transformations for spreadsheet applications, [6], learning and optimising recursive robot strategies [1] and learning tactics for proving correctness of programs [5]. The paper concludes by pointing to challenges which remain to be addressed within this new area.

2 Simple Worked Example

Suppose we machine learn a set of kinship relations such as those in Fig. 1. If examples of the ancestor relation are provided and the background contains only father and mother facts, then a system must not only be able to learn ancestor as a recursive definition but also simultaneously *invent* parent to learn these definitions.

S. Costantini et al. (Eds.): RuleML+RR 2017, LNCS 10364, pp. 1–6, 2017.
DOI: 10.1007/978-3-319-61252-2_1

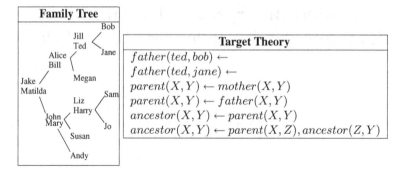

First-order	Metalogical substitutions
Examples $ancestor(jake, bob) \leftarrow$ $ancestor(alice, jane) \leftarrow$	N/A
Background Knowledge $father(jake, alice) \leftarrow$ $mother(alice, ted) \leftarrow$	N/A
Instantiated Hypothesis $father(ted, bob) \leftarrow$ $father(ted, jane) \leftarrow$ $p1(X, Y) \leftarrow father(X, Y)$ $p1(X, Y) \leftarrow mother(X, Y)$ $ancestor(X, Y) \leftarrow p1(X, Y)$ $ancestor(X, Y) \leftarrow p1(X, Z),$ $ancestor(Z, Y)$	$metasub(instance, [father, ted, bob])$ $metasub(instance, [father, ted, jane])$ $metasub(base, [p1, father])$ $metasub(base, [p1, mother])$ $metasub(base, [ancestor, p1])$ $metasub(tailrec, [ancestor, p1, ancestor])$

Fig. 1. Kinship example. *p1* invented, representing *parent*.

Although the topic of Predicate Invention was investigated in early Inductive Logic Programming (ILP) research [8,18] it is still seen as hard and under-explored [14]. ILP systems such as ALEPH [17] and FOIL [15] have no predicate invention and limited recursion learning and therefore cannot learn recursive grammars from example sequences. By contrast, in [11] definite clause grammars were learned with predicate invention using Meta-Interpretive Learning (MIL). MIL [6,9,10] is a technique which supports efficient predicate invention and learning of recursive logic programs built as a set of metalogical substitutions by a modified Prolog meta-interpreter (see Fig. 2) which acts as the central part of the ILP learning engine. The meta-interpreter is provided by the user with *meta-rules* (see Fig. 3) which are higher-order expressions describing the forms of clauses permitted in hypothesised programs. As shown in Fig. 3 each meta-rule has an associated Order constraint, which is designed to ensure termination of the proof. The meta-interpreter attempts to prove the examples and, for any successful proof, saves the substitutions for existentially quantified variables found in the associated meta-rules. When these substitutions are applied to the meta-rules they result in a first-order definite program which is an inductive

Generalised meta-interpreter
$prove([\,], Prog, Prog)$.
$prove([Atom\mid As], Prog1, Prog2) : -$
$\quad metarule(Name, MetaSub, (Atom :- Body), Order),$
$\quad Order,$
$\quad save\_subst(metasub(Name, MetaSub), Prog1, Prog3),$
$\quad prove(Body, Prog3, Prog4),$
$\quad prove(As, Prog4, Prog2)$.

Fig. 2. Prolog code for the generalised meta-interpreter. The interpreter recursively proves a series of atomic goals by matching them against the heads of meta-rules. After testing the Order constraint *save_subst* checks whether the meta-substitution is already in the program and otherwise adds it to form an augmented program. On completion the returned program, by construction, derives all the examples.

generalisation of the examples. For instance, the two examples shown in the upper part of Fig. 1 could be proved by the meta-interpreter in Fig. 2 from the Background Knowledge BK by generating the Hypothesis H using the Prolog goal

$$\leftarrow prove([ancestor, jake, bob], [ancestor, alice, jane], BK, H).$$

H is constructed by applying the metalogical substitutions in Fig. 1 to the corresponding meta-rules found in Fig. 3. Note that $p1$ is an invented predicate corresponding to *parent*.

Name	Meta-Rule	Order
Instance	$P(X, Y) \leftarrow$	$True$
Base	$P(x, y) \leftarrow Q(x, y)$	$P \succ Q$
Chain	$P(x, y) \leftarrow Q(x, z), R(z, y)$	$P \succ Q, P \succ R$
TailRec	$P(x, y) \leftarrow Q(x, z), P(z, y)$	$P \succ Q,$ $x \succ z \succ y$

Fig. 3. Examples of dyadic meta-rules with associated Herbrand ordering constraints. $\succ$ is a pre-defined ordering over symbols in the signature.

Completeness of SLD resolution ensures that *all* hypotheses consistent with the examples can be constructed. Moreover, unlike many ILP systems, *only* hypotheses consistent with all examples are considered. Owing to the efficiency of Prolog backtracking MIL implementations have been demonstrated to search the hypothesis space 100–1000 times faster than state-of-the-art ILP systems [11] in the task of learning recursive grammars[1].

---

[1] Metagol$_R$ and Metagol$_{CF}$ learn Regular and Context-Free grammars respectively.

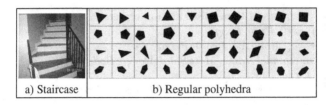

| a) Staircase | b) Regular polyhedra |

Fig. 4. MIL vision applications: (a) learning a recursion definition of a staircase from a single image [11] and (b) learning definition relating regular polygons [3].

3   Vision Applications

Figure 4 illustrates two applications in which MIL has been used to analyse images. The staircase learning in Fig. 4a was based on data from Claude Sammut's group [4]. However, the original author's approach, using ALEPH was not entirely general since it does not involve recursion. Using MIL it was possible to learn a general recursive definition of a staircase using predicate invention. A staircase is represented as a set of ordered planes, where the background predicates *vertical* and *horizontal* describe adjacent planes. The resulting hypothesis is shown in Fig. 5, where a is an invented predicate corresponding to *step*. Due to its recursive form, this definition has shorter description length than those found by ALEPH. It is also general in its applicability and easily understood.

> **stair(X,Y)** :- a(X,Y).
> **stair(X,Y)** :- a(X,Z), **stair(Z,Y)**.
> a(X,Y) :- vertical(X,Z), horizontal(Z,Y).

Fig. 5. Definition of staircase learned in 0.08 s on a laptop from single image. Note predicate invention and recursion.

4   Challenges

A number of open challenges exist for Meta-Interpretive Learning. These include the following.

Generalise beyond Dyadic logic. The dyadic fragment of Prolog has provided an efficient approach to selecting a compact and efficient universal set of metarules [2] for MIL. However, many Prolog programs are more natural to represent when represented with more than two arguments.

Deal with classification noise. Most data sources for machine learning contain both classification and attribute noise. We are presently developing variants of the Metagol system which act robustly in the face of such noise.

Active learning. Most forms of machine learning are *passive* in the sense that they take a given training data set and generate a model. Active learning involves proposing and testing instances which are classified either by a user of by carrying out experiments in the real world. We are developing probabilistic variants of Meta-Interpretive Learning [10] which could be adapted for efficient Active Learning.

Efficient problem decomposition. Finding efficient ways of decomposing the definitions in MIL is one of the hardest open problems in the field.

Meaningful hypotheses. In ongoing work [16] we are investigating the issues which are most important for improving the understandability of learned programs.

References

1. Cropper, A., Muggleton, S.: Learning efficient logical robot strategies involving composable objects. In: Proceedings of the 24th International Joint Conference Artificial Intelligence (IJCAI 2015), pp. 3423–3429. IJCAI (2015). http://www.doc.ic.ac.uk/~shm/Papers/metagolo.pdf
2. Cropper, A., Muggleton, S.H.: Logical minimisation of meta-rules within meta-interpretive learning. In: Davis, J., Ramon, J. (eds.) ILP 2014. LNCS, vol. 9046, pp. 62–75. Springer, Cham (2015). doi:10.1007/978-3-319-23708-4_5
3. Dai, W.Z., Muggleton, S., Zhou, Z.H.: Logical vision: meta-interpretive learning for simple geometrical concepts. In: Late Breaking Paper Proceedings of the 25th International Conference on Inductive Logic Programming, pp. 1–16. CEUR (2015). http://ceur-ws.org/Vol-1636
4. Farid, R., Sammut, C.: Plane-based object categorization using relational learning. ILP2012 MLJ special issue (2012)
5. Farquhar, C., Cropper, G.G.A., Muggleton, S., Bundy, A.: Typed meta-interpretive learning for proof strategies. In: Short Paper Proceedings of the 25th International Conference on Inductive Logic Programming. National Institute of Informatics, Tokyo (2015). http://www.doc.ic.ac.uk/~shm/Papers/typemilproof.pdf
6. Lin, D., Dechter, E., Ellis, K., Tenenbaum, J., Muggleton, S.: Bias reformulation for one-shot function induction. In: Proceedings of the 23rd European Conference on Artificial Intelligence (ECAI 2014), pp. 525–530. IOS Press, Amsterdam (2014). http://www.doc.ic.ac.uk/~shm/Papers/metabias.pdf
7. Muggleton, S.: Inductive logic programming. New Gener. Comput. **8**(4), 295–318 (1991). http://www.doc.ic.ac.uk/~shm/Papers/ilp.pdf
8. Muggleton, S., Buntine, W.: Machine invention of first-order predicates by inverting resolution. In: Proceedings of the 5th International Conference on Machine Learning, pp. 339–352. Kaufmann (1988). http://www.doc.ic.ac.uk/~shm/Papers/cigol.pdf
9. Muggleton, S., Lin, D.: Meta-interpretive learning of higher-order dyadic datalog: predicate invention revisited. In: Proceedings of the 23rd International Joint Conference Artificial Intelligence (IJCAI 2013), pp. 1551–1557 (2013). http://www.doc.ic.ac.uk/~shm/Papers/metagold.pdf
10. Muggleton, S.H., Lin, D., Chen, J., Tamaddoni-Nezhad, A.: MetaBayes: bayesian meta-interpretative learning using higher-order stochastic refinement. In: Zaverucha, G., Santos Costa, V., Paes, A. (eds.) ILP 2013. LNCS, vol. 8812, pp. 1–17. Springer, Heidelberg (2014). doi:10.1007/978-3-662-44923-3_1

11. Muggleton, S., Lin, D., Pahlavi, N., Tamaddoni-Nezhad, A.: Meta-interpretive learning: application to grammatical inference. Mach. Learn. **94**, 25–49 (2014). http://www.doc.ic.ac.uk/~shm/Papers/metagolgram.pdf
12. Muggleton, S., Lin, D., Tamaddoni-Nezhad, A.: Meta-interpretive learning of higher-order dyadic datalog: predicate invention revisited. Mach. Learn. **100**(1), 49–73 (2015). http://www.doc.ic.ac.uk/~shm/Papers/metagolDMLJ.pdf
13. Muggleton, S., Raedt, L.D.: Inductive logic programming: theory and methods. J. Logic Program. **19**(20), 629–679 (1994). http://www.doc.ic.ac.uk/~shm/Papers/lpj.pdf
14. Muggleton, S., Raedt, L.D., Poole, D., Bratko, I., Flach, P., Inoue, K.: ILP turns 20: biography and future challenges. Mach. Learn. **86**(1), 3–23 (2011). http://www.doc.ic.ac.uk/~shm/Papers/ILPturns20.pdf
15. Quinlan, J.: Learning logical definitions from relations. Mach. Learn. **5**, 239–266 (1990)
16. Schmid, U., Zeller, C., Besold, T., Tamaddoni-Nezhad, A., Muggleton, S.: How does predicate invention affect human comprehensibility? In: Russo, A., Cussens, J. (eds.) Proceedings of the 26th International Conference on Inductive Logic Programming (ILP 2016). Springer, Berlin (2016)
17. Srinivasan, A.: The ALEPH manual. Machine Learning at the Computing Laboratory, Oxford University (2001)
18. Stahl, I.: Constructive induction in inductive logic programming: an overview. Fakultat Informatik, Universitat Stuttgart, Technical report (1992)

Dischargeable Obligations in Abductive Logic Programming

Marco Alberti[1]([⊠]), Marco Gavanelli[2], Evelina Lamma[2], Fabrizio Riguzzi[1], and Riccardo Zese[2]

[1] Dipartimento di Matematica e Informatica, University of Ferrara,
Via Saragat 1, 44122 Ferrara, Italy
{marco.alberti,fabrizio.riguzzi}@unife.it
[2] Dipartimento di Ingegneria, University of Ferrara,
Via Saragat 1, 44122 Ferrara, Italy
{marco.gavanelli,evelina.lamma,riccardo.zese}@unife.it

Abstract. Abductive Logic Programming (ALP) has been proven very effective for formalizing societies of agents, commitments and norms, in particular by mapping the most common deontic operators (obligation, prohibition, permission) to abductive expectations.

In our previous works, we have shown that ALP is a suitable framework for representing norms. Normative reasoning and query answering were accommodated by the same abductive proof procedure, named $\mathcal{S}$CIFF.

In this work, we introduce a defeasible flavour in this framework, in order to possibly discharge obligations in some scenarios. Abductive expectations can also be qualified as dischargeable, in the new, extended syntax. Both declarative and operational semantics are improved accordingly, and proof of soundness is given under syntax allowedness conditions.

The expressiveness and power of the extended framework, named $\mathcal{S}$CIFF$^{\mathcal{D}}$, is shown by modeling and reasoning upon a fragment of the Japanese Civil Code. In particular, we consider a case study concerning manifestations of intention and their rescission (Sect. 2 of the Japanese Civil Code).

1 Introduction

A normative system is a set of norms encoded in a formal language, together with mechanisms to reason about, apply, and modify them. Since norms preserve the autonomy of the interacting parties (which ultimately decide whether or not to comply), normative systems are an appropriate tool to regulate interaction in multi-agent systems [15]. Usually, norm definitions build upon notions of obligation, permission and prohibition, in the tradition of Deontic Logic [36].

When formalizing norms, a natural approach is to encode them as implications; semantically, implications naturally represent conditional norms, where the antecedent is read as a property of a state of affairs and the consequent as its deontic consequence, and operationally rule-based systems offer support for reasoning and drawing conclusions from norms and a description of the system they

© Springer International Publishing AG 2017
S. Costantini et al. (Eds.): RuleML+RR 2017, LNCS 10364, pp. 7–21, 2017.
DOI: 10.1007/978-3-319-61252-2_2

regulate. Applications of computational logic to formalize norms include logic programming for the British Nationality Act [35], argument-based extended logic programming with defeasible priorities [33], defeasible logic [27].

As mentioned above, normative systems have been applied in multi-agent systems [15]. Among the organizational models and [18,19] exploit Deontic Logic to specify the society norms and rules. Significant portions of EU research projects were devoted to formalizing norms for multiagent systems; namely, the ALFEBI-ITE project [11] was focused on the formalization of an open society of agents using Deontic Logic, and in the IMPACT project [12,20] an agent's obligations, permissions and prohibitions were specified by corresponding deontic operators.

The EU IST Project SOCS proposed various Abductive Logic Programming (ALP) languages and proof procedures to specify and implement both individual agents [17] and their interaction [4]; both approaches have later been applied to modeling and reasoning about norms with deontic flavours [7,34].

ALP has been proved a powerful tool for knowledge representation and reasoning [30], taking advantage of ALP operational support as a (static or dynamic) verification tool. ALP languages are usually equipped with a declarative (model-theoretic) semantics, and an operational semantics given in terms of a proof-procedure. Fung and Kowalski proposed the IFF abductive proof-procedure [23] to deal with forward rules, and with non-ground abducibles. It has been later extended [5], and the resulting proof procedure, named $\mathcal{S}$CIFF, can deal with both existentially and universally quantified variables in rule heads and Constraint Logic Programming (CLP) constraints [28]. The resulting system was used for modeling and implementing several knowledge representation frameworks, such as deontic logic [7], where the deontic notions of obligation and permission are mapped into special $\mathcal{S}$CIFF abducible predicates, normative systems [6], interaction protocols for multi-agent systems [8], Web services choreographies [3], and Datalog$^{\pm}$ ontologies [24].

In this work, we present $\mathcal{S}$CIFF$^{\mathcal{D}}$, an extension of the $\mathcal{S}$CIFF framework, which introduces a defeasible flavour in the norm portion of the framework, as a mechanism for discharging obligations: intuitively, rather than removing an abductive expectation representing obligation with a sort of contraction [10], we mark it as discharged to indicate that the lack of a fulfilling act is not a violation of the norms. Both declarative and operational semantics are extended accordingly, and a proof of soundness is given under syntax allowedness conditions.

Thanks to this extension, we are better able to cope with real-life norms, even in the legal domain.

The paper is organized as follows. In Sect. 2, we first recall the $\mathcal{S}$CIFF language, also mentioning its declarative semantics and its underlying proof procedure, and discuss a case study from Sect. 2 of the Japanese Civil Code. Then, in Sect. 3, we introduce the $\mathcal{S}$CIFF$^{\mathcal{D}}$ syntax, with a novel abducible for discharging obligations (namely, expectations); we also discuss the formalization of a further article from the Japanese Civil Code. Section 4 extends the declarative and operational semantics accordingly, and presents the proof of soundness for the extended framework. In Sect. 5 we discuss related work and in Sect. 6 we conclude the paper.

2 $\mathcal{S}$CIFF language and semantics

As a running example, we consider, throughout the paper, article 96 ("Fraud or duress") of the Japanese civil code (see, for example, [29]). In order to model, and discuss it, we first provide an informal description of the $\mathcal{S}$CIFF language; for formal definitions, we refer the reader to [7].

The $\mathcal{S}$CIFF language. In $\mathcal{S}$CIFF, the agent behaviour is described by means of events (actual behaviour) and expectations (expected behaviour):

- events are atoms of the form **H**(*Content*, *Time*)
- expectations are abducible atoms of the following possible forms, which, while not being modal operators, can be given a deontic reading as shown in [7]: **E**(*Content*, *Time*): positive expectations, with a deontic reading of obligation; **EN**(*Content*, *Time*): negative expectations, read as prohibition; ¬**E**(*Content*, *Time*): negation of positive expectation, or explicit absence of obligation; ¬**EN**(*Content*, *Time*): negation of negative expectation, or explicit permission.

where *Content* is a logic term that describes the event and *Time* is a variable or a term representing the time of the event. CLP constraints can be imposed over variables; for time variables, they represent time constraints, such as deadlines.

A $\mathcal{S}$CIFF program is a pair $\langle KB, \mathcal{IC} \rangle$, where KB is a set of logic programming clauses (used to express domain specific knowledge) which can have expectations, but not events, in their bodies, and $\mathcal{IC}$ is a set of implications called Integrity Constraints, which implicitly define the expected behaviour of the interacting parties. Function symbols and arbitrary nesting of terms are allowed. Each Integrity Constraint (IC) in $\mathcal{IC}$ has the form $Body \rightarrow Head$, where $Body$ is a conjunction of literals defined in KB, events and expectations, while $Head$ is a disjunction of conjunctions of expectations.

Thanks to their implication structure and the deontic reading of expectations shown in [7], ICs can be read as conditional norms [6].

Case Study. In order to model article 96 ("Fraud or duress" from the Japanese Civil Code), we describe the content of events and expectations by means of the following terms:

- *intention*(A, B, I, Id_I): person A utters a manifestation of intention to person B, with identifier Id_I for action I;
- *do*(A, B): person A performs act B;
- *induce*(A, B): act A induces act B;
- *rescind*(A, B, I, F, Id_I, Id_R): person A rescinds, with identifier Id_R, his or her intention, uttered to B and identified by Id_I, to perform action I, due to fraud or duress F;

- $know(A, F)$: person A becomes aware of fact F;
- $assertAgainst(A, B, Id_R)$: person A asserts the legal act identified by Id_R against person B.

Legally relevant acts (*intention, rescind, assertAgainst*) have identifiers.

The following integrity constraint states that a manifestation of intention should, in general, be followed by the performance of the act.

$$\mathbf{H}(intention(A, B, I, Id_I), T_1) \rightarrow \mathbf{E}(do(A, I), T_2) \wedge T_2 > T_1 \tag{1}$$

Each of the following integrity constraints models one of the paragraphs of Article 96. Here, $fraudOrDuress/1$ is a predicate, defined in KB, which specifies which actions count as fraud or duress.

1. Manifestation of intention which is induced by any fraud or duress may be rescinded.

$$\mathbf{H}(intention(A, B, I, Id_I), T_1) \wedge \mathbf{H}(do(B, F), T_3) \wedge \mathbf{H}(induce(F, I), T_2)$$
$$\wedge\, fraudOrDuress(F) \wedge T_3 < T_2 \wedge T_2 < T_1 \wedge T_1 < T_4$$
$$\rightarrow \neg\mathbf{EN}(rescind(A, B, I, F, Id_I, Id_R), T_4)$$
$$\tag{2}$$

2. In cases any third party commits any fraud inducing any person to make a manifestation of intention to the other party, such manifestation of intention may be rescinded only if the other party knew such fact.

$$\mathbf{H}(intention(A, B, I, Id_I), T_1) \wedge \mathbf{H}(do(C, F), T_3) \wedge C \neq B$$
$$\wedge\, \mathbf{H}(know(B, F), T_5) \wedge \mathbf{H}(induce(F, I), T_2)$$
$$\wedge\, fraudOrDuress(F) \wedge T_2 < T_1 \wedge T_3 \leq T_5 \wedge T_5 < T_1$$
$$\rightarrow \neg\mathbf{EN}(rescind(A, B, I, F, Id_I, Id_R), T_4) \wedge T_4 > T_1 \tag{3}$$

3. The rescission of the manifestation of intention induced by the fraud pursuant to the provision of the preceding two paragraphs may not be asserted against a third party without knowledge.

$$\mathbf{H}(rescind(A, B, I, F, Id_I, Id_R), T_1) \wedge \mathbf{not}\ \mathbf{H}(know(C, F), T_2)$$
$$\rightarrow \mathbf{EN}(assertAgainst(A, C, Id_R), T_3) \wedge T_1 < T_3 \tag{4}$$

Declarative Semantics. The abductive semantics of the $\mathcal{S}$CIFF language defines, given a set $\mathbf{HAP}$ of H atoms called history and representing the actual behaviour, an abductive answer, i.e., a ground set $\mathbf{EXP}$ of expectations that

- together with the history and KB, entails $\mathcal{IC}$:

$$KB \cup \mathbf{HAP} \cup \mathbf{EXP} \models \mathcal{IC} \tag{5}$$

where $\models$ is entailment according to the in 3-valued completion semantics.

– is consistent with respect to explicit negation;

$$\{\mathbf{E}(\textit{Content, Time}), \neg\mathbf{E}(\textit{Content, Time})\} \nsubseteq \mathbf{EXP}\wedge$$
$$\wedge\{\mathbf{EN}(\textit{Content, Time}), \neg\mathbf{EN}(\textit{Content, Time})\} \nsubseteq \mathbf{EXP} \tag{6}$$

– is consistent with respect to the meaning of expectations

$$\{\mathbf{E}(\textit{Content, Time}), \mathbf{EN}(\textit{Content, Time})\} \nsubseteq \mathbf{EXP} \tag{7}$$

– is fulfilled by the history, i.e.

$$\text{if } \mathbf{E}(\textit{Content, Time}) \in \mathbf{EXP} \text{ then } \mathbf{H}(\textit{Content, Time}) \in \mathbf{HAP} \text{ and} \tag{8}$$
$$\text{if } \mathbf{EN}(\textit{Content, Time}) \in \mathbf{EXP} \text{ then } \mathbf{H}(\textit{Content, Time}) \notin \mathbf{HAP} \tag{9}$$

Operational Semantics. Operationally, the $\mathcal{S}$CIFF abductive proof procedure finds an abductive answer if one exists, or detects that no one exists (see [5] for soundness and completeness statements), meaning that the history violates the $\mathcal{S}$CIFF program. We call the two cases success and failure, respectively. The $\mathcal{S}$CIFF proof-procedure is defined through a set of transitions, each rewriting one node of a proof tree into one or more nodes. The basic transitions of $\mathcal{S}$CIFF are inherited from the IFF [23], and they account for the core of abductive reasoning. Other transitions deal with CLP constraints, and are inherited from the CLP [28] transitions. Due to lack of space, we cannot describe in detail all transitions; we sketch those dealing with the concept of expectation, that are most relevant for the rest of the paper.

In order to deal with the concept of expectation, in each node of the proof tree, the set of abduced expectations **EXP** is partitioned into two sets: the fulfilled (**FULF**), and pending (**PEND**) expectations.

Transition *Fulfillment* **E** deals with the fulfillment of **E** expectations: if an expectation $\mathbf{E}(E, T_E) \in \mathbf{PEND}$ and the event $\mathbf{H}(H, T_H)$ is in the current history **HAP**, two nodes are generated: one in which $E = H$, $T_E = T_H$ and $\mathbf{E}(E, T_E)$ is moved to **FULF**, the other in which $E \neq H$ or $T_E \neq T_H$ (where $\neq$ stands for the constraint of disunification).

Transition *Violation* **EN** deals with the violation of **EN** expectations: if an expectation $\mathbf{EN}(E, T_E) \in \mathbf{PEND}$ and the event $\mathbf{H}(H, T_H) \in \mathbf{HAP}$, one node is generated where the constraint $E \neq H \vee T_E \neq T_H$ is imposed, possibly leading to failure.

When there are no more relevant events, *history closure* is applied; in this case, all remaining **E** expectations in **PEND** are considered as violated and failure occurs.

As regards complexity, the $\mathcal{S}$CIFF language is an extension of Prolog, and, as such, it is Turing-complete; so a $\mathcal{S}$CIFF evaluation, in general, may not terminate. Even in the propositional case, Gottlob and Eiter [21] proved that the complexity of abduction is Σ_2^P-complete.

3 $\mathcal{S}$CIFF$^{\mathcal{D}}$ Language

In legal reasoning, expectations can be discharged not only because they become fulfilled by matching the actual behaviour of the agent, but also for other reasons. For example, in case a contract is declared null, the agents are no longer expected to perform the actions required in the contract.

We introduce an extension of the $\mathcal{S}$CIFF language to deal with expectations that do not hold any longer. We introduce two new abducible atoms, $\mathbf{D}(\mathbf{E})$ and $\mathbf{D}(\mathbf{EN})$, which mean that an expectation is discharged; for example, the atom

$$\mathbf{D}(\mathbf{E}(X, T))$$

means that the expectation $\mathbf{E}(X, T)$ is no longer required to be fulfilled, as it has been discharged.

The integrity constraints can have $\mathbf{D}$ atoms, which can be abduced.

Example 1. The user might write an IC saying that, if a contract with identifier Id_C is null (represented in this example with an abducible $\mathbf{NULL}$, carrying the identifier of the contract and that of the reason for nullification), all expectations requiring an action in the context of that contract are discharged:

$$\mathbf{NULL}(Id_C, Id_{null}) \wedge \mathbf{E}(do(Agent, Action, Id_C), T_{do})$$
$$\rightarrow \mathbf{D}(\mathbf{E}(do(Agent, Action, Id_C), T_{do})). \tag{10}$$

We can express that a contract that is explicitly permitted to be rescinded can be nullified as

$$\neg\mathbf{EN}(rescind(A, I, F, Id_I, Id_R), T_r) \wedge \mathbf{H}(rescind(A, I, F, Id_I, Id_R), T_r)$$
$$\rightarrow \mathbf{NULL}(Id_I, Id_R) \tag{11}$$

The combined effect of ICs (10) and (11) is that rescission is only effective when the circumstances grant an explicit permission.

Example 2. As a second case study from the Japanese Civil Code, we consider Article 130, which states "In cases any party who will suffer any detriment as a result of the fulfillment of a condition intentionally prevents the fulfillment of such condition, the counterparty may deem that such condition has been fulfilled". Article 130 can be modeled as follows:

$$\mathbf{H}(do(Agent_1, Action_1), T_1) \wedge \mathbf{E}(do(Agent_2, Action_2), T_2)$$
$$\wedge\, detrimental(Action_2, Agent_1) \wedge prevent(Action_1, Action_2) \tag{12}$$
$$\rightarrow \mathbf{D}(\mathbf{E}(do(Agent_2, Action_2), T_2))$$

where detrimental/2 and prevent/2 are predicates defined in the KB to specify when, respectively, an action is detrimental to an agent and when an action prevents another.

Syntactic Restrictions. The following syntactic restriction is used in the proof of soundness.

Definition 1. *Weak* **D**-*allowedness. An IC containing a* **D** *atom is weakly* **D**-*allowed if there is only one* **D** *atom, it occurs in the head, and the head contains only that atom.*

A *KB is weakly* **D**-*allowed if none of its clauses contains* **D** *atoms.*

A $\mathcal{S}CIFF^{\mathcal{D}}$ *program* $\langle KB, \mathcal{IC} \rangle$ *is weakly* **D**-*allowed if KB is weakly* **D**-*allowed and all the ICs in* $\mathcal{IC}$ *are weakly* **D**-*allowed.*

The following restriction is not necessary for the soundness results proved in Sect. 4.3, but it allows a more efficient treatment of the **D** atoms. Note that all the examples presented in this paper satisfy the restriction.

Definition 2. *Strong* **D**-*allowedness. An IC containing a* **D** *atom is strongly* **D**-*allowed if it is weakly* **D**-*allowed and the (only) expectation in the* **D** *atom occurs identically in the body of the IC.*

Intuitively, the given notion of strong **D**-allowedness allows one to define ICs that select one expectation and make it discharged, subject to conditions occurring in the body. This syntactic restriction is aimed at capturing the most common scenarios while trying to maintain an efficient execution.

In fact, if the strong allowedness condition is lifted, it is not required for an atom $\mathbf{E}(X)$ to have been abduced before declaring it discharged. If two atoms $\mathbf{E}(X)$ and $\mathbf{D}(\mathbf{E}(Y))$ are abduced, two options have to be explored, as alternatives: either X unifies with Y, and the expectation $\mathbf{E}(X)$ becomes discharged, or X and Y do not unify (e.g., by imposing a dis-unification constraint $X \neq Y$). These cases, the $\mathcal{S}$CIFF proof-procedure opens a choice point; this means that, in case $|E|$ expectations **E** are abduced and $|D|$ **D** atoms are abduced, $|E||D|$ choice points will be created, each opening 2 alternative branches, which would generate $2^{|E||D|}$ branches (of course, the same could be said for **EN** expectations).

We performed an experiment to verify this worst-case analysis. We generated a number of $\mathbf{E}(X)$ and $\mathbf{D}(\mathbf{E}(Y))$ atoms, and measured the time $\mathcal{S}CIFF^{\mathcal{D}}$ took to find the first solution and all solutions (all experiments were run on a Intel Core i7-3720QM CPU @ 2.60 GHz running SWI-Prolog version 7.4.0-rc1 on Linux Mint 18.1 Serena 64 bits). For all solutions (Fig. 1 right), the running time follows closely the foreseen $2^{|E||D|}$, while for one solution (Fig. 1 left), the running time seems dependent mainly on the number of raised expectations and almost independent from the number of **D** atoms. Note also the different scales: finding one solution takes at most 3 s with 100 expectations and discharge atoms, while finding all solutions takes almost 3 h with $|E| = |D| = 8$.

From a language viewpoint, the strong allowedness condition restricts the set of expectations that can be discharged to those that have been raised. Without such restriction, one could abduce a generic atom $\mathbf{D}(\mathbf{E}(X))$ saying that one expectation is discharged. Semantically, this would mean that one of the expectations might be discharged, although it is not said which one.

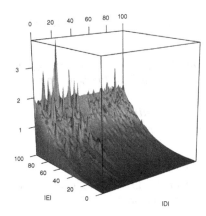 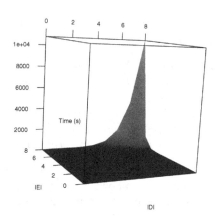

Fig. 1. Experiments with different numbers $|D|$ of $\mathbf{D}$ atoms and $|E|$ of $\mathbf{E}$ atoms; time in seconds for finding one solution (left) or all solutions (right).

Dischargement Scenarios. The remainder of this section is devoted to discuss an example concerning manifestation of intention (Sect. 2 of the Japanese Civil Code), modeled in $\mathcal{SCIFF}^{\mathcal{D}}$ and one concerning prevention of fulfillment of conditions. Sections presenting the declarative and operational semantics of the extended framework and proof of soundness then follow.

Example 3. (Example 1 continued). Let us consider the case study of Sect. 2 again, and assume that work on an acquired good G is to be paid by the good's owner O, unless O rescinds the good's purchase and asserts the rescission against the performer of the work M (which, due to integrity constraint (4), is only allowed if the performer was aware of the rescission's cause, such as a fraud). We can express this norm by means of the following integrity constraint:

$$\mathbf{H}(work(M, G, O, W), T_1)$$
$$\rightarrow \mathbf{E}(pay(O, M, W), T_2) \wedge T_1 < T_2$$
$$\vee (\mathbf{E}(rescind(O, B, buy(G), F, Id_I, Id_R), T_3) \tag{13}$$
$$\wedge \mathbf{E}(assertAgainst(O, M, Id_R), T_4)$$
$$\wedge T_1 < T_3 \wedge T_3 < T_4)$$

where the term $work(M, G, O, W)$ represents mechanic M doing work W on the good G owned by O, and the term $pay(O, M, W)$ represents owner O paying mechanic M for work W.

The KB states that fixing a car's mileage constitutes fraud or duress.

$$fraudOrDuress(fixMileage(C)) \tag{14}$$

In the scenario defined by the following history

$$\mathbf{H}(do(bob, fixMileage(car)), 1)$$
$$\mathbf{H}(induce(fixMileage(car), buy(car)), 2)$$
$$\mathbf{H}(intention(alice, bob, buy(car), i1), 3) \tag{15}$$
$$\mathbf{H}(work(mechanic, car, alice, lpgSystem), 4)$$
$$\mathbf{H}(rescind(alice, bob, buy(car), fixMileage(car), i1, i2), 5)$$

Alice's rescission is explicitly permitted by IC (2), because her manifestation of intention was induced by Bob's fraudulent act of fixing the car's mileage; the expectation $\mathbf{E}(do(alice, buy(car)), T)$, raised because of IC (1), is discharged because of ICs (10) and (11).

However, since the mechanic was not aware of Bob's fraud, IC (4) prevents Alice from asserting the rescission against him, so the second disjunct in IC (13) cannot hold, and Alice still has to pay him for installing the LPG system ($\mathbf{E}(pay(alice, mechanic, lpgSystem, T_2))$). For the history that contains all the events in formula (15), plus $\mathbf{H}(know(mechanic, fixMileage(car)), 1)$ (i.e., the mechanic is now aware of the car's mileage being fixed), alice is not prohibited from asserting the rescission against the mechanic by integrity constraint (4). With the event $\mathbf{H}(assertAgainst(alice, mechanic, i2), 6)$, the second disjunct in the head of integrity constraint (13), is satisfied and alice is not obliged to pay the mechanic for his work.

Example 4. Consider the following scenario, where an order by a customer should be followed by a delivery by the seller:

$$\mathbf{H}(order(Customer, Seller, Good), T_{order})$$
$$\rightarrow \mathbf{E}(do(Seller, deliver(Good)), T_{delivery}) \wedge T_{delivery} > T_{order}. \tag{16}$$

Suppose that Alice placed an order, but in the meanwhile she was diagnosed a rare immunodeficiency, and she cannot meet people, except her family members. Her mother usually lives with her, but today she went out, so Alice locked the door, as it would be detrimental for her if any person got in the house. This prevents any delivery, but it is a minor issue for her compared to the consequences that Alice should face in case she met a stranger.

$$detrimental(deliver(Good), alice).$$
$$prevent(lockDoor, deliver(Good)). \tag{17}$$

Given the following history

$$\mathbf{H}(order(alice, bob, computer), 1)$$
$$\mathbf{H}(do(alice, lockDoor), 2) \tag{18}$$

the expectation for Bob to deliver the good, raised by IC (16), is discharged by IC (12), because Alice performed an action that prevents the fulfillment.

4 $\mathcal{S}$CIFF$^{\mathcal{D}}$ Declarative and Operational Semantics

4.1   Declarative Semantics

We now show how to deal with the discharge of expectations in the context of ALP. We first give an intuitive definition, then show its pitfalls and finally provide a correct definition.

In order to accept histories in which expectations may not have matching events, we need to extend the definition of fulfillment of expectations given in Eqs. (8) and (9); intuitively, a positive expectation is fulfilled if either there is a matching event or if the expectation has been discharged:

$$\begin{aligned}&\text{if } \mathbf{E}(\textit{Content, Time}) \in \mathbf{EXP} \\ &\text{then } \mathbf{H}(\textit{Content, Time}) \in \mathbf{HAP} \vee \mathbf{D}(\mathbf{E}(\textit{Content, Time})) \in \mathbf{EXP}\end{aligned} \qquad (19)$$

and symmetrically for a negative expectation:

$$\begin{aligned}&\text{if } \mathbf{EN}(\textit{Content, Time}) \in \mathbf{EXP} \\ &\text{then } \mathbf{H}(\textit{Content, Time}) \notin \mathbf{HAP} \vee \mathbf{D}(\mathbf{EN}(\textit{Content, Time})) \in \mathbf{EXP}\end{aligned} \qquad (20)$$

However in this way there could exist abductive answers with $\mathbf{D}$ literals even if there is no explicit rule introducing them. For example, in the history of formula (15) an abductive answer would be[1]

$\neg\mathbf{EN}(rescind(alice, bob, buy(car), fixMileage(car), i1, \_), T2),$
$\mathbf{D}(\mathbf{EN}(assertAgainst(alice, \_, i2), \_))$
$\mathbf{D}(\mathbf{E}(do(alice, buy(car), i1), \_))$
$\mathbf{D}(\mathbf{E}(pay(alice, mechanic, lpgsystem), \_))$
$\mathbf{NULL}(i1, i2)$

since it satisfies Eq. (5) (which takes into account knowledge base and integrity constraints), (6), (7), (19) and (20). Note that Alice is no longer required to pay the mechanic, because although no IC introduces explicitly the dischargement of the expectation that she should pay, the abductive semantics accepts the introduction of the literal $\mathbf{D}(\mathbf{E}(pay(alice, mechanic, lpgsystem), \_))$.

We propose the following semantics.

Definition 3. *Abductive answer.*
If there is a set $\mathbf{EXP}$ *such that*

1. *satisfies Eqs. (5), (6), and (7)*
2. *is minimal with respect to set inclusion within the sets satisfying point 3, considering only $\mathbf{D}$ atoms; more precisely: there is no set $\mathbf{EXP}'$ satisfying point 3 and such that $\mathbf{EXP}' \subset \mathbf{EXP}$ and $\mathbf{EXP} = \mathbf{EXP}' \cup F$, where F contains only $\mathbf{D}$ atoms*
3. *satisfies Eqs. (19) and (20)*

then the set $\mathbf{EXP}$ *is an abductive answer, and we write* $\langle KB, \mathcal{IC} \rangle \models_{\mathbf{EXP}} true.$

---

[1] For brevity, we omit an expectation $\mathbf{E}(x)$ if we have already its discharged version $\mathbf{D}(\mathbf{E}(x))$.

4.2   Operational Semantics

Operationally, the proof procedure is extended with transition *Dischargement*.

If **EXP** contains two atoms $\mathbf{E}(x,T) \in \mathbf{PEND}$ and $\mathbf{D}(\mathbf{E}(x,T))$, then atom $\mathbf{E}(x,T)$ is moved to the set **FULF** of fulfilled expectations.

Similarly, if **EXP** contains two atoms $\mathbf{EN}(x,T) \in \mathbf{PEND}$ and $\mathbf{D}(\mathbf{EN}(x,T))$, then atom $\mathbf{EN}(x,T)$ is moved to the set **FULF** of fulfilled expectations.

Another modification is that transition **EN** *violation* is postponed after all other transitions (including the closure of the history). In fact, if we have $\mathbf{H}(x,1)$, $\mathbf{EN}(x,T)$ and $\mathbf{D}(x,T)$, a failure would occur if the proof-procedure applied first **EN** *violation*. Instead, if *Dischargement* is applied first, expectation $\mathbf{EN}(x,T)$ is moved to the **FULF** set and transition **EN** *violation* is no longer applicable.

In case, at the end of a derivation, there are still expectations that are not fulfilled, the derivation is a failure derivation (and backtracking might occur to explore another branch, if available).

If a computation terminates with success, we write $\langle KB,\mathcal{IC}\rangle \vdash_{\mathbf{EXP}} true$.

4.3   Soundness

We are now ready to give the soundness statements; these statements rely on the soundness and completeness theorems of the $\mathcal{S}$CIFF proof-procedure, so they hold in the same cases; for the $\mathcal{S}$CIFF allowedness conditions over knowledge base and integrity constraints, we refer the reader to [5].

Theorem 1 *(Soundness of success). If $\langle KB,\mathcal{IC}\rangle$ is weakly $\mathbf{D}$-allowed and $\langle KB,\mathcal{IC}\rangle \vdash_{\mathbf{EXP}} true$ then $\langle KB,\mathcal{IC}\rangle \models_{\mathbf{EXP}} true$.*

Proof. If no **D** atoms occur in $\mathcal{IC}$, the procedure coincides with $\mathcal{S}$CIFF, which is sound [5]. In the case with **D** atoms in $\mathcal{IC}$, the procedure might report success in cases in which $\mathcal{S}$CIFF reports failure due to the extended notion of fulfillment (Eqs. (19) and (20)). In such a case, the **D** atom must have been generated, and the only way to generate it is through an IC having such atom in the head (see Definition 1).

The procedure generates the atom only if the body of the IC is true. If the body is true, it means (from the soundness of $\mathcal{S}$CIFF) that it is true also in the declarative semantics, so the **D** atom must be true also declaratively. In such a case, Eq. (19) (or (20)) is satisfied, meaning that the success was sound.   □

Theorem 2 *(Soundness of failure). If $\langle KB,\mathcal{IC}\rangle$ is weakly $\mathbf{D}$-allowed and $\langle KB,\mathcal{IC}\rangle \models_{\mathbf{EXP}} true$, then $\exists \mathbf{EXP}' \subseteq \mathbf{EXP}$ such that $\langle KB,\mathcal{IC}\rangle \vdash_{\mathbf{EXP}'} true$.*

Proof. If there are no **D** atoms in $\mathcal{IC}$, the procedure coincides with $\mathcal{S}$CIFF, so the completeness theorem of $\mathcal{S}$CIFF holds [5]. In the case with **D** atoms in $\mathcal{IC}$, the declarative semantics allows as abductive answers some sets that would not have been returned by $\mathcal{S}$CIFF, and in which expectations are not fulfilled by actual events, but discharged through an abduced **D** atom.

Consider such an abductive answer **EXP**. We prove by contradiction that each **D** atom in **EXP** occurs in the head of an IC whose body is true. In fact, if a **D** atom in **EXP** was not in the head of an IC whose body is true, then the set **EXP**$'$ obtained by removing the **D** atom from **EXP** would satisfy Eq. (5). On the other hand, since **EXP** satisfies Eqs. (6) and (7) and those equations do not involve **D** atoms, also **EXP**$'$ satisfies those equations. This means that **EXP** does not satisfy condition 2 of Definition 3, which means that **EXP** was not an abductive answer and we get a contradiction.

Since each **D** atom occurs in the head of an IC whose body is true, the procedure applies such IC and abduces that atom. This means that the corresponding expectation becomes discharged, and hence it does not cause failure.   □

5   Related Work

Many authors have investigated legal and normative applications of deontic logics. The use of such logics was initially debated when taking into account permissions. For example, in [16] the authors present an approach based on input/output logics [32] for formalizing conditional norms, obligations and permissions in a scenario where many hierarchically organized authorities are present. In such a scenario, there can be norms that are more important than others and therefore the authors consider a hierarchy of norms, defined by "meta-norms", and different types of permissions with different strengths. However, the focus of [16] is on helping the legislator to understand how the modification of a norm or the definition of a new one may change the whole normative system. In fact, following the input/output logic's semantics, [16] is not concerned about the truth value of formulae representing (part of) norms but defines a cause-effect link between inputs and obligatory outputs in an abductive-like way.

Recently deontic logics have been increasingly applied to legal domains. In [26] the authors discuss the impact new contracts, which introduce new constraints, may have on already existing business processes. The authors present a logic called FCL (Formal Contract Language), based on RuleML, for representing contracts in a formal way. The language allows automatic checking and debugging, analysis and reasoning [25]. In [26] a normal form of FCL, called NFCL, is presented with the aim of having a clean, complete and non-redundant representation of a contract. This normal form is obtained by merging the new constraints with the existing ones and cleaning up the redundancies by using the notion of subsumption. The result points out possible conflicts among contracts and how each contract is intertwined with the whole business process. Similar results can be accomplished with $\mathcal{S}$CIFF$^{\mathcal{D}}$ which allows checking the consistency of the $\mathcal{S}$CIFF$^{\mathcal{D}}$ program representing the constraints of the business process.

A different approach is the combination of temporal logics with deontic logics. An example is given in [1], where the authors define Normative Temporal Logic (NTL) which replaces the standard operators of the well-known CTL [22] with deontic operators. The use of time, which forces the sequentiality of the constraints, avoids many paradoxes typical of standard deontic logic, such as those involving contrary-of-duty. Moreover, the authors present the Simple Reactive Modules Language (SRML) which follows NTL and allows the execution of model checking in four different scenarios depending on the presence or absence of an interpretation of the normative system and on the definition of the model under examination. Similarly, $\mathcal{SCIFF}^\mathcal{D}$ can manage time although it does not follow the temporal logic semantics. A similar approach is proposed by the same authors in [2] where they present the Norm Compliance CTL (NCCTL). This logic extends CTL by adding a new deontic-like operator P modeling coalitions between norms which cooperate in the normative system. NCCTL is equipped with a model checker, called NORMC [31]. Since $\mathcal{SCIFF}$ performs on-the-fly checking of compliance, the two systems cannot be directly compared.

The **AD** system [9] is a deontic logic that supports defeasibile obligations by means a revision operator (called f), which represents the assumptions that normally come with an explicitly stated condition. Intuitively, $fA \Rightarrow O(B)$ means that A implies that B is obligatory, as long as the usual assumptions about A are true. The $\mathcal{SCIFF}^\mathcal{D}$ semantics implements an implicit assumption that an expectation is not discharged (and is therefore required to be fulfilled), which can be defeated by an explicit dischargement atom (which allows for the expectation not to be fulfilled).

This paper shows that representing and reasoning with norms facilitate for the adoption of such approaches in many scenarios. Checking whether certain facts are compliant with the normative system in use is in fact often needed. Abductive frameworks such as $\mathcal{SCIFF}^\mathcal{D}$ can also be used, for example, in forensics for analysing and arguing on evidence of a crime or for explaining causal stories, sequence of states and events forming (part of) a case. Such stories must be coherent and there must be a process, usually abductive, able to prove their truthfulness. These necessities are pointed out for example in [13,14], where the authors present a hybrid framework which combines the two most used approaches in reasoning about criminal evidences: argumentative and story-based analysis. Both of them could benefit from the use of normative systems.

6 Conclusions

In this article we continue our line of research that applies abductive logic programming to the formalization of normative systems.

We introduced the $\mathcal{SCIFF}^\mathcal{D}$ language, extending the $\mathcal{SCIFF}$ abductive framework with the notion of dischargeable obligation. Dischargeable obligations can occur in the head of forward rules (named ICs), fired under specific conditions mentioned in the body of the rules. The $\mathcal{SCIFF}^\mathcal{D}$ declarative semantics and its operational counterpart for verification accordingly extend $\mathcal{SCIFF}$'s, and soundness is proved under syntactic conditions over these (discharging) constraints.

To experiment the framework we considered case studies requiring the notion of discharging of an obligation. In particular, we considered the articles in the Japanese Civil Code that deal with the rescission of manifestation of intentions and prevention of fulfillment of conditions. We also show - informally - the result of running the operational support upon this example in some simple scenarios.

Acknowledgements. This work was partially supported by the "GNCS-INdAM".

References

1. Ågotnes, T., van der Hoek, W., Rodríguez-Aguilar, J.A., Sierra, C., Wooldridge, M.: On the logic of normative systems. In: Veloso, M.M. (ed.) 20th International Joint Conference on Artificial Intelligence, Hyderabad, India (IJCAI 2007), vol. 7, pp. 1175–1180. AAAI Press, Palo Alto (2007)
2. Ågotnes, T., van der Hoek, W., Wooldridge, M.: Robust normative systems and a logic of norm compliance. Log. J. IGPL 18(1), 4–30 (2010)
3. Alberti, M., Chesani, F., Gavanelli, M., Lamma, E., Mello, P., Montali, M.: An abductive framework for a-priori verification of web services. In: Maher, M. (ed.) Proceedings of the 8th Symposium on Principles and Practice of Declarative Programming, pp. 39–50. ACM Press, New York, July 2006
4. Alberti, M., Chesani, F., Gavanelli, M., Lamma, E., Mello, P., Torroni, P.: Compliance verification of agent interaction: a logic-based software tool. Appl. Artif. Intell. 20(2–4), 133–157 (2006)
5. Alberti, M., Chesani, F., Gavanelli, M., Lamma, E., Mello, P., Torroni, P.: Verifiable agent interaction in abductive logic programming: the SCIFF framework. ACM T. Comput. Log. 9(4), 29:1–29:43 (2008)
6. Alberti, M., Gavanelli, M., Lamma, E.: $Deon^+$: abduction and constraints for normative reasoning. In: Artikis, A., Craven, R., Kesim Çiçekli, N., Sadighi, B., Stathis, K. (eds.) Logic Programs, Norms and Action. LNCS, vol. 7360, pp. 308–328. Springer, Heidelberg (2012). doi:10.1007/978-3-642-29414-3_17
7. Alberti, M., Gavanelli, M., Lamma, E., Mello, P., Sartor, G., Torroni, P.: Mapping deontic operators to abductive expectations. Comput. Math. Organ. Th. 12(2–3), 205–225 (2006)
8. Alberti, M., Gavanelli, M., Lamma, E., Mello, P., Torroni, P.: Specification and verification of agent interactions using social integrity constraints. Electr. Notes Theor. Comput. Sci. 85(2), 94–116 (2003)
9. Alchourrón, C.E.: Detachment and defeasibility in deontic logic. Studia Logica 57(1), 5–18 (1996)
10. Alchourrón, C.E., Gärdenfors, P., Makinson, D.: On the logic of theory change: partial meet contraction and revision functions. J. Symbolic Logic 50(2), 510–530 (1985)
11. ALFEBIITE: A Logical Framework for Ethical Behaviour Between Infohabitants in the Information Trading Economy of the Universal Information Ecosystem. IST-1999-10298 (1999)
12. Arisha, K.A., Ozcan, F., Ross, R., Subrahmanian, V.S., Eiter, T., Kraus, S.: IMPACT: a platform for collaborating agents. IEEE Intell. Syst. 14(2), 64–72 (1999)
13. Bex, F., Prakken, H., Reed, C., Walton, D.: Towards a formal account of reasoning about evidence: argumentation schemes and generalisations. Artif. Intell. Law 11(2–3), 125–165 (2003)
14. Bex, F.J., van Koppen, P.J., Prakken, H., Verheij, B.: A hybrid formal theory of arguments, stories and criminal evidence. Artif. Intell. Law 18(2), 123–152 (2010)
15. Boella, G., van der Torre, L., Verhagen, H.: Introduction to normative multiagent systems. Comput. Math. Organ. Th. 12, 71–79 (2006)
16. Boella, G., van der Torre, L.W.N.: Permissions and obligations in hierarchical normative systems. In: Zeleznikow, J., Sartor, G. (eds.) 9th International Conference on Artificial Intelligence and Law (ICAIL 2003), Edinburgh, Scotland, UK, Proceedings, pp. 109–118. ACM Press (2003)

17. Bracciali, A., et al.: The KGP model of agency for global computing: computational model and prototype implementation. In: Priami, C., Quaglia, P. (eds.) GC 2004. LNCS, vol. 3267, pp. 340–367. Springer, Heidelberg (2005). doi:10.1007/978-3-540-31794-4_18
18. Dignum, V., Meyer, J.J., Weigand, H.: Towards an organizational model for agent societies using contracts. In: Castelfranchi, C., Lewis Johnson, W. (eds.) 1st International Joint Conference on Autonomous Agents and Multiagent Systems (AAMAS 2002), Part II, pp. 694–695. ACM Press (2002)
19. Dignum, V., Meyer, J.J., Weigand, H., Dignum, F.: An organizational-oriented model for agent societies. In: 1st International Joint Conference on Autonomous Agents and Multiagent Systems (AAMAS 2002). ACM Press (2002)
20. Eiter, T., Subrahmanian, V., Pick, G.: Heterogeneous active agents, I: semantics. Artif. Intell. **108**(1–2), 179–255 (1999)
21. Eiter, T., Gottlob, G.: The complexity of logic-based abduction. J. ACM **42**(1), 3–42 (1995)
22. Emerson, E.A.: Temporal and modal logic. In: Handbook of Theoretical Computer Science, Volume B: Formal Models and Sematics (B), pp. 995–1072. Elsevier (1990)
23. Fung, T.H., Kowalski, R.A.: The IFF proof procedure for abductive logic programming. J. Logic Program. **33**(2), 151–165 (1997)
24. Gavanelli, M., Lamma, E., Riguzzi, F., Bellodi, E., Zese, R., Cota, G.: An abductive framework for Datalog+− ontologies. In: De Vos, M., Eiter, T., Lierler, Y., Toni, F. (eds.) Technical Communications of the 31st International Conference on Logic Programming (ICLP 2015), No. 1433 in CEUR-WS, Sun SITE Central Europe, Aachen, Germany (2015)
25. Governatori, G.: Representing business contracts in RuleML. Int. J. Coop. Inf. Syst. **14**(2–3), 181–216 (2005)
26. Governatori, G., Milosevic, Z., Sadiq, S.W.: Compliance checking between business processes and business contracts. In: 10th IEEE International Enterprise Distributed Object Computing Conference (EDOC), Hong Kong, China, pp. 221–232. IEEE Computer Society (2006)
27. Governatori, G., Rotolo, A.: BIO logical agents: norms, beliefs, intentions in defeasible logic. Auton. Agent Multi Ag. **17**(1), 36–69 (2008)
28. Jaffar, J., Maher, M.: Constraint logic programming: a survey. J. Logic Program. **19–20**, 503–582 (1994)
29. Japanese Civil Code, Part I. https://en.wikisource.org/wiki/Civil_Code_of_Japan/Part_I. Accessed 19 July 2016
30. Kakas, A.C., Kowalski, R.A., Toni, F.: Abductive logic programming. J. Logic Comput. **2**(6), 719–770 (1993)
31. Kazmierczak, P., Pedersen, T., Ågotnes, T.: NORMC: a norm compliance temporal logic model checker. In: Kersting, K., Toussaint, M. (eds.) 6th Starting AI Researchers' Symposium (STAIR 2012), FRONTIERS, Montpellier, France, vol. 241, pp. 168–179. IOS Press (2012)
32. Makinson, D., van der Torre, L.W.N.: Constraints for input/output logics. J. Philos. Logic **30**(2), 155–185 (2001)
33. Prakken, H., Sartor, G.: Argument-based extended logic programming with defeasible priorities. J. Appl. Non Classical Logics **7**(1), 25–75 (1997)
34. Sadri, F., Stathis, K., Toni, F.: Normative KGP agents. Comput. Math. Organ. Th. **12**(2–3), 101–126 (2006)
35. Sergot, M.J., Sadri, F., Kowalski, R.A., Kriwaczek, F., Hammond, P., Cory, H.T.: The British Nationality Act as a logic program. Commun. ACM **29**, 370–386 (1986)
36. Wright, G.: Deontic logic. Mind **60**, 1–15 (1951)

Using Rule-Based Reasoning for RDF Validation

Dörthe Arndt$^{(\boxtimes)}$, Ben De Meester, Anastasia Dimou, Ruben Verborgh,
and Erik Mannens

Ghent University - imec - IDLab, Sint-Pietersnieuwstraat 41, 9000 Ghent, Belgium
doerthe.arndt@ugent.be

Abstract. The success of the Semantic Web highly depends on its ingredients. If we want to fully realize the vision of a machine-readable Web, it is crucial that Linked Data are actually useful for machines consuming them. On this background it is not surprising that (Linked) Data validation is an ongoing research topic in the community. However, most approaches so far either do not consider reasoning, and thereby miss the chance of detecting implicit constraint violations, or they base themselves on a combination of different formalisms, e.g. Description Logics combined with SPARQL. In this paper, we propose using Rule-Based Web Logics for RDF validation focusing on the concepts needed to support the most common validation constraints, such as Scoped Negation As Failure (SNAF), and the predicates defined in the Rule Interchange Format (RIF). We prove the feasibility of the approach by providing an implementation in Notation3 Logic. As such, we show that rule logic can cover both validation and reasoning if it is expressive enough.

Keywords: N3 · RDF validation · Rule-based reasoning

1 Introduction

The amount of publicly available Linked Open Data (LOD) sets is constantly growing[1], however, the diversity of the data employed in applications is mostly very limited: only a handful of RDF data is used frequently [27]. One of the reasons for this is that the datasets' quality and consistency varies significantly, ranging from expensively curated to relatively low quality data [33], and thus need to be validated carefully before use.

One way to assess data quality is to check them against constraints: users can verify that certain data are fit for their use case, if the data abide to their requirements. First approaches to do that were implementations with hard coded validation rules, such as Whoknows? [13]. Lately, attention has been drawn to formalizing RDF quality assessment, more specifically, formalizing RDF constraints languages, such as Shape Expressions (ShEx) [30] or Resource Shapes (ReSh) [28]. This detaches the specification of the constraints from its implementation.

---

[1] See, e.g. statistics at: http://lod-cloud.net/.

© Springer International Publishing AG 2017
S. Costantini et al. (Eds.): RuleML+RR 2017, LNCS 10364, pp. 22–36, 2017.
DOI: 10.1007/978-3-319-61252-2_3

Constraint languages allow users dealing with RDF data and vocabularies to express, communicate, and test their particular expectations. Such languages can either be (i) existing frameworks designed for different purposes, e.g. the query language SPARQL [12,21], or the description logic based Web Ontology Language (OWL) [31], or they can be (ii) languages only designed for validation, e.g. ShEx [30], ReSh [28], Description Set Profiles (DSP) [23], or the forthcoming W3C recommendation candidate Shapes Constraint Language (SHACL) [19]. These different languages can be compared by testing them on commonly supported constraints [9,21], as conducted by Hartmann (né Bosch) et al. [8].

Depending on the users' needs, constraint languages have to be able to cope with very diverse kinds of constraints which imply certain *logical requirements*. Such requirements were investigated by Hartmann et al. [8] who identified the Closed World Assumption (CWA) and the Unique Name Assumption (UNA) as crucial for validation. Since both are not supported by many Web Logics, Hartmann et al. particularly emphasize the difference between reasoning and validation languages and favour SPARQL based approaches for validation which – if needed – can be combined with OWL DL or QL reasoning. In this paper, we take a closer look into these findings from a rule-based perspective: We show that neither UNA nor CWA are necessary for validation if a rule-based framework containing predicates to compare URIs and literals, and supporting Scoped Negation as Failure (SNAF) is used. This enables us to – instead of combining separate, successive systems – do both RDF validation *and* reasoning in only one system which acts directly on a constraint language. We show the feasibility of this approach by providing an implementation. This proof-of-concept is implemented in Notation3 Logic (N3Logic) and tackles the subset of the constraints identified by Hartmann et al. [8] which are covered in RDFUnit [21].

The remainder of this paper is structured as follows: In Sect. 2 we discuss related work. In Sect. 3 we give an overview of common RDF validation constraints. In Sect. 4, we discuss how different requirements for RDF validation are met by rule-based logics. Section 5 explains the details of our proof of concept and Sect. 6 concludes the paper and provides an outlook for future work.

2   Related Work

In this section, first, we will present the state of the art around validation constraint languages. Then, we will give an overview of different languages and approaches used for RDF validation.

Data quality can be described in many dimensions, one of them being the intrinsic dimension, namely, the adherence to a data schema [33]. In the case of RDF data, this implies adhering to certain constraints. These have been carefully investigated by several authors (e.g. Hartmann [12]). The formulation of (a subset of) these constraints can be done using existing languages (e.g. the Web Ontology Language (OWL) [7], the SPARQL Inferencing Notation (SPIN) [18], or SPARQL [26])), or via dedicated languages (e.g. Shape Expressions (ShEx) [30], Resource Shapes (ReSh) [28], Description Set Profiles

(DSP) [23], or Shapes Constraint Language (SHACL) [19]. Their execution is either based on reasoning frameworks, or querying frameworks.

On the one hand, Motik et al. [22] and Sirin and Tau [29] propose alternative semantics for OWL which support the Closed World Assumption, and are therefore more suited for constraint validation than the original version. To know which semantics apply, constraints have to be marked as such. Using one standard to express both, validation and reasoning, is a strong point of this approach, however, this leads to ambiguity: If the exact same formula can have different meanings, one of the key properties of the Semantics Web – interoperability – is in danger. Another disadvantage of using (modified) OWL as a constraint language is its limited expressiveness. Common constraints such as mathematical operations or specific checks on language tags are not covered by OWL [12].

On the other hand, SPARQL based querying frameworks for validation execution emerged (e.g. Hartmann [12] or Kontokostas et al. [21]). Where Hartmann proposes SPIN as base language to support validation constraints, Kontokostas introduces a similar but distinct language to SPIN, more targeted to validation, so-called Data Quality Test Patterns (DQTP). DQTPs are generalized SPARQL queries containing an extra type of variables. In an extra step, these variables are instantiated based on the RDFS and OWL axioms used by the data schema and can then be employed for querying. As such, the authors assume a closed world semantics for OWL but in contrast to the approaches mentioned above, this special semantics cannot be marked in the ontology itself. They thus change the semantics of the common Web standard OWL. To also find implicit constraint validation an extra reasoning step could be added, but this step would then most probably assume the standard semantics of OWL, further increasing the possibly of experiencing conflicts between the two contradicting versions of the semantics. Hartmann proposes a dedicated ontology to express integrity constraints, and as such, this method does not involve changing existing semantics. For both, involving reasoning is not possible without inclusion of a secondary system.

3   RDF Validation Constraints

Based on the collaboration of the W3C RDF Data Shapes Working Group[2] and the DCMI RDF Application Profiles Task Group[3] with experts from industry, government, and academia, a set of validation requirements has been defined, based on which, 81 types of constraints were published, each of them corresponding to at least one of the validation requirements [9]. This set thus gives a realistic and comprehensive view of what validation systems should support.

Prior to this, the creators of RDFUnit [21] had provided their own set of constraint types they support. Given the usage of RDFUnit in real-world use

---

[2] https://www.w3.org/2014/data-shapes/wiki/Main_Page.
[3] http://wiki.dublincore.org/index.php/RDF_Application_Profiles.

cases [20], this set gives a good overview of what validation systems should minimally cover.

Table 1 shows the alignment of the 17 types of constraints as supported by RDFUnit with the relevant constraint types as identified by Hartmann et al. [8]. As can be seen, these types are not mapped one-to-one. One constraint from RDFUnit maps to at least one constraint as identified by Hartmann, except for PVT and TRIPLE, which are both not very complex constraints and could thus easily be added to the work of Hartmann et al. In this paper, we mainly focus on these 17 constraints which are all covered by our implementation. To make the topic of constraint validation more concrete, we discuss the examples (TYPEDEP), (INVFUNC) and (MATCH) in more detail later in this paper and refer the interested reader to the above mentioned sources.

Table 1. Constraints Alignment. The first column lists the codes as used in RDFUnit; the second column lists the constraints of Hartmann following the numbering [12, Appendix]; and the third column lists the description taken from RDFUnit.

RDFUnit	Constraint code	Description
COMP	A11	Comparison between two literal values of a resource
MATCH	A20, A21	A resource's literal value (does not) matches a RegEx
LITRAN	A17, A18	The literal value of a resource (having a certain type) must (not) be within a specific range
TYPEDEP	A4	Type dependency: the type of a resource may imply the attribution of another type
TYPRODEP	A41	A resource of specific type should have a certain property
PVT	B1	If a resource has a certain value V assigned via a property P1 that in some way classifies this resource, one can assume the existence of another property P2
TRIPLE	B2	A resource can be considered erroneous if there are corresponding hints contained in the dataset
ONELANG	A28	A literal value has at most one literal for a language
RDFS-DOMAIN	A13	The attribution of a resource's property (with a certain value) is only valid if the resource is of a certain type
RDFS-RANGE	A14, A15	The attribution of a resource's property is only valid if the value is of a certain type
RDFS-RANGED	A23	The attribution of a resource's property is only valid if the literal value has a certain Datatype
INVFUNC	A2	Some values assigned to a resource are considered to be unique for this particular resource and must not occur in Connection with other resources
OWL-CARD	A1, A32–37	Cardinality restriction on a property
OWLDISJC	A70	Disjoint class constraint
OWLDISJP	A69	Disjoint property constraint
OWL-ASYMP	A57	Asymmetric property constraint
OWL-IRREFL	A64	Irreflexive property constraint

4   Features Required for Validation

After having listed the kind of constraints relevant for RDF validation in the previous section, we will now focus on the suitability of rule-based logics for that task. Based on the work of Sirin and Tao [29], and Hartmann et al. [8] who identified the logical requirements constraint languages need to fulfil, we discuss why rule-based logic is a reasonable choice to validate RDF datasets.

4.1   Reasoning

We start our discussion with reasoning. Hartmann [12, p. 181] points out that performing reasoning in combination with RDF validation brings several benefits: constraint violations may be solved, violations which otherwise would stay undetected can be found, and datasets do not need to contain redundant data to be accepted by a validation engine. To better understand these benefits, consider the following ontology example:

$$\texttt{:Reseacher rdfs:subClassOf :Person.} \tag{1}$$

And the instance:

$$\texttt{:Kurt a :Researcher; :name"Kurt01".} \tag{2}$$

If we now have a type dependency constraint (TYPEDEP) saying that every instance of the class `:Researcher` should also be an instance of the class `:Person`, which we test on the data above, a constraint validation error would be raised since `:Kurt` is not declared as a `:Person`. If we perform the same constraint check after reasoning, the triple

$$\texttt{:Kurt a :Person.} \tag{3}$$

would be derived and the constraint violation would be solved. Without the reasoning, Triple 3 would need to be inserted into the dataset to solve the constraint, leading to redundant data.

To understand how reasoning can help to detect implicit constraints, consider another restriction: suppose that we have a constraint stating that a person's name should not contain numbers[4]. Without reasoning, no constraint validation would be detected because even though the `:name` of `:Kurt` contains numbers, `:Kurt` would not be detected as an instance of `:Person`.

Hartmann's and many other validation approaches thus suggest to first perform a reasoning step and then do an extra validation step via SPARQL querying. The advantage of using rule-based reasoning instead is that validation can take place during the reasoning process *in one single step*. Relying on a rule which supports `rdfs:subClassOf` as for example presented in [2] the aforementioned problem could be detected. In general, OWL-RL [10] can be applied since it is supported by every rule language. If higher complexity is needed, rule languages with support for existential quantification can be used for OWL QL reasoning.

---

[4] This could be expressed by an extended version of MATCH as for example the constraint "Negative Literal Pattern Matching" in [12].

4.2   Scoped Negation as Failure

Another aspect which is important for constraint validation is negation. Hartmann et al. claim that the Closed World Assumption is needed to perform validation tasks. Given that most Web logics assume the Open World Assumption, that would form a barrier for the goal of combining reasoning and validation mentioned in the previous section. Luckily, that is not the case. As constraint validation copes with the local knowledge base, Scoped Negation as Failure (SNAF), inter alia discussed in [11,16,25], is enough. Among the logics which support this concept are for example FLORA-2 [14] or N3Logic [6].

In order to understand the idea behind Scoped Negation as Failure, consider the triples that form Formula 2 and suppose that these are the only triples in a knowledge base we want to validate. We now want to test the constraint from above that every individual which is declared as a researcher is also declared as a person (TYPEDEP). This means our system needs to give a warning if it finds an individual which is declared as a researcher, but not as a person:

$$\forall x : ((\text{ x a :Researcher}) \land \neg (\text{ x a :Person}))$$
$$\rightarrow (\text{:constraint :is :violated.}) (4)$$

In the form it is stated before, the constraint cannot be tested with the Open World Assumption. The knowledge base contains the triple

$$\text{:Kurt a :Researcher.}$$

but not Triple 3, but the rule is more general: given its open nature, we cannot guarantee that there is no document in the entire Web which declares Triple 3. This changes if we make an addition. Suppose that $\mathcal{K}$ is the the set of triples we can derive (either with or without reasoning) from our knowledge base consisting of Formula 2. Having $\mathcal{K}$ at our disposal, we can test:

$$\forall x : ((\text{ x a :Researcher}) \in \mathcal{K}) \land \neg ((\text{ x a :Person}) \in \mathcal{K}))$$
$$\rightarrow (\text{:constraint :is :violated.}) (5)$$

The second conjunct is not a simple negation, it is a negation with a certain scope, in this case $\mathcal{K}$. If we added new data to our knowledge like for example Triple 3, we would have different knowledge $\mathcal{K}'$ for which other statements hold. The truth value of the formula above would not be touched since this formula explicitly mentions $\mathcal{K}$. The logic stays monotonic. Scoped negation as failure is the kind of negation we actually need in RDF validation: we do not want to make and test statements in the Web in general, we just want to test the information contained in a local file or knowledge base.

4.3   Predicates for Name Comparison

Next to the Open World Assumption, Hartmann et al. [8] identify the fact that most Web logics do not base themselves on the Unique Names Assumption (UNA) as a barrier for them being used for constraint validation. This assumption is for example present in F-Logic [17] and basically states that every element in the domain of discourse can only have one single name (URI or Literal in our case). The reason, why this assumption is in general problematic for the Semantic Web lies in its distributed nature: different datasets can – and actually do – use different names for the same individual or concept. For instance, the URI dbpedia:London refers to the same place in England as for example dbpedia-nl:London. In this case this fact is even stated in the corresponding ontologies using the predicate owl:sameAs.

The impact of the Unique Name Assumption for RDF validation becomes clear if we take a closer look at OWL's inverse functional property and the related constraint (INVFUNC). Let us assume that dbo:capital is an owl:InverseFunctionalProperty and our knowledge base contains:

$$:England\ dbo:capital\ :London.\ :Britain\ dbo:capital\ :London. \qquad (6)$$

Since :England and :Britain are both stated as having :London as their capital and dbo:capital is an inverse functional property, an OWL reasoner would derive

$$:England\ owl:sameAs\ :Britain. \qquad (7)$$

Such a derivation cannot be made if the Unique Name Assumption is valid, since the former explicitly excludes this possibility.

The constraint (INVFUNC) is related to the OWL concept above, but it is slightly different: while OWL's inverse functional property refers to the elements of the domain of discourse denoted by the name, the validation constraint (INVFUNC) refers to the representation itself. Formula 6 thus violates the constraint. Even if our logic does not follow the Unique Name Assumption, this violation can be detected if the logic offers predicates to compare names. In N3Logic, log:equalTo and log:notEqualTo[5] are such predicates: in contrast to owl:sameAs and owl:differentFrom, they do not compare the resources they denote, but their representation. The idea to support these kinds of predicates is very common. So does, for example, the Rule Interchange Format (RIF) cover several functions which can handle URIs and strings, as we will discuss in the next subsection.

4.4   RIF Built-Ins

In the previous subsection we indicated that a special predicate of a logic, in this case log:notEqualTo, can be used to do URI comparisons and thereby support a concept which would otherwise be difficult to express. Such built-in functions are widely spread in rule-based logics and play an important role in RDF validation which very often deals with string comparisons, calculations or operations on URI level. While it normally depends on the designers of a logic which features are supported, there are also common standards.

---

[5] https://www.w3.org/2000/10/swap/doc/CwmBuiltins.

One of them is the Rule Interchange Format (RIF) [15] whose aim it is to provide a formalism to exchange rules in the Web. Being the result of a W3C working group consisting of developers and users of different rule-based languages, RIF can also be understood as a reference for the most common features rule based logics might have. This makes the list of predicates [24] supported by the different RIF dialects particularly interesting for our analysis. And it is indeed the case that by only using RIF predicates many of the constraints listed in Sect. 3 can already be checked: negative pattern matching (MATCH) can be implemented by using the predicate `pred:matches`, the handling of language tags as required for the constraint ONELANG can be done using `func:lang-from-PlainLiteral`, and for the comparison of literal values (COMP) there are several predicates to compare strings, numbers or dates.

To illustrate how powerful RIF is when it comes to string validation, we take a closer look at the predicate `log:notEqualTo` from the previous section. In the example above it is used to compare two URI representations and succeeds if these two are different. To refer to a URI value, RIF provides the predicate `pred:iri-string` which converts a URI to a string and vice versa. In N3 notation[6] that could be expressed by:

$$(\text{:England "http://exmpl.com/England") pred:iri-string true.} \quad (8)$$

To compare the newly generated strings, the function `func:compare` can be used. This function takes two string values as input, and returns -1 if the first string is smaller than the second one regarding a string order, 0 if the two strings are the same, and 1 if the second is smaller than the first. The example above gives:

$$(\text{"http://exmpl.com/Britain""http://exmpl.com/England")}$$
$$\text{func:compare } -1. \quad (9)$$

To enable a rule to detect whether the two URI names are equal, one additional function is needed: the reasoner has to detect whether the result of the comparison is not equal to zero. That can be checked using the predicate `pred:numeric-not-equal` which is the RIF version of $\neq$ for numeric values. In the present case the output of the comparison would be **true** since $0 \neq 1$, a rule checking for the name equality of :England and :Britain using the three predicates would therefore be triggered.

Even though we needed three RIF predicates to express one N3 predicate, the previous example showed how powerful built-ins in general – but also the very common RIF predicates in particular – are. Whether a rule based Web logic is suited for RDF validation highly depends on its built-ins. If it supports all RIF predicates, this can be seen as a strong indication that it is expressive enough.

---

[6] More about that in Sect. 5.1.

5   Validation with N3Logic

In the previous section we analysed the requirements on a rule-based Web logic to be able to combine validation and reasoning: it should support scoped negation as failure, it should provide predicates to compare different URIs and strings, and its built-in functions should be powerful enough to, inter alia, access language tags and do string comparison as they are supported by RIF. N3Logic as it is implemented in the EYE reasoner [32] fulfils all these conditions. With that logic, we were able to implement rules for all the constraints listed in Sect. 3, and thus provide similar functionality as RDFUnit using rule-based Web logics. Below we discuss the details of this implementation starting by providing more information about N3Logic and EYE. The code of our implementation can be accessed at https://github.com/IDLabResearch/data-validation.

5.1   N3Logic

N3Logic was introduced in 2008 by Berners-Lee et al. [6] and is an extension of RDF: All RDF turtle triples are also valid in N3. As in RDF, blanknodes are understood as existentially quantified variables and the co-occurrence of two triples as in Formula 6 is understood as their conjunction. N3 furthermore supports universally quantified variables. These are indicated by a leading question mark ?.

$$?x \; :\texttt{likes} \; :\texttt{IceCream}. \tag{10}$$

stands for *"Everyone likes ice cream."*, or in first order logic

$$\forall x : \text{likes}(x, \text{ice-cream})$$

Rules are written using curly brackets { } and the implication symbol =>. The `rdfs:subClassOf` relation from Formula 1 can be expressed as:

$$\{?x \; \texttt{a} \; :\texttt{Researcher}\} \; => \; \{?x \; \texttt{a} \; :\texttt{Person}\}. \tag{11}$$

Applied on Formula 2 the rule results in Formula 3. More details about syntax and semantics of N3 can be found in our previous paper [4].

There are several reasoners supporting N3: FuXi [1] is a forward-chaining production system for Notation3 whose reasoning is based on the RETE algorithm. The forward-chaining cwm [5] reasoner is a general-purpose data processing tool which can be used for querying, checking, transforming and filtering information. EYE [32] is a reasoner enhanced with Euler path detection. It supports backward and forward reasoning and also a user-defined mixture of both. Amongst its numerous features are the option to skolemise blank nodes and the possibility to produce and reuse proofs for further reasoning. The reason why we use EYE in our implementation is its generous support for built-ins[7]: next to N3's native built-ins[8], RIF, but also several other functions and concepts are implemented.

---

[7] http://eulersharp.sourceforge.net/2003/03swap/eye-builtins.html.
[8] https://www.w3.org/2000/10/swap/doc/CwmBuiltins.

5.2   Expressing Constraints

Before we can detect violations of constraints using N3 logic, these constraints first need to be stated. This could either be done by directly expressing them in rules – and thereby creating a new constraint language next to the ones presented in Sect. 2 – or on top of existing RDF-based conventions. We opt for the latter and base our present implementation on the work of Hartmann [12, p. 167 ff]: in his PhD thesis, Hartmann presents a lightweight vocabulary to describe any constraint, the RDF Constraints Vocabulary (RDF-CV)[9]. The reason why we chose that vocabulary over the upcoming standard SHACL is its expressiveness. We aim to tackle the 81 constraints identified by Hartmann which are not all expressible in SHACL or any other of the constraint languages mentioned in Sect. 2 [12, p. 52, Appendix]. As will be shown in the following section, it is not difficult to adopt the rules to different constraint languages as long as they are based on RDF and as such valid N3 expressions.

RDF-CV supports the concept of so called *simple constraints* which are all the constraints expressible by the means of the vocabulary, in particular the ones mentioned in Sect. 3. Each simple constraint has a constraining element. Where applicable, the names of these elements are inspired by their related DL names, but the constraining element can also be for example the name of a SPARQL function. In some cases, the same constraint type can be marked by different constraining elements as for example the constraint COMP whose constraining element is the relation used to compare values (e.g. the usual numerical orders: $<, >, \leq$, and $\geq$) or there can be different constraint types sharing the same constraining element. To be sure that cases like this do not cause any ambiguity we additionally assign a *constraint type* to every constraint. The names of these types follow the names used by Hartmann [12, Appendix]. The TYPEDEP constraint from Sect. 4.1 is for example of constraint type :Subsumption.

In addition to constraining element and constraint type, there are several predicates to assign the constraints to individuals and classes: *context class*, *classes, leftProperties, rightProperties*, and *constraining values*. The *context class* of a constraint fixes the set of individuals for which a constraint must hold. For the subsumption constraint mentioned above, that would be the class :Researcher, the constraint talks about *every* individual labelled as *researcher*. There could be other classes involved. In our subsumption example that is the superclass the individuals should belong to, :Person. Every researcher should also be labelled as *person*. Since these kinds of properties can be multiple, they are given in a list. How and if the predicate *classes* is used depends on the constraint. The predicates *leftProperties* and *rightProperties* are used to do similar statements about properties. The constraint INVFUNC as displayed in Listing 1 makes for example use of it to relate the constraint specified to the predicate it is valid for. The objects of the predicates *leftProperties* and *rightProperties* are lists. The predicate *constraining value* is used for the predicates where a literal value is needed to further specify a constraint. An example for such a constraint

---

[9] https://github.com/boschthomas/RDF-Constraints-Vocabulary.

```
1  @prefix rdfcv: <http://www.dr-thomashartmann.de/phd-thesis/
     rdf-validation/vocabularies/rdf-constraints-vocabulary#>.
2  @prefix : <http://example.com/constraints#>.
3  @prefix dbo: <http://dbpedia.org/ontology/> .
4
5  :example_constraint a rdfcv:SimpleConstraint;
6    :constraintType  :InverseFunctionalProperties;
7    rdfcv:constrainingElement  :inverse-functional-properties;
8    rdfcv:leftProperties ( dbo:capital );
9    rdfcv:contextClass  dbo:Country.
```

Listing 1. Example inverse functional property constraint: No city can be the capital of two countries.

is MATCH as described in Sect. 4.1. To express, that a name should not contain numbers, the predicate *constraining value* connects the constraint to the string pattern, "[1-9]" in the present case.

5.3 Constraint Rules

Having seen in the last section one possible way to describe constraints on RDF datasets, this section explains how these descriptions can be used. We employ rules which take the expressed constraints and the RDF dataset to be tested into account and generate triples indicating constraint validations, if present. We illustrate that by an example: In Listing 2 we provide a rule handling the constraint INVFUNC. Lines 7–11 contain the details of the constraint. The rule applies for simple constraints of the type *inverse functional properties* for which a context class ?Class and a list ?list of left properties is specified. This part of the rule's antecedence unifies with the constraint given in Listing 1. Lines 13–18 describe which situation in the tested data causes a constraint violation: for an ?object which is an instance of ?Class, there are two subjects, ?x1 and ?x2, defined which are both connected to ?object via ?property. This ?property is an element of ?list, and the names, i.e. the URI- or string-representations, of ?x1 and ?x differ. The latter is expressed using the predicate log:notEqualTo[10] (Line 18). Together with Listing 1 that violation is thus detected if two different resource names for resources of the class dbo:Country are connected via the predicate dbo:capital to the same object. Assuming that :Britain and :England are both instances of the class dbo:Country, the triples in Formula 6 lead to the violation:

$$\text{\_:x a :violaton; :violatedConstraint :example\_constraint.} \quad (12)$$

The example shown relies on descriptions following the vocabulary Hartmann suggests, but our approach can easily be adapted for other RDF based constraint

---

[10] As explained in Sect. 4.4 there are alternative ways to express the predicate log:notEqualTo in N3, the antecedence of the entire rule could also be expressed only using RIF predicates.

```
 1  @prefix rdfcv: <http://www.dr-thomashartmann.de/phd-thesis/
    rdf-validation/vocabularies/rdf-constraints-vocabulary#> .
 2  @prefix : <http://example.com/constraints#> .
 3  @prefix list: <http://www.w3.org/2000/10/swap/list#>.
 4  @prefix log: <http://www.w3.org/2000/10/swap/log#> .
 5
 6  {
 7  ?constraint a rdfcv:SimpleConstraint;
 8    :constraintType  :InverseFunctionalProperties;
 9    rdfcv:constrainingElement  :inverse-functional-properties;
10    rdfcv:leftProperties ?list;
11    rdfcv:contextClass  ?Class.
12
13  ?object a ?Class.
14  ?property list:in ?list.
15  ?x1 ?property ?object.
16  ?x2 ?property ?object.
17  ?x1 log:notEqualTo ?x2
18  }
19  =>
20  {
21  [] a :constraintViolation;
22     :violatedConstraint ?constraint.
23  }.
```

Listing 2. Rule for inverse functional property (INVFUNC). The predicate `log:notEqualTo` compares the resources based on their URI and thereby supports the Unique Name Assumption.

vocabularies. All we need is a consistent way to express constraints in RDF. Note that our rules act directly on constraint descriptions and RDF datasets: while the SPARQL based approaches [12,21] mentioned in Sect. 2 rely on an extra mapping step to instantiate the search patterns. If reasoning needs to be included into the data validation, a rule based system can do reasoning, mapping and constraint validation in one single step where other systems need to perform three.

6   Conclusion and Future Work

In this paper we investigated the requirements a rule based Web logic needs to fulfil to be suitable for RDF validation: it should support Scoped Negation as Failure, it should provide predicates for name comparison, and its built-ins should be powerful enough to, for example, do string comparisons or access language tags. Together with the capability to meet its primary purpose, Web reasoning, such a Web logic is a strong alternative to the common approach of either combining reasoning and validation in two different steps, for example by first performing OWL reasoning and then executing SPARQL queries on top of the result as done by Hartmann [12], or only executing SPARQL queries and thereby ignoring possible implicit constraint violations as done in

RDFUnit [21]. Rule based Web logics fulfilling the requirements still provide the same expressivity as SPARQL with the additional advantage of supporting reasoning. Validation and reasoning can thus be done by *one single system* in *one single step*. The practical feasibility of this approach has been shown by providing a proof-of-concept in N3Logic which supports all RDFUnit constraint types. As such, we allow users to assess their data quality more easily using a single rule based validation system, and potentially uncovering more errors. Thus, improving data quality on the Semantic Web overall.

In future work, we are planning to extend our implementation: we aim to cover all of the 81 constraints identified by Hartmann et al. [8] which are not specific to SPARQL. We furthermore envisage to extend the supported RDF constraint vocabularies and to align our efforts with SHACL. Another direction of future research will be a better combination of performant reasoning and validation, following the ideas provided in previous work [3]. Further evaluation on performance is also to be conducted.

Acknowledgements. The described research activities were funded by Ghent University, imec, Flanders Innovation & Entrepreneurship (AIO), the Fund for Scientific Research Flanders (FWO Flanders), and the European Union, in the context of the project "DiSSeCt", which is a collaboration by SMIT, DistriNet, and IDLab.

References

1. FuXi 1.4: A Python-based, bi-directional logical reasoning system for the semantic web. http://code.google.com/p/fuxi/
2. Arndt, D., et al.: Ontology reasoning using rules in an ehealth context. In: Bassiliades, N., Gottlob, G., Sadri, F., Paschke, A., Roman, D. (eds.) RuleML 2015. LNCS, vol. 9202, pp. 465–472. Springer, Cham (2015). doi:10.1007/978-3-319-21542-6_31
3. Arndt, D., et al.: Improving OWL RL reasoning in N3 by using specialized rules. In: Tamma, V., Dragoni, M., Gonçalves, R., Lawrynowicz, A. (eds.) OWLED 2015. LNCS, vol. 9557, pp. 93–104. Springer, Cham (2016). doi:10.1007/978-3-319-33245-1_10
4. Arndt, D., Verborgh, R., Roo, J., Sun, H., Mannens, E., Walle, R.: Semantics of Notation3 logic: a solution for implicit quantification. In: Bassiliades, N., Gottlob, G., Sadri, F., Paschke, A., Roman, D. (eds.) RuleML 2015. LNCS, vol. 9202, pp. 127–143. Springer, Cham (2015). doi:10.1007/978-3-319-21542-6_9
5. Berners-Lee, T.: *cwm* (2000–2009). http://www.w3.org/2000/10/swap/doc/cwm.html
6. Berners-Lee, T., Connolly, D., Kagal, L., Scharf, Y., Hendler, J.: N3Logic: a logical framework for the world wide web. Theory Pract. Logic Programm. 8(3), 249–269 (2008)
7. Bock, C., Fokoue, A., Haase, P., Hoekstra, R., Horrocks, I., Ruttenberg, A., Sattler, U., Smith, M.: OWL 2 Web Ontology Language. w3c Recommendation, December 2012. http://www.w3.org/TR/owl2-syntax/
8. Bosch, T., Acar, E., Nolle, A., Eckert, K.: The role of reasoning for RDF validation. In: Proceedings of the 11th International Conference on Semantic Systems, pp. 33–40. SEMANTICS 2015, ACM, New York (2015). http://doi.acm.org/10.1145/2814864.2814867

9. Bosch, T., Nolle, A., Acar, E., Eckert, K.: RDF validation requirements-evaluation and logical underpinning. arXiv preprint arXiv:1501.03933 (2015)
10. Calvanese, D., Carroll, J., Di Giacomo, G., Hendler, J., Herman, I., Parsia, B., Patel-Schneider, P.F., Ruttenberg, A., Sattler, U., Schneider, M.: OWL 2 Web Ontology Language Profiles, 2nd edn. W3C Recommendation, December 2012. www.w3.org/TR/owl2-profiles/
11. Damásio, C.V., Analyti, A., Antoniou, G., Wagner, G.: Supporting open and closed world reasoning on the web. In: Alferes, J.J., Bailey, J., May, W., Schwertel, U. (eds.) PPSWR 2006. LNCS, vol. 4187, pp. 149–163. Springer, Heidelberg (2006). doi:10.1007/11853107_11
12. Hartmann, T.: Validation Framework for RDF-based Constraint Languages. Ph.D. thesis, Dissertation, Karlsruhe, Karlsruher Institut für Technologie (KIT) 2016 (2016)
13. Ketterl, M., Knipping, L., Ludwig, N., Mertens, R., Waitelonis, J., Ludwig, N., Knuth, M., Sack, H.: Whoknows? Evaluating linked data heuristics with a quiz that cleans up dbpedia. Interact. Technol. Smart Educ. **8**(4), 236–248 (2011)
14. Kifer, M.: Nonmonotonic reasoning in FLORA-2. In: Baral, C., Greco, G., Leone, N., Terracina, G. (eds.) LPNMR 2005. LNCS, vol. 3662, pp. 1–12. Springer, Heidelberg (2005). doi:10.1007/11546207_1
15. Kifer, M.: Rule interchange format: the framework. In: Bassiliades, N., Governatori, G., Paschke, A. (eds.) RuleML 2008. LNCS, vol. 5321, pp. 1–2. Springer, Heidelberg (2008). doi:10.1007/978-3-540-88808-6_1
16. Kifer, M., Bruijn, J., Boley, H., Fensel, D.: A realistic architecture for the semantic web. In: Adi, A., Stoutenburg, S., Tabet, S. (eds.) RuleML 2005. LNCS, vol. 3791, pp. 17–29. Springer, Heidelberg (2005). doi:10.1007/11580072_3
17. Kifer, M., Lausen, G., Wu, J.: Logical foundations of object-oriented and frame-based languages. J. ACM **42**(4), 741–843 (1995). http://doi.acm.org/10.1145/210332.210335
18. Knublauch, H., Hendler, J.A., Idehen, K.: SPIN – overview and motivation. Technical report, W3C, February 2011. https://www.w3.org/Submission/2011/SUBM-spin-overview-20110222/. Accessed 18 April 2016
19. Knublauch, H., Kontokostas, D.: Shapes constraint language (shacl). Technical report, W3C (2017). https://www.w3.org/TR/shacl/. Accessed 3 March 2017
20. Kontokostas, D., Mader, C., Dirschl, C., Eck, K., Leuthold, M., Lehmann, J., Hellmann, S.: Semantically enhanced quality assurance in the jurion business use case. In: 13th International Conference, ESWC 2016, Heraklion, Crete, Greece, May 2016, pp. 661–676 (2016). http://svn.aksw.org/papers/2016/ESWC_Jurion/public.pdf
21. Kontokostas, D., Westphal, P., Auer, S., Hellmann, S., Lehmann, J., Cornelissen, R., Zaveri, A.: Test-driven evaluation of linked data quality. In: Proceedings of the 23rd International Conference on World Wide Web, pp. 747–758. ACM (2014)
22. Motik, B., Horrocks, I., Sattler, U.: Adding integrity constraints to OWL. In: OWLED, vol. 258 (2007)
23. Nilsson, M.: Description set profiles: a constraint language for dublin core application profiles. DCMI Working Draft (2008)
24. Polleres, A., Boley, H., Kifer, M.: RIF datatypes and built-ins 1.0, 2nd edn. W3C Recommendation, February 2013. https://www.w3.org/TR/rif-dtb/
25. Polleres, A., Feier, C., Harth, A.: Rules with contextually scoped negation. In: Sure, Y., Domingue, J. (eds.) ESWC 2006. LNCS, vol. 4011, pp. 332–347. Springer, Heidelberg (2006). doi:10.1007/11762256_26

26. Prud'hommeaux, E., Seaborne, A.: SPARQL Query Language for RDF. W3C Recommendation, January 2008. http://www.w3.org/TR/rdf-sparql-query/
27. Rietveld, L., Beek, W., Schlobach, S.: LOD lab: experiments at LOD scale. In: Arenas, M., et al. (eds.) ISWC 2015. LNCS, vol. 9367, pp. 339 355. Springer, Cham (2015). doi:10.1007/978-3-319-25010-6_23
28. Ryman, A.: Resource shape 2.0. w3c member submission. In: World Wide Web Consortium, February 2014
29. Sirin, E., Tao, J.: Towards integrity constraints in OWL. In: Proceedings of the 6th International Conference on OWL: Experiences and Directions, vol. 529, pp. 79–88. OWLED 2009, CEUR-WS.org, Aachen, Germany, Germany (2009). http://dl.acm.org/citation.cfm?id=2890046.2890055
30. Solbrig, H., Prud'hommeaux, E.: Shape expressions 1.0 definition. w3c member submission. World Wide Web Consortium, June 2014
31. Tao, J.: Integrity constraints for the semantic web: an OWL 2 DL extension. Ph.D. thesis, Rensselaer Polytechnic Institute (2012)
32. Verborgh, R., De Roo, J.: Drawing conclusions from linked data on the web. IEEE Softw. **32**(5), 23–27 (2015). http://online.qmags.com/ISW0515?cid=3244717&eid=19361&pg=25
33. Zaveri, A., Rula, A., Maurino, A., Pietrobon, R., Lehmann, J., Auer, S.: Quality assessment for linked data: a survey. Semant. Web **7**(1), 63–93 (2015). http://www.semantic-web-journal.net/system/files/swj556.pdf

Three Methods for Revising Hybrid Knowledge Bases

Sebastian Binnewies$^{(\boxtimes)}$, Zhiqiang Zhuang, and Kewen Wang

Institute for Integrated and Intelligent Systems,
Griffith University, Brisbane, Australia
{s.binnewies,z.zhuang,k.wang}@griffith.edu.au

Abstract. Contemporary approaches for the Semantic Web include *hybrid knowledge bases* that combine ontologies with rule-based languages. Despite a number of existing combination approaches, little attention has been given to change mechanisms for hybrid knowledge bases that can appropriately handle the dynamics of information on the Web. We present here three methods for *revising* hybrid knowledge bases in light of new information. We show by means of representation theorems that two of them fit properly into the classic belief change framework and that each of the two generalises the third method.

Keywords: Belief revision · Hybrid knowledge bases · Logic programs · Ontologies · Here-and-there logic · Semantic web

1   Introduction

In the last decade, ontologies [9] have become widely accepted as knowledge engineering artefacts in the Semantic Web for modelling domains of expertise. For example, SNOMED CT[1], the Gene Ontology[2], and OBO Foundry Ontologies[3] represent standardised biomedical terminologies and are well-established within their field of application. They are usually specified in a fragment of first-order logic and can be viewed as first-order theories in restricted form. More recently, ontologies have been integrated with logic programs [4,13] into *hybrid knowledge bases* to combine monotonic reasoning over the former component with nonmonotonic reasoning over the latter. A wide array of such integrations have been proposed (overviews can be found in [7,12,14]), which differ in the way ontologies and rules are combined. We concentrate here on hybrid knowledge bases under quantified here-and-there logic [3], because they place no restriction on the fragment of first-order logic or the class of logic programs to be used in the composition and capture several other integration approaches.

---

[1] http://www.snomed.org/snomed-ct.

[2] http://www.geneontology.org/.

[3] http://www.obofoundry.org/.

© Springer International Publishing AG 2017
S. Costantini et al. (Eds.): RuleML+RR 2017, LNCS 10364, pp. 37–52, 2017.
DOI: 10.1007/978-3-319-61252-2_4

For hybrid knowledge bases to be successfully adopted in practical applications, it is crucial that they are not only static entities but also responsive to changes as required within the domain. It may be necessary to add new knowledge or retract some existing knowledge. We focus on this problem by framing it within the traditional *belief change* framework [1,8,10], which provides sets of postulates that any rational change operator should satisfy. While the framework has been applied to a variety of knowledge representation formalisms (e.g., [2,6,23,24]), a particular challenge in constructing appropriate belief change mechanisms for hybrid knowledge bases lies in their bi-component nature. Any change operator must be able to handle changes to the theory component, the logic program component, or both, depending on the new information acquired. When either component is changed, it may have an effect on the other component and cause the hybrid knowledge base to become inconsistent.

In the following, we address this gap by first adapting a partial meet revision operator from classical logics to hybrid knowledge bases. We then define a special case of partial meet revision, called protected revision, allowing to preferably revise only one component of the hybrid knowledge base. Finally, we present prioritised revision, a more fine-grained method, where a priority ordering over individual elements of the hybrid knowledge base determines the outcome. By evaluating our operators with respect to each other and the revision postulates, we find that partial meet revision and prioritised revision are interdefinable and comply with the belief change framework, whereas protected revision is a restricted version of partial meet revision.

2   Preliminaries

We first formally introduce hybrid knowledge bases under here-and-there logic and then briefly cover relevant belief change fundamentals.

2.1   Hybrid Knowledge Bases Under Here-and-There Logic

Let $\mathcal{L} = (\mathcal{C}, \mathcal{P}_T \cup \mathcal{P}_P)$ be a function-free, first-order language, in which $\mathcal{C}$ is a set of constant symbols and $\mathcal{P}_T, \mathcal{P}_P$ are sets of predicate symbols such that $\mathcal{C}, \mathcal{P}_T, \mathcal{P}_P$ are pairwise disjoint. Let $\mathcal{L}$ further include the symbols '$\wedge$', '$\vee$', '$\rightarrow$', '$\neg$', '$\forall$', '$\exists$', the predicate symbol '$\approx$' for equality, a countably infinite set of variables, and the standard punctuation marks, as well as the symbols '; ', ', ', '*not*', '$\leftarrow$', and '$\perp$'. Atoms, formulas, closed formulas, and theories are defined in the usual way. A *(first-order) rule r* over $\mathcal{L}$ has the form

$$a_1; \ldots ; a_k; not\, b_1; \ldots ; not\, b_l \leftarrow c_1, \ldots, c_m, not\, d_1, \ldots, not\, d_n. \qquad (1)$$

Here, all a_i, b_i, c_i, d_i are atoms from $\mathcal{L}$ and $k, l, m, n \geq 0$. If $m = n = 0$, then we omit '$\leftarrow$'. A *hybrid knowledge base (HKB)* [3] $K = (K_T, K_P)$ over $\mathcal{L}$ consists of a classical first-order theory K_T over the language subset $\mathcal{L}_T = (\mathcal{C}, \mathcal{P}_T)$, and a set of rules of the form (1) over $\mathcal{L}$ that constitute a program K_P. We write $\mathcal{K}_{\mathcal{L}}$ for the class of all HKBs over $\mathcal{L}$.

A HKB can be used to combine specific constraints that hold in a domain, expressed by a program component K_P, with more general information, captured by a theory component K_T. For instance, a personal assistant system on a mobile phone may have in its HKB some general information about gender and marriage as well as some specific information about its user Chris, shown in Example 1.

Example 1. Let $\mathcal{C} = \{Chris, Alex\}$, $\mathcal{P}_T = \{male, female, married\}$, $\mathcal{P}_P = \emptyset$, and $K = (K_T, K_P)$ be a HKB over $(\mathcal{C}, \mathcal{P}_T \cup \mathcal{P}_P)$ such that

$$K_T = \{\, \forall x : male(x) \rightarrow \neg female(x),$$
$$\forall x, y : married(x, y) \rightarrow married(y, x),$$
$$\forall x, y : married(x, y) \wedge female(x) \rightarrow male(y) \,\},$$
$$K_P = \{\, female(Chris).\,\}.$$

∎

We extend the usual set operations to HKBs as follows. For any pairs of sets $K^1 = (K_T^1, K_P^1), \ldots, K^n = (K_T^n, K_P^n)$, let $K^1 \odot \cdots \odot K^n = (\{K_T^1 \odot \cdots \odot K_T^n\}, \{K_P^1 \odot \cdots \odot K_P^n\})$ for $\odot \in \{\cap, \cup\}$, $K^1 \setminus K^2 = (K_T^1 \setminus K_T^2, K_P^1 \setminus K_P^2)$, and for $i, j \in \{T, P\}$ with $i \neq j$:

$$K^1 \subseteq K^2 \text{ iff } K_i^1 \subseteq K_i^2 \text{ and } K_j^1 \subseteq K_j^2,$$
$$K^1 \subseteq_i K^2 \text{ iff } K_i^1 \subseteq K_i^2, \text{ and if } K_i^1 = K_i^2, \text{ then } K_j^1 \subseteq K_j^2, \text{ and}$$
$$K^1 \subset_\circ K^2 \text{ iff } K^1 \subseteq_\circ K^2 \text{ and } K^2 \not\subseteq_\circ K^1 \text{ where } \subseteq_\circ \in \{\subseteq, \subseteq_T, \subseteq_P\}.$$

For any $K \in \mathcal{K}_\mathcal{L}$, let $K|_T = (K_T, \emptyset)$, $K|_P = (\emptyset, K_P)$, and, for any $\mathbb{K} \subseteq 2^K$, $\mathbb{K}|_T = \{(\tau, \emptyset) \mid (\tau, \rho) \in \mathbb{K}\}$ and $\mathbb{K}|_P = \{(\emptyset, \rho) \mid (\tau, \rho) \in \mathbb{K}\}$.

An $\mathcal{L}$ *structure* is a pair $\mathcal{I} = (U, I)$, where the universe $U = (\mathcal{D}, \sigma)$ consists of a non-empty domain $\mathcal{D}$ and a function σ from $\mathcal{C} \cup \mathcal{D}$ to $\mathcal{D}$ such that $\sigma(D) = D$ for all $D \in \mathcal{D}$, and an interpretation I is a set of variable-free atoms that can be constructed from $(\mathcal{C} \cup \mathcal{D}, \mathcal{P}_T \cup \mathcal{P}_P)$. For a tuple $t = (D_1, \ldots, D_n)$, we define $\sigma(t) = (\sigma(D_1), \ldots, \sigma(D_n))$. To obtain a ground instance of a rule in K_P, we replace each constant symbol C in the rule by $\sigma(C)$ and each variable in the rule by an element from $\mathcal{D}$. The set of all ground instances of rules in K_P is written $ground(K_P)$.

A **QHT$_=^s$** *(quantified here-and-there logic with static domains and equality)* *structure with respect to* $\mathcal{L}$ [18] (or simply **QHT$_=^s$** structure if $\mathcal{L}$ is clear from the context) is a triple $\mathcal{M} = (U, H, T)$ such that (U, H) and (U, T) are $\mathcal{L}$ structures with $H \subseteq T$. Let $\mathcal{QHT}$ be the set of all **QHT$_=^s$** structures over $\mathcal{L}$. For any set S of **QHT$_=^s$** structures, by $\overline{S}$ we denote the complement of S with respect to $\mathcal{QHT}$, that is, $\overline{S} = \mathcal{QHT} \setminus S$. We define the satisfaction relation for a **QHT$_=^s$** structure $\mathcal{M}$ recursively as follows. Let $p(t_1, \ldots, t_n)$ be an atom and ϕ, ψ closed formulas built from $(\mathcal{C} \cup \mathcal{D}, \mathcal{P}_T \cup \mathcal{P}_P)$, x be a variable, and $w \in \{H, T\}$. Then

$\mathcal{M} \models_w p(t_1, \ldots, t_n)$ iff $p(\sigma(t_1), \ldots, \sigma(t_n)) \in w$,

$\mathcal{M} \models_w \phi \wedge \psi$ iff $\mathcal{M} \models_w \phi$ and $\mathcal{M} \models_w \psi$,

$\mathcal{M} \models_w \phi \vee \psi$ iff $\mathcal{M} \models_w \phi$ or $\mathcal{M} \models_w \psi$,

$\mathcal{M} \models_T \phi \rightarrow \psi$ iff $\mathcal{M} \not\models_T \phi$ or $\mathcal{M} \models_T \psi$,

$\mathcal{M} \models_H \phi \rightarrow \psi$ iff (i) $\mathcal{M} \models_T \phi \rightarrow \psi$ and (ii) $\mathcal{M} \not\models_H \phi$ or $\mathcal{M} \models_H \psi$,

$\mathcal{M} \models_w \neg\phi$ iff $\mathcal{M} \not\models_T \phi$,

$\mathcal{M} \models_T \forall x\phi(x)$ iff $\mathcal{M} \models_T \phi(D)$ for all $D \in \mathcal{D}$,

$\mathcal{M} \models_H \forall x\phi(x)$ iff $\mathcal{M} \models_T \forall x\phi(x)$ and $\mathcal{M} \models_H \phi(D)$ for all $D \in \mathcal{D}$,

$\mathcal{M} \models_w \exists x\phi(x)$ iff $\mathcal{M} \models_w \phi(D)$ for some $D \in \mathcal{D}$,

$\mathcal{M} \models_w t_1 \approx t_2$ iff $\sigma(t_1) = \sigma(t_2)$.

A $\mathbf{QHT}^s_=$ structure $\mathcal{M}$ is a $\mathbf{QHT}^s_=$-*model* of a closed formula ϕ, denoted $\mathcal{M} \models \phi$, iff $\mathcal{M} \models_w \phi$ for each $w \in \{H, T\}$. A $\mathbf{QHT}^s_=$ structure $\mathcal{M}$ is a:

- $\mathbf{QHT}^s_=$ model of a theory K_T iff it is a model of all formulas in K_T;
- $\mathbf{QHT}^s_=$ model of a program K_P iff it is a $\mathbf{QHT}^s_=$ model of all rules in $ground(K_P)$ where each rule of the form (1) is interpreted as

$$c_1 \wedge \cdots \wedge c_m \wedge \neg d_1 \wedge \cdots \wedge \neg d_n \rightarrow a_1 \vee \cdots \vee a_k \vee \neg b_1 \vee \cdots \vee \neg b_l \,;$$

- $\mathbf{QHT}^s_=$ model of a HKB $K = (K_T, K_P)$ iff it is a $\mathbf{QHT}^s_=$ model of K_T and K_P.

The set of all $\mathbf{QHT}^s_=$ models of K is denoted by $QHT(K)$ and K is *satisfiable* iff $QHT(K) \neq \emptyset$.

Example 2. For K from Example 1, we obtain $QHT(K) = \{\mathcal{M}_1, \mathcal{M}_2, \mathcal{M}_3, \mathcal{M}_4, \mathcal{M}_5, \mathcal{M}_6, \mathcal{M}_7, \mathcal{M}_8\}$ such that, for $i = \{1, \ldots, 8\}$, $U_i = (\{Chris, Alex\}, \sigma)$ for each $\mathcal{M}_i$, where σ is the identity function, and H_i, T_i contain the atoms marked with a H (here) or T (there), respectively, in Table 1. ∎

Table 1. (H, T)-elements for models of K in Example 1

	$\mathcal{M}_1$	$\mathcal{M}_2$	$\mathcal{M}_3$	$\mathcal{M}_4$	$\mathcal{M}_5$	$\mathcal{M}_6$	$\mathcal{M}_7$	$\mathcal{M}_8$
male(Chris)								
male(Alex)	H,T	H,T	T	H,T	T			
female(Chris)	H,T	H,T	H,T	H,T	H,T	H,T	H,T	H,T
female(Alex)						H,T	T	
married(Chris, Alex)	H,T	T	T					
married(Alex, Chris)	H,T	T	T					

2.2 Belief Change

The *belief base framework* [8,10,19] of belief change defines *expansion, revision*, and *contraction* as the operations on a body of beliefs held by an agent, called a belief base, in light of some new information. In an expansion, new beliefs are simply added to an existing belief base, regardless of any inconsistencies that may arise. A revision operation also incorporates new beliefs into a belief base, but may discard some existing beliefs to ensure consistency of the outcome. During a contraction, some beliefs are removed from a belief base but no new beliefs are added. Particularly, and contrary to other frameworks, a belief base is not required to be closed under logical consequence, which makes this framework suitable for consideration regarding belief change in HKBs.

For propositional logic, Hansson [11] defined a *partial meet (base) contraction operator* $-_\gamma$ for a belief base B and a sentence ϕ as $B -_\gamma \phi = \bigcap \gamma(B \bot \phi)$, where $B \bot \phi = \{ B' \subseteq B \mid B' \nvdash \phi$ and, for all B'', $B' \subset B'' \subseteq B$ implies $B'' \vdash \phi \}$ and γ is a selection function such that $\gamma(B \bot \phi) = \{B\}$ if $B \bot \phi = \emptyset$, and $\emptyset \neq \gamma(B \bot \phi) \subseteq B \bot \phi$ otherwise. He determined a set of four postulates that exactly characterises the class of partial meet contraction operators. He further defined a corresponding *partial meet (base) revision operator* $*_\gamma$ as $B *_\gamma \phi = (B -_\gamma \neg \phi) \cup \{\phi\}$ and showed that a set of five postulates exactly characterises the class of partial meet revision operators.

We now translate these five revision postulates to HKBs, so that we can later evaluate the rationality of our proposed operators. Let $+$ be an expansion operator for $K \in \mathcal{K}_\mathcal{L}$ such that for any $K' \in \mathcal{K}_\mathcal{L}$, $K + K' = K \cup K'$. The postulates are as follows, where we assume $K, K', K'' \in \mathcal{K}_\mathcal{L}$ and a revision operator $*$ to be a function from $\mathcal{K}_\mathcal{L} \times \mathcal{K}_\mathcal{L}$ to $\mathcal{K}_\mathcal{L}$.

($*$1) $K' \subseteq K * K'$
($*$2) $K * K' \subseteq K + K'$
($*$3) If $\kappa \subseteq K \setminus (K * K')$, then there exists a $\kappa' \in \mathcal{K}_\mathcal{L}$ such that $K * K' \subseteq \kappa' \subset K + K'$ and κ' is satisfiable but $\kappa' \cup \kappa$ is not satisfiable
($*$4) If it holds for all $\kappa \subseteq K$ that $\kappa + K'$ is satisfiable iff $\kappa + K''$ is satisfiable, then $K \cap (K * K') = K \cap (K * K'')$
($*$5) If K' is satisfiable, then $K * K'$ is satisfiable

3 Revision in Hybrid Knowledge Bases

In this section, we introduce three new methods for revising HKBs. We begin with an adaptation of *partial meet revision* (Sect. 3.1), then define a method that prioritises either component of a HKB in its entirety during a revision, called *protected revision* (Sect. 3.2), and finally propose a method that prioritises individual elements of a HKB, termed *prioritised revision* (Sect. 3.3).

3.1 Partial Meet Revision

As the foundation of our revision operations, we define the subsets of a HKB that are consistent with another HKB.

Definition 1 (Compatible Set). *Let* $K, K' \in \mathcal{K}_{\mathcal{L}}$ *and* $\subseteq_{\circ} \in \{\subseteq, \subseteq_T, \subseteq_P\}$. *The set of compatible sets of* K *regarding* K' *is*

$$\mathbb{K}_{K',\subseteq_{\circ}} = \{\, \kappa = (\tau, \rho) \mid \kappa \subseteq K, QHT(\kappa) \cap QHT(K') \neq \emptyset, \text{ and,}$$
$$\text{for all } \kappa' = (\tau', \rho'), \kappa \subset_{\circ} \kappa' \subseteq K \text{ implies}$$
$$QHT(\kappa') \cap QHT(K') = \emptyset \,\}.$$

To construct our revision, we will further make use of a selection function that chooses from a set of compatible sets the most suitable ones. As we aim to employ our selection function for different types of compatible sets, we define it here with respect to an arbitrary set.

Definition 2 (Selection Function). *A selection function* γ *for a set* S *is a function such that (i)* $\mathbb{S} \subseteq 2^S$, *(ii)* $\gamma(\mathbb{S}) \subseteq \mathbb{S}$, *and (iii) if* $\mathbb{S} \neq \emptyset$, *then* $\gamma(\mathbb{S}) \neq \emptyset$.

We are now ready to introduce a *partial meet revision* operator for HKBs as follows.

Definition 3 (Partial Meet Revision). *Let* $K \in \mathcal{K}_{\mathcal{L}}$ *and* γ *be a selection function for* K. *A partial meet revision operator* $*_\gamma$ *for* K *is defined such that for any* $K' \in \mathcal{K}_{\mathcal{L}}$:

$$K *_\gamma K' = \begin{cases} K + K' & \text{if } K' \text{ is not satisfiable,} \\ \bigcap \gamma(\mathbb{K}_{K',\subseteq}) + K' & \text{otherwise.} \end{cases}$$

Since one of the maxims for belief revision is to ensure primacy of new information [5], our revision operator $*_\gamma$ always includes the information expressed by the revising HKB K' in the outcome. In addition, the main characteristic that distinguishes a revision from an expansion is that the former aims at providing a consistent outcome. In the case that K' is itself not satisfiable, our revision operator returns the combination of K' and the initial HKB K in its entirety, since no removal of any part of K would lead to a satisfiable outcome. This behaviour adheres to the maxim of persistence of prior knowledge [5]. In all other cases, the revision operator returns the intersection of the selected compatible sets of K added to K'.

We obtain the following representation theorem, stating that our partial meet revision operator $*_\gamma$ is exactly characterised by the postulates (*1)–(*5).

Lemma 1. *Let* $K, K' \in \mathcal{K}_{\mathcal{L}}$ *and* γ *be a selection function for* K. *If* $\kappa \subseteq K \cap K'$, *then* $\kappa \subseteq_{\circ} \bigcap \gamma(\mathbb{K}_{K',\subseteq_{\circ}})$.

Theorem 1. *An operator* $*_\gamma$ *is a partial meet revision operator for* $K \in \mathcal{K}_{\mathcal{L}}$ *determined by a selection function* γ *for* K *iff* $*_\gamma$ *satisfies (*1)–(*5).*

Proof. We first show that a partial meet revision operator $*_\gamma$ for K determined by a given selection function γ for K satisfies (*1)–(*5).

(*1): Follows directly from Definition 3.

($*2$): If K' is not satisfiable, then $K *_\gamma K' = K + K$ by Definition 3. Otherwise, since $\bigcap \gamma(\mathbb{K}_{K',\subseteq}) \subseteq K$ we have $\bigcap \gamma(\mathbb{K}_{K',\subseteq}) + K' \subseteq K + K'$.

($*3$): Let $\kappa \subseteq K$. Assume that for all κ' with $K *_\gamma K' \subseteq \kappa' \subset K + K'$ and κ' being satisfiable, it holds that $\kappa' \cup \kappa$ is satisfiable. In particular, for each $\kappa'' \in \mathbb{K}_{K',\subseteq}$ with $K *_\gamma K' \subseteq \kappa'' \cup K'$, this implies $\kappa'' \cup K' \cup \kappa$ is satisfiable. As each κ'' is $\subseteq$-maximal, it follows that $\kappa \subseteq \kappa''$ and thus $\kappa \subseteq \bigcap \gamma(\mathbb{K}_{K',\subseteq})$. From Definition 3 we can then conclude $\kappa \not\subseteq K \setminus (K *_\gamma K')$.

($*4$): For all $\kappa \subseteq K$, let $\kappa + K'$ be satisfiable iff $\kappa + K''$ is satisfiable. Then $\mathbb{K}_{K',\subseteq} = \mathbb{K}_{K'',\subseteq}$ by Definition 1 and so $\bigcap \gamma(\mathbb{K}_{K',\subseteq}) = \bigcap \gamma(\mathbb{K}_{K'',\subseteq})$ as well as $K \cap \bigcap \gamma(\mathbb{K}_{K',\subseteq}) = K \cap \bigcap \gamma(\mathbb{K}_{K'',\subseteq})$. By Lemma 1 we obtain $(K \cap \bigcap \gamma(\mathbb{K}_{K',\subseteq})) \cup (K \cap K') = (K \cap \bigcap \gamma(\mathbb{K}_{K'',\subseteq})) \cup (K \cap K'')$. This means $K \cap (\bigcap \gamma(\mathbb{K}_{K',\subseteq}) \cup K') = K \cap (\bigcap \gamma(\mathbb{K}_{K'',\subseteq}) \cup K'')$. Thus, $K \cap (K *_\gamma K') = K \cap (K *_\gamma K'')$.

($*5$): If K' is satisfiable, then, for any $\kappa \in \mathbb{K}_{K',\subseteq}$, $\kappa + K'$ is satisfiable, which implies $K *_\gamma K'$ is satisfiable.

We now show that any operator $\circ_\gamma$ for K satisfying ($*1$)–($*5$) is a partial meet revision operator for K determined by some selection function for K. We first find a selection function γ for K. Let γ be such that (i) if $\mathbb{K}_{K',\subseteq} = \emptyset$, then $\gamma(\mathbb{K}_{K',\subseteq}) = \emptyset$ and (ii) $\gamma(\mathbb{K}_{K',\subseteq}) = \{ \kappa \in \mathbb{K}_{K',\subseteq} \mid K \cap (K \circ_\gamma K') \subseteq \kappa \}$ otherwise.

We begin by showing that γ is a function. For any $K', K'' \in \mathcal{K}_{\mathcal{L}}$, if $\mathbb{K}_{K',\subseteq} = \mathbb{K}_{K'',\subseteq}$, then $K \cap (K \circ_\gamma K') = K \cap (K \circ_\gamma K'')$ by ($*4$). This means $\gamma(\mathbb{K}_{K',\subseteq}) = \gamma(\mathbb{K}_{K'',\subseteq})$ according to our definition of γ.

We next show that γ is a selection function. Clearly, $\gamma(\mathbb{K}_{K',\subseteq}) \subseteq \mathbb{K}_{K',\subseteq}$ by our definition of γ. If $\mathbb{K}_{K',\subseteq} \neq \emptyset$, then K' is satisfiable by Definition 1 and thus $K \circ_\gamma K'$ is satisfiable by ($*5$). Since $K' \subseteq K \circ_\gamma K'$ by ($*1$) and $K \circ_\gamma K' \subseteq K \cup K'$ by ($*2$), it follows that $(K \cap (K \circ_\gamma K')) \cup K'$ is satisfiable. This means that there exists $\kappa \in \mathbb{K}_{K',\subseteq}$ such that $K \cap (K \circ_\gamma K') \subseteq \kappa$. From our definition of γ we therefore obtain that $\gamma(\mathbb{K}_{K',\subseteq}) \neq \emptyset$.

Finally, we show that $\circ_\gamma$ is a partial meet revision operator for K, that is, $K \circ_\gamma K' = K \cup K'$ if K' is not satisfiable and $K \circ_\gamma K' = \bigcap \gamma(\mathbb{K}_{K',\subseteq}) \cup K'$ otherwise. Consider first the limiting case that K' is not satisfiable. If $\kappa \subseteq K \setminus (K \circ_\gamma K')$, then there exists κ' such that $K \circ_\gamma K' \subseteq \kappa' \subset K \cup K'$ and κ' is satisfiable but $\kappa' \cup \kappa$ is not satisfiable by ($*3$). This is a contradiction since $K' \subseteq \kappa'$ by ($*1$). Therefore, it holds for all $\kappa \subseteq K$ that $\kappa \subseteq K \circ_\gamma K'$, that is, $K \subseteq K \circ_\gamma K'$. Since $K' \subseteq K \circ_\gamma K'$ by ($*1$) and $K \circ_\gamma K' \subseteq K \cup K'$ by ($*2$), we can conclude $K \circ_\gamma K' = K \cup K'$.

Assume now that K' is satisfiable. Let $\kappa \subseteq K \setminus (K \circ_\gamma K')$. If $\mathbb{K}_{K',\subseteq} = \emptyset$, then it follows from ($*1$) and ($*3$) that $K \circ_\gamma K' = K'$. Since $\gamma(\mathbb{K}_{K',\subseteq}) = \emptyset$ by our definition of γ, we thus have $K \circ_\gamma K' = K' = \bigcap \gamma(\mathbb{K}_{K',\subseteq}) \cup K'$. If $\mathbb{K}_{K',\subseteq} \neq \emptyset$, then it follows directly from our definition of γ that $K \cap (K \circ_\gamma K') \subseteq \bigcap \gamma(\mathbb{K}_{K',\subseteq})$. From ($*1$) and ($*2$) we then obtain $K \circ_\gamma K' \subseteq \bigcap \gamma(\mathbb{K}_{K',\subseteq}) \cup K'$. To show the converse inclusion, first assume the case that $K \cup K'$ is satisfiable. This implies that for any $\kappa' \subseteq K \cup K'$ it holds that κ' is satisfiable. Applying ($*3$), we obtain $K \setminus (K \circ_\gamma K') = \emptyset$ and thus $K \subseteq K \circ_\gamma K'$. From ($*1$) and ($*2$) it follows that $K \circ_\gamma K' = K \cup K'$. Moreover, due to the assumption that $K \cup K'$ is satisfiable and Definition 1, we have $\mathbb{K}_{K',\subseteq} = \{K\}$. By our definition of γ, we obtain $\gamma(\mathbb{K}_{K',\subseteq}) = \{K\}$ and thus

$\bigcap \gamma(\mathbb{K}_{K',\subseteq}) = K$ and can conclude $K \circ_\gamma K' = \bigcap \gamma(\mathbb{K}_{K',\subseteq}) \cup K'$. Lastly, assume the case that $K \cup K'$ is not satisfiable. We will show that $\kappa \not\subseteq K \circ_\gamma K'$ implies $\kappa \not\subseteq \bigcap \gamma(\mathbb{K}_{K',\subseteq}) \cup K'$. If $\kappa \not\subseteq K$, then $\kappa \not\subseteq (K \circ_\gamma K') \setminus K'$ by $(*1)$ and $(*2)$ and $\kappa \not\subseteq \bigcap \gamma(\mathbb{K}_{K',\subseteq})$ by Definition 1. Since $\kappa \not\subseteq K \circ_\gamma K'$ implies $\kappa \not\subseteq K'$ by $(*1)$, it follows that $\kappa \not\subseteq ((K \circ_\gamma K') \setminus K') \cup K') = K \circ_\gamma K'$ and $\kappa \subseteq \bigcap \gamma(\mathbb{K}_{K',\subseteq}) \cup K'$. Now assume $\kappa \subseteq K \setminus (K \circ_\gamma K')$. According to $(*3)$, then there exists κ' such that $K \circ_\gamma K' \subseteq \kappa' \subset K \cup K'$ and κ' is satisfiable but $\kappa' \cup \kappa$ is not satisfiable. This means that there exists $\kappa'' \in \mathbb{K}_{K',\subseteq}$ such that $K \cap \kappa' \subseteq \kappa''$ and $\kappa \not\subseteq \kappa''$. Since $K \cap (K \circ_\gamma K') \subseteq K \cap \kappa' \subseteq \kappa''$, we obtain from our definition of γ that $\kappa'' \in \gamma(\mathbb{K}_{K',\subseteq})$. We can thus conclude from $\kappa \not\subseteq \kappa''$ that $\kappa \not\subseteq \bigcap \gamma(\mathbb{K}_{K',\subseteq})$.   □

3.2   Protected Revision

As a HKB consists of two components, it may be desirable to emphasise one component over the other during a revision operation. We can achieve this by a *protected revision*, which keeps the theory (or program) component of the initial HKB intact as much as possible whenever the theory (or program) component of the revising HKB is compatible with the initial HKB.

Definition 4 (Protected Revision). *Let $K \in \mathcal{K}_\mathcal{L}$ and γ be a selection function for K. A protected revision operator $*_{\gamma,\subseteq_\circ}$ for K is defined such that for any $K' \in \mathcal{K}_\mathcal{L}$:*

$$K *_{\gamma,\subseteq_\circ} K' = \begin{cases} K + K' & \text{if } K' \text{ is not satisfiable,} \\ \bigcap \gamma(\mathbb{K}_{K',\subseteq_\circ}) + K & \text{otherwise,} \end{cases}$$

where $\subseteq_\circ = \subseteq_T$ if $K + K'|_T$ is satisfiable, $\subseteq_\circ = \subseteq_P$ if $K + K'|_P$ is satisfiable, and $\subseteq_\circ = \subseteq$ otherwise.

In contrast to our partial meet revision operator, the protected revision operator $*_{\gamma,\subseteq_\circ}$ relies on selecting only among those compatible sets that have a maximal theory (or program) component, whenever $K + K'|_T$ ($K + K'|_P$, respectively) is satisfiable. The two revision operators coincide whenever neither $K + K'|_T$ nor $K + K'|_P$ is satisfiable. Obviously, the parameter $\subseteq_\circ$ could also be fixed to $\subseteq_T$ (or $\subseteq_P$) in settings where the theory (program, respectively) component is required to have absolute priority over the other. We illustrate the operation of protected revision in the following example.

Example 3. Consider again K from Example 1. Suppose the user Chris now states the command: "Call my wife Alex." This input by the user contains new information, i.e., Alex is female and Chris is married to Alex, to be added to K. Formally, let $K' = (K'_T, K'_P) \in \mathcal{K}_\mathcal{L}$ with $K'_T = \emptyset$ and $K'_P = \{ female(Alex).,$ $married(Chris, Alex). \}$. Since $K'_T = \emptyset$, $K + K'|_T$ is satisfiable and we obtain $\mathbb{K}_{K',\subseteq_T} = \{(K_T, \emptyset)\}$. Thus, $K *_{\gamma,\subseteq_T} K' = (K_T, K'_P)$.   ∎

The next proposition establishes that partial meet revision is a generalisation of protected revision.

Proposition 1. *Let $K, K' \in \mathcal{K}_\mathcal{L}$. For any selection function γ for K, there exists a selection function γ' for K such that $K *_{\gamma, \subseteq_\circ} K' = K *_{\gamma'} K'$.*

Proof. Let $K, K' \in \mathcal{K}_\mathcal{L}$ and γ be a selection function for K. In the limiting case that K' is not satisfiable, it holds by Definitions 3 and 4 that $K *_{\gamma, \subseteq_\circ} K' = K + K' = K *_\gamma K'$ for any selection function γ'. Otherwise, since $\mathbb{K}_{K', \subseteq_\circ} \subseteq \mathbb{K}_{K', \subseteq}$ for $\subseteq_\circ \in \{\subseteq, \subseteq_T, \subseteq_P\}$ by Definition 1, we can choose a selection function γ' for K such that $\gamma'(\mathbb{K}_{K', \subseteq}) = \gamma(\mathbb{K}_{K', \subseteq_\circ})$. From Definitions 3 and 4 it then follows that $K *_{\gamma, \subseteq_\circ} K' = K *_{\gamma'} K'$. $\qquad\square$

The other direction of the proposition does not hold because the use of the parameter $\subseteq_\circ$ in Definition 4 restricts the compatible sets to be included in $\mathbb{K}_{K', \subseteq_\circ}$. Due to this restriction, protected revision also does not satisfy (∗4). If we consider the weaker postulate (∗4c) below, then we can show that our protected revision operator $*_{\gamma, \subseteq_\circ}$ satisfies (∗1)–(∗3), (∗4c), and (∗5).

(∗4c) If it holds for all $\kappa \subseteq K$ that $\kappa + K'|_T$ is satisfiable iff $\kappa + K''|_T$ is satisfiable and $\kappa + K'|_P$ is satisfiable iff $\kappa + K''|_P$ is satisfiable, then $K \cap (K * K') = K \cap (K * K'')$

Theorem 2. *Let $K \in \mathcal{K}_\mathcal{L}$ and γ be a selection function for K. If $*_{\gamma, \subseteq_\circ}$ is a protected revision operator for K, then $*_{\gamma, \subseteq_\circ}$ satisfies (∗1)–(∗3), (∗4c), and (∗5).*

Proof. (∗1)–(∗3) and (∗5): Follow analogously to the proofs for Theorem 1.
(∗4c): Assume that for all $\kappa \subseteq K$, it holds that $\kappa + K'|_T$ is satisfiable iff $\kappa + K''|_T$ is satisfiable and $\kappa + K'|_P$ is satisfiable iff $\kappa + K''|_P$ is satisfiable. We proceed by cases.
Case 1: $K + K'|_T$ is satisfiable. This implies $K + K''|_T$ is satisfiable by the assumption and thus $\mathbb{K}_{K'|_T, \subseteq_\circ} = K = \mathbb{K}_{K''|_T, \subseteq_\circ}$ by Definition 1. In particular, $\mathbb{K}_{K'|_T, \subseteq_T} = K = \mathbb{K}_{K''|_T, \subseteq_T}$ as Definition 4 requires $\subseteq_\circ = \subseteq_T$. Since $\kappa + K'|_P$ is satisfiable iff $\kappa + K''|_P$ is satisfiable for all $\kappa \subseteq K$ by the assumption, we obtain $\mathbb{K}_{K', \subseteq_T} = \mathbb{K}_{K'', \subseteq_T}$ by Definition 1. Then $\bigcap \gamma(\mathbb{K}_{K', \subseteq_T}) = \bigcap \gamma(\mathbb{K}_{K'', \subseteq_T})$ as well as $K \cap \bigcap \gamma(\mathbb{K}_{K', \subseteq_T}) = K \cap \bigcap \gamma(\mathbb{K}_{K'', \subseteq_T})$. By Lemma 1 we obtain $(K \cap \bigcap \gamma(\mathbb{K}_{K', \subseteq_T})) \cup (K \cap K') = (K \cap \bigcap \gamma(\mathbb{K}_{K'', \subseteq_T})) \cup (K \cap K'')$. This means $K \cap (\bigcap \gamma(\mathbb{K}_{K', \subseteq_T}) \cup K') = K \cap (\bigcap \gamma(\mathbb{K}_{K'', \subseteq_T}) \cup K'')$. Thus, $K \cap (K *_{\gamma, \subseteq_T} K') = K \cap (K *_{\gamma, \subseteq_T} K'')$.
Case 2: $K + K'|_P$ is satisfiable. Follows symmetrically to Case 1.
Case 3: Neither $K + K'|_T$ nor $K + K'|_P$ is satisfiable. This implies neither $K + K''|_T$ nor $K + K''|_P$ is satisfiable by the assumption as well as $\subseteq_\circ = \subseteq$ by Definition 4. Thus, $*_{\gamma, \subseteq_\circ} = *_\gamma$ and the proof reduces to the one for satisfaction of (∗4) in Theorem 1. $\qquad\square$

At this point it becomes interesting to investigate how protected revision relates to a "stepwise" application of partial meet revision, that is, $K|_P *_\gamma (K|_T *_\gamma K')$ or $K|_T *_\gamma (K|_P *_\gamma K')$. It turns out that the result of protected revision $K *_{\gamma, \subseteq_T} K'$ is a subset of the result of stepwise revision $K|_P *_\gamma (K|_T *_\gamma K')$, provided that the selection function chooses similar sets in each respective operation, more specifically, the same theory-maximal compatible sets for protected revision as for the first step of stepwise revision and only those compatible sets for the second step of stepwise revision that include the program component of a selected compatible set for protected revision (analogously for $K|_T *_\gamma (K|_P *_\gamma K')$ and $K *_{\gamma, \subseteq_P} K'$). Before we show these results formally in Propositions 2 and 3, we introduce some useful notation. For any $K, K' \in \mathcal{K}_\mathcal{L}$, let

$$\mathbb{T}_{K'} = \{(\tau, \emptyset) \mid \tau \subseteq K_T, QHT((\tau, \emptyset)) \cap QHT(K') \neq \emptyset, \text{and, for all } \tau',$$
$$\tau \subset \tau' \subseteq K_T \text{ implies } QHT((\tau', \emptyset)) \cap QHT(K') = \emptyset\},$$
$$\mathbb{P}_{K'} = \{(\emptyset, \rho) \mid \rho \subseteq K_P, QHT((\emptyset, \rho)) \cap QHT(K') \neq \emptyset, \text{and, for all } \rho',$$
$$\rho \subset \rho' \subseteq K_P \text{ implies } QHT((\emptyset, \rho')) \cap QHT(K') = \emptyset\}.$$

Proposition 2. *Let $K, K' \in \mathcal{K}_\mathcal{L}$ and $K + K'|_T$ be satisfiable. There exists a selection function γ for K such that $K *_{\gamma, \subseteq_T} K' \subseteq K|_P *_\gamma (K|_T *_\gamma K')$.*

Proof. Let $K, K' \in \mathcal{K}_\mathcal{L}$ and $K + K'|_T$ be satisfiable. Assume that γ is a selection function for K such that $\gamma(\mathbb{T}_{K'}) = \gamma(\mathbb{K}_{K', \subseteq_T})|_T$ and $\gamma(\mathbb{P}_{K|_T *_\gamma K'}) = \{(\emptyset, \rho) \mid (\emptyset, \rho') \in \gamma(\mathbb{K}_{K', \subseteq_T})|_P$ and $(\emptyset, \rho') \subseteq (\emptyset, \rho)\}$. If K' is not satisfiable, then it follows directly from Definitions 3 and 4 that $K *_{\gamma, \subseteq_T} K' = K + K' = K|_P *_\gamma (K|_T *_\gamma K')$. Otherwise, it follows from Definition 1 and our definition of $\mathbb{T}_{K'}$ that $\mathbb{T}_{K'} = \mathbb{K}_{K', \subseteq_T}|_T$. Due to the assumption, this implies $\bigcap \gamma(\mathbb{T}_{K'}) = \bigcap \gamma(\mathbb{K}_{K', \subseteq_T})|_T$. For each $(\tau, \emptyset) \in \gamma(\mathbb{K}_{K', \subseteq_T})|_T$, since $\bigcap \gamma(\mathbb{T}_{K'}) \subseteq (\tau, \emptyset)$ it holds that $QHT((\tau, \emptyset)) \cap QHT(K') \subseteq QHT(\bigcap \gamma(\mathbb{T}_{K'})) \cap QHT(K')$. Thus, for each $(\emptyset, \rho) \in \gamma(\mathbb{K}_{K', \subseteq_T})|_P$ there exists a $(\emptyset, \rho') \in \mathbb{P}_{K|_T *_\gamma K'}$ such that $(\emptyset, \rho) \subseteq (\emptyset, \rho')$. From the assumption we then obtain $\bigcap \gamma(\mathbb{K}_{K', \subseteq_T})|_P \subseteq \bigcap \gamma(\mathbb{P}_{K|_T *_\gamma K'})$, which implies $K *_{\gamma, \subseteq_T} K' \subseteq K|_P *_\gamma (K|_T *_\gamma K')$ by Definitions 3 and 4. $\qquad \square$

Proposition 3. *Let $K, K' \in \mathcal{K}_\mathcal{L}$ and $K + K'|_P$ be satisfiable. There exists a selection function γ for K such that $K *_{\gamma, \subseteq_P} K' \subseteq K|_T *_\gamma (K|_P *_\gamma K')$.*

Proof. Let $K, K' \in \mathcal{K}_\mathcal{L}$ and $K + K'|_P$ be satisfiable. Assume that γ is a selection function for K such that $\gamma(\mathbb{P}_{K'}) = \gamma(\mathbb{K}_{K', \subseteq_P})|_P$ and $\gamma(\mathbb{T}_{K|_P *_\gamma K'}) = \{(\tau, \emptyset) \mid (\tau', \emptyset) \in \gamma(\mathbb{K}_{K', \subseteq_P})|_T$ and $(\tau', \emptyset) \subseteq (\tau, \emptyset)\}$. The proof then follows symmetrically to the proof of Proposition 2. $\qquad \square$

For completeness, we also show here the relationship between stepwise revision and partial meet revision in Propositions 4 and 5, namely, that the result of stepwise revision is a subset of the result of partial meet revision, given that the selection function behaves similarly in each operation. Particularly, this is the case for $K|_P *_\gamma (K|_T *_\gamma K')$ whenever the theory part of K retained in the first step of stepwise revision is included in each selected compatible set for partial meet revision and the set of selected compatible sets for the second step of stepwise revision is the same as the set of program parts in the selected compatible sets for partial meet revision (analogously for $K|_T *_\gamma (K|_P *_\gamma K')$).

Proposition 4. *Let $K, K' \in \mathcal{K}_\mathcal{L}$. There exists a selection function γ for K such that $K|_P *_\gamma (K|_T *_\gamma K') \subseteq K *_\gamma K'$.*

Proof. Let $K, K' \in \mathcal{K}_{\mathcal{L}}$. Assume that γ is a selection function for K such that, for any $(\tau, \rho) \in \gamma(\mathbb{K}_{K', \subseteq})$, $\bigcap \gamma(\mathbb{T}_{K'}) \subseteq (\tau, \emptyset)$ and $\gamma(\mathbb{P}_{K|_T *_\gamma K'}) = \gamma(\mathbb{K}_{K', \subseteq})|_P$. If K' is not satisfiable, then it follows directly from Definition 3 that $K|_P *_\gamma (K|_T *_\gamma K') = K + K' = K *_\gamma K'$. Otherwise, for any $(\emptyset, \rho') \in \mathbb{P}_{K|_T *_\gamma K'}$, there exists a $(\tau'', \rho'') \in \mathbb{K}_{K', \subseteq}$ such that $(\emptyset, \rho') = (\emptyset, \rho'')$ by Definition 1 and our definition of $\mathbb{P}_{K'}$ and $(K|_T *_\gamma K') \setminus K' = \bigcap \gamma(\mathbb{T}_{K'}) \subseteq (\tau'', \emptyset)$ by Definitions 1 and 3. Due to the assumption, it then follows that $\bigcap \gamma(\mathbb{K}_{K', \subseteq})|_P = \bigcap \gamma(\mathbb{P}_{K|_T *_\gamma K'})$ and $\bigcap \gamma(\mathbb{T}_{K'}) \subseteq \bigcap \gamma(\mathbb{K}_{K', \subseteq})|_T$. This implies $K|_P *_\gamma (K|_T *_\gamma K') \subseteq K *_\gamma K'$ by Definition 3. □

Proposition 5. *Let $K, K' \in \mathcal{K}_{\mathcal{L}}$ There exists a selection function γ for K such that $K|_T *_\gamma (K|_P *_\gamma K') \subseteq K *_\gamma K'$.*

Proof. Let $K, K' \in \mathcal{K}_{\mathcal{L}}$. Assume that γ is a selection function for K such that, for any $(\tau, \rho) \in \gamma(\mathbb{K}_{K', \subseteq})$, $\bigcap \gamma(\mathbb{P}_{K'}) \subseteq (\emptyset, \rho)$ and $\gamma(\mathbb{T}_{K|_P *_\gamma K'}) = \gamma(\mathbb{K}_{K', \subseteq})|_T$. The proof then follows symmetrically to the proof of Proposition 4. □

3.3   Prioritised Revision

While protected revision allows us to emphasise entire components of a HKB during a revision, its flexibility is somewhat limited. Specifically, in Example 3 above we saw that the theory component of K was fully preserved due to the structure of the new information K'. Intuitively, the revision outcome states that the unisex name Chris was incorrectly identified or entered as female. Yet, what if Chris is actually female and she married Kate after the law changed to allow same-sex marriage? In that case, we need to have a more fine-grained method than protected revision to allow the theory component to be changed. We therefore define *prioritised revision* now, based on an idea by Nebel [17].

Definition 5 (Priority Level). *Let $K \in \mathcal{K}_{\mathcal{L}}$ and $\leq$ be a total preorder on $K_T \cup K_P$. A priority level of K is*

$$\lambda = \{ (\tau, \rho) \subseteq K \mid e_1 \leq e_2 \text{ and } e_2 \leq e_1 \text{ for all } e_1, e_2 \in \tau \cup \rho \}.$$

We call $\leq$ defined as above a *prioritisation of K*. Furthermore, for all $e_1 \in \lambda_1$ and $e_2 \in \lambda_2$, we write $\lambda_1 \leq \lambda_2$ iff $e_1 \leq e_2$, and $\lambda_1 < \lambda_2$ iff $e_1 \leq e_2$ and $e_2 \not\leq e_1$. A prioritisation partitions K into a hierarchical sequence of levels and places each formula or rule of K in a particular level. We modify our definition of compatible sets to include priority levels.

Definition 6 (Prioritised Compatible Set). *Let $K, K' \in \mathcal{K}_{\mathcal{L}}$ and $\leq$ be a prioritisation of K. The set of prioritised compatible sets of K regarding K' is*

$$\mathbb{K}_{K', \leq} = \{ (\tau, \rho) \mid (\tau, \rho) = \bigcup_{\lambda \subseteq K} (\tau_\lambda, \rho_\lambda) \},$$

such that for all $\lambda \subseteq K$:

(a) $(\tau_\lambda, \rho_\lambda) \subseteq \lambda$,

(b) $QHT(\bigcup_{\lambda < \lambda'}(\tau_{\lambda'}, \rho_{\lambda'})) \cap QHT(K') \neq \emptyset$, *and*

(c) *for all* $(\tau_\lambda^\mathsf{T}, \rho_\lambda') \subseteq \lambda$, $(\tau_\lambda, \rho_\lambda) \subset (\tau_\lambda', \rho_\lambda')$ *implies* $QHT(\bigcup_{\lambda < \lambda'}(\tau_{\lambda'}, \rho_{\lambda'})) \cap QHT((\tau_\lambda', \rho_\lambda')) \cap QHT(K') = \emptyset$.

Each prioritised compatible set is composed of a maximal subset of the highest level that is compatible with K', a maximal subset of the next highest level that is compatible with K' and the subsets formed previously in higher levels, and so on. With these concepts established, we can now define a prioritised revision operator as follows.

Definition 7 (Prioritised Revision). *Let $K \in \mathcal{K}_\mathcal{L}$ and $\leq$ be a prioritisation of K. A prioritised revision operator $*_\leq$ for K is defined such that for any $K' \in \mathcal{K}_\mathcal{L}$:*

$$K *_\leq K' = \begin{cases} K + K' & \textit{if } K' \textit{ is not satisfiable,} \\ \bigcap \mathbb{K}_{K', \leq} + K' & \textit{otherwise.} \end{cases}$$

Whenever K' is satisfiable, our prioritised revision operator $*_\leq$ returns those elements of K that are common to all prioritised compatible sets together with K'. The following example illustrates the operation of prioritised revision and shows that it can indeed return the desired result with respect to our running example, that is, appropriately represent a change in marriage legislation.

Example 4. Consider again K from Example 1 and K' from Example 3. Let $\leq$ be a prioritisation of K such that assertion of the user's gender is given higher priority than prohibition of same-sex marriage. Formally, let $\lambda_1 = (\{ \forall x, y : married(x, y) \wedge female(x) \rightarrow male(y) \}, \emptyset)$, $\lambda_2 = (\emptyset, \{ female(Chris). \})$, $\lambda_3 = K \setminus (\lambda_1 \cup \lambda_2)$, and $\lambda_1 < \lambda_2 < \lambda_3$. It then follows that $\mathbb{K}_{K', \leq} = \{\lambda_2 \cup \lambda_3\}$ and thus $K *_\leq K' = \lambda_2 \cup \lambda_3 \cup K'$. ∎

Comparing our prioritised revision operator to our partial meet revision operator, we find that they coincide, as stated in Propositions 6 and 7.

Proposition 6. *Let $K, K' \in \mathcal{K}_\mathcal{L}$. For any selection function γ for K, there exists a prioritisation $\leq$ of K such that $K *_\gamma K' = K *_\leq K'$.*

Proof. Let $K, K' \in \mathcal{K}_\mathcal{L}$ and γ be a selection function for K that determines the outcome of $K *_\gamma K'$. By $S = \bigcap \gamma(\mathbb{K}_{K', \subseteq})$ we denote the part of K that is preserved in the partial meet revision and by $S' = K \setminus S$ the part of K that is discarded. We can then create a prioritisation $\leq$ of K as follows. In the limiting case that $S = \emptyset$, let $\leq$ consist of one level $\lambda_1 = S'$ only. From Definitions 1 and 6 it then follows that $\mathbb{K}_{K', \subseteq} = \mathbb{K}_{K', \leq}$. Since $\gamma(\mathbb{K}_{K', \subseteq}) \subseteq \mathbb{K}_{K', \subseteq}$ by Definition 2 and $\bigcap \gamma(\mathbb{K}_{K', \subseteq}) = \emptyset$ by the assumption, we obtain $\bigcap \mathbb{K}_{K', \leq} = \emptyset$ and consequently $K *_\gamma K' = K *_\leq K'$. Otherwise, let $\leq$ consist of exactly two levels λ_1 and λ_2 such that $\lambda_1 = S'$, $\lambda_2 = S$, and $\lambda_1 < \lambda_2$. We now show that $\bigcap \mathbb{K}_{K', \leq} = S$. For any $\kappa \in \mathbb{K}_{K', \leq}$, it follows from Definition 6 and our choice of $\leq$ that $S \subseteq \kappa$, which implies $S \subseteq \bigcap \mathbb{K}_{K',\leq}$ by Definition 7. Assume that there exists a $\kappa' \subseteq S'$ such that $\kappa' \subseteq \bigcap \mathbb{K}_{K',\leq}$. Then for each compatible set $\kappa'' \in \mathbb{K}_{K',\subseteq}$ with $S \subseteq \kappa''$ it would hold that $\kappa' \subseteq \kappa''$ because κ'' is maximal by Definition 1. Yet, this would imply $\kappa' \subseteq \bigcap \gamma(\mathbb{K}_{K',\subseteq})$ and thus $\kappa' \subseteq S$, a contradiction.   □

Proposition 7. *Let* $K, K' \in \mathcal{K}_{\mathcal{L}}$. *For any prioritisation* $\leq$ *of* K, *there exists a selection function* γ *for* K *such that* $K *_{\leq} K' = K *_{\gamma} K'$.

Proof. Let $K, K' \in \mathcal{K}_{\mathcal{L}}$ and $\leq$ be a prioritisation of K that determines the outcome of $K *_{\gamma} K'$. In the trivial case that K' is not satisfiable, we have $K *_{\leq} K' = K + K' = K *_{\gamma} K'$. Let K' be satisfiable in the following. We first show that for any prioritised compatible set $\kappa_1 \in \mathbb{K}_{K',\leq}$, there exists a compatible set $\kappa_2 \in \mathbb{K}_{K',\subseteq}$ such that $\kappa_1 = \kappa_2$. It follows directly from Definitions 1 and 6 that $\kappa_1 \subseteq \kappa_2$. Assume that $\kappa_1 \subset \kappa_2$. From Definition 6 it would then follow that $QHT(\kappa_1) \cap QHT(\kappa_2 \setminus \kappa_1) \cap QHT(K') = \emptyset$. Yet, this is a contradiction since $QHT(\kappa_2) \cap QHT(K') \neq \emptyset$ by Definition 1 and κ_1 is required to be maximal by Definition 6. Thus, for any $\kappa_1 \in \mathbb{K}_{K',\leq}$ it holds that $\kappa_1 \in \mathbb{K}_{K',\subseteq}$, that is, $\mathbb{K}_{K',\leq} \subseteq \mathbb{K}_{K',\subseteq}$. We can now set γ as a selection function for K such that $\gamma(\mathbb{K}_{K',\subseteq}) = \mathbb{K}_{K',\leq}$ and consequently obtain $K *_{\leq} K' = K *_{\gamma} K'$.   □

Since prioritised revision and partial meet revision coincide, it also holds that prioritised revision generalises protected revision and further that prioritised revision is exactly characterised by the postulates $(*1)$–$(*5)$.

Corollary 1. *Let* $K, K' \in \mathcal{K}_{\mathcal{L}}$. *For any selection function* γ *for* K, *there exists a prioritisation* $\leq$ *of* K *such that* $K *_{\gamma,\subseteq_\circ} K' = K *_{\leq} K'$.

Proof. Follows directly from Propositions 1 and 6.   □

Theorem 3. *Let* $K \in \mathcal{K}_{\mathcal{L}}$. *An operator* $*_{\leq}$ *is a prioritised revision operator for* K *determined by a prioritisation* $\leq$ *of* K *iff* $*_{\leq}$ *satisfies* $(*1)$–$(*5)$.

Proof. Follows directly from Theorem 1 and Propositions 6 and 7.   □

4 Related Work

Closest related work concerns itself with belief update, a relative of belief revision, in hybrid MKNF knowledge bases [21], which combine first-order theories and logic programs in a different semantic composition to the one considered here. That approach takes the combination of an initial HKB and an updating HKB and splits it into hierarchical levels, similar to the process of logic program stratification, such that updating information is given priority. It then applies given ontology update and rule update semantics to the respective components to evaluate the models of the updated HKB. In contrast to our prioritised revision, the update method does not allow arbitrary combinations of formulas and rules on the same level. In addition, since the update operation preserves all existing information and relies on the chosen semantics to determine a satisfiable outcome, the initial

HKB grows with each operation and may contain duplicate elements to express information that was first asserted, then contradicted, and later asserted again.

Multi-context systems allow reasoning over two or more knowledge bases, specified in some monotonic or nonmonotonic logic, by connecting them via nonmonotonic bridge rules. An adaptation of Dalal's [5] and Satoh's [20] classic belief revision operators to multi-context systems [22] computes the outcome of revising one multi-context system by another as the set of those models of the revising multi-context system that are closest to the ones of the initial multi-context system, where closeness is determined by Dalal's or Satoh's notion of distance. The adaptation to multi-context systems exhibits the same properties as the classic construction with respect to the belief revision postulates.

To assist with the task of rule authoring in HKBs, inductive logic programming can be used to learn new rules from the existing rules and formulas in a HKB [15]. As any induced rule is consistent with existing knowledge and no existing knowledge is removed, this process can be compared to screened revision [16] where the entire existing HKB is protected.

5   Conclusion

In this study, we proposed three operators to revise hybrid knowledge bases, namely, a general partial meet revision operator that does not assume any ordering of the elements of a hybrid knowledge base, a protected revision operator that emphasises the theory or program component of a hybrid knowledge base depending on the structure of information in the revising hybrid knowledge base, and lastly a prioritised revision operator that computes the outcome based on a pre-defined priority ordering among the elements in a hybrid knowledge base. We demonstrated the interdefinability between our operators, provided representation theorems for partial meet revision and prioritised revision with respect to the belief revision postulates, and showed that partial meet revision as well as prioritised revision are generalisations of protected revision.

It is straightforward to define corresponding partial meet, protected, and prioritised *contraction* operators, by using the complement of $QHT(K')$ in the definitions of compatible sets. Properties and representation theorems analogous to revision can then be obtained, after translating the classic contraction postulates in a similar manner as the ones for revision.

While our operators return a revised hybrid knowledge base, they do not specify how a selection function or prioritisation changes during the operation. In future work, we aim to investigate such an extension to our approach.

References

1. Alchourrón, C.E., Gärdenfors, P., Makinson, D.: On the logic of theory change: partial meet contraction and revision functions. J. Symbolic Logic **50**(2), 510–530 (1985)

2. Binnewies, S., Zhuang, Z., Wang, K.: Partial meet revision and contraction in logic programs. In: Proceedings of the Twenty-Ninth AAAI Conference on Artificial Intelligence, AAAI 2015, pp. 1439–1445. AAAI Press, Palo Alto (2015)
3. de Bruijn, J., Pearce, D., Polleres, A., Valverde, A.: A semantical framework for hybrid knowledge bases. Knowl. Inf. Syst. **25**(1), 81–104 (2010)
4. Colmerauer, A., Roussel, P.: The birth of prolog. In: Bergin Jr., T.J., Gibson Jr., R.G. (eds.) History of Programming Languages–II, pp. 331–367. ACM, New York (1996)
5. Dalal, M.: Investigations into a theory of knowledge base revision: preliminary report. In: Proceedings of the Seventh National Conference on Artificial Intelligence, pp. 475–479 (1988)
6. Delgrande, J.P., Schaub, T., Tompits, H., Woltran, S.: A model-theoretic approach to belief change in answer set programming. ACM Trans. Comput. Logic **14**(2), 14:1–14:46 (2013)
7. Drabent, W., Eiter, T., Ianni, G., Krennwallner, T., Lukasiewicz, T., Małuszyński, J.: Hybrid reasoning with rules and ontologies. In: Bry, F., Małuszyński, J. (eds.) Semantic Techniques for the Web. LNCS, vol. 5500, pp. 1–49. Springer, Heidelberg (2009). doi:10.1007/978-3-642-04581-3_1
8. Fuhrmann, A.: Theory contraction through base contraction. J. Philos. Logic **20**(2), 175–203 (1991)
9. Guarino, N., Oberle, D., Staab, S.: What is an ontology? In: Staab, S., Studer, R. (eds.) Handbook on Ontologies. International Handbooks on Information Systems, pp. 1–17. Springer, Berlin Heidelberg (2009)
10. Hansson, S.O.: New operators for theory change. Theoria **55**(2), 114–132 (1989)
11. Hansson, S.O.: Reversing the levi identity. J. Philos. Logic **22**(6), 637–669 (1993)
12. Hitzler, P., Parsia, B.: Ontologies and rules. In: Staab, S., Studer, R. (eds.) Handbook on Ontologies. International Handbooks on Information Systems, pp. 111–132. Springer, Berlin Heidelberg (2009)
13. Kowalski, R.: Predicate logic as a programming language. In: Proceedings of the IFIP Congress, pp. 569–574 (1974)
14. Krisnadhi, A., Maier, F., Hitzler, P.: OWL and Rules. In: Polleres, A., d'Amato, C., Arenas, M., Handschuh, S., Kroner, P., Ossowski, S., Patel-Schneider, P. (eds.) Reasoning Web 2011. LNCS, vol. 6848, pp. 382–415. Springer, Heidelberg (2011). doi:10.1007/978-3-642-23032-5_7
15. Lisi, F.A.: Learning onto-relational rules with inductive logic programming. In: Lehmann, J., Völker, J. (eds.) Perspectives on Ontology Learning, pp. 93–111. IOS Press Amsterdam, Studies on the Semantic Web (2014)
16. Makinson, D.: Screened revision. Theoria **63**(1–2), 14–23 (1997)
17. Nebel, B.: Belief revision and default reasoning: syntax-based approaches. In: Proceedings of the 2nd International Conference on Principles of Knowledge Representation and Reasoning (KR'91). pp. 417–428. Morgan Kaufmann, San Francisco (1991)
18. Pearce, D., Valverde, A.: Quantified equilibrium logic and foundations for answer set programs. In: Garcia de la Banda, M., Pontelli, E. (eds.) ICLP 2008. LNCS, vol. 5366, pp. 546–560. Springer, Heidelberg (2008). doi:10.1007/978-3-540-89982-2_46
19. Rott, H.: Modellings for belief change: base contraction, multiple contraction, and epistemic entrenchment (preliminary report). In: Pearce, D., Wagner, G. (eds.) JELIA 1992. LNCS, vol. 633, pp. 139–153. Springer, Heidelberg (1992). doi:10.1007/BFb0023426

20. Satoh, K.: Nonmonotonic reasoning by minimal belief revision. In: Proceedings of the International Conference on Fifth Generation Computer Systems, pp. 455–462 (1988)
21. Slota, M., Leite, J., Swift, T.: On updates of hybrid knowledge bases composed of ontologies and rules. Artif. Intell. **229**, 33–104 (2015)
22. Wang, Y., Zhuang, Z., Wang, K.: Belief change in nonmonotonic multi-context systems. In: Cabalar, P., Son, T.C. (eds.) LPNMR 2013. LNCS, vol. 8148, pp. 543–555. Springer, Heidelberg (2013). doi:10.1007/978-3-642-40564-8_54
23. Wassermann, R.: On AGM for non-classical logics. J. Philos. Logic **40**(2), 271–294 (2011)
24. Zhuang, Z., Wang, Z., Wang, K., Qi, G.: DL-lite contraction and revision. J. Artif. Intell. Res. **56**(1), 329–378 (2016)

Can My Test Case Run on Your Test Plant? A Logic-Based Compliance Check and Its Evaluation on Real Data

Daniela Briola[1]([✉]) and Viviana Mascardi[2]

[1] DISCO Department, Università degli Studi di Milano Bicocca, Milan, Italy
daniela.briola@unimib.it
[2] DIBRIS Department, Università degli Studi di Genova, Genoa, Italy
viviana.mascardi@unige.it

Abstract. Test automation is adopted by the majority of software and hardware producers since it speeds up the testing phase and allows to design and perform a large bunch of tests that would be hardly manageable in a manual way. When dealing with the testing of hardware instruments, different physical environments have to be created so that the instruments under test can be analyzed in different scenarios, involving disparate components and software configurations.

Creating a test case is a time consuming activity: test cases should be reused as much as possible. Unfortunately, when a physical test plant changes or a new one is created, understanding if existing test cases can be executed over the updated or new test plant is extremely difficult.

In this paper we present our approach for checking the compliance of a test case w.r.t. a physical test plant characterized by its devices and their current configuration. The compliance check, which is fully automated and exploits a logic-based approach, answers the query "Can the test case A run over the physical configured test plant B"?

Keywords: Test automation · Test case compliance · Logic programming

1 Introduction

Defects, or so-called bugs, are very common in software development and cause enormous economic losses. According to a research carried out by Cambridge University in 2013[1], the global cost of debugging software has risen to \$312 billion annually. The research found that, on average, software developers spend 50% of their programming time finding and fixing bugs.

Nowadays, software organizations invest a lot of time and money in analyzing and testing software, trying to keep up with developers who have to continuously modify the product throughout the entire software testing life cycle. For a long

---

[1] http://www.prweb.com/releases/2013/1/prweb10298185.htm.

© Springer International Publishing AG 2017
S. Costantini et al. (Eds.): RuleML+RR 2017, LNCS 10364, pp. 53–69, 2017.
DOI: 10.1007/978-3-319-61252-2_5

time, software testing has been conducted manually: a human tester runs the application using predefined processes to verify the correct behavior of the code. Nowadays manual testing is definitely less popular because some tasks are difficult to face manually, they can be repetitive and boring and, most important, they are often uselessly time consuming and error prone.

Today, to improve the testing phase, automation frameworks are widely adopted: they are integrated systems that automatically perform a set of tests over a specific product, offering scheduling policies, reports, test creation facilities and many other services. Scientists addressed the problem of automating the software testing stage starting from the end of the nineties [7,8] and the benefits of test automation, at least for some kind of processes and situations, were soon clear [12]. The research area became more and more important, with the birth of many conferences and workshops[2] and the publication of tens of books and manuals over the years [10,11,20,26]. Test automation is still an extremely lively research field, and recent works confirm the favorable impacts of software test automation in software cost, quality and time to market [16].

One of the most important aspects in test automation is tests reusability: companies that perform tests on entities that have similar internal structure have particular interest in this issue. These companies can use an equipment that changes its architecture from build to build, or pieces of software changing from release to release. These changes can either fix minor bugs or introduce new features, but the overall system remains stable and performs its core activity. Redesigning and rewriting tests when the system undergoes minor changes is an extremely time-consuming activity: for this reason, tests written for testing a specific area of the system under test, a part of an equipment, or a specific portion of code should be adaptive, flexible and reusable. A good practice to achieve this goal would be to keep the test itself and its configuration separate from each other. Configuration includes all necessary parameters, variables and constraints that should be isolated from the test. In this way, the test would contain the description of the steps that should be performed in order to test a specific area of a system, while the configuration would describe the test scope. This approach enables scalability of a test and provides the context of this work.

Tests reuse can be resorted to checking the compliance of a test case w.r.t. a physical test plant characterized by its devices and their current configuration. The compliance check should answer the query "Can the test case A run over the physical configured test plant B"?

The research activity described in this paper addresses test compliance using Prolog and has been carried out in collaboration with a world-leading provider of telecommunication equipments and services to mobile and fixed network operators. We will name this big company "BlindedCompany" throughout the paper, to respect the NDA signed with its legal representatives. We will also modify the name of some components of the System Under Test, to avoid disclosing BlindedCompany's identity. The experiments carried out together with BlindedCom-

---

pany's engineers show that the logic based algorithm we designed and developed solves the compliance check problem.

The paper is organized in the following way: Sect. 2 introduces the BlindedCompany test automation domain and Sect. 3 discusses how we modeled it. Section 4 explains the compliance check algorithm, Sect. 5 presents the experiments we run and how we hid the Prolog details to the BlindedCompany testers, and finally Sect. 6 presents related work and conclusions.

2   Test Plants and Test Cases in BlindedCompany

The first activity we carried out with BlindedCompany was to identify a shared terminology in the test automation domain. Although we agreed on an almost standard one, understanding the vocabulary used in the company and reaching this agreement required some effort. In the end, we set the following definitions:

- **Test Case (TC)**: a sequence of operations used to test the correct behavior of a software functionality;
- **Test Suite (TS)**: a set of TCs usually related to a specific fragment or component of the software application;
- **Test Plant (TP)**: a physical system representing a significant portion of BlindedCompany's telecommunications network or of its clients' products;
- **Physical Configured Test Plant (PCTP)**: the actual, physical test plant under test along with its configuration; it should be possible to represent the PCTP in some suitable modeling language $\mathcal{L}$ (discussed later on);
- **Minimal Configured Test Plant of a Test Case (MCTP(TC))**: the representation, in the same language $\mathcal{L}$ used for representing PCTP, of the minimal set of components, links among them and their configuration, which is required to run a given test case. MCTP(TC) states the minimal requirements that a configured TP should satisfy to support the run of TC.

In the sequel we describe the TPs and the unstructured data (such as text files) used by BlindedCompany to describe the elements that a TP should include in order for a TC to run on it, and that would allow us to extract the MCTP(TC). Section 3 discusses how we modeled both TCs and MCTP(TC)s in a formal way.

2.1   Test Plants

A TP is a physical system that represents a significant part of BlindedCompany network or a part of product for clients; it is subject to tests execution. TPs include Packet Optical Transport Platforms, AttachedUnitType1, AttachedUnitType2, and third-party instruments. The first three elements are developed by BlindedCompany and for this reason we changed their names.

Packet Optical Transport Platforms (POTPs). BlindedCompany designs and develops a family of products providing the management of metropolitan networks. POTPs are compact multiservice and packet optical transport elements. They are optimized to be used in Access and Metro networks and provide Ethernet and TDM (Time Division Multiplexing) services interworking with metro and core Networks based on Ethernet or WDM (Wavelength Division Multiplexing) connectivity. The POTP flexibility of installation and configuration makes it perfect for both the implementation of a new network architecture and for the renewal of existing ones.

A POTP is a shelf hosting cards for the management of data traffic in a metropolitan network. The shelf also accommodates control cards (usually inserted in specific positions by default), cooling fans and power supplies: a POTP can be seen as a set of cards (traffic cards or control cards, inserted into slots), each characterized by different Module Modes (MM), or modes of operation. Typically, each card has a set of ports whose configuration depends on the Module Mode loaded on the card. The Module Mode can be set by the Local Craft Terminal, a web Graphical User Interface (GUI) that allows the system developer or the tester to interact with the device and configure it to suit his or her purposes.

Attached Units. The shelf can accommodate one or more attached units of type 1, AttachedUnitType1, either connected directly to a shelf or integrated into a hierarchic system of attached units of type 1. They provide the photonics part. Attached units of type 2, AttachedUnitType2 in the sequel, also belong to the POTP family and are usually connected to one or more AttachedUnitType1. They amplify an optical signal directly, without the need to first convert it into an electrical signal. Attached units provide a variety of Dense Wavelength Division Multiplexing (DWDM) networking functions for building the POTP photonics network layer. Different configurations are loaded into ports of the cards and are used to connect POTPs.

Instruments. Some third-party devices, generically called "Instruments" in the sequel, may be part of the TP as well and may undergo a testing process. Their architecture is a "black box": we only possess information about their integration with the other elements of the POTP. Instruments can be used for example to simulate traffic events (traffic generator instrument) or the degradation of a wire and, as a result, of an optical signal.

Figure 1 shows the architecture of a real TP installed in BlindedCompany, called WDM2: the two elements shown on top represent two POTPs (POTP1 and POTP2); AU1_1 and AU1_2 are two AttachedUnitType1 elements connected to POTP1 and POTP2, respectively. The third component (AttachedUnitType2 named AU2) is shown in the middle of the picture. The POTPs are connected to AU2 thanks to AU1_1 and AU1_2. Some instruments are connected to the POTPs and AUs to register/create traffic, evaluate performances and so on.

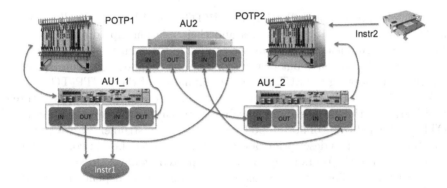

Fig. 1. WDM2 TP.

2.2   Current Representations of TPs and TCs in BlindedCompany

To design the compliance check, the first input we needed from BlindedCompany was a model of all the entities involved in the testing process in general, and in TCs and MCTP(TC)s in particular. It turned out that BlindedCompany used different models, represented in different languages and formats, for some of the tests portions only, and that it did not model in an explicit way the physical plant under test. We started a deep analysis of the different modeling approaches used in the company, in order to design a unified one. This activity represented a relevant part of the domain elicitation phase and required almost two man-months of a student who carried out his Bachelor's Thesis in BlindedCompany, supported by the authors and by the engineers from BlindedCompany's test automation team.

BlindedCompany does not use any formal representation of TCs: they are just source code files with the actual test code to be executed, plus some natural language documents describing them.

Even if the TC itself is not properly modeled, BlindedCompany uses an XML file to model the elements that should be available in the TP in order to run the TC, including the foreseen configurations, equipments, instruments and connections of the elements. This file is called, following a standard terminology, SUT (System Under Test) file. The SUT file helps testers to focus on what they are actually testing. It is used by the test automation tool to automate the execution of tests, and by testers to configure the TP as needed. After analyzing different SUT files and making interviews with many testers we understood that, given a TC associated with a SUT file, the information contained in the SUT file corresponds to a superset of the information characterizing MCTP(TC).

Identifying the MCTP(TC) based on the SUT file of TC may lead to some overestimation. For example, the SUT file might list more entities than those actually "solicited" by TC: these entities should not appear there, but our analysis shows that the presence of useless entities in the SUT file is very common and we must be aware of it.

Another approach for extracting MCTP(TC) would be to statically analyze the TC code and extract the entities and their relationships directly from it. This activity would lead to more precise results, but it is known to be extremely complex [1,13,14] and was out of the scope of our collaboration: consequently, we agreed on adopting the SUT as an approximation of the MCTP(TC).

Although the SUT is neither structured nor formalized, it follows a three levels hierarchy that makes it processable in an automatic way: at Level one, POTPs, Attached Units of both type 1 and type 2 and Instruments are described, then for each of them a description of their cards appears in Level two, and finally the description of the ports for each card is reported at Level three.

To make the reading of the remainder easier, the domain-dependent acronyms used in this paper are summarized below:

- **AUx**: Attached Unit of type "x".
- **DWDM**: Dense Wavelength Division Multiplexing.
- **MCTP(TC)**: Minimal Configured Test Plant of a Test Case.
- **MM**: Module Mode.
- **PCTP**: Physical Configured Test Plant.
- **POTP**: Packet Optical Transport Platform.
- **SUT**: System Under Test.
- **TC**: Test Case.
- **TP**: Test Plant.
- **WDM**: Wavelength Division Multiplexing.

3   Modeling PCTPs and MCTP(TC)s in UML and Prolog

Given a TC and a PCTP, if we choose the language $\mathcal{L}$ in a suitable way, we should be able to:

1. extract (either manually, semi-automatically, or automatically) MCTP(TC) from TC and describe it in $\mathcal{L}$;
2. describe PCTP using $\mathcal{L}$.

The objective of the compliance check is to answer the question:

given a set of TCs, which of them can run on a given PCTP?

If we are able to model both MCTP(TC) and PCTP in the same machine-readable language $\mathcal{L}$, an algorithm able to perform a smart comparison between the two models would allow us to find compliant ones.

Among the possible candidates as languages for modeling MCTP(TC) and PCTP, we took under consideration UML [24], OWL [25] and Prolog [23]. Since BlindedCompany's documentation describing the POTP was already in UML and the test automation engineers were more familiar with UML than with the other languages, we decided to adopt UML for sharing the model representation with them. Then we designed an ad-hoc manual translation mechanism from

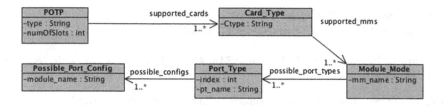

Fig. 2. UML representation of the POTP family with its main related classes.

UML to Prolog to make the specification suitable for undergoing a Prolog-based compliance check[3].

In the remainder of this section, we describe the models of POTP, PCTPs and of MCTP(TC)s in both UML and Prolog.

3.1 POTP

The most complex among the TP elements is the POTP. Figure 2 shows the UML class diagram for the POTP instruments family. The diagram consists of 5 classes modeling the architecture of the different types of POTPs, formalizing which cards each POTP type can contain in its slots. Class POTP models the POTP and its slots. The attribute **type** indicates a type of POTP, for example POTP1410, POTP1460, POTP1485, etc., while the numOfSlots attribute stores the number of available slots for the current type of POTP: the relation supported_cards relates the POTP with the possible cards that can be installed, belonging to class Card_Type. Each card has several possible Module_Modes (or modes of operation), which represent the interfaces of the card, used to manage it. A Module Mode defines, for that specific mode of operation, the available ports with their possible configurations. For each port, class Port_Type defines its number (**index**) and name (**pt_name**) plus its possible configurations (**possible_configs**). Class Possible_Port_Config represents one configuration of a port, and is identified with a unique name.

The main difference among POTP types lies in the cards they support: supported cards will be used to make a comparison between the POTPs in the MCTP and those in the PCTP to check their compliance.

The UML classes in Fig. 2 were manually translated into Prolog predicates. As customary, we use "?" to denote arguments that can be either (partially) bound or unbound. Since we use mainly cards and module modes in our compliance algorithm, we report here an example of these predicates; we will focus on the POTP details later on.

potp(?type_of_potp, ?list_of_attributes_including_installed_cards).
card_type(?card, ?list_of_supported_mm).

---

[3] This manual translation was enough for the purpose of our work, but if we had to generalize and automatize our approach, a logic-based language supporting a declarative representation of the structural aspects of object-oriented and frame-based languages like F-logic [15] might be taken into account in the modeling stage.

module_mode(?mm, ?list_of_possible_port_types).
port_type(?port_type, ?list_of_possible_port_config).

For example, a card type `SM-1xS64-4xS16-AH`, with one of its possible module mode, is described as:

```
card_type('SM-1xS64-4xS16-AH', supported_mms(['1xSTM64/OTU2(SM)',
   '4xSTM16/OTU1(SM)', '2xSTM16/OTU1(SM)', '4xXFP(SM)'])).

module_mode('4xXFP(SM)', port_types([
   (1, [
     ('OTN',possible_configs(['klevel2','klevel2e'])),
     ('CBR',possible_configs(['lan 10g','oc192','stm64','wan 10g']))]),
   (2, [
     ('OTN',possible_configs(['klevel2','klevel2e'])),
     ('CBR',possible_configs(['lan 10g','oc192','stm64','wan 10g']))]),
])).
```

For space constraints we do not provide examples of `port_type`, and we do not discuss the UML and Prolog models of AUs and instruments.

When dealing with PCTPs and MCPTs, we have to manage concrete instances of POTPs, each containing different installed cards, all coherent with those foreseen in the general model in Fig. 2: we speak of POTP Instances, as modeled in Fig. 3, where a concrete instance of a POTP (a `POTP_instance`) is described. The classes and their relationships come from those in Fig. 2 and formalize which elements are concretely, physically, installed in a specific POTP instance, among those foreseen for that POTP type. Attribute `type` in class `POTP_instance` recalls the UML Class modeling the generic POTP; besides the type, a POTP instance could also have a name, and the IP and NTP addresses. A POTP instance has a set of `Slots` with one installed `Card`, each configured with a specific `Module_Mode` (`installed_interface`). Ports and their configuration come together with the selected MM.

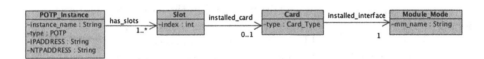

Fig. 3. UML representation of a POTP Instance.

As an example, a POTP instance named 'ne1' is represented by the following ground fact meaning that it has type `POTP1415,IP1` and `NTP1` addresses, and three slots, identified by number 1, 2 and 3, the first two hosting cards of type `SCM` with no installed interfaces, the third hosting a card with type `SM-1xS64-4xS16-AH` with module mode `4xXFP(SM)`.

```
potp_instance('ne1', attributes([
  ('TYPE', 'POTP1415'), ('IPADDR', 'IP1'), ('NTPADDR', 'NTP1'),
  ('INSTALLED_CARDS', [
    slot(1, card('SCM'),installed_int([])),
    slot(2, card('SCM'),installed_int([])),
    slot(3, card('SM-1xS64-4xS16-AH'),installed_int([(1,'4xXFP(SM)')]))
  ])])).
```

3.2   Test Plant (PCTP) and Test Case (MCTP) Representation

A PCTP, denoted by the `pctp` predicate, is identified by a name (such as WDM1, WDM2, etc.) and by four lists containing the identifiers of POTP Instances, Instruments, AttachedUnitType1 and AttachedUnitType2. Each list can be empty, meaning that a PCTP may not have elements of a particular type at all.

The PCTP representation must come along with the predicates describing the `POTP_instances` (like `ne1` described before), and the predicates describing the AU1s, AU2s and Instruments. AttachedUnitType1 and AttachedUnitType2 instances have an attribute `connected_to` which lists connections between them and POTPs. An example of predicate describing a PCTP is reported below.

```
pctp('wdm1',
  popt(['ne1', 'ne2', 'ne4']),
  instrument(['ONT_506_H', 'VOA_MAP200_S2P2']),
  au2([(('AU2_138', connected_to(['ne1', 'ne2']))]),
  au1([
      ('AU1_15', connected_to(['ne1'])),
      ('AU1_40', connected_to(['ne2'])),
      ('AU1_25', connected_to(['ne4'])),
      ('AU1_28', connected_to(['ne4'])),
      ('AU1_35', connected_to(['ne4'])) ])     ).
```

The Prolog representations of MCTP(TC), `mctp/5`, is identical in structure to the PCTP Prolog representation. Some of its arguments might be modeled by variables, whereas a PCTP representation is always a ground fact. As far as the POTP components of MCTP(TC) are concerned, we face the same situation: some of the arguments of a `potp_instance` of MCTP(TC) might be represented by variables, whereas the arguments of a `potp_instance` characterizing the PCTP must be ground since they represent physical running elements, with all the parameters already configured.

Since TCs operate on TPs with specific element types (POTPs, cards, AUs and so on) and not on specific instances, some concrete details like the IP address and the slots numbers are not relevant in their representation.

An example of a `potp_instance` for a MCTP is shown below.

```
potp_instance('potp1', attributes([
 ('TYPE', 'POTP1415'), ('IPADDR', _IP), ('NTPADDR', _NTP),
 ('INSTALLED_CARDS', [
 slot(_S1, card('SM-1xS64-4xS16-AH'),installed_int([(1,'OTU2_DWDM')])),
 slot(_S2, card('SM-1xS64-4xS16-AH'),installed_int([(1,'OTU2_DWDM')])),
 slot(_S3, card('SM-2x10GE-10xGE-A'),installed_int([(1,'10GBASE_LW')])),
 slot(_S4, card('SM-2xXFP-16xSFP'),installed_int([(1,'OTU2_DWDM')]))
 ])  ])).
```

4 Compliance Algorithm

A TC is fully compliant with a PCTP if the following four conditions are satisfied:

1. Each POTP in MCTP(TC) is compliant with one POTP in PCTP, which is not already compliant with another POTP in MCTP(TC). A POTP P1 is compliant with a POTP P2 if all cards of P1 are compliant with some (or all) distinct cards of POTP P2. From now on, we will use the notion of mapping. If a POTP P1 is compliant with POTP P2, all cards of P1 can be mapped to some (or all) cards of P2. The compliance check of POTPs is done through the exploration of the space of all possible solutions via backtracking. Two cards C1 and C2 are compliant if the installed interface (MM) of C1 is exactly the one installed in C2 or if it is supported by the `card_type` of C2.
2. Each Instrument in MCTP(TC) is present in PCTP.
3. Each AttachedUniteType1 in MCTP(TC) is compliant with one in PCTP (not already compliant with another AUType1 in MCTP(TC)) and its connections are correct.
4. Each AttachedUniteType2 in MCTP(TC) is compliant with one in PCTP (not already compliant with another AUType2 in MCTP(TC)) and its connections are correct.

The compliance algorithm is implemented by the `can_run_on` Prolog predicate which retrieves the PCTP and MCTP(TC) models, and operates a pairwise compliance check between pairs of homogeneous entities; for presentation purposes we ignore the possibility of a `setof` failure, and due to space limitation we do not show the code for the compliance between AttachedUnits and Instruments. That code is simpler than the one for the POTPs since it only checks that, for each $e \in AttachedUniteType1 \bigcup AttachedUniteType2 \bigcup Instrument$, if $e \in MCTP(TC)$, then there must exist $e' \in PCTP$ whose attributes are equivalent to those in e (and all the e' are distinct) and connection are correct (this for attached units only).

```prolog
can_run_on(MCTP, PCTP) :-

    % get the description of a PCTP by means of the pctp/5 predicate
    pctp(PCTP, potp(PCTP_POTPS), instrument(PCTP_INSTRUMENTS),
                au2(PCTP_AU2), au1(PCTP_AU1)),

    % get the description of the MCTP(TC) by means of the mctp/5 predicate
    mctp(MCTP, potp(MCTP_POTPS), instrument(MCTP_INSTRUMENTS),
                au2(MCTP_AU2), au1(MCTP_AU1)),

    % perform the compliance check of Instruments and Attached Units
    compliance_INSTRUMENTS(MCTP_INSTRUMENTS, PCTP_INSTRUMENTS),
    compliance_AU1(MCTP_AU1, PCTP_AU1),
    compliance_AU2(MCTP_AU2, PCTP_AU2),

    % unify [MinNotMapped|_] with the list of couples (NotMapped,Res),
    % ordered in increasing order of not mapped cards (the lower,
    % the better) such that Res is a List containing couples (MCTP_POTP,
    % PCTP_POTP) of succesfully mapped POTPs obtained by calling the
    % compliance_potps/3 predicate and NotMapped is the number of cards
    % that remained unmapped, as computed by compute_efficiency/2
    setof((Eff,Res),
          (compliance_potps(MCTP_POTPS, PCTP_POTPS, Res),
           compute_efficiency(Res, Eff)),
        [MinNotMapped|_]),

    % print the MinNotMapped result on screen ...
```

The compliance of POTPs implemented by the `compliance_potps` predicate is the core part of the algorithm.

```prolog
compliance_potps([], _, []).
compliance_potps([H|T], List, Res) :-
    compliance_card_aux(H,List,(H,PCTP_POTP)),
    delete(List, PCTP_POTP, Removed),
    compliance_potps(T,Removed,Sol),
    append([(H,PCTP_POTP)],Sol,Res).

compliance_card_aux(POTP,[Head|Tail],(POTP,Head)) :-
    compliance_cards(POTP,Head,(POTP,Head)).
compliance_card_aux(POTP,[Head|Tail],R) :-
    compliance_card_aux(POTP,Tail,R).

compliance_cards(Id_MCTP, Id_PCTP, (Id_MCTP, Id_PCTP)) :-
    potp_instance(Id_MCTP,
        attributes([TYPE_MCTP, IP_ADDR_MCTP, NTP_ADDR_MCTP,
                    ('INSTALLED_CARDS', CARDS_MCTP)])),
    potp_instance(Id_PCTP,
        attributes([TYPE_PCTP, IP_ADDR_PCTP, NTP_ADDR_PCTP,
                    ('INSTALLED_CARDS', CARDS_PCTP)])),
    cards(CARDS_MCTP, CARDS_PCTP, Result).
```

The predicate `cards`, not reported here for space limitation, checks if two cards are compliant. The best candidate for mapping of POTPs is selected based on "Minimal not mapped cards" parameter which shows how good a mapping is. The best POTP's mapping is the one with the minimal number of non-mapped cards. Below is a formula for computation of this parameter along with its implementation. Only mappable POTPs are taken into account.

Efficiency = (#CardsPCTP_POTP1 - #CardsMCTP_POTP1) + (#CardsPCTP_POTP2 - #CardsMCTP_POTP2) + ... + (#CardsPCTP_POTPn - #CardsMCTP_POTPn) where #CardsXXX is the number of successfully mapped cards.

```
compute_efficiency([], 0).
compute_efficiency([(POTP_A, POTP_B)|T], Eff) :-
    potp_instance(POTP_A,
        attributes([_, _, _, ('INSTALLED_CARDS', CARDS_MCTP)])),
    potp_instance(POTP_B,
        attributes([_, _, _, ('INSTALLED_CARDS', CARDS_PCTP)])),
    length(CARDS_MCTP, Length_MCTP),
    length(CARDS_PCTP, Length_PCTP),
    K is Length_PCTP-Length_MCTP,
    compute_efficiency(T, Rest),
    Eff is K+Rest.
```

The Prolog code defining `can_run_on` and its auxiliary predicates can be downloaded from http://www.disi.unige.it/person/MascardiV/Software/ RuleML17Code.zip. It consists of 194 lines of code, including predicates for computing the best mapping and for pretty-printing the output. The total number of predicates in the program is 23, defined by means of 33 clauses (including both rules and facts). Among the 23 predicates, 10 are defined recursively: 4 are tail recursive, 6 are not. Only 4 predicates defined recursively call in their body another recursively defined predicate. In only one case there is a double nesting, with recursive predicate P1 calling recursive predicate P2, which in turn calls recursive predicate P3.

5   Implementation and Experiments

During the interviews with BlindedCompany's testers it turned out that none of them was familiar with Prolog. Hence, we implemented an easy to use web application providing a GUI, hiding the details of the Prolog algorithm discussed in Sect. 4. To the BlindedCompany's testers, the compliance check tool was proposed as a black box with a GUI. The model of a POTP instance, as well as of instances of Attached Units and Instruments that make up a PCTP, can be entered by the test designer via that GUI. Because of space constraints, we cannot go into the details of the web application implementation. It uses Java Servlets able to communicate with Prolog thanks to JPL[4]. For the implementation of the View Layer we adopted HTML plus CSS, JavaScript to perform

---

[4] http://www.swi-prolog.org/packages/jpl.

some action callbacks, and AJAX for asynchronous communication with the server and for performing background tasks.

To test the correctness of the algorithm, we first created fictional MCTPs and PCTPs that were simple enough to allow a manual check of the algorithm behavior, but complex enough to demonstrate all the features of the compliance checking mechanism.

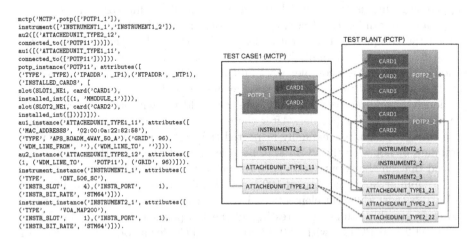

```
mctp('MCTP',potp(['POTP1_1']),
instrument(['INSTRUMENT1_1','INSTRUMENT1_2']),
au2([('ATTACHEDUNIT_TYPE2_12',
connected_to(['POTP11']))]),
au1([('ATTACHEDUNIT_TYPE1_11',
connected_to(['POTP11']))])]).
potp_instance('POTP11', attributes([
('TYPE', _TYPE),('IPADDR', _IP1),('NTPADDR', _NTP1),
('INSTALLED_CARDS', [
slot(SLOT1_NE1, card('CARD1'),
installed_int([(1, 'MMODULE_1')])),
slot(SLOT2_NE1, card('CARD2'),
installed_int([]))])]))).
au1_instance('ATTACHEDUNIT_TYPE1_11', attributes([
('MAC_ADDRESSS', '02:00:0a:22:82:58'),
('TYPE', 'APS_ROADM_4WAY_50_A'),('GRID', 96),
('WDM_LINE_FROM', ''),('WDM_LINE_TO', '')])).
au2_instance('ATTACHEDUNIT_TYPE2_12', attributes([
(1, ('WDM_LINE_TO', 'POTP11'), ('GRID', 96))])).
instrument_instance('INSTRUMENT1_1', attributes([
('TYPE', 'ONT_506_SC'),
('INSTR_SLOT', 4),('INSTR_PORT', 1),
('INSTR_BIT_RATE', 'STM64')])).
instrument_instance('INSTRUMENT2_1', attributes([
('TYPE', 'VOA_MAP200'),
('INSTR_SLOT', 1),('INSTR_PORT', 1),
('INSTR_BIT_RATE', 'STM64')])).
```

Fig. 4. Fictional TC, modeled in Prolog by mctp, and PCTP (Prolog model not shown).

For example, in Fig. 4 one couple of fictional TCs and PCTPs is reported[5]: the TC needs one POTP with two cards, two instruments (INSTRUMENT1_1 and INSTRUMENT2_1), one AttachedUnitType1 (ATTACHEDUNIT_TYPE1_11) and one AttachedUnitType2 (ATTACHEDUNIT_TYPE2_12) both connected (continuous arrows) to POTP1_1, while in the TP there are two POTPs, three Instruments, one AttachedUnitType1 and two AttachedUnitType2. The dotted arrows connect the equivalent elements (that is, those elements that are compatible: for example, CARD3 in POTP2_1 is not compatible with those in POTP1_1).

On the left of Fig. 4 the Prolog representation of MCTP(TC) is reported; for space limitations we cannot show the PCTP Prolog model, which has the same structure.

If we execute the compliance algorithm, it answers that the POTP1_1 is compatible with both the POTPs in the PCTP, but the best mapping is the one with POTP2_2 since all its cards are mapped into those of POTP1_1.

Many similar tests with fictional data where performed to assess the compliance check, all built to be similar to the real data but with simplified entities and properties name and connections.

---

[5] Since TC is the actual test case and MCTP(TC) is its representation, in the sequel we prefer TC to MCTP(TC) to stress the fact that our experiments involved real or fictional but realistic TCs.

Then, we performed two kinds of tests on real data, those where we already knew the results and those whose results were unknown, involving randomly chosen TCs and PCTPs. Both were based on actual data collected with the collaboration of BlindedCompany: we started testing a large set of TCs currently used on two PCTPs, which we manually formalized in Prolog. Since we used PCTPs and TCs whose compliance was already known by our partner, we only had to verify that all the compliance check runs gave the expected result. This happened, giving us an empirical validation of the algorithm correctness.

Finally, we randomly selected ten TCs from different Test Suites and we performed the compliance check with the two PCTPs used in the previous tests. These experiments were limited to twenty because creating the Prolog representation of the PCTP is a complex work and, above all, because in order to execute the TCs we needed physical test plants available, and the two PCTPs that we previously formalized were the only ones we could use without interfering with the normal job of our partner. After the experiments were set and the compliance check was run, we manually inspected the TCs to understand if they were compliant or not with the PCTPs, to be able to check the algorithm results. We verified that all the twenty tests gave the correct results.

To summarize, we performed 100 tests with fictional data using 10 TCs and 10 PCTPs (with different elements and values, to cover all the involved entities and their possible values), and testing all the 100 possible combinations. Then, we tested 2 real PCTPs with 100 different real TCs, for a total of 200 tests. In these tests, we knew in advance the expected results and we could verify that the computed results were the same. Finally, we used the same 2 PCTPs employed in the previous experiments to execute 20 more tests on 10 randomly selected TCs, which had to be physically executed on the company PCTPs.

Based on the experiments outcomes, we are confident that the compliance algorithm correctly performs its task, since we selected TCs to cover all the involved entities and all the configurations used in the Test Suites: the "Compliance Check Web Application" has been delivered to BlindedCompany, which is currently integrating it in its test automation tools suite and process.

6 Related Works and Conclusions

We presented a logic based algorithm able to verify the compliance of a MCTP with a PCTP, which represents a real problem faced by our industrial partner and in general by several hardware developers: starting from BlindedCompany's real data, we created a model expressive enough to be used to solve this problem, and our tests verified that the algorithm works correctly.

The main contribution of our work is on "exporting" Prolog to a big company. The task we faced is "easy" for academic researchers working in the computational logic field: we did not use meta-programming capabilities, cyclic terms, coinduction, constraints, or other sophisticated features. Nevertheless, the easy Prolog program we developed turned out to be extremely promising for the company, and this is a relevant result.

We were not able to find works sharing the same goal and exploiting the same logic-based approach as ours in the literature. The test automation experts in BlindedCompany helped us in this search making queries to colleagues in other test automation units and looking for patents. The result was the same.

Our compliance check is aimed at TC reuse [3, 6, 27], a problem whose importance was understood many years ago and improved in the last few years with the increased importance of software product lines, and which has been addressed using techniques different from ours. To the best of our knowledge, this makes our proposal original: Logic Programming and related approaches including constraint programming and CLP are used in the test automation domain since the mid eighties. Many works discuss how Prolog, CP and CLP programs are used either as generators of inputs for the SUT, or as a validators of the SUT outputs (test oracle), or both, in particular in conjunction with model-based testing [9, 17, 19, 21, 22], but TC reuse is never addressed.

As a future work we see the following improvements that, thanks to Prolog and its meta-programming abilities, should be implemented with little effort:

- Automation of the extraction of MCTP and PCTP models;
- Integration of a "suggestion module" that provides suggestions on how to reconfigure a TP in order to support a given TC;
- Extension of the model with more detailed information about Instruments and Attached Units, to make their compliance check more sophisticated.

Finally, we are considering how the lessons learned from this experience could be generalized and ported to other domains including planning ("is an actual course of activities compliant with a planned one?") and interactions in multiagent systems ("is an actual conversation among agents compliant with an expected one?"). The problems are different since in the test automation domain compliance is "structural/static", whereas in the agent interaction protocol and in the planning domains it must take the dynamics of the protocol/plan into account. Nevertheless, using Prolog for coping with compliance in dynamic domains is not a novelty, and we are exploiting it in our research on monitoring the communicative behavior of a set of agents w.r.t. the expected one [2, 4, 5, 18]. Being able to generalize this work with BlindedCompany and to unify it with our research activities in the agents field would demonstrate the suitability and the flexibility of logic-based approaches to generic compliance problems.

Acknowledgements. We thank Vladimir Zaikin who contributed to the realization of some parts of this work, and the engineers from BlindedCompany's test automation team involved in the project. We also thank the reviewers for their valuable comments.

References

1. Ackermann, C., Cleaveland, R., Huang, S., Ray, A., Shelton, C., Latronico, E.: Automatic requirement extraction from test cases. In: Barringer, H., et al. (eds.) RV 2010. LNCS, vol. 6418, pp. 1–15. Springer, Heidelberg (2010). doi:10.1007/978-3-642-16612-9_1

2. Ancona, D., Drossopoulou, S., Mascardi, V.: Automatic generation of self-monitoring mass from multiparty global session types in Jason. In: Baldoni, M., Dennis, L., Mascardi, V., Vasconcelos, W. (eds.) DALT 2012. LNCS (LNAI), vol. 7784, pp. 76–95. Springer, Heidelberg (2013). doi:10.1007/978-3-642-37890-4_5

3. Asaithambi, S.P.R., Jarzabek, S.: Towards test case reuse: a study of redundancies in android platform test libraries. In: Favaro, J., Morisio, M. (eds.) ICSR 2013. LNCS, vol. 7925, pp. 49–64. Springer, Heidelberg (2013). doi:10.1007/978-3-642-38977-1_4

4. Briola, D., Mascardi, V., Ancona, D.: Distributed runtime verification of JADE and Jason multiagent systems with Prolog. In: Italian Conference on Computational Logic, CEUR Workshop Proceedings, vol. 1195, pp. 319–323 (2014)

5. Briola, D., Mascardi, V., Ancona, D.: Distributed runtime verification of JADE multiagent systems. In: Camacho, D., Braubach, L., Venticinque, S., Badica, C. (eds.) Intelligent Distributed Computing VIII. SCI, vol. 570, pp. 81–91. Springer, Cham (2015). doi:10.1007/978-3-319-10422-5_10

6. Cai, L., Tong, W., Liu, Z., Zhang, J.: Test case reuse based on ontology. In: 15th IEEE Pacific Rim International Symposium on Dependable Computing, 2009. PRDC 2009, pp. 103–108. IEEE (2009)

7. Dustin, E., Rashka, J., Paul, J., Testing, A.S.: Introduction, Management, and Performance. Addison-Wesley, Boston (1999)

8. Fewster, M., Graham, D.: Software Test Automation. Addison-Wesley, Reading (1999)

9. Gorlick, M.M., Kesselman, C.F., Marotta, D.A., Parker, D.S.: Mockingbird: a logical methodology for testing. J. Log. Program. 8(1–2), 95–119 (1990)

10. Graham, D., Fewster, M.: Experiences of Test Automation: Case Studies of Software Test Automation. Addison-Wesley, Upper Saddle River (2012)

11. Hayes, L.G.: Automated Testing Handbook. Software Testing Inst, Dallas (2004)

12. Hoffman, D.: Cost benefits analysis of test automation. Report of Software Quality Methods, LLC (1999). https://www.agileconnection.com/sites/default/files/article/file/2014/Cost-Benefit

13. Jääskeläinen, A.: Towards model construction based on test cases and GUI extraction. In: Wotawa, F., Nica, M., Kushik, N. (eds.) ICTSS 2016. LNCS, vol. 9976, pp. 225–230. Springer, Cham (2016). doi:10.1007/978-3-319-47443-4_15

14. Jääskeläinen, A., Kervinen, A., Katara, M., Valmari, A., Virtanen, H.: Synthesizing test models from test cases. In: Chockler, H., Hu, A.J. (eds.) HVC 2008. LNCS, vol. 5394, pp. 179–193. Springer, Heidelberg (2009). doi:10.1007/978-3-642-01702-5_18

15. Kifer, M., Lausen, G., Wu, J.: Logical foundations of object-oriented and frame-based languages. J. ACM 42(4), 741–843 (1995)

16. Kumar, D., Mishra, K.K.: The impacts of test automation on software's cost, quality and time to market. In: 7th International Conference on Communication Procedia Computer Science, Computing and Virtualization 2016, vol. 79, pp. 8–15 (2016)

17. Lucio, L., Pedro, L., Buchs, D.: A methodology and a framework for model-based testing. In: Guelfi, N. (ed.) RISE 2004. LNCS, vol. 3475, pp. 57–70. Springer, Heidelberg (2005). doi:10.1007/11423331_6

18. Mascardi, V., Ancona, D.: Attribute global types for dynamic checking of protocols in logic-based multiagent systems. TPLP **13**(4-5-Online-Supplement) (2013)
19. Meudec, C.: Atgen: automatic test data generation using constraint logic programming and symbolic execution. Softw. Test. Verif. Reliab. **11**(2), 81–96 (2001)
20. Mosley, D.J., Posey, B.A.: Just Enough Software Test Automation. Prentice Hall, Upper Saddle River (2002)
21. Pesch, H., Schnupp, P., Schaller, H., Spirk, A.P.: Test case generation using Prolog. In: 8th International Conference on Software Engineering, ICSE 1985, pp. 252–258. IEEE Computer Society Press (1985)
22. Philipps, J., Pretschner, A., Slotosch, O., Aiglstorfer, E., Kriebel, S., Scholl, K.: Model-based test case generation for smart cards. Electron. Notes Theoret. Comput. Sci. **80**, 170–184 (2003)
23. Sterling, L., Shapiro, E.Y.: The Art of Prolog - Advanced Programming Techniques, 2nd edn. MIT Press, Cambridge (1994)
24. The Object Management Group: OMG Unified Modeling Language^{TM} (OMG UML). Version 2.5. OMG Document Number formal/2015-03-01 (2015). http://www.omg.org/spec/UML/2.5/PDF/
25. The W3C OWL Working Group: OWL 2 Web Ontology Language Document Overview, 2nd Ed. W3C Recommendation, 11 December 2012. https://www.w3.org/TR/owl2-overview/
26. Unmesh, G.: Selenium Testing Tools Cookbook. Packt Publishing, Burmingham (2012)
27. Von Mayrhauser, A., Mraz, R., Walls, J., Ocken, P.: Domain based testing: increasing test case reuse. In: IEEE International Conference on Computer Design: VLSI in Computers and Processors. ICCD 1994, pp. 484–491. IEEE (1994)

Semantic DMN: Formalizing Decision Models with Domain Knowledge

Diego Calvanese[1](✉), Marlon Dumas[2], Fabrizio M. Maggi[2],
and Marco Montali[1]

[1] Free University of Bozen-Bolzano, Bolzano, Italy
{calvanese,montali}@inf.unibz.it
[2] University of Tartu, Tartu, Estonia
{marlon.dumas,f.m.maggi}@uu.ee

Abstract. The Decision Model and Notation (DMN) is a recent OMG standard for the elicitation and representation of decision models. DMN builds on the notion of decision table, which consists of columns representing the inputs and outputs of a decision, and rows denoting rules. DMN models work under the assumption of complete information, and do not support integration with background domain knowledge. In this paper, we overcome these issues, by proposing *decision knowledge bases* (DKBs), where decisions are modeled in DMN, and domain knowledge is captured by means of first-order logic with datatypes. We provide a logic-based semantics for such an integration, and formalize how the different DMN reasoning tasks introduced in the literature can be lifted to DKBs. We then consider the case where background knowledge is expressed as an $\mathcal{ALC}$ description logic ontology equipped with datatypes, and show that in this setting, all reasoning tasks can be actually decided in EXP-TIME. We discuss the effectiveness of our framework on a case study in maritime security.

1 Introduction

The Decision Model and Notation (DMN) [11] is a recent OMG standard for the elicitation and representation of decision models, and for managing their interconnection with business processes, separating decision and control-flow logic [4]. The standard is already receiving widespread adoption in the industry, and an increasing number of tools and techniques are being developed to assist users in modeling, checking, and applying DMN models. DMN builds on the notion of a *decision table* (cf. [13]), which consists of columns representing the inputs and outputs of a decision, and rows denoting rules. Each rule is a conjunction of basic expressions, which in our case are captured in a language known as S-FEEL, which is also part of the DMN standard itself.

According to the standard, DMN models work under the assumption of complete information, and do not support integration with background domain knowledge. In this paper, we overcome this limitation, by proposing a combined framework, which we call *Semantic DMN*, that is based on *decision*

© Springer International Publishing AG 2017
S. Costantini et al. (Eds.): RuleML+RR 2017, LNCS 10364, pp. 70–86, 2017.
DOI: 10.1007/978-3-319-61252-2_6

Table 1. Ontology of cargo ships and their features.

Ship type	Short name	Length (m)	Draft (m)	Capacity (TEU)
Converted Cargo Vessel	*CCV*	135	0–9	500
Converted Tanker	*CT*	200	0–9	800
Cellular Containership	*CC*	215	10	1000–2500
Small Panamax Class	*SPC*	250	11–12	3000
Large Panamax Class	*LPC*	290	11–12	4000
Post Panamax	*PP*	275–305	11–13	4000–5000
Post Panamax Plus	*PPP*	335	13–14	5000–8000
New Panamax	*NP*	397	15.5	11000–14500

knowledge bases (DKBs). In a DKB, decisions are modeled in DMN, and background domain knowledge[1] is captured by means of an ontology expressed in multi-sorted first-order logic. The different sorts are used to seamlessly integrate abstract domain objects with the data values belonging to the concrete domains used in the DMN rules (such as strings, integers, and reals).

For the enriched setting of Semantic DMN, we provide a logic-based semantics, and we formalize how the different DMN reasoning tasks that have been introduced in the literature can be lifted to DKBs. We then approach the problem of actually reasoning on DKBs, and of devising effective algorithms for the different reasoning tasks captured by our formalization. For this purpose, we need to put restrictions on how to express background knowledge, and we consider the significant case where such knowledge is formulated in terms of an ontology expressed in a description logic (DL) [3] equipped with *datatypes* [2,9,10,14]. In such a DL, besides the domain of abstract objects, one can refer to concrete domains of data values (such as strings, integers, and reals) accessed through functional relations, and one can express conditions on such values by making use of *unary* predicates[2] over the concrete domains. Specifically, we prove that for the case where the DL ontology is epressed in $\mathcal{ALC}(\mathfrak{D})$, i.e., $\mathcal{ALC}$ [3] extended with multiple datatypes, all reasoning tasks can be actually decided in ExpTime.

We show the effectiveness of our framework by considering a case study in maritime security, arguing that our approach facilitates modularity and separation of concerns.

---

[1] We remark that our notion of *domain knowledge* is different from that of *business knowledge model* in DMN. The latter is a reusable decision logic, with a purely operational meaning.

[2] The restriction to unary predicates only, is what distinguishes DLs with datatypes from the richer setting of DLs with concrete domains, where in general arbitrary predicates over the datatype/concrete domain can be specified.

2   Case Study

Our case study is inspired by the international Ship and Port Facility Security Code[3], used by port authories to determine whether a ship can enter a Dutch port.

2.1   Domain Description

As shown in Table 1, there are several types of cargo ships that may enter a port, with different characteristics: *(i) Length* of the ship (in *m*); *(ii) Draft* size (in *m*); *(iii) Capacity* of the ship (in *TEU*, for Twenty-foot Equivalent Units). Such characteristics, together with other data about the ships, allow the port managers to decide whether to grant entrance permission to an incoming ship or not. More specifically, a ship can enter the port only if it complies with the requirements of the inspection, which is the case if it is equipped with a *valid certificate of registry*, and it meets the *safety requirements*.

The ship's certificate is valid if its expiration date is after the current date. The rules for establishing whether a ship meets the safety requirements depend on its characteristics, and the amount of its residual cargo. In particular, small ships (with length $\leq$260 m and draft $\leq$10 m) may enter only if their capacity is $\leq$1000 TEU. Ships with a small length ($\leq$260 m), medium draft >10 and $\leq$12 m, and capacity $\leq$4000 TEU, may enter only if cargo residuals have $\leq$0.75 mg dry weight per cm^2. Medium-sized ships (with length >260 m and <320 m, and draft >10 m and $\leq$13 m), and with a cargo capacity <6000 TEU, may enter only if their residuals have $\leq$0.5 mg dry weight per cm^2. Big ships with length between 320 m and 400 m, draft >13 m, and capacity >4000 TEU, may enter only if their carried residuals have $\leq$0.25 mg dry weight per cm^2.

2.2   Challenges

The first challenge posed by this case study concerns modeling, representation, management, and actual application of the decision rules that relate the numerical inputs capturing the characteristics of ships, to the boolean, clearance output. All these issues are tackled by the DMN standard. In particular, the standard defines clear guidelines to encode and graphically represent the input/output attributes and the rules of interest in the form of a DMN decision table. This table, in turn, may be used to document the decision logic for clearance determination, and to match the data of a ship with the modeled rules, computing the corresponding output(s), i.e., whether the ship can enter or not. this latter mechanism is backed up by a formal semantics in predicate logic [5].

In addition, DMN allows the modeler to decorate the decision with meta-information: *completeness* indicates that rules cover all possible input configurations, while the *hit policy* describes how input may match with the rules. Different hit policies are used to declare whether rules are non-overlapping, or may instead simultaneously match with the same input, then also specifying how to calculate the final output.

---

[3] https://dmcommunity.wordpress.com/challenge/challenge-march-2016/.

A crucial aspect is that such meta-information is declared in DMN without actually checking whether it suitably captures how the decision logic behaves. Dedicated algorithms have been thus developed to accomplish this task (see, e.g., [5,12,15–17]). There are, however, a number of additional crucial challenges that cannot be tackled by capturing the decision logic alone. Let us imagine how a decision table for ship clearance could actually be employed in an actual Dutch port, when a ship is approaching the port. How would the port authority know about all ship characteristics needed to take the decision? An immediate, but quite inconvenient, solution would be to measure all required characteristics on a per ship basis, then applying the decision table directly so as to compute the clearance outcome. A more pragmatic and feasible approach is to exploit the *domain knowledge* captured in Table 1, by acquiring from the ship only the information regarding *ship type* and *cargo residuals*, while using Table 1 to infer from the ship type the information about length, draft, and capacity. It is important to stress that the possibility of interconnecting multiple DMN tables (so that the output of one table is used as input of another table), also supported by the standard, is not applicable here: Table 1 is not a decision table, since it is not always possible to univocally compute the ship characteristics from the type (see, e.g., the case of *Post Panamax* ship type). In fact, the domain knowledge captured by Table 1 is a set of *constraints*, implicitly discriminating between allowed combinations of ship types and characteristics, from those that are impossible. In this light, Table 1 captures a *domain ontology*.

The interplay between such a domain ontology and the ship clearance decision model is far from trivial. On the one hand, it requires to lift from an approach working under complete information to one that works under *incomplete information*, and where the background knowledge is used to complement the known inputs, before the corresponding outputs are inferred. On the other hand, it does not only impact how decision table outputs are computed, but it also changes the interpretation of the completeness and hit policy indicators: they cannot be checked anymore by analyzing the decision table in isolation (as in [5]), but *in the context of the domain knowledge*.

In particular, by elaborating on the rules above, one would understand that rules are non-overlapping regardless of the domain knowledge, since their input conditions are mutually exclusive. However, one would also conclude, by mistake, that they are not complete, since, e.g., they do not cover the case of a long ship ($\geq 320\,\mathrm{m}$) with small draft ($\leq 10\,\mathrm{m}$). However, under the assumption that all possible ship types are those listed in Table 1, one would know that such a combination of parameters is impossible and, more in general, that the set of rules is indeed complete w.r.t. the domain knowledge.

3   Sources of Decision Knowledge

We now generalize the discussion in Sect. 2 by introducing the two main sources of decision knowledge: background knowledge expressed using a logical theory enriched with datatypes, and decision logic captured in DMN.

3.1   Logics with Datatypes

To capture background knowledge, we resort to a variant of multi-sorted first-order logic (see, e.g., [6]), which we call $FOL(\mathfrak{D})$, where one sort Δ denotes a domain of abstract objects, while the remaining sorts represent a finite collection $\mathfrak{D}$ of datatypes. We consider a countably infinite set Σ of predicates, where each $p \in \Sigma$ comes with an arity n, and a signature $\mathsf{Sig}_p : \{1,\ldots,n\} \to \mathfrak{D} \uplus \{\Delta\}$, mapping each position of p to one of the sorts. $FOL(\mathfrak{D})$ contains unary and binary predicates only. A unary predicate N with $\mathsf{Sig}_N(1) = \Delta$ is called a *concept*, a binary predicates P with $\mathsf{Sig}_P(1) = \mathsf{Sig}_P(2) = \Delta$ a *role*, and a binary predicate F with $\mathsf{Sig}_F(1) = \Delta$ and $\mathsf{Sig}_F(2) \in \mathfrak{D}$ a *feature*.

Example 1. The cargo ship ontology in Table 1 should be interpreted as follows: each entry applies to a ship, and expresses how the specific ship type constrains the other features of the ship, namely length, draft, and capacity. Thus the first table entry is encoded in $FOL(\mathfrak{D})$ as

$$\forall s.CCV(s) \to Ship(s) \wedge \forall l.(length(s,l) \to l = 135) \wedge$$
$$\forall d.(draft(s,d) \to d \geq 0 \wedge d \leq 9) \wedge \forall c.(capacity(s,c) \to c = 500),$$

where CCV and $Ship$ are concepts, while *length*, *draft*, and *capacity* are features whose second component is of sort *real*. ∎

We consider also well-behaved fragments of $FOL(\mathfrak{D})$ that are captured by description logics (DLs) extended with datatypes. For details on DLs, we refer to [3], and for a survey of DLs equipped with datatypes (also called, in fact, *concrete domain*), to [9]. Here we adopt the DL $\mathcal{ALC}(\mathfrak{D})$, a slight extension of the DL $\mathcal{ALC}(\mathcal{D})$ [9] with multiple datatypes. As for datatypes, we follow [1], which is based on the OWL 2 datatype map [10, Sect. 4], but we adopt some simplifications that suffice for our purposes.

A *(primitive) datatype* $\mathcal{D}$ is a pair $\langle \Delta_{\mathcal{D}}, \Gamma_{\mathcal{D}} \rangle$, where $\Delta_{\mathcal{D}}$ is the *domain* of values[4] of $\mathcal{D}$, and $\Gamma_{\mathcal{D}}$ is a (possibly infinite) set of *facets*, denoting unary predicate symbols. Each facet $S \in \Gamma_{\mathcal{D}}$ comes with a set $S^{\mathcal{D}} \subseteq \Delta_{\mathcal{D}}$ that rigidly defines the semantics of S as a subset of $\Delta_{\mathcal{D}}$. Given a primitive datatype $\mathcal{D}$, datatypes $\mathcal{E}$ *derived from* $\mathcal{D}$ are defined according to the following syntax

$$\mathcal{E} \longrightarrow \mathcal{D} \mid \mathcal{E}_1 \cup \mathcal{E}_2 \mid \mathcal{E}_1 \cap \mathcal{E}_2 \mid \mathcal{E}_1 \setminus \mathcal{E}_2 \mid \{d_1,\ldots,d_m\} \mid \mathcal{D}[S]$$

where S is a facet for $\mathcal{D}$, and $d_1,\ldots,d_m$ are datatype values in $\Delta_{\mathcal{D}}$. The domain of a derived datatype is obtained for $\cup$, $\cap$, and $\setminus$, by applying the corresponding set operator to the domains of the component datatypes, for $\{d_1,\ldots,d_m\}$ as the set $\{d_1,\ldots,d_m\}$, and for $\mathcal{D}[S]$ as $S^{\mathcal{D}}$. In the remainder of the paper, we consider the (primitive) datatypes present in the S-FEEL language of the DMN standard: strings equipped with equality, and numerical datatypes, i.e., naturals, integers,

---

[4] We blur the distinction between *value space* and *lexical space* of OWL 2 datatypes, and consider the datatype domain elements as elements of the lexical space interpreted as themselves.

rationals, and reals equipped with their usual comparison operators (which, for simplicity, we all illustrate using the same set of standard symbols $=$, $<$, $\leq$, $>$, $\geq$). We denote this core set of datatypes as $\mathfrak{D}$. Other S-FEEL datatypes, such as that of datetime, are syntactic sugar on top of $\mathfrak{D}$.

A facet for one of these datatypes $\mathcal{D}$ is specified using a binary comparison predicate $\approx$, together with a *constraining value* v, and is denoted as $\approx_v$. E.g., using the facet $\leq_9$ of the primitive datatype *real*, we can define the derived datatype *real*$[\leq_9]$, whose value domain are the real numbers that are ≤ 9. In the following, we abbreviate $\mathcal{D}[S_1] \cap \mathcal{D}[S_2]$ as $\mathcal{D}[S_1 \wedge S_2]$, $\mathcal{D}[S_1] \cup \mathcal{D}[S_2]$ as $\mathcal{D}[S_1 \vee S_2]$, and $\mathcal{D}[S_1] \setminus \mathcal{D}[S_2]$ as $\mathcal{D}[S_1 \wedge \neg S_2]$, where S_1 and S_2 are either facets or their combinations with boolean/set operators.

Let Δ be a countably infinite universe of objects. A (DL) *knowledge base with datatypes* (KB hereafter) is a tuple $\langle \Sigma, T, A \rangle$, where Σ is the *KB signature*, T is the *TBox* (capturing the intensional knowledge of the domain of interest), and A is the *ABox* (capturing extensional knowledge). When the focus is on the intensional knowledge only, we omit the ABox, and call the pair $\langle \Sigma, T \rangle$ *intensional KB* (IKB). The form of T and A depends on the specific DL of interest. We review each component next.

Signature. $\Sigma = \Sigma_C \uplus \Sigma_R \uplus \Sigma_F$ consists of: *(i)* a finite set Σ_C of *concept names*, i.e., unary predicates interpreted over Δ, *(ii)* a finite set Σ_R of *role names*, binary predicates connecting pairs of objects in Δ; and *(iii)* a finite set Σ_F of *features*, i.e., binary predicates connecting objects to corresponding typed values. In particular, each feature F comes with its datatype $\mathcal{D}_F \in \mathfrak{D}$.

TBox. T is a finite set of universal FO axioms based on predicates in Σ, and on predicates and values of datatypes in $\mathfrak{D}$. To capture such axioms, we employ the usual DL syntax, using the boolean connectives $\sqcap$, $\sqcup$ and $\neg$ for intersection, union and complement, and $\exists R. C$ for qualified existential restriction. In the case of $\mathcal{ALC}(\mathfrak{D})$, such axioms are built from $\mathcal{ALC}(\mathfrak{D})$ *concepts*, inductively defined as follows:

- An atomic concept $N \in \Sigma_C$ is a concept;
- $\top$ and $\bot$ are concepts, respectively denoting the top and empty concepts;
- given a concept C, its complement $\neg C$ is a concept;
- given two concepts C and D, their conjunction $C \sqcap D$ is a concept;
- given a role $R \in \Sigma_R$ and a concept C, the qualified existential restriction $\exists R. C$ is a concept;
- given a feature $F \in \Sigma_F$, and a datatype r that is either $\mathcal{D}_F$ or a datatype derived from $\mathcal{D}_F$, the feature restriction $\exists F. r$ is a concept.

Intuitively, $\exists F. r$ allows the modeler to single out those objects having an F-feature that satisfies condition r, interpreted in accordance with the underlying datatype. We adopt the usual abbreviations $C \sqcup D$ for $\neg(\neg C \sqcap \neg D)$, and $\forall R. C$ for $\neg \exists R. \neg C$.

An $\mathcal{ALC}(\mathfrak{D})$ TBox is a finite set of *inclusion assertions* of the form $C \sqsubseteq D$, where C and D are $\mathcal{ALC}(\mathfrak{D})$ concepts. Intuitively, such assertions model that whenever an individual is an instance of C, then it is also an instance of D.

Example 2. The $\mathcal{ALC}(\mathfrak{D})$ encoding of the first entry in Table 1 is:

$$CCV \sqsubseteq Ship \sqcap \forall length.\, real[=_{135}] \sqcap \forall draft.\, real[\geq_0 \wedge \leq_9] \sqcap \forall capacity.\, real[=_{500}]$$

All other table entries can be formalized in a similar way. The entire table is then captured by the union of all so-obtained inclusion assertions, plus an assertion expressing that the types mentioned in Table 1 exhaustively *cover* all possible ship types:

$$Ship \sqsubseteq CCV \sqcup CT \sqcup CC \sqcup SPC \sqcup LPC \sqcup PP \sqcup PPP \sqcup NP \qquad \blacksquare$$

ABox. The ABox A is a finite set of *assertions*, or *facts*, of the form $N(d)$, $P(d, d')$, or $F(d, \mathrm{v})$, with N a concept name, P a role name, F a feature, $d, d' \in \Delta$, and $\mathrm{v} \in \Delta_{\mathcal{D}_F}$.

Semantics. The semantics of an $\mathcal{ALC}(\mathfrak{D})$ KB $\mathcal{K} = \langle \Sigma, T, A \rangle$ relies, as usual, on first-order interpretations $\mathcal{I} = \langle \Delta, \cdot^{\mathcal{I}} \rangle$ over the fixed domain Δ, where $\cdot^{\mathcal{I}}$ is an interpretation function mapping each atomic concept N in T to a set $N^{\mathcal{I}} \subseteq \Delta$, $\top$ to Δ, $\bot$ to $\emptyset$, each role R to a relation $R^{\mathcal{I}} \subseteq \Delta \times \Delta$, and each feature F to a relation $F^{\mathcal{I}} \subseteq \Delta \times \Delta_{\mathcal{D}_F}$. Complex concepts are interpreted as follows:

- $(\neg C)^{\mathcal{I}} = \Delta \setminus C^{\mathcal{I}}$;
- $(C \sqcap D)^{\mathcal{I}} = C^{\mathcal{I}} \cap D^{\mathcal{I}}$;
- $(\exists R.\, C)^{\mathcal{I}} = \{x \in \Delta \mid \exists y \in \Delta \text{ s.t. } \langle x, y \rangle \in R^{\mathcal{I}} \text{ and } y \in C^{\mathcal{I}}\}$;
- $(\exists F.\, r)^{\mathcal{I}} = \{x \in \Delta \mid \exists \mathrm{v} \in \Delta_{\mathcal{D}_F} \text{ s.t. } \langle x, \mathrm{v} \rangle \in F^{\mathcal{I}} \text{ and } r(\mathrm{v}) \text{ holds}\}$.

When an interpretation $\mathcal{I}$ *satisfies* an assertion is defined as follows:

$$C \sqsubseteq D \quad \text{if} \quad C^{\mathcal{I}} \subseteq D^I; \qquad P(d_1, d_2) \quad \text{if} \quad \langle d_1, d_2 \rangle \in P^{\mathcal{I}};$$
$$N(d) \quad \text{if} \quad d \in N^{\mathcal{I}}; \qquad F(d, \mathrm{v}) \quad \text{if} \quad \langle d, \mathrm{v} \rangle \in F^{\mathcal{I}}.$$

Finally, we say that $\mathcal{I}$ is a *model* of T if it satisfies all inclusion assertions of T, and a *model* of $\mathcal{K}$ if it satisfies all assertions of T and A.

Reasoning in $\mathcal{ALC}(\mathfrak{D})$. Reasoning in $\mathcal{ALC}$ with a single concrete domain is decidable in EXPTIME (and hence EXPTIME-complete) under the assumption that *(i)* the logic allows for unary concrete domain predicates only, *(ii)* the concrete domain is *admissible* [7,8], and *(iii)* checking the satisfiability of conjunctions of predicates of the datatype is decidable in EXPTIME. This follows from a slightly more general result shown in [9, Sect. 2.4.1]. Admissibility requires that the set of predicate names is closed under negation and that it contains a predicate name denoting the entire domain. Hence, reasoning in $\mathcal{ALC}$ extended with one of the concrete domains used in DMN (e.g., integers or reals, with facets based on comparison predicates together with a constraining value), is EXPTIME-complete. The variant of DL with concrete domains that we consider here, $\mathcal{ALC}(\mathfrak{D})$, makes only use of unary concrete domain (i.e., datatype) predicates, but allows for multiple datatypes. Hence, the above decidability results do not directly apply. However, exploiting the absence of non-unary datatype predicates, and considering that each feature is *typed* with a specified datatype, it is easy to see that the various datatypes essentially do not interact with each other, and that therefore the complexity of reasoning is not affected.

Theorem 1. *Checking satisfiability of an $\mathcal{ALC}(\mathfrak{D})$ KB is decidable in* EXP-
TIME *(and so are the problems of deciding instance checking and subsumption
w.r.t. a KB).*

Rich KBs. We also consider rich KBs where axioms are specified in full FOL($\mathfrak{D}$)
(and the signature is that of a FOL($\mathfrak{D}$) theory). We call such KBs FOL($\mathfrak{D}$) *KBs.*

3.2 DMN Decision Tables

To capture the business logic of a complex decision, we rely on the DMN standard
and its S-FEEL language [11]. Specifically, we resort to [5] for a formal definition
of the notion of decision as specified in the standard. We do not consider priorities
here. An *S-FEEL DMN decision table* $\mathcal{M}$ (called simply *decision table* in the
following) is a tuple $\langle Name, I, O, \mathsf{AType}, \mathsf{AFacet}, R, C, H \rangle$, where:

- *Name* is the *table name*.
- I and O are disjoint, finite sets of *input* and *output attributes*.
- $\mathsf{AType} : I \uplus O \to \mathfrak{D}$ is a *typing function* that associates each input/output
  attribute to its corresponding data type.
- AFacet is a *facet function* that associates each input/output attribute $\mathbf{a} \in I \uplus O$
  to an S-FEEL condition over $\mathsf{AType}(\mathbf{a})$ (see below).
- R is a finite set $\{r_1, \ldots, r_p\}$ of *rules*. Each rule r_k is a pair $\langle \mathsf{If}_k, \mathsf{Then}_k \rangle$, where
  If_k is an *input entry function* that associates each input attribute $\mathbf{a}^{\mathbf{in}} \in I$ to
  an S-FEEL condition over $\mathsf{AType}(\mathbf{a}^{\mathbf{in}})$, and Then_k is an *output entry function*
  that associates each output attribute $\mathbf{a}^{\mathbf{out}} \in O$ to an object in $\mathsf{AType}(\mathbf{a}^{\mathbf{out}})$.
- $C \in \{\mathsf{c}, \mathsf{i}\}$ is the *completeness indicator* - c (resp., i) stands for *(in)complete*
  table.
- H is the *(single) hit indicator* defining the policy for the rule application. Since
  we do not focus on priorities, the interesting policies are: *(i)* u for *unique hit
  policy, (ii)* a for *any hit policy.*

In the following, we use a dot notation to single out an element of a decision
table. For example, $\mathcal{M}.I$ denotes the set of input attributes for decision $\mathcal{M}$.

An *(S-FEEL) condition* $\mathcal{Q}$ over type $\mathcal{D}$ is inductively defined as follows:

- "$-$" is an S-FEEL condition representing *any value* (i.e., it evaluates to true
  for every object in $\Delta_{\mathcal{D}}$);
- given a constant v, expressions "v" and "$\mathsf{not}(\mathsf{v})$" are S-FEEL conditions
  respectively denoting that the value shall (not) match with v.
- if $\mathcal{D}$ is a numerical datatype, given two numbers $\mathsf{v}_1, \mathsf{v}_2 \in \Delta_{\mathcal{D}}$, the interval
  expressions "$[\mathsf{v}_1, \mathsf{v}_2]$", "$[\mathsf{v}_1, \mathsf{v}_2)$", "$(\mathsf{v}_1, \mathsf{v}_2]$", and "$(\mathsf{v}_1, \mathsf{v}_2)$" are S-FEEL conditions (interpeted in the usual, mathematical way);
- given two S-FEEL conditions $\mathcal{Q}_1$ and $\mathcal{Q}_2$, "$\mathcal{Q}_1, \mathcal{Q}_2$" is an S-FEEL condition
  representing their disjunction (i.e., it evaluates to true for a value $\mathsf{v} \in \Delta_{\mathcal{D}}$ if
  either $\mathcal{Q}_1$ or $\mathcal{Q}_2$ evaluates to true for v).

Table 2. Decision table for determining vessel clearance in Dutch ports; symbol `today` is a shortcut for the milliseconds representing time 00:00:00 of the current date.

Vessel Clearance						
C U	*Cer. Exp.* (date)	*Length* (m)	*Draft* (m)	*Capacity* (TEU)	*Cargo* (mg/cm^2)	*Enter*
	≥ 0	≥ 0	≥ 0	≥ 0	≥ 0	Y,N
1	$\leq$ today	–	–	–	–	N
2	> today	<260	<10	<1000	–	Y
3	> today	<260	<10	$\geq$1000	–	N
4	> today	<260	[10,12]	<4000	$\leq$0.75	Y
5	> today	<260	[10,12]	<4000	>0.75	N
6	> today	[260,320)	(10,13]	<6000	$\leq$0.5	Y
7	> today	[260,320)	(10,13]	<6000	>0.5	N
8	> today	[320,400)	$\geq$13	>4000	$\leq$0.25	Y
9	> today	[320,400)	$\geq$13	>4000	>0.25	N

Example 3. We use our case study to illustrate how a complex decision can be captured in DMN. Table 2 depicts the decision table for ship clearance, formalizing Sect. 2.1. The first two rows (below the table title) indicate the table meta-information. In particular, the leftmost cell indicates that the table is meant to be complete, and that rules are declared to not overlap.[5] Blue-colored cells (i.e., all other cells but the rightmost one), together with the cells below, respectively model the input attributes used to determine ship clearance, and the facets over their corresponding datatypes. In particular, the input attributes are: *(i)* the certificate expiration date, *(ii)* the length, *(iii)* the size, *(iv)* the capacity, and *(v)* the amount of cargo residuals of a ship. Such attributes are nonnegative real numbers; this is captured by typing them as reals, adding restriction "≥ 0" as facet. The rightmost, red cell represents the output attribute, i.e., whether the ship under scrutiny may enter the port. This is modeled by typing the output attribute as string, allowing only values **Y** and **N**. Every other row models a rule. The intuitive interpretation of such rules relies on the usual "if . . . then . . . " pattern. For example, the first rule states that if the certificate of the ship is expired, then the ship cannot enter the port (regardless of the other input attributes). The second rule, instead, states that if the ship has a valid certificate, a length shorter than 260 m, a draft smaller than 10 m, a capacity smaller than 1000 TEU, then the ship is allowed to enter the port (regardless of the cargo residuals it carries). Other rules are interpreted similarly. ∎

4   Semantic Decision Models

We now combine the two knowledge sources discussed in Sect. 3.1, namely FOL($\mathfrak{D}$) knowledge bases and DMN decision tables, into an integrated *decision knowledge base* (DKB) that *empowers DMN with semantics*.

---

[5] Recall that such indicators are provided by the user, and may not reflect the actual table content.

4.1 Decision Knowledge Bases

The intuition behind our proposal for integration is to consider decision tables as a sort of enhancement of a KB describing a domain of interest. In this respect, a decision table $\mathcal{M}$ is linked to a specific concept. The idea is that given an object o of the specified type, $\mathcal{M}$ inspects all features of o that correspond to its input attributes $\mathcal{M}.I$, matching their values against the decision rules. Depending on which rule(s) match, $\mathcal{M}$ then dictates which are the values to which o must be connected via those features that correspond to the output attributes $\mathcal{M}.O$. Hence, the KB and the decision table "interact" on (some of) the input attributes of the decision, while the output attributes exclusively belong to the decision table, which is in fact used to infer new knowledge about the domain.

Formally, a *decision knowledge base* over datatypes $\mathfrak{D}$ ($\mathfrak{D}$-DKB, or DKB for short) is a tuple $\langle \Sigma, T, \mathcal{M}, C, A \rangle$, where:

- T is a $\mathsf{FOL}(\mathfrak{D})$ IKB with signature Σ.
- $\mathcal{M}$ is a decision table that satisfies the following two typing conditions:
  (output uniqueness) $\mathcal{M}.O \cap \Sigma = \emptyset$;
  (input type compatibility) for every binary predicate $P \in \Sigma$ whose name appears in $\mathcal{M}.I$, their types are compatible, i.e., $\mathcal{M}.\mathsf{AType}(P) = \mathsf{Sig}_P(2)$.
- $C \in \Sigma_C$ is a *bridge concept*, that is, a concept from Σ that links T with $\mathcal{M}$.
- A is an ABox over the extended signature $\Sigma \cup \mathcal{M}.I$.

When the focus is on the intensional decision knowledge only, we omit the ABox, and call the tuple $\langle \Sigma, T, \mathcal{M}, C \rangle$ intensional DKB (IDKB).

Example 4. The combination of Tables 1 and 2 using "ship" as bridge concept gives rise to a DKB for the ship clearance domain. On the one hand, Table 1 introduces different types of ships, which can be modeled as subtype concepts of the generic concept of "ship", together with a set of axioms constraining the length, draft, and capacity features depending on the specific subtype (cf. Example 1). On the other hand, Table 2 extends the signature of Table 1 with three additional features for ships, namely certificate expiration and cargo, as well as the indication of whether a ship can enter a port or not. This latter feature is the output of the decision, and is in fact inferred by applying the ship clearance decision table in the context of a specific port. ∎

4.2 Formalizing DKBs

From the formal point of view, the integration between a KB and a decision table is obtained by encoding the latter into $\mathsf{FOL}(\mathfrak{D})$, consequently enriching the KB with additional axioms that capture its intended semantics. The purpose of this section is to provide such an encoding. To this end, we use the predicate logic-based formalization of DMN introduced in [5] as a starting point. However, we cannot simply rely on it, since it does not interpret input and output attributes as features of a certain type of object, but directly encodes decisions as formulae relating tuples of input values to corresponding tuples of output values.

This "objectification" is essential in our setting: it is the basis for the integration between the two sources of knowledge.

Technically, we introduce a translation function τ that transforms a DKB $\mathcal{X} = \langle \Sigma, T, \mathcal{M}, C, A \rangle$ into a corresponding FOL($\mathfrak{D}$) KB $\tau(\mathcal{X}) = \langle \Sigma', T', A \rangle$ (or an IDKB $\overline{\mathcal{X}} = \langle \Sigma, T, \mathcal{M}, C \rangle$ into a corresponding FOL($\mathfrak{D}$) IKB $\tau(\overline{\mathcal{X}})$) as follows. Signature $\Sigma' = \Sigma \cup \Sigma_{\mathcal{M}}^i \cup \Sigma_{\mathcal{M}}^o$ is the signature obtained from the original DKB by incorporating a set $\Sigma_{\mathcal{M}}^i = \{P^i/2 \mid P^i \in \mathcal{M}.I\}$ of binary predicates that account for the input attributes of the table, and a set $\Sigma_{\mathcal{M}}^o = \{P^{o,k}/2 \mid P^o \in \mathcal{M}.O, k \in \{1, \ldots, |\mathcal{M}.R|\}\}$ of predicates that account for the output attributes. Specifically, each input attribute becomes a binary predicate with the same name, while each output attribute gives rise to a series of corresponding binary predicates, one per rule in the table. In this way, an output value retains information about its provenance, i.e., which rule was applied to produce it. All so-generated predicates have first component typed with Δ, and second component typed according to the type assigned by $\mathcal{M}$ to their corresponding attribute.

TBox $T' = T \cup \tau_C(\mathcal{M})$ extends the original axioms in T with a set of additional axioms that encode $\mathcal{M}$ into FOL($\mathfrak{D}$), relativizing the encoding to the bridge concept C.

The encoding $\tau_C(\mathcal{M})$ of decision table $\mathcal{M}$ consists of the union of formulae obtained by encoding: (i) input/output attributes of $\mathcal{M}$; (ii) the facet conditions attached to such attributes; (iii) rules in $\mathcal{M}$.

In the following, given a predicate $P \in \Sigma_{\mathcal{M}}^i \cup \Sigma_{\mathcal{M}}^o$, we denote by $attr(P)$ the attribute in $\mathcal{M}.I \cup \mathcal{M}.O$ from which P has been obtained. In addition, given $m \in \{1, \ldots, |\mathcal{M}.R|\}$, we denote by $\Sigma_{\mathcal{M}}^o|_m = \{P^{o,k} \mid P^{o,k} \in \Sigma_{\mathcal{M}}^o, k = m\}$ the subset of $\Sigma_{\mathcal{M}}^o$ containing only the predicates associated to index m.

Encoding of attributes. For each predicate $P \in \Sigma_{\mathcal{M}}^i \cup \Sigma_{\mathcal{M}}^o$, function τ_C produces two formulae: (i) a typing formula $\forall x, y. P(x, y) \to C(x)$, declaring that the domain of the attribute is the bridge concept; (ii) a functionality formula $\forall x, y, z. P(x, y) \wedge P(x, z) \to x = z$, declaring that every object of the bridge concept cannot be connected to more than one value through P. If $attr(P)$ is an input attribute, functionality guarantees that the application of the decision table is unambiguous. If $attr(P)$ is an output attribute, functionality simply captures that there is a single value present in an output cell of the decision table. In general, multiple outputs for the same column may in fact be obtained when applying a decision, but if so, they would be generated by different rules.

Encoding of facet conditions. For each attribute predicate $P \in \Sigma_{\mathcal{M}}^i \cup \Sigma_{\mathcal{M}}^o$, function τ_C produces the facet formula imposing that the range of the predicate must satisfy the restrictions imposed by the S-FEEL condition attached to attribute $attr(P)$:

$$\forall x, y. P(x, y) \to \tau^y(\mathcal{M}.\mathsf{AFacet}(attr(P))),$$

where, given an S-FEEL condition Q, function $\tau^x(Q)$ builds a unary FOL($\mathfrak{D}$) formula that encodes the application of Q to x. This is defined as follows:

$$\tau^x(Q) \triangleq \begin{cases} true & \text{if } Q = \text{``}-\text{''} \\ x \neq v & \text{if } Q = \text{``}\mathtt{not}(v)\text{''} \\ x = v & \text{if } Q = \text{``}v\text{''} \\ x \approx v & \text{if } Q = \text{``}\approx v\text{''} \text{ and } \approx \in \{<,>,\leq,\geq\} \\ x > v_1 \wedge x < v_2 & \text{if } Q = \text{``}(v_1..v_2)\text{''} \\ \ldots & \text{(similarly for the other types of intervals)} \\ \tau^x(Q_1) \vee \tau^x(Q_2) & \text{if } Q = \text{``}Q_1,Q_2\text{''} \end{cases}$$

Example 5. Consider the length attribute in Table 2. Assuming that *Ship* acts as bridge concept, its typing and facet $\mathsf{FOL}(\mathfrak{D})$ formulae are:

$$\forall x, y.length(x, y) \to Ship(x). \qquad \forall x, y.length(x, y) \to y \geq 0. \qquad \blacksquare$$

Encoding of rules. Each rule is translated into a formula expressing that whenever an object belonging to the bridge concept is related, via predicates accounting for the input attributes, to values that satisfy the S-FEEL conditions associated by the rule to such attributes, then the same object must be related, via predicates accounting for the output attributes, to the values associated by the rule to such attributes. Formally, fix an ordering over the rules $\mathcal{M}.R$. For every $m \in \{1, \ldots, |\mathcal{M}.R|\}$, given the m-rule $r_m = \langle \mathsf{If}, \mathsf{Then} \rangle \in R$, function τ_C produces:

$$\forall x, y. \bigwedge_{P_j^i \in \Sigma_\mathcal{M}^i} \left(P_j^i(x, y_j) \wedge \tau^{y_j}\left(attr(\mathsf{If}(P_j^i))\right) \right) \to \bigwedge_{P_k^{o,m} \in \Sigma_\mathcal{M}^o|m} \left(\exists z_k. P_k^{o,m} \wedge \tau^{z_k}\left(\mathsf{Then}(attr(P_k^{o,m}))\right) \right)$$

Example 6. Rule 2 in Table 2 is encoded in $\mathsf{FOL}(\mathfrak{D})$ as:

$$\begin{aligned} \forall x, e, l, d, c. \; exp(x, e) \wedge e > \mathbf{today} \wedge length(x, l) \wedge l < 260 \wedge \\ draft(x, d) \wedge d < 10 \wedge cap(x, c) \wedge c < 1000 \; \to \; \exists o.enter_2(x, o) \wedge o = \mathbf{Y}. \end{aligned}$$

where $enter_2$ is obtained from output attribute **enter** in the context of Rule 2. $\blacksquare$

We close this section by arguing that our encoding can be seen as a sort of "objectification" of the encoding in [5], where a tuple of values is now reified into an explicit object, together with corresponding predicates pointing to the different tuple components.

4.3 Reasoning Tasks

We formally revisit the main reasoning tasks introduced in [5] for DMN, in the presence of background knowledge. Such reasoning tasks aim at understanding whether the metadata attached to a DMN decision to indicate completeness and hit policies, indeed reflect the semantics of the DKB of interest. In the following, we fix a DKB $\mathcal{X} = \langle \Sigma, T, \mathcal{M}, C, A \rangle$, and denote by $\overline{\mathcal{X}} = \langle \Sigma, T, \mathcal{M}, C \rangle$ its corresponding IDKB.

I/O relationship. The first and most fundamental reasoning task is to check whether the DKB induces a certain input/output relationship over a given object. The *I/O relationship problem* for DKBs is defined as follows:

Input: (i) DKB $\mathcal{X}$, (ii) object $c \in \Delta$ of type C, (iii) output attribute $P^o \in \mathcal{M}.O$, (iv) value $v \in \mathcal{M}.\mathsf{AType}(P^o)$.

Question: Is it the case that $\mathcal{X}$ assigns output v for attribute P^o to object c? Formally, this amounts to check whether fact $P^{o,k}(c,v)$ is implied for some rule k, i.e., whether: $\tau(\mathcal{X}) \models \bigvee_{P^{o,k} \in \Sigma^o_{\mathcal{M}}} P^{o,k}(c,v)$.

Table completeness. Completeness is declared by setting $\mathcal{M}.C = c$, and indicates that the rules in $\mathcal{M}$ cover all possible configurations for the input values. The *table completeness problem* is then defined as follows:

Input: IDKB $\overline{\mathcal{X}}$.

Question: Is it the case that at least one rule of $\mathcal{M}$ is guaranteed to trigger? Formally:

$$\tau(\overline{\mathcal{X}}) \models \forall x, y. \bigvee_{\langle \mathsf{If}, \mathsf{Then} \rangle \in \mathcal{M}.R} \bigwedge_{P^i_j \in \Sigma^i_{\mathcal{M}}} \left(P^i_j(x, y_j) \rightarrow \tau^{y_j}(\mathsf{If}(attr(P^i_j))) \right)?$$

Correctness of unique hit. Unique hit is declared by setting $\mathcal{M}.H = u$, and indicates that at most one rule of $\mathcal{M}$ may trigger on a given input object. The *correctness of unique hit problem* is hence defined as follows:

Input: IDKB $\overline{\mathcal{X}}$.

Question: Is it the case that rules in $\mathcal{M}$ do not overlap? Formally: is it the case that, for every pair $\langle \mathsf{If}_1, \mathsf{Then}_1 \rangle$ and $\langle \mathsf{If}_2, \mathsf{Then}_2 \rangle$ of rules in $\mathcal{M}.R$,

$$\tau(\overline{\mathcal{X}}) \models \forall x, y. \bigvee_{P^i_j \in \mathcal{M}.I} \left(P^i_j(x, y_j) \rightarrow \neg \left(\bigwedge_{k \in \{1,2\}} \tau^{y_j}(\mathsf{If}_k(attr(P^i_j))) \right) \right)?$$

Correctness of any hit. Any hit is declared by setting $\mathcal{M}.H = a$, and states that whenever multiple rules may simultaneously trigger, they need to agree on the produced output. In this light, checking whether this policy is correct can be directly reduced to the case of unique hit, but considering only those pairs of rules that differ in output.

DMN reasoning tasks. We conclude by pointing out that, in the case where background knowledge is absent, i.e., $T = \emptyset$, the different reasoning tasks reduce to the case of pure DMN (as defined in [5]). The reduction is direct for table completeness, and also for checking correctness of unique/any hit. Checking I/O relationship is obtained instead by fixing A to contain exactly the following facts: (i) a fact $C(c)$ where c is an arbitrary object from Δ; (ii) a set of facts of the form $\{P^i_j(c, v_j) \mid P^i_j \in \mathcal{M}.I\}$, denoting the assignment of input attributes for c to the corresponding values of interest.

5   Reasoning on Decision Knowledge Bases

While the translation from DKBs to FOL($\mathfrak{D}$) presented in Sect. 4.2 provides the logic-based semantics of DKBs, it does not give any insight on how to actually approach the different reasoning tasks of Sect. 4.3. Obviously, decidability and complexity of such reasoning tasks depend on the background knowledge and on the decision component. Since the decision component comes with the fixed S-FEEL language, we approach this problem as follows. First, we show that DMN decision tables based on S-FEEL can be encoded in $\mathcal{ALC}(\mathfrak{D})$. Then, we show that all reasoning tasks defined in Sect. 4.3 can be reduced to (un)satisfiability of an $\mathcal{ALC}(\mathfrak{D})$ concept w.r.t. a KB consisting of the union of the background knowledge with the $\mathcal{ALC}(\mathfrak{D})$ formalization of the decision table. We consequently obtain that such satisfiability checks can be carried out in ExpTime, whenever the background knowledge is expressed in $\mathcal{ALC}(\mathfrak{D})$.

5.1   Encoding Decision Tables in $\mathcal{ALC}(\mathfrak{D})$

We revisit the translation from DKBs to FOL($\mathfrak{D}$) introduced in Sect. 4.2, showing that the translation of decision tables can be reformulated so as to obtain an $\mathcal{ALC}(\mathfrak{D})$ IKB. Given a bridge concept C and a decision table $\mathcal{M}$, we introduce a translation function ρ_C that encodes $\mathcal{M}$ into the corresponding $\mathcal{ALC}(\mathfrak{D})$ IKB $\rho_C(\mathcal{M}) = \langle \Sigma_\mathcal{M}, T_\mathcal{M} \rangle$, using C to provide a context for the encoding. Specifically, the signature of the target IKB is simply obtained from the bridge concept and the input/output attributes of $\mathcal{M}$, adopting exactly the same strategy followed for the encoding into FOL($\mathfrak{D}$): input attributes become binary predicates, and output attributes become binary predicates relativized w.r.t. the different rules present in $\mathcal{M}$. In formulae, $\Sigma_\mathcal{M} = C \cup \Sigma_\mathcal{M}^i \cup \Sigma_\mathcal{M}^o$. The encoding of $T_\mathcal{M}$ reconstructs that of Sect. 4.2, and in fact deals with: *(i)* input/output attributes of $\mathcal{M}$; *(ii)* the facet conditions attached to such attributes; *(iii)* rules in $\mathcal{M}$.

Encoding of attributes. For each attribute $P \in \Sigma_\mathcal{M}^i \cup \Sigma_\mathcal{M}^o$, function ρ_C produces the typing axiom $\exists P \sqsubseteq C$. Note that functionality is not explicitly asserted, since $\mathcal{ALC}(\mathfrak{D})$ features are functional by default.

Encoding of facet conditions. For each attribute $P \in \Sigma_\mathcal{M}^i \cup \Sigma_\mathcal{M}^o$, function ρ_C produces a derived datatype declaration of the form: $C \sqsubseteq \rho^P(\mathcal{M}.\mathsf{AFacet}(attr(P)))$, where, given an S-FEEL condition Q, and assuming that $\mathcal{M}.\mathsf{AType} = type$, $\rho^P(Q)$ builds an $\mathcal{ALC}(\mathfrak{D})$ concept application of Q to x. This is defined as follows:

$$\rho^P(Q) \triangleq \begin{cases} \top & \text{if } Q = \text{``--''} \\ \neg \exists P.type[=_\mathsf{v}] & \text{if } Q = \text{``not(v)''} \\ \forall P.type[=_\mathsf{v}] & \text{if } Q = \text{``v''} \\ \forall P.type[COP_\mathsf{v}] & \text{if } Q = \text{``}COP\ \mathsf{v}\text{''} \text{ and } COP \in \{<,>,\leq,\geq\} \\ \forall P.type[>_{\mathsf{v}_1} \wedge <_{\mathsf{v}_2}] & \text{if } Q = \text{``}(\mathsf{v}_1..\mathsf{v}_2)\text{''} \\ \dots & \text{(similarly for the other types of intervals)} \\ \rho^P(Q_1) \sqcup \rho^P(Q_2) & \text{if } Q = \text{``}Q_1,Q_2\text{''} \end{cases}$$

Example 7. Consider the length attribute in Table 2. Assuming that *Ship* acts as bridge concept, its typing and facet FOL($\mathfrak{D}$) formulae are $\exists length \sqsubseteq Ship$ and $Ship \sqsubseteq \forall length.real[>_0]$. ∎

Encoding of rules. Fix an ordering over the rules $\mathcal{M}.R$. For every $m \in \{1, \ldots, |\mathcal{M}.R|\}$, given the m-rule $r_m = \langle \mathsf{If}, \mathsf{Then} \rangle \in R$, function ρ_C produces an inclusion assertion of the form:

$$\prod_{P_j^i \in \Sigma_{\mathcal{M}}^i} \left(\rho^{P_j^i}\left(attr(\mathsf{If}(P_j^i))\right) \right) \sqsubseteq \prod_{P_k^{o,m} \in \Sigma_{\mathcal{M}}^o |_m} \left(\exists P_k^{o,m} \sqcap \rho^{P_k^{o,m}}\left(\mathsf{Then}(attr(P_k^{o,m}))\right) \right)$$

Example 8. Rule 2 in Table 2 is encoded in $\mathcal{ALC}(\mathfrak{D})$ as:

$$\forall exp.real[>_{\mathsf{today}}] \sqcap \forall length.real[<_{260}] \sqcap \forall draft.real[<_{10}] \sqcap \forall cap.real[<_{1000}]$$
$$\sqsubseteq \exists enter_2 \sqcap \forall enter_2.string[=_{\mathsf{Y}}] \quad ∎$$

Thanks to the fact that $\mathcal{ALC}(\mathfrak{D})$ can be seen as a fragment of FOL($\mathfrak{D}$), we can directly establish that the $\mathcal{ALC}(\mathfrak{D})$ encoding of decision tables is indeed correct.

Theorem 2. *For every decision table $\mathcal{M}$, and (bridge) concept C, we have that the* FOL($\mathfrak{D}$) *IKB $\tau_C(\mathcal{M})$ is logically equivalent to the $\mathcal{ALC}(\mathfrak{D})$ IKB $\rho_C(\mathcal{M})$.*

Proof. Direct by construction of the translation functions τ_C and ρ_C, noting that, once the standard FOL($\mathfrak{D}$) encoding of $\mathcal{ALC}(\mathfrak{D})$ is applied to the $\mathcal{ALC}(\mathfrak{D})$ IKB $\rho_C(\mathcal{M})$, it becomes syntactically identical to the FOL($\mathfrak{D}$) IKB $\tau_C(\mathcal{M})$. ◻

5.2   Reasoning over $\mathcal{ALC}(\mathfrak{D})$ Decision Knowledge Bases

In this section, we leverage the possibility of encoding decision tables into $\mathcal{ALC}(\mathfrak{D})$ so as to obtain a characterization of the decidability and complexity of reasoning in the case of $\mathcal{ALC}(\mathfrak{D})$ *DKBs*, i.e., DKBs whose background knowledge is specified in $\mathcal{ALC}(\mathfrak{D})$. Formally, a DKB $\mathcal{X} = \langle \Sigma, T, \mathcal{M}, C, A \rangle$ is an $\mathcal{ALC}(\mathfrak{D})$ *DKB* if $\langle \Sigma, T, A \rangle$ is an $\mathcal{ALC}(\mathfrak{D})$ KB. We extend the translation function of Sect. 5 to handle the entire $\mathcal{ALC}(\mathfrak{D})$ KB as follows: $\rho(\mathcal{X}) = \langle \Sigma \cup \Sigma_{\mathcal{M}}, T \cup T_{\mathcal{M}}, A \rangle$, where $\langle \Sigma_{\mathcal{M}}, T_{\mathcal{M}} \rangle = \rho_C(\mathcal{M})$ (similarly for an $\mathcal{ALC}(\mathfrak{D})$ IKB). With these notions at hand, we show the following.

Theorem 3. *The I/O relationship, table completeness, and correctness of unique hit problems can all be decided in* EXPTIME *for $\mathcal{ALC}(\mathfrak{D})$ DKBs.*

Proof. The proof is based on a reduction from the three decision problems to a polynomial number of instance or subsumption checks w.r.t. an $\mathcal{ALC}(\mathfrak{D})$ KB, which can be decided in EXPTIME (cf. Theorem 1). Let $\mathcal{X} = \langle \Sigma, T, \mathcal{M}, C, A \rangle$ be an $\mathcal{ALC}(\mathfrak{D})$ DKB, and let $\overline{\mathcal{X}} = \langle \Sigma, T, \mathcal{M}, C \rangle$ be its corresponding IDKB.

  (*I/O relationship*) Fix an ordering over the rules $\mathcal{M}.R$. Given (*i*) $\mathcal{X}$, (*ii*) object $\mathsf{c} \in \Delta$ of type C, (*iii*) output attribute $P^o \in \mathcal{M}.O$, and (*iv*) value

$\mathbf{v} \in \mathcal{M}.\mathsf{AType}(P^o)$, we have that $\mathcal{X}$ assigns output $\mathbf{v}$ for attribute P^o to object $\mathbf{c}$ iff there exists $k \in \{1, \ldots, |\mathcal{M}.R|\}$ such that instance checking for fact $P^{o,k}(\mathbf{c}, \mathbf{v})$ w.r.t. KB $\rho(\mathcal{X})$ succeeds.

(*Table completeness*) Decision rules in $\overline{\mathcal{X}}$ are complete iff the following $\mathcal{ALC}(\mathfrak{D})$ subsumption holds with respect to KB $\rho(\overline{\mathcal{X}})$:

$$\top \sqsubseteq \bigsqcup_{\langle \mathsf{If}, \mathsf{Then} \rangle \in \mathcal{M}.R} \bigcap_{P_j^i \in \Sigma_{\mathcal{M}}^i} \left(\rho^{P_j^i}(\mathsf{If}(attr(P_j^i))) \right)$$

(*Unique hit*) Decision rules in $\overline{\mathcal{X}}$ do not overlap iff for every pair $\langle \mathsf{If}_1, \mathsf{Then}_1 \rangle$ and $\langle \mathsf{If}_2, \mathsf{Then}_2 \rangle$ of rules in $\mathcal{M}.R$, the following subsumption holds w.r.t KB $\rho(\overline{\mathcal{X}})$:

$$\top \sqsubseteq \bigsqcup_{P_j^i \in \mathcal{M}.I} \neg \bigcap_{k \in \{1,2\}} \rho^{P_j^i}(\mathsf{If}_k(attr(P_j^i)))$$

$\square$

Example 9. As discussed in Example 2, the ship ontology in Table 1 can be formalized in $\mathcal{ALC}(\mathfrak{D})$. Hence, the maritime security DKB of Example 4 is actually an $\mathcal{ALC}(\mathfrak{D})$ DKB. Thanks to Theorem 3, standard $\mathcal{ALC}(\mathfrak{D})$ reasoning tasks can then be used to check that such a DKB guarantees table completeness and the correctness of the unique hit indicators, as specified in Table 2. Recall that completeness holds because the table is interpreted w.r.t. the ship ontology. ∎

6 Conclusions

In this work, we have provided a threefold contribution to the area of decision management, recently revived by the introduction of the DMN OMG standard. First, we have introduced decision knowledge bases (DKBs) as a framework to integrate DMN decision tables with background knowledge, captured by means of a DL KB. Second, we have formalized the framework, as well as different fundamental reasoning tasks, in $\mathsf{FOL}(\mathfrak{D})$. Third, we have shown that, in the case where background knowledge is expressed in $\mathcal{ALC}(\mathfrak{D})$, all such reasoning tasks are decidable in ExpTime. Before delving into the implementation of such reasoning tasks, we are interested in refining the analysis of their complexity, by varying the DL used to capture the background knowledge. On the one hand, we argue that DMN decision tables can actually be integrated with more expressive DLs, such as OWL 2, by retaining the complexity of reasoning that comes with the DL. On the other hand, we note that the DL encoding of DMN decision tables falls within the lightweight fragment of $\mathcal{ALC}(\mathfrak{D})$ constituted by the $DL\text{-}Lite_{bool}^{(\mathcal{HN})}(\mathfrak{D})$ logic extended with qualified existentials on the left-hand side of inclusions. This logic has been very recently introduced in [1, Sect. 4.3], and although upper bounds for the standard DL reasoning services are not yet established for such logic, we conjecture that it is strictly less complex than $\mathcal{ALC}(\mathfrak{D})$. This paves the way towards the study of lightweight DKBs.

Acknowledgements. This work is supported by the Euregio IPN12 project *Knowledge-Aware Operational Support* (KAOS), funded by the "European Region Tyrol-South Tyrol-Trentino" (EGTC) under the first call for basic research projects, and by the unibz project *Knowledge-driven ENterprise Distributed cOmputing* (KENDO).

References

1. Artale, A., Calvanese, D., Kontchakov, R., Ryzhikov, V., Savković, O.: Datatypes in DL-Lite. Technical report KRDB17-1, KRDB Research Centre for Knowledge and Data, Free Univ. of Bozen-Bolzano. https://www.inf.unibz.it/krdb/pub/TR/KRDB17-1.pdf
2. Artale, A., Kontchakov, R., Ryzhikov, V.: DL-Lite with attributes and datatypes. In: Proceedings of ECAI, pp. 61–66 (2012)
3. Baader, F., Calvanese, D., McGuinness, D., Nardi, D., Patel-Schneider, P.F. (eds.): The Description Logic Handbook: Theory, Implementation and Applications. Cambridge University Press, 2nd edn. (2007)
4. Batoulis, K., Meyer, A., Bazhenova, E., Decker, G., Weske, M.: Extracting decision logic from process models. In: Zdravkovic, J., Kirikova, M., Johannesson, P. (eds.) CAiSE 2015. LNCS, vol. 9097, pp. 349–366. Springer, Cham (2015). doi:10.1007/978-3-319-19069-3_22
5. Calvanese, D., Dumas, M., Laurson, Ü., Maggi, F.M., Montali, M., Teinemaa, I.: Semantics and analysis of DMN decision tables. In: La Rosa, M., Loos, P., Pastor, O. (eds.) BPM 2016. LNCS, vol. 9850, pp. 217–233. Springer, Cham (2016). doi:10.1007/978-3-319-45348-4_13
6. Enderton, H.B.: A Mathematical Introduction to Logic, 2nd edn. Academic Press (2001)
7. Haarslev, V., Möller, R., Wessel, M.: The description logic $\mathcal{ALCNH}_{R+}$ extended with concrete domains: a practically motivated approach. In: Proceedings of IJCAR, pp. 29–44 (2001)
8. Horrocks, I., Sattler, U.: Ontology reasoning in the $\mathcal{SHOQ}$(D) description logic. In: Proceedings of IJCAI, pp. 199–204 (2001)
9. Lutz, C.: Description logics with concrete domains-A survey. Advances in Modal Logic, pp. 265–206 (2002)
10. Motik, B., Parsia, B., Patel-Schneider, P.F.: OWL 2 Web Ontology Language structural specification and functional-style syntax, 2nd edn. W3C Recommendation, W3C, December 2012. http://www.w3.org/TR/owl2-syntax/
11. Object Management Group: Decision Model and Notation (DMN) 1.0 (2015). http://www.omg.org/spec/DMN/1.0/
12. Pawlak, Z.: Decision tables - a rough set approach. Bull. EATCS **33**, 85–95 (1987)
13. Pooch, U.W.: Translation of decision tables. ACM Comput. Surv. **6**(2), 125–151 (1974)
14. Savkovic, O., Calvanese, D.: Introducing datatypes in DL-Lite. In: Proceedings of ECAI, pp. 720–725 (2012)
15. Vanthienen, J., Dries, E.: Illustration of a decision table tool for specifying and implementing knowledge based systems. Int. J. Artif. Intell. Tools **3**(2), 267–288 (1994)
16. Vanthienen, J., Mues, C., Aerts, A.: An illustration of verification and validation in the modelling phase of KBS development. DKE **27**(3), 337–352 (1998)
17. Zaidi, A.K., Levis, A.H.: Validation and verification of decision making rules. Automatica **33**(2), 155–169 (1997)

A Set-Theoretic Approach
to ABox Reasoning Services

Domenico Cantone, Marianna Nicolosi-Asmundo,
and Daniele Francesco Santamaria[(✉)]

Department of Mathematics and Computer Science,
University of Catania, Catania, Italy
{cantone,nicolosi,santamaria}@dmi.unict.it

Abstract. In this paper we consider the most common ABox reasoning services for the description logic $\mathcal{DL}\langle\mathsf{4LQS}^{\mathsf{R},\times}\rangle(\mathbf{D})$ ($\mathcal{DL}_{\mathbf{D}}^{4,\times}$, for short) and prove their decidability via a reduction to the satisfiability problem for the set-theoretic fragment $\mathsf{4LQS}^{\mathsf{R}}$. The description logic $\mathcal{DL}_{\mathbf{D}}^{4,\times}$ is very expressive, as it admits various concept and role constructs and data types that allow one to represent rule-based languages such as SWRL.

Decidability results are achieved by defining a generalization of the conjunctive query answering (CQA) problem that can be instantiated to the most widespread ABox reasoning tasks. We also present a KE-tableau based procedure for calculating the answer set from $\mathcal{DL}_{\mathbf{D}}^{4,\times}$-knowledge bases and higher order $\mathcal{DL}_{\mathbf{D}}^{4,\times}$-conjunctive queries, thus providing means for reasoning on several well-known ABox reasoning tasks. Our calculus extends a previously introduced KE-tableau based decision procedure for the CQA problem.

1 Introduction

Recently, results from Computable Set Theory have been applied to knowledge representation for the semantic web in order to define and reason about description logics and rule languages. Such a study is motivated by the fact that Computable Set Theory is a research field full of interesting decidability results and that there exists a natural translation map between some set-theoretic fragments and description logics and rule languages.

In particular, the decidable four-level stratified fragment of set theory $\mathsf{4LQS}^{\mathsf{R}}$, involving variables of four sorts, pair terms, and a restricted form of quantification over variables of the first three sorts (cf. [4]), has been used in [3] to represent the description logic $\mathcal{DL}\langle\mathsf{4LQS}^{\mathsf{R}}\rangle(\mathbf{D})$ ($\mathcal{DL}_{\mathbf{D}}^{4}$, for short). The logic $\mathcal{DL}_{\mathbf{D}}^{4}$ admits concept constructs such as full negation, union and intersection of concepts, concept domain and range, existential quantification and min cardinality on the left-hand side of inclusion axioms. It also supports role constructs such as role chains on the left hand side of inclusion axioms, union, intersection, and

---

This work has been partially supported by the Polish National Science Centre research project DEC-2011/02/A/HS1/00395.

S. Costantini et al. (Eds.): RuleML+RR 2017, LNCS 10364, pp. 87–102, 2017.
DOI: 10.1007/978-3-319-61252-2_7

complement of abstract roles, and properties on roles such as transitivity, symmetry, reflexivity, and irreflexivity. As briefly shown in [3], $\mathcal{DL}_{\mathbf{D}}^4$ is particularly suitable to express a rule language such as the Semantic Web Rule Language (SWRL), an extension of the Ontology Web Language (OWL). It admits data types, a simple form of concrete domains that are relevant in real world applications. In [3], the consistency problem for $\mathcal{DL}_{\mathbf{D}}^4$-knowledge bases has been proved decidable by means of a reduction to the satisfiability problem for 4LQS$^\mathsf{R}$, whose decidability has been established in [4]. It has also been shown that, under not very restrictive constraints, the consistency problem for $\mathcal{DL}_{\mathbf{D}}^4$-knowledge bases is **NP**-complete. Such a low complexity result is motivated by the fact that existential quantification cannot appear on the right-hand side of inclusion axioms. Nonetheless, $\mathcal{DL}_{\mathbf{D}}^4$ turns out to be more expressive than other low complexity logics such as OWL RL and therefore it is suitable for representing real world ontologies. For example, the restricted version of $\mathcal{DL}_{\mathbf{D}}^4$ mentioned above allows one to express several ontologies, such as Ontoceramic [9], for the classification of ancient pottery.

In [7], the description logic $\mathcal{DL}\langle 4\text{LQS}^{\mathsf{R},\times}\rangle(\mathbf{D})$ ($\mathcal{DL}_{\mathbf{D}}^{4,\times}$, for short), extending $\mathcal{DL}_{\mathbf{D}}^4$ with Boolean operations on concrete roles and with the product of concepts, has been introduced and the *Conjunctive Query Answering* (CQA) problem for $\mathcal{DL}_{\mathbf{D}}^{4,\times}$ has been proved decidable via a reduction to the CQA problem for 4LQS$^\mathsf{R}$, whose decidability follows from that of 4LQS$^\mathsf{R}$ (see [4]). CQA is a powerful way to query ABoxes, particularly relevant in the context of description logics and for real world applications based on semantic web technologies, as it provides mechanisms for interacting with ontologies and data. The CQA problem for description logics has been introduced in [1,2] (further references on the problem can be found in [8]). Finally, we mention also a terminating KE-tableau based procedure that, given a $\mathcal{DL}_{\mathbf{D}}^{4,\times}$-query Q and a $\mathcal{DL}_{\mathbf{D}}^{4,\times}$-knowledge base $\mathcal{KB}$ represented in set-theoretic terms, determines the answer set of Q with respect to $\mathcal{KB}$. KE-tableau systems [10] allow the construction of trees whose distinct branches define mutually exclusive situations, thus preventing the proliferation of redundant branches, typical of semantic tableaux.

In this paper we extend the results presented in [7] by considering also the main ABox reasoning tasks for $\mathcal{DL}_{\mathbf{D}}^{4,\times}$, such as *instance checking* and *concept retrieval*, and study their decidability via a reduction to the satisfiability problem for 4LQS$^\mathsf{R}$. Specifically, we define *Higher Order* (HO) $\mathcal{DL}_{\mathbf{D}}^{4,\times}$-conjunctive queries admitting variables of three sorts: individual and data type variables, concept variables, and role variables. HO $\mathcal{DL}_{\mathbf{D}}^{4,\times}$-conjunctive queries can be instantiated to any of the ABox reasoning tasks we are considering in the paper. Then, we define the *Higher Order Conjunctive Query Answering* (HOCQA) problem for $\mathcal{DL}_{\mathbf{D}}^{4,\times}$ and prove its decidability by reducing it to the HOCQA problem for 4LQS$^\mathsf{R}$. Decidability of the latter problem follows from that of the satisfiability problem for 4LQS$^\mathsf{R}$. 4LQS$^\mathsf{R}$ representation of $\mathcal{DL}_{\mathbf{D}}^{4,\times}$-knowledge bases is defined according to [7]. 4LQS$^\mathsf{R}$ turns out to be naturally suited for the HOCQA problem since HO $\mathcal{DL}_{\mathbf{D}}^{4,\times}$-conjunctive queries are easily translated into 4LQS$^\mathsf{R}$-formulae. In particular, individual and data type variables are mapped into 4LQS$^\mathsf{R}$ variables of sort 0, concept variables into 4LQS$^\mathsf{R}$ variables of sort 1, and role variables into 4LQS^R variables of sort 3. Finally, we present an extension of the KE-tableau presented in [7], which provides a decision procedure for the HOCQA task for $\mathcal{DL}_{\mathbf{D}}^{4,\times}$.

2 Preliminaries

2.1 The Set-Theoretic Fragment 4LQS^R

It is convenient to first introduce the syntax and semantics of the more general four-level quantified language 4LQS. Then we provide some restrictions on the quantified formulae of 4LQS to characterize 4LQS^R. The interested reader can find more details in [4] together with the decision procedure for the satisfiability problem for 4LQS^R.

4LQS involves four collections, $\mathcal{V}_i$, of variables of sort $i = 0, 1, 2, 3$, respectively. These will be denoted by $X^i, Y^i, Z^i, \ldots$ (in particular, variables of sort 0 will also be denoted by $x, y, z, \ldots$). In addition to variables, 4LQS involves also *pair terms* of the form $\langle x, y \rangle$, for $x, y \in \mathcal{V}_0$.

4LQS-*quantifier-free atomic formulae* are classified as:

- level 0: $x = y$, $x \in X^1$, $\langle x, y \rangle = X^2$, $\langle x, y \rangle \in X^3$;
- level 1: $X^1 = Y^1$, $X^1 \in X^2$;
- level 2: $X^2 = Y^2$, $X^2 \in X^3$.

4LQS-*purely universal formulae* are classified as:

- level 1: $(\forall z_1) \ldots (\forall z_n)\varphi_0$, where $z_1, \ldots, z_n \in \mathcal{V}_0$ and φ_0 is any propositional combination of quantifier-free atomic formulae of level 0;
- level 2: $(\forall Z_1^1) \ldots (\forall Z_m^1)\varphi_1$, where $Z_1^1, \ldots, Z_m^1 \in \mathcal{V}_1$ and φ_1 is any propositional combination of quantifier-free atomic formulae of levels 0 and 1, and of purely universal formulae of level 1;
- level 3: $(\forall Z_1^2) \ldots (\forall Z_p^2)\varphi_2$, where $Z_1^2, \ldots, Z_p^2 \in \mathcal{V}_2$ and φ_2 is any propositional combination of quantifier-free atomic formulae and of purely universal formulae of levels 1 and 2.

4LQS-formulae are all the propositional combinations of quantifier-free atomic formulae of levels 0, 1, 2, and of purely universal formulae of levels 1, 2, 3.

The variables $z_1, \ldots, z_n$ are said to occur *quantified* in $(\forall z_1) \ldots (\forall z_n)\varphi_0$. Likewise, $Z_1^1, \ldots, Z_m^1$ and $Z_1^2, \ldots, Z_p^2$ occur quantified in $(\forall Z_1^1) \ldots (\forall Z_m^1)\varphi_1$ and in $(\forall Z_1^2) \ldots (\forall Z_p^2)\varphi_2$, respectively. A variable occurs *free* in a 4LQS-formula φ if it does not occur quantified in any subformula of φ. For $i = 0, 1, 2, 3$, we denote with $\text{Var}_i(\varphi)$ the collections of variables of level i occurring free in φ and we put $\text{Vars}(\varphi) := \bigcup_{i=0}^{3} \text{Var}_i(\varphi)$.

A substitution $\sigma := \{\boldsymbol{x}/\boldsymbol{y}, \ \boldsymbol{X}^1/\boldsymbol{Y}^1, \ \boldsymbol{X}^2/\boldsymbol{Y}^2, \ \boldsymbol{X}^3/\boldsymbol{Y}^3\}$ is the mapping $\varphi \mapsto \varphi\sigma$ such that, for any given 4LQS-formula φ, $\varphi\sigma$ is the 4LQS-formula obtained from φ by replacing the free occurrences of the variables x_i in $\boldsymbol{x}$ (for $i = 1, \ldots, n$) with the corresponding y_i in $\boldsymbol{y}$, of X_j^1 in $\boldsymbol{X}^1$ (for $j = 1, \ldots, m$) with Y_j^1 in $\boldsymbol{Y}^1$, of

X_k^2 in $\boldsymbol{X}^2$ (for $k = 1, \ldots, p$) with Y_k^2 in $\boldsymbol{Y}^2$, and of X_h^3 in $\boldsymbol{X}^3$ (for $h = 1, \ldots, q$) with Y_h^3 in $\boldsymbol{Y}^3$, respectively. A substitution σ is *free* for φ if the formulae φ and $\varphi\sigma$ have exactly the same occurrences of quantified variables. The *empty substitution*, denoted with ϵ, satisfies $\varphi\epsilon = \varphi$, for every 4LQS-formula φ.

A 4LQS-*interpretation* is a pair $\boldsymbol{\mathcal{M}} = (D, M)$, where D is a non-empty collection of objects (called *domain* or *universe* of $\boldsymbol{\mathcal{M}}$) and M is an assignment over the variables in $\mathcal{V}_i$, for $i = 0, 1, 2, 3$, such that:

$$MX^0 \in D, \quad MX^1 \in \mathcal{P}(D), \quad MX^2 \in \mathcal{P}(\mathcal{P}(D)), \quad MX^3 \in \mathcal{P}(\mathcal{P}(\mathcal{P}(D))),$$

where $X^i \in \mathcal{V}_i$, for $i = 0, 1, 2, 3$, and $\mathcal{P}(s)$ denotes the powerset of s.

Pair terms are interpreted *à la* Kuratowski, and therefore we put

$$M\langle x, y \rangle := \{\{Mx\}, \{Mx, My\}\}.$$

Quantifier-free atomic formulae and purely universal formulae are evaluated in a standard way according to the usual meaning of the predicates '$\in$' and '$=$'. The interpretation of quantifier-free atomic formulae and of purely universal formulae is given in [4].

Finally, compound formulae are interpreted according to the standard rules of propositional logic. If $\boldsymbol{\mathcal{M}} \models \varphi$, then $\boldsymbol{\mathcal{M}}$ is said to be a 4LQS-*model* for φ. A 4LQS-formula is said to be *satisfiable* if it has a 4LQS-model. A 4LQS-formula is *valid* if it is satisfied by all 4LQS-interpretations.

We are now ready to present the fragment 4LQS^R of 4LQS of our interest. This is the collection of the formulae ψ of 4LQS fulfilling the restrictions:

1. for every purely universal formula $(\forall Z_1^1) \ldots (\forall Z_m^1)\varphi_1$ of level 2 occurring in ψ and every purely universal formula $(\forall z_1) \ldots (\forall z_n)\varphi_0$ of level 1 occurring negatively in φ_1, φ_0 is a propositional combination of quantifier-free atomic formulae of level 0 and the condition

$$\neg\varphi_0 \rightarrow \bigwedge_{i=1}^{n} \bigwedge_{j=1}^{m} z_i \in Z_j^1$$

   is a valid 4LQS-formula (in this case we say that $(\forall z_1) \ldots (\forall z_n)\varphi_0$ is *linked to the variables* $Z_1^1, \ldots, Z_m^1$);

2. for every purely universal formula $(\forall Z_1^2) \ldots (\forall Z_p^2)\varphi_2$ of level 3 in ψ:
   - every purely universal formula of level 1 occurring negatively in φ_2 and not occurring in a purely universal formula of level 2 is only allowed to be of the form

$$(\forall z_1) \ldots (\forall z_n)\neg(\bigwedge_{i=1}^{n} \bigwedge_{j=1}^{n} \langle z_i, z_j \rangle = Y_{ij}^2),$$

with $Y_{ij}^2 \in \mathcal{V}^2$, for $i, j = 1, \ldots, n$;
- purely universal formulae $(\forall Z_1^1) \ldots (\forall Z_m^1) \varphi_1$ of level 2 may occur only positively in φ_2.[1]

Restriction 1 has been introduced for technical reasons related to the decidability of the satisfiability problem for the fragment, while restriction 2 allows one to define binary relations and several operations on them (see [4] for details). The semantics of 4LQS^R plainly coincides with that of 4LQS.

2.2   The Logic $\mathcal{DL}\langle$4LQS$^{R,\times}\rangle$(D)

The description logic $\mathcal{DL}\langle$4LQS$^{R,\times}\rangle$(D) (which, as already remarked, will be more simply referred to as $\mathcal{DL}_{\mathbf{D}}^{4,\times}$) is an extension of the logic $\mathcal{DL}\langle$4LQS$^R\rangle$(D) presented in [3], where Boolean operations on concrete roles and the product of concepts are introduced. In addition to other features, $\mathcal{DL}_{\mathbf{D}}^{4,\times}$ admits also *data types*, a simple form of concrete domains that are relevant in real-world applications. In particular, it treats derived data types by admitting data type terms constructed from data ranges by means of a finite number of applications of the Boolean operators. Basic and derived data types can be used inside inclusion axioms involving concrete roles.

Data types are introduced through the notion of *data type map*, defined according to [12] as follows. Let $\mathbf{D} = (N_D, N_C, N_F, \cdot^{\mathbf{D}})$ be a data type map, where N_D is a finite set of data types, N_C is a function assigning a set of constants $N_C(d)$ to each data type $d \in N_D$, N_F is a function assigning a set of facets $N_F(d)$ to each $d \in N_D$, and $\cdot^{\mathbf{D}}$ is a function assigning a data type interpretation $d^{\mathbf{D}}$ to each data type $d \in N_D$, a facet interpretation $f^{\mathbf{D}} \subseteq d^{\mathbf{D}}$ to each facet $f \in N_F(d)$, and a data value $e_d^{\mathbf{D}} \in d^{\mathbf{D}}$ to every constant $e_d \in N_C(d)$. We shall assume that the interpretations of the data types in N_D are non-empty pairwise disjoint sets.

Let $\mathbf{R_A}$, $\mathbf{R_D}$, $\mathbf{C}$, $\mathbf{I}$ be denumerable pairwise disjoint sets of abstract role names, concrete role names, concept names, and individual names, respectively. We assume that the set of abstract role names $\mathbf{R_A}$ contains a name U denoting the universal role.

(a) $\mathcal{DL}_{\mathbf{D}}^{4,\times}$-data types, (b) $\mathcal{DL}_{\mathbf{D}}^{4,\times}$-concepts, (c) $\mathcal{DL}_{\mathbf{D}}^{4,\times}$-abstract roles, and (d) $\mathcal{DL}_{\mathbf{D}}^{4,\times}$-concrete role terms are constructed according to the following syntax rules:

(a) $t_1, t_2 \longrightarrow dr \mid \neg t_1 \mid t_1 \sqcap t_2 \mid t_1 \sqcup t_2 \mid \{e_d\}$,
(b) $C_1, C_2 \longrightarrow A \mid \top \mid \bot \mid \neg C_1 \mid C_1 \sqcup C_2 \mid C_1 \sqcap C_2 \mid \{a\} \mid \exists R.Self \mid \exists R.\{a\} \mid \exists P.\{e_d\}$,
(c) $R_1, R_2 \longrightarrow S \mid U \mid R_1^- \mid \neg R_1 \mid R_1 \sqcup R_2 \mid R_1 \sqcap R_2 \mid R_{C_1|} \mid R_{|C_1} \mid R_{C_1 \mid C_2} \mid id(C) \mid$
$\quad C_1 \times C_2$,
(d) $P_1, P_2 \longrightarrow T \mid \neg P_1 \mid P_1 \sqcup P_2 \mid P_1 \sqcap P_2 \mid P_{C_1|} \mid P_{|t_1} \mid P_{C_1|t_1}$,

---

[1] Definitions of positive and of negative occurrences of a formula within another formula can be found in [4].

where dr is a data range for $\mathbf{D}$, t_1, t_2 are data type terms, e_d is a constant in $N_C(d)$, a is an individual name, A is a concept name, C_1, C_2 are $\mathcal{DL}_\mathbf{D}^{4,\times}$-concept terms, S is an abstract role name, R, R_1, R_2 are $\mathcal{DL}_\mathbf{D}^{4,\times}$-abstract role terms, T is a concrete role name, and P, P_1, P_2 are $\mathcal{DL}_\mathbf{D}^{4,\times}$-concrete role terms. We remark that data type terms are introduced in order to represent derived data types.

A $\mathcal{DL}_\mathbf{D}^{4,\times}$-knowledge base is a triple $\mathcal{K} = (\mathcal{R}, \mathcal{T}, \mathcal{A})$ such that $\mathcal{R}$ is a $\mathcal{DL}_\mathbf{D}^{4,\times}$-RBox, $\mathcal{T}$ is a $\mathcal{DL}_\mathbf{D}^{4,\times}$-TBox, and $\mathcal{A}$ a $\mathcal{DL}_\mathbf{D}^{4,\times}$-ABox. These are defined as follows.

A $\mathcal{DL}_\mathbf{D}^{4,\times}$-RBox is a collection of statements of the following forms: $R_1 \equiv R_2$, $R_1 \sqsubseteq R_2$, $R_1 \ldots R_n \sqsubseteq R_{n+1}$, $\mathsf{Sym}(R_1)$, $\mathsf{Asym}(R_1)$, $\mathsf{Ref}(R_1)$, $\mathsf{Irref}(R_1)$, $\mathsf{Dis}(R_1, R_2)$, $\mathsf{Tra}(R_1)$, $\mathsf{Fun}(R_1)$, $R_1 \equiv C_1 \times C_2$, $P_1 \equiv P_2$, $P_1 \sqsubseteq P_2$, $\mathsf{Dis}(P_1, P_2)$, $\mathsf{Fun}(P_1)$, where R_1, R_2 are $\mathcal{DL}_\mathbf{D}^{4,\times}$-abstract role terms, C_1, C_2 are $\mathcal{DL}_\mathbf{D}^{4,\times}$-abstract concept terms, and P_1, P_2 are $\mathcal{DL}_\mathbf{D}^{4,\times}$-concrete role terms. Any expression of the type $w \sqsubseteq R$, where w is a finite string of $\mathcal{DL}_\mathbf{D}^{4,\times}$-abstract role terms and R is an $\mathcal{DL}_\mathbf{D}^{4,\times}$-abstract role term, is called a *role inclusion axiom (RIA)*.

A $\mathcal{DL}_\mathbf{D}^{4,\times}$-TBox is a set of statements of the following types:

- $C_1 \equiv C_2$, $C_1 \sqsubseteq C_2$, $C_1 \sqsubseteq \forall R_1.C_2$, $\exists R_1.C_1 \sqsubseteq C_2$, $\geq_n R_1.C_1 \sqsubseteq C_2$, $C_1 \sqsubseteq \leq_n R_1.C_2$,
- $t_1 \equiv t_2$, $t_1 \sqsubseteq t_2$, $C_1 \sqsubseteq \forall P_1.t_1$, $\exists P_1.t_1 \sqsubseteq C_1$, $\geq_n P_1.t_1 \sqsubseteq C_1$, $C_1 \sqsubseteq \leq_n P_1.t_1$,

where C_1, C_2 are $\mathcal{DL}_\mathbf{D}^{4,\times}$-concept terms, t_1, t_2 data type terms, R_1 a $\mathcal{DL}_\mathbf{D}^{4,\times}$-abstract role term, P_1 a $\mathcal{DL}_\mathbf{D}^{4,\times}$-concrete role term. Any statement of the form $C \sqsubseteq D$, with C, D $\mathcal{DL}_\mathbf{D}^{4}$-concept terms, is a *general concept inclusion axiom*.

A $\mathcal{DL}_\mathbf{D}^{4,\times}$-ABox is a set of *individual assertions* of the forms: $a : C_1$, $(a, b) : R_1$, $a = b$, $a \neq b$, $e_d : t_1$, $(a, e_d) : P_1$, with C_1 a $\mathcal{DL}_\mathbf{D}^{4,\times}$-concept term, d a data type, t_1 a data type term, R_1 a $\mathcal{DL}_\mathbf{D}^{4,\times}$-abstract role term, P_1 a $\mathcal{DL}_\mathbf{D}^{4,\times}$-concrete role term, a, b individual names, and e_d a constant in $N_C(d)$.

The semantics of $\mathcal{DL}_\mathbf{D}^{4,\times}$ is given by means of an interpretation $\mathbf{I} = (\Delta^\mathbf{I}, \Delta_\mathbf{D}, \cdot^\mathbf{I})$, where $\Delta^\mathbf{I}$ and $\Delta_\mathbf{D}$ are non-empty disjoint domains such that $d^\mathbf{D} \subseteq \Delta_\mathbf{D}$, for every $d \in N_D$, and $\cdot^\mathbf{I}$ is an interpretation function. The definition of the interpretation of concepts and roles, axioms and assertions is illustrated in [8, Table 1].

Let $\mathcal{R}$, $\mathcal{T}$, and $\mathcal{A}$ be as above. An interpretation $\mathbf{I} = (\Delta^\mathbf{I}, \Delta_\mathbf{D}, \cdot^\mathbf{I})$ is a $\mathbf{D}$-*model* of $\mathcal{R}$ (resp., $\mathcal{T}$), and we write $\mathbf{I} \models_\mathbf{D} \mathcal{R}$ (resp., $\mathbf{I} \models_\mathbf{D} \mathcal{T}$) if $\mathbf{I}$ satisfies each axiom in $\mathcal{R}$ (resp., $\mathcal{T}$) according to the semantic rules in [8, Table 1]. Analogously, $\mathbf{I} = (\Delta^\mathbf{I}, \Delta_\mathbf{D}, \cdot^\mathbf{I})$ is a $\mathbf{D}$-model of $\mathcal{A}$, and we write $\mathbf{I} \models_\mathbf{D} \mathcal{A}$ if $\mathbf{I}$ satisfies each assertion in $\mathcal{A}$, according to the semantic rules in [8, Table 1]. A $\mathcal{DL}_\mathbf{D}^{4,\times}$-knowledge base $\mathcal{K} = (\mathcal{A}, \mathcal{T}, \mathcal{R})$ is *consistent* if there is an interpretation $\mathbf{I} = (\Delta^\mathbf{I}, \Delta_\mathbf{D}, \cdot^\mathbf{I})$ that is a $\mathbf{D}$-model of $\mathcal{A}$, $\mathcal{T}$, and $\mathcal{R}$ (we write $\mathbf{I} \models_\mathbf{D} \mathcal{K}$).

Some considerations on the expressive power of $\mathcal{DL}_\mathbf{D}^{4,\times}$ are in order. As illustrated in [8, Table 1] existential quantification is admitted only on the left hand side of inclusion axioms. Thus $\mathcal{DL}_\mathbf{D}^{4,\times}$ is less powerful than logics such as $\mathcal{SROIQ}(\mathbf{D})$ [11] as far as the generation of new individuals is concerned. On the other hand, $\mathcal{DL}_\mathbf{D}^{4,\times}$ is more liberal than $\mathcal{SROIQ}(\mathbf{D})$ in the definition of role inclusion axioms since the roles involved are not required to be subject to any ordering relationship, and the notion of simple role is not needed. For example, the role hierarchy presented in [11, p. 2] is not expressible in $\mathcal{SROIQ}(\mathbf{D})$ but can be represented in $\mathcal{DL}_{\mathbf{D}}^{4,\times}$. In addition, $\mathcal{DL}_{\mathbf{D}}^{4,\times}$ is a powerful rule language able to express rules with negated atoms such as

$$Person(?p) \wedge \neg hasCar(?p, ?c) \implies CarlessPerson(?p).$$

Notice that rules with negated atoms are not supported by the SWRL language.

3   ABox Reasoning Services for $\mathcal{DL}_{\mathbf{D}}^{4,\times}$-Knowledge Base

The most important feature of a knowledge representation system is the capability of providing reasoning services. Depending on the type of the application domains, there are many different kinds of implicit knowledge that is desirable to infer from what is explicitly mentioned in the knowledge base. In particular, reasoning problems regarding ABoxes consist in querying a knowledge base in order to retrieve information concerning data stored in it. In this section we study the decidability for the most widespread ABox reasoning tasks for the logic $\mathcal{DL}_{\mathbf{D}}^{4,\times}$ by resorting to a general problem, called *Higher Order Conjunctive Query Answering* (HOCQA), that can be instantiated to each of them.

Let $V_i = \{v_1, v_2, \ldots\}$, $V_c = \{c_1, c_2, \ldots\}$, $V_{ar} = \{r_1, r_2, \ldots\}$, and $V_{cr} = \{p_1, p_2, \ldots\}$ be pairwise disjoint denumerably infinite sets of variables which are disjoint from **Ind**, $\bigcup\{N_C(d) : d \in N_{\mathbf{D}}\}$, **C**, $\mathbf{R_A}$, and $\mathbf{R_D}$. A HO $\mathcal{DL}_{\mathbf{D}}^{4,\times}$-*atomic formula* is an expression of one of the following types: $R(w_1, w_2)$, $P(w_1, u_1)$, $C(w_1)$, $r(w_1, w_2)$, $p(w_1, u_1)$, $c(w_1)$, $w_1 = w_2$, $u_1 = u_2$, where $w_1, w_2 \in V_i \cup \mathbf{Ind}$, $u_1, u_2 \in V_i \cup \bigcup\{N_C(d) : d \in N_{\mathbf{D}}\}$, R is a $\mathcal{DL}_{\mathbf{D}}^{4,\times}$-abstract role term, P is a $\mathcal{DL}_{\mathbf{D}}^{4,\times}$-concrete role term, C is a $\mathcal{DL}_{\mathbf{D}}^{4,\times}$-concept term, $r \in V_{ar}$, $p \in V_{cr}$, and $c \in V_c$. A HO $\mathcal{DL}_{\mathbf{D}}^{4,\times}$-atomic formula containing no variables is said to be *ground*. A HO $\mathcal{DL}_{\mathbf{D}}^{4,\times}$-*literal* is a HO $\mathcal{DL}_{\mathbf{D}}^{4,\times}$-atomic formula or its negation. A HO $\mathcal{DL}_{\mathbf{D}}^{4,\times}$-*conjunctive query* is a conjunction of HO $\mathcal{DL}_{\mathbf{D}}^{4,\times}$-literals. We denote with λ the *empty* HO $\mathcal{DL}_{\mathbf{D}}^{4,\times}$-conjunctive query.

Let $v_1, \ldots, v_n \in V_i$, $c_1, \ldots, c_m \in V_c$, $r_1, \ldots, r_k \in V_{ar}$, $p_1, \ldots, p_h \in V_{cr}$, $o_1, \ldots, o_n \in \mathbf{Ind} \cup \bigcup\{N_C(d) : d \in N_{\mathbf{D}}\}$, $C_1, \ldots, C_m \in \mathbf{C}$, $R_1, \ldots, R_k \in \mathbf{R_A}$, and $P_1, \ldots, P_h \in \mathbf{R_D}$. A substitution

$$\sigma := \{v_1/o_1, \ldots, v_n/o_n, c_1/C_1, \ldots, c_m/C_m, r_1/R_1, \ldots, r_k/R_k, p_1/P_1, \ldots, p_h/P_h\}$$

is a map such that, for every HO $\mathcal{DL}_{\mathbf{D}}^{4,\times}$-literal L, $L\sigma$ is obtained from L by replacing the occurrences of v_i in L with o_i, for $i = 1, \ldots, n$; the occurrences of c_j in L with C_j, for $j = 1, \ldots, m$; the occurrences of r_ℓ in L with R_ℓ, for $\ell = 1, \ldots, k$; the occurrences of p_t in L with P_t, for $t = 1, \ldots, h$.

Substitutions can be extended to HO $\mathcal{DL}_{\mathbf{D}}^{4,\times}$-conjunctive queries in the usual way. Let $Q := (L_1 \wedge \ldots \wedge L_m)$ be a HO $\mathcal{DL}_{\mathbf{D}}^{4,\times}$-conjunctive query, and $\mathcal{KB}$ a $\mathcal{DL}_{\mathbf{D}}^{4,\times}$-knowledge base. A substitution σ involving *exactly* the variables occurring in Q is a *solution for Q w.r.t. $\mathcal{KB}$* if there exists a $\mathcal{DL}_{\mathbf{D}}^{4,\times}$-interpretation $\mathbf{I}$ such that $\mathbf{I} \models_{\mathbf{D}} \mathcal{KB}$ and $\mathbf{I} \models_{\mathbf{D}} Q\sigma$. The collection Σ of the solutions for Q w.r.t. $\mathcal{KB}$ is the *higher order answer set of Q w.r.t. $\mathcal{KB}$*. Then the *higher order conjunctive query answering problem* for Q w.r.t. $\mathcal{KB}$ consists in finding the HO answer set Σ of Q w.r.t. $\mathcal{KB}$. We shall solve the HOCQA problem just stated by reducing it to the analogous problem formulated in the context of the fragment 4LQS^{R} (and in turn to the decision procedure for 4LQS^{R} presented in [4]). The HOCQA problem for 4LQS^{R}-formulae can be stated as follows. Let ϕ be a 4LQS^{R}-formula and let ψ be a conjunction of 4LQS^{R}-quantifier-free atomic formulae of level 0 of the types $x = y$, $x \in X^1$, $\langle x, y \rangle \in X^3$, or their negations.

The *HOCQA problem for ψ w.r.t. ϕ* consists in computing the HO *answer set of ψ w.r.t. ϕ*, namely the collection Σ' of all the substitutions σ' such that $\mathcal{M} \models \phi \wedge \psi\sigma'$, for some 4LQS^{R}-interpretation $\mathcal{M}$.

In view of the decidability of the satisfiability problem for 4LQS^{R}-formulae, the HOCQA problem for 4LQS^{R}-formulae is decidable as well. Indeed, let ϕ and ψ be two 4LQS^{R}-formulae fulfilling the above requirements. To calculate the HO answer set of ψ w.r.t. ϕ, for each candidate substitution

$$\sigma' := \{x/z, X^1/Y^1, X^2/Y^2, X^3/Y^3\}$$

one has just to check the 4LQS^{R}-formula $\phi \wedge \psi\sigma'$ for satisfiability. Since the number of possible candidate substitutions is $|\mathtt{Vars}(\phi)|^{|\mathtt{Vars}(\psi)|}$ and the satisfiability problem for 4LQS^{R}-formulae is decidable, the HO answer set of ψ w.r.t. ϕ can be computed effectively. Summarizing,

Lemma 1. *The HOCQA problem for* 4LQS^{R}-*formulae is decidable.* □

The following theorem states decidability of the HOCQA problem for $\mathcal{DL}_{\mathbf{D}}^{4,\times}$.

Theorem 1. *Given a $\mathcal{DL}_{\mathbf{D}}^{4,\times}$-knowledge base $\mathcal{KB}$ and a HO $\mathcal{DL}_{\mathbf{D}}^{4,\times}$- conjunctive query Q, the HOCQA problem for Q w.r.t. $\mathcal{KB}$ is decidable.* □

The proof of Theorem 1 is much along the same lines of [7, Theorem 1] and, for space reasons, is omitted. However, the interested reader can find it in the extended version of this paper [8]. Here, we just sketch the main ideas of the proof to ease the understanding of the rest of the paper. As mentioned above, the $\mathcal{DL}_{\mathbf{D}}^{4,\times}$-HOCQA problem can be solved by reducing it effectively to the HOCQA problem for 4LQS^{R}-formulae and then exploiting Lemma 1. The reduction is carried out by means of a transformation function θ that maps the $\mathcal{DL}_{\mathbf{D}}^{4,\times}$-knowledge base $\mathcal{KB}$ in a 4LQS^R-formula $\phi_{\mathcal{KB}}$ in Conjunctive Normal Form (CNF) and the HO $\mathcal{DL}_D^{4,\times}$-conjunctive query Q in the 4LQS^R-formula ψ_Q. Specifically,[2]

$$\phi_{\mathcal{KB}} := \bigwedge\nolimits_{H \in \mathcal{KB}} \theta(H) \wedge \bigwedge\nolimits_{i=1}^{12} \xi_i, \qquad \psi_Q := \theta(Q).$$

Let Σ be the HO answer set of Q w.r.t. $\mathcal{KB}$ and Σ' the HO answer set of ψ_Q w.r.t. $\phi_{\mathcal{KB}}$. Then Σ consists of all substitutions σ (involving exactly the variables occurring in Q) such that $\theta(\sigma) \in \Sigma'$. By Lemma 1, Σ' can be calculated effectively and thus Σ can be calculated effectively as well.

Next, we list the most widespread reasoning services for $\mathcal{DL}_D^{4,\times}$ -ABox and then show how to define them as particular cases of the HOCQA task.

1. *Instance checking*: the problem of deciding whether or not an individual a is an instance of a concept C.
2. *Instance retrieval*: the problem of retrieving all the individuals that are instances of a given concept.
3. *Role filler retrieval*: the problem of retrieving all the fillers x such that the pair (a, x) is an instance of a role R.
4. *Concept retrieval*: the problem of retrieving all concepts which an individual is an instance of.
5. *Role instance retrieval*: the problem of retrieving all roles which a pair of individuals (a, b) is an instance of.

The instance checking problem is a specialisation of the HOCQA problem admitting HO $\mathcal{DL}_D^{4,\times}$-conjunctive queries of the form $Q_{IC} = C(w_1)$, with $w_1 \in \mathbf{Ind}$. The instance retrieval problem is a particular case of the HOCQA problem in which HO $\mathcal{DL}_D^{4,\times}$-conjunctive queries have the form $Q_{IR} = C(w_1)$, where w_1 is a variable in V_i. The HOCQA problem can be instantiated to the role filler retrieval problem by admitting HO $\mathcal{DL}_D^{4,\times}$-conjunctive queries $Q_{RF} = R(w_1, w_2)$, with $w_1 \in \mathbf{Ind}$ and w_2 a variable in V_i. The concept retrieval problem is a specialization of the HOCQA problem allowing HO $\mathcal{DL}_D^{4,\times}$-conjunctive queries of the form $Q_{QR} = c(w_1)$, with $w_1 \in \mathbf{Ind}$ and c a variable in V_c. Finally, the role instance retrieval problem is a particularization of the HOCQA problem, where HO $\mathcal{DL}_D^{4,\times}$-conjunctive queries have the form $Q_{RI} = r(w_1, w_2)$, with $w_1, w_2 \in \mathbf{Ind}$ and r a variable in V_{cr}.

Notice that the CQA problem for $\mathcal{DL}_D^{4,\times}$ defined in [7] is an instance of the HOCQA problem admitting HO $\mathcal{DL}_D^{4,\times}$-conjunctive queries of the form $(L_1 \wedge \ldots \wedge L_m)$, where the conjuncts L_i are atomic formulae of any of the types $R(w_1, w_2)$,

---

[2] The map θ coincides with the transformation function defined in [7] as far as it concerns the translation of each axiom or assertion H of $\mathcal{KB}$ in a 4LQS^R-formula $\theta(H)$. The map θ extends the function introduced in [7] for what regards the translation of the HO query Q and of the substitutions σ of the HO answer set Σ. In particular it maps effectively variables in V_c in variables of sort 1 (in the language of 4LQS^R), and variables in V_{ar} and in V_{cr} in variables of sort 3. The constraints ξ_1-ξ_{12} are added to make sure that each 4LQS^R-model of $\phi_{\mathcal{KB}}$ can be transformed into a $\mathcal{DL}_D^{4,\times}$-interpretation (cf. [7, Theorem 1]).

$C(w_1)$, and $w_1 = w_2$ (or their negation), with $w_1, w_2 \in (\mathbf{Ind} \cup V_i)$. Notice also that problems 1, 2, and 3 are instances of the CQA problem for $\mathcal{DL}_{\mathbf{D}}^{4,\times}$, whereas problems 4 and 5 fall outside the definition of CQA. As shown above, they can be treated as specializations of HOCQA.

4   An Algorithm for the HOCQA Problem for $\mathcal{DL}_{\mathbf{D}}^{4,\times}$

In this section we introduce an effective set-theoretic procedure to compute the answer set of a HO $\mathcal{DL}_{\mathbf{D}}^{4,\times}$-conjunctive query Q w.r.t. a $\mathcal{DL}_{\mathbf{D}}^{4,\times}$ knowledge base $\mathcal{KB}$. Such procedure, called HOCQA-$\mathcal{DL}_{\mathbf{D}}^{4,\times}$, takes as input $\phi_{\mathcal{KB}}$ (i.e., the 4LQS^{R}-translation of $\mathcal{KB}$) and ψ_Q (i.e., the 4LQS^{R}-formula representing the HO $\mathcal{DL}_{\mathbf{D}}^{4,\times}$-conjunctive query Q), and returns a KE-tableau $\mathcal{T}_{\mathcal{KB}}$, representing the saturation of $\mathcal{KB}$, and the answer set Σ' of ψ_Q w.r.t. $\phi_{\mathcal{KB}}$, namely the collection of all substitutions σ' such that $\mathcal{M} \models \phi_{\mathcal{KB}} \wedge \psi_Q \sigma'$, for some 4LQS^{R}-interpretation $\mathcal{M}$. Specifically, HOCQA-$\mathcal{DL}_{\mathbf{D}}^{4,\times}$ constructs for each open branch of $\mathcal{T}_{\mathcal{KB}}$ a decision tree whose leaves are labelled with elements of Σ'.

Let us first introduce some definitions and notations useful for the presentation of Procedure HOCQA-$\mathcal{DL}_{\mathbf{D}}^{4,\times}$.

Assume without loss of generality that universal quantifiers in $\phi_{\mathcal{KB}}$ occur as inward as possible and that universally quantified variables are pairwise distinct. Let $S_1, \ldots, S_m$ be the conjuncts of $\phi_{\mathcal{KB}}$ having the form of 4LQS^{R}-purely universal formulae. For each $S_i := (\forall z_1^i) \ldots (\forall z_{n_i}^i) \chi_i$, with $i = 1, \ldots, m$, we put

$$Exp(S_i) := \bigwedge_{\{x_{a_1}, \ldots, x_{a_{n_i}}\} \subseteq \mathtt{Var}_0(\phi_{\mathcal{KB}})} S_i \{z_1^i / x_{a_1}, \ldots, z_{n_i}^i / x_{a_{n_i}}\}.$$

We also define the *expansion* $\Phi_{\mathcal{KB}}$ of $\phi_{\mathcal{KB}}$ by putting

$$\Phi_{\mathcal{KB}} := \{F_j : i = 1, \ldots, k\} \cup \bigcup_{i=1}^{m} Exp(S_i), \tag{1}$$

where $F_1, \ldots, F_k$ are the conjuncts of $\phi_{\mathcal{KB}}$ having the form of 4LQS^{R}-quantifier free atomic formulae.

To prepare for Procedure $HOCQA\text{-}\mathcal{DL}_{\mathbf{D}}^{4,\times}$ to be described next, a brief introduction to KE-tableau systems is in order (see [10] for a detailed overview of KE-tableaux). KE-tableaux are a refutation system inspired to Smullyan's semantic tableaux [14]. The main characteristic distinguishing KE-tableaux from the latter is the introduction of an analytic cut rule (PB-rule) that permits to reduce inefficiencies of semantic tableaux. In fact, firstly, the classic tableau system can not represent the use of auxiliary lemmas in proofs; secondly, it can not express the bivalence of classical logic. Thirdly, it is highly inefficient, as witnessed by the fact that it can not polynomially simulate the truth-tables. None of these anomalies occurs if the cut rule is allowed. Procedure HOCQA-$\mathcal{DL}_{\mathbf{D}}^{4,\times}$ constructs a complete KE-tableau $\mathcal{T}_{\mathcal{KB}}$ for the expansion $\Phi_{\mathcal{KB}}$ of $\phi_{\mathcal{KB}}$ (cf. (1)), representing the saturation of the $\mathcal{DL}_{\mathbf{D}}^{4,\times}$-knowledge base $\mathcal{KB}$.

Let $\Phi := \{C_1, \ldots, C_p\}$ be a collection of disjunctions of 4LQS^R-quantifier free atomic formulae of level 0 of the types: $x = y$, $x \in X^1$, $\langle x, y \rangle \in X^3$. $\mathcal{T}$ is a KE-tableau for Φ if there exists a finite sequence $\mathcal{T}_1, \ldots, \mathcal{T}_t$ of trees such that (i) $\mathcal{T}_1$ is a one-branch tree consisting of the sequence $C_1, \ldots, C_p$, (ii) $\mathcal{T}_t = \mathcal{T}$, and (iii) for each $i < t$, $\mathcal{T}_{i+1}$ is obtained from $\mathcal{T}_i$ either by an application of one of the rules in Fig. 1 or by applying a substitution σ to a branch ϑ of $\mathcal{T}_i$ (in particular, the substitution σ is applied to each formula X of ϑ; the resulting branch will be denoted by $\vartheta\sigma$). The set of formulae $\mathcal{S}_i^{\overline{\beta}} := \{\overline{\beta}_1, \ldots, \overline{\beta}_n\} \setminus \{\overline{\beta}_i\}$ occurring as premise in the E-rule contains the complements of all the components of the formula β with the exception of the component β_i.

$$\frac{\beta_1 \vee \ldots \vee \beta_n \qquad \mathcal{S}_i^{\overline{\beta}}}{\beta_i} \quad \textbf{E-Rule} \qquad\qquad \frac{}{A \mid \overline{A}} \quad \textbf{PB-Rule}$$

where $\mathcal{S}_i^{\overline{\beta}} := \{\overline{\beta}_1, ..., \overline{\beta}_n\} \setminus \{\overline{\beta}_i\}$, $\qquad$ with A a literal
for $i = 1, ..., n$

Fig. 1. Expansion rules for the KE-tableau.

Let $\mathcal{T}$ be a KE-tableau. A branch ϑ of $\mathcal{T}$ is *closed* if it contains either both A and $\neg A$, for some formula A, or a literal of type $\neg(x = x)$. Otherwise, the branch is *open*. A KE-tableau is *closed* if all its branches are closed. A formula $\beta_1 \vee \ldots \vee \beta_n$ is *fulfilled* in a branch ϑ, if β_i is in ϑ, for some $i = 1, \ldots, n$; otherwise it is *unfulfilled*. A branch ϑ is *fulfilled* if every formula $\beta_1 \vee \ldots \vee \beta_n$ occurring in ϑ is fulfilled; otherwise it is *unfulfilled*. A branch ϑ is *complete* if either it is closed or it is open, fulfilled, and it does not contain any literal of type $x = y$, with x, y distinct variables. A KE-tableau is *complete* (resp., *fulfilled*) if all its branches are complete (resp., fulfilled or closed). A 4LQS^R-interpretation $\mathcal{M}$ *satisfies* a branch ϑ of a KE-tableau (or, equivalently, ϑ *is satisfied* by $\mathcal{M}$), and we write $\mathcal{M} \models \vartheta$, if $\mathcal{M} \models X$ for every formula X occurring in ϑ.

A 4LQS^R-interpretation $\mathcal{M}$ satisfies a KE-tableau $\mathcal{T}$ (or, equivalently, $\mathcal{T}$ *is satisfied* by $\mathcal{M}$), and we write $\mathcal{M} \models \mathcal{T}$, if $\mathcal{M}$ satisfies a branch ϑ of $\mathcal{T}$. A branch ϑ of a KE-tableau $\mathcal{T}$ is *satisfiable* if there exists a 4LQS^R-interpretation $\mathcal{M}$ that satisfies ϑ. A KE-tableau is satisfiable if at least one of its branches is satisfiable.

Let ϑ be a branch of a KE-tableau. We denote with $<_\vartheta$ an arbitrary but fixed total order on the variables in $\mathsf{Var}_0(\vartheta)$.

Procedure HOCQA-$\mathcal{DL}_{\mathbf{D}}^{4,\times}$ takes care of literals of type $x = y$ occurring in the branches of $\mathcal{T}_{\mathcal{KB}}$ by constructing, for each open and fulfilled branch ϑ of $\mathcal{T}_{\mathcal{KB}}$, a substitution σ_ϑ such that $\vartheta\sigma_\vartheta$ does not contain literals of type $x = y$ with distinct x, y. Then, for every open and complete branch $\vartheta' := \vartheta\sigma_\vartheta$ of $\mathcal{T}_{\mathcal{KB}}$, Procedure HOCQA-$\mathcal{DL}_{\mathbf{D}}^{4,\times}$ constructs a decision tree $\mathcal{D}_{\vartheta'}$ such that every maximal branch of $\mathcal{D}_{\vartheta'}$ induces a substitution σ' such that $\sigma_\vartheta\sigma'$ belongs to the answer set of ψ_Q with respect to $\phi_{\mathcal{KB}}$. $\mathcal{D}_{\vartheta'}$ is defined as follows.

Let d be the number of literals in ψ_Q. Then $\mathcal{D}_{\vartheta'}$ is a finite labelled tree of depth $d + 1$ whose labelling satisfies the following conditions, for $i = 0, \ldots, d$:

(i) every node of $\mathcal{D}_{\vartheta'}$ at level i is labelled with $(\sigma_i', \psi_Q \sigma_\vartheta \sigma_i')$; in particular, the root is labelled with $(\sigma_0', \psi_Q \sigma_\vartheta \sigma_0')$, where σ_0' is the empty substitution;

(ii) if a node at level i is labelled with $(\sigma_i', \psi_Q \sigma_\vartheta \sigma_i')$, then its s successors, with $s \geq 1$, are labelled with $\big(\sigma_i' \varrho_1^{q_{i+1}}, \psi_Q \sigma_\vartheta (\sigma_i' \varrho_1^{q_{i+1}})\big), \dots, \big(\sigma_i' \varrho_s^{q_{i+1}}, \psi_Q \sigma_\vartheta (\sigma_i' \varrho_s^{q_{i+1}})\big)$, where q_{i+1} is the $(i+1)$-st conjunct of $\psi_Q \sigma_\vartheta \sigma_i'$ and $\mathcal{S}_{q_{i+1}} := \{\varrho_1^{q_{i+1}}, \dots, \varrho_s^{q_{i+1}}\}$ is the collection of the substitutions $\varrho = \{v_1/o_1, \dots, v_n/o_n, c_1/C_1, \dots, c_m/C_m, r_1/R_1, \dots, r_k/R_k, p_1/P_1, \dots, p_h/P_h\}$, with $\{v_1, \dots, v_n\} = \mathrm{Var}_0(q_{i+1})$, $\{c_1, \dots, c_m\} = \mathrm{Var}_1(q_{i+1})$, and $\{p_1, \dots, p_h, r_1, \dots, r_k\} = \mathrm{Var}_3(q_{i+1})$, such that $t = q_{i+1} \varrho$, for some literal t on ϑ'. If $s = 0$, the node labelled with $(\sigma_i', \psi_Q \sigma_\vartheta \sigma_i')$ is a leaf node and, if $i = d$, $\sigma_\vartheta \sigma_i'$ is added to Σ'.

We are now ready to define Procedure HOCQA-$\mathcal{DL}_D^{4,\times}$.

```
 1: procedure HOCQA-DL_D^{4,×} (ψ_Q, φ_KB);
 2:     Σ' := ∅;
 3:     - let Φ_KB be the expansion of φ_KB (cf. (1));
 4:     T_KB := Φ_KB;
 5:     while T_KB is not fulfilled do
 6:         - select an unfulfilled open branch ϑ of T_KB and an unfulfilled formula
              β_1 ∨ ... ∨ β_n in ϑ;
 7:         if S_j^β̄ is in ϑ, for some j ∈ {1, ..., n} then
 8:             - apply the E-Rule to β_1 ∨ ... ∨ β_n and S_j^β̄ on ϑ;
 9:         else
10:             - let B^β̄ be the collection of the formulae present in ϑ and let
                  h be the lowest index such that β̄_h ∉ B^β̄;
11:             - apply the PB-rule to β̄_h on ϑ;
12:         end if;
13:     end while;
14:
        while T_KB has open branches containing literals of type x = y, with distinct x and y do
15:         - select such an open branch ϑ of T_KB;
16:         σ_ϑ := ε (where ε is the empty substitution);
17:         Eq_ϑ := {literals of type x = y occurring in ϑ};
18:         while Eq_ϑ contains x = y, with distinct x, y do
19:             - select a literal x = y in Eq_ϑ, with distinct x, y;
20:             z := min_{<_ϑ}(x, y);
21:             σ_ϑ := σ_ϑ · {x/z, y/z};
22:             Eq_ϑ := Eq_ϑ σ_ϑ;
23:         end while;
24:         ϑ := ϑσ_ϑ;
25:         if ϑ is open then
26:             - initialize S to the empty stack;
27:             - push (ε, ψ_Q σ_ϑ) in S;
28:             while S is not empty do
29:                 - pop (σ', ψ_Q σ_ϑ σ') from S;
30:                 if ψ_Q σ_ϑ σ' ≠ λ then
31:                     - let q be the leftmost conjunct of ψ_Q σ_ϑ σ';
32:                     ψ_Q σ_ϑ σ' := ψ_Q σ_ϑ σ' deprived of q;
33:                     Lit_Q^M := {t ∈ ϑ : t = qρ, for some substitution ρ};
34:                     while Lit_Q^M is not empty do
35:                         - let t ∈ Lit_Q^M, t = qρ;
36:                         Lit_Q^M := Lit_Q^M \ {t};
37:                         - push (σ'ρ, ψ_Q σ_ϑ σ'ρ) in S;
38:                     end while;
39:                 else
40:                     Σ' := Σ' ∪ {σ_ϑ σ'};
41:                 end if;
42:             end while;
43:         end if;
44:     end while;
45:     return (T_KB, Σ');
46: end procedure;
```

$\{\overline{\beta}_1, \ldots, \overline{\beta}_n\}$ that is included in ϑ

For each open branch ϑ of $\mathcal{T}_{\mathcal{KB}}$, Procedure HOCQA-$\mathcal{DL}_\mathbf{D}^{4,\times}$ computes the corresponding $\mathcal{D}_\vartheta$ by constructing a stack of its nodes. Initially the stack contains the root node $(\epsilon, \psi_Q \sigma_\vartheta)$ of $\mathcal{D}_\vartheta$, as defined in condition (i). Then, iteratively, the following steps are executed. An element $(\sigma', \psi_Q \sigma_\vartheta \sigma')$ is popped out of the stack. If the last literal of the query ψ_Q has not been reached, the successors of the current node are computed according to condition (ii) and inserted in the stack. Otherwise the current node must have the form (σ', λ) and the substitution $\sigma_\vartheta \sigma'$ is inserted in Σ'.

Correctness of Procedure HOCQA-$\mathcal{DL}_\mathbf{D}^{4,\times}$ follows from Theorem 2, which show that $\phi_{\mathcal{KB}}$ is satisfiable if and only if $\mathcal{T}_{\mathcal{KB}}$ is a non-closed KE-tableau, and from Theorem 3, which shows that the set Σ' coincides with the HO answer set of ψ_Q w.r.t. $\phi_{\mathcal{KB}}$. Theorems 2 and 3 are stated below. In particular, Theorem 2, requires the following technical lemmas.

Lemma 2. *Let ϑ be a branch of $\mathcal{T}_{\mathcal{KB}}$ selected at step 15 of Procedure HOCQA-$\mathcal{DL}_\mathbf{D}^{4,\times}$ $(\psi_Q, \phi_{\mathcal{KB}})$, let σ_ϑ be the associated substitution constructed during the execution of the while-loop 18–23, and let $\mathcal{M} = (D, M)$ be a 4LQS^R-interpretation satisfying ϑ. Then, for every $x \in \mathsf{Var}_0(\vartheta)$, $Mx = Mx\sigma_\vartheta$ is an invariant of the while-loop 18–23.* $\square$

Lemma 3. *Let $\mathcal{T}_0, \ldots, \mathcal{T}_h$ be a sequence of KE-tableaux such that $\mathcal{T}_0 = \Phi_{\mathcal{KB}}$, and where, for $i = 1, \ldots, h-1$, $\mathcal{T}_{i+1}$ is obtained from $\mathcal{T}_i$ by applying either the rule of step 8, or the rule of step 10, or the substitution of step 24 of Procedure HOCQA-$\mathcal{DL}_\mathbf{D}^{4,\times}$ $(\psi_Q, \phi_{\mathcal{KB}})$. If $\mathcal{T}_i$ is satisfied by a 4LQS^R-interpretation $\mathcal{M}$, then $\mathcal{T}_{i+1}$ is satisfied by $\mathcal{M}$ as well, for $i = 1, \ldots, h-1$.* $\square$

Then we have:

Theorem 2. *The formula $\phi_{\mathcal{KB}}$ is satisfiable if and only if the tableau $\mathcal{T}_{\mathcal{KB}}$ is not closed.* $\square$

The proof of Theorem 3 below requires the following technical lemma.

Lemma 4. *Let $\psi_Q := q_1 \wedge \ldots \wedge q_d$ be a HO 4LQS^R-conjunctive query, $(\mathcal{T}_{\mathcal{KB}}, \Sigma')$ the output of HOCQA-$\mathcal{DL}_\mathbf{D}^{4,\times}$ $(\psi_Q, \phi_{\mathcal{KB}})$, and ϑ an open and complete branch of $\mathcal{T}_{\mathcal{KB}}$. Then, for any substitution σ, we have*

$$\sigma \in \Sigma' \iff \{q_1\sigma, \ldots, q_d\sigma\} \subseteq \vartheta.$$
$\square$

Theorem 3. *Let Σ' be the set of substitutions returned by Procedure HOCQA-$\mathcal{DL}_\mathbf{D}^{4,\times}$ $(\psi_Q, \phi_{\mathcal{KB}})$. Then Σ' is the HO answer set of ψ_Q w.r.t. $\phi_{\mathcal{KB}}$.*

Due to space limitations, we do not include here the proofs of Theorems 2 and 3 and of Lemmas 2, 3, and 4, which can be found in the extended version of the paper [8].

Termination of Procedure HOCQA-$\mathcal{DL}_\mathbf{D}^{4,\times}$ is based on the fact that the while-loops 5–13 and 14–44 terminate. Termination of the while-loop 5–13 can be shown much in the same way as for Procedure 1 in [7].

Concerning the while-loop 14–44, its termination can be proved by observing that the number of branches of the KE-tableau resulting from the execution of the previous while-loop 5–13 is finite and then showing that the internal while-loops 18–23 and 28–42 always terminate. Indeed, initially the set Eq_ϑ contains a finite number of literals of type $x = y$, and σ_ϑ is the empty substitution. It is then enough to show that the number of literals of type $x = y$ in Eq_ϑ, with distinct x and y, strictly decreases during the execution of the internal while-loop 18–23. But this follows immediately, since at each of its iterations one puts $\sigma_\vartheta := \sigma_\vartheta \cdot \{x/z, y/z\}$, with $z := \min_{<_\vartheta}(x, y)$, according to a fixed total order $<_\vartheta$ over the variables of $\mathsf{Var}_0(\vartheta)$ and then the application of σ_ϑ to Eq_ϑ replaces a literal of type $x = y$ in Eq_ϑ, with distinct x and y, with a literal of type $x = x$.

The while-loop 28–42 terminates when the stack $\mathcal{S}$ of the nodes of the decision tree gets empty. Since the query ψ_Q contains a finite number of conjuncts and the number of literals on each open and complete branch of $\mathcal{T}_{\mathcal{KB}}$ is finite, the number of possible matches (namely the size of the set Lit_Q^M) computed at step 33 is finite as well. Thus, in particular, the internal while-loop 34–38 terminates at each execution. Once the procedure has processed the last conjunct of the query, the set Lit_Q^M of possible matches is empty and thus no element gets pushed in the stack $\mathcal{S}$ anymore. Since the first instruction of the while-loop 28–42 removes an element from $\mathcal{S}$, the stack gets empty after a finite number of "pops". Hence Procedure HOCQA-$\mathcal{DL}_\mathbf{D}^{4,\times}$ terminates, as we wished to prove.

We provide now some complexity results. Let r be the maximum number of universal quantifiers in each S_i ($i = 1, \ldots, m$), and put $k := |\mathsf{Var}_0(\phi_{\mathcal{KB}})|$. Then, each S_i generates at most k^r expansions. Since the knowledge base contains m such formulae, the number of disjunctions in the initial branch of the KE-tableau is bounded by $m \cdot k^r$. Next, let ℓ be the maximum number of literals in each S_i. Then, the height of the KE-tableau (which corresponds to the maximum size of the models of $\Phi_{\mathcal{KB}}$ constructed as illustrated above) is $\mathcal{O}(\ell m k^r)$ and the number of leaves of the tableau (namely, the number of such models of $\Phi_{\mathcal{KB}}$) is $\mathcal{O}(2^{\ell m k^r})$. Notice that the construction of Eq_ϑ and of σ_ϑ in the lines 16–23 of Procedure HOCQA-$\mathcal{DL}_\mathbf{D}^{4,\times}$ takes $\mathcal{O}(\ell m k^r)$ time, for each branch ϑ.

Let $\eta(\mathcal{T}_{\mathcal{KB}})$ and $\lambda(\mathcal{T}_{\mathcal{KB}})$ be, respectively, the height of $\mathcal{T}_{\mathcal{KB}}$ and the number of leaves of $\mathcal{T}_{\mathcal{KB}}$ computed by Procedure HOCQA-$\mathcal{DL}_\mathbf{D}^{4,\times}$. Plainly, $\eta(\mathcal{T}_{\mathcal{KB}}) = \mathcal{O}(\ell m k^r)$ and $\lambda(\mathcal{T}_{\mathcal{KB}}) = \mathcal{O}(2^{\ell m k^r})$, as computed above. It is easy to verify that $s = \mathcal{O}(\ell k^r)$ is the maximum branching of $\mathcal{D}_\vartheta$. Since the height of $\mathcal{D}_\vartheta$ is h, where h is the number of literals in ψ_Q, and the successors of a node are computed in $\mathcal{O}(\ell k^r)$ time, the number of leaves in $\mathcal{D}_\vartheta$ is $\mathcal{O}(s^h) = \mathcal{O}((\ell k^r)^h)$ and they are computed in $\mathcal{O}(s^h \cdot \ell k^r \cdot h) = \mathcal{O}(h \cdot (\ell k^r)^{h+1})$ time. Finally, since we have $\lambda(\mathcal{T}_{\mathcal{KB}})$ of such decision trees, the answer set of ψ_Q w.r.t. $\phi_{\mathcal{KB}}$ is computed in time $\mathcal{O}(h \cdot (\ell k^r)^{h+1} \cdot \lambda(\mathcal{T}_{\mathcal{KB}})) = \mathcal{O}(h \cdot (\ell k^r)^{h+1} \cdot 2^{\ell m k^r})$.

Since the size of $\phi_{\mathcal{KB}}$ and of ψ_Q are related to those of $\mathcal{KB}$ and of Q, respectively (see the proof of Theorem 1 in [8] for details on the reduction), the construction of the HO answer set of Q with respect to $\mathcal{KB}$ can be done in double-exponential time. In case $\mathcal{KB}$ contains neither role chain axioms nor qualified cardinality restrictions, the complexity of our $HOCQA$ problem is in

EXPTIME, since the maximum number of universal quantifiers in $\phi_{\mathcal{KB}}$, namely r, is a constant (in particular $r = 3$). The latter complexity result is a clue to the fact that the HOCQA problem is intrinsically more difficult than the consistency problem (proved to be NP-complete in [3]). In fact, the consistency problem simply requires to guess a model of the knowledge base, whereas the $HOCQA$ problem forces the construction of all the models of the knowledge base and the computation of a decision tree for each of them.

We remark that such result compares favourably with the complexity of the usual CQA problem for a wide collection of description logics such as the Horn fragment of $\mathcal{SHOIQ}$ and of $\mathcal{SROIQ}$, which are EXPTIME- and 2EXPTIME-complete respectively (see [13] for details).

5   Conclusions and Future Work

We have considered an extension of the CQA problem for the description logic $\mathcal{DL}_{\mathbf{D}}^{4,\times}$ to more general queries on roles and concepts. The resulting problem, called HOCQA, can be instantiated to the most widespread ABox reasoning services such as instance retrieval, role filler retrieval, and instance checking. We have proved the decidability of the HOCQA problem by reducing it to the satisfiability problem for the set-theoretic fragment 4LQS^{R}.

We have introduced an algorithm to compute the HO answer set of a 4LQS^{R}-formula ψ_Q representing a HO $\mathcal{DL}_{\mathbf{D}}^{4,\times}$-conjunctive query Q w.r.t. a 4LQS^{R}-formula $\phi_{\mathcal{KB}}$ representing a $\mathcal{DL}_{\mathbf{D}}^{4,\times}$ knowledge base. Our procedure, called HOCQA-$\mathcal{DL}_{\mathbf{D}}^{4,\times}$, is based on the KE-tableau system and on decision trees. It takes as input ψ_Q and $\phi_{\mathcal{KB}}$, and yields a KE-tableau $\mathcal{T}_{\mathcal{KB}}$ representing the saturation of $\phi_{\mathcal{KB}}$ and the requested HO answer set Σ'. Procedure HOCQA-$\mathcal{DL}_{\mathbf{D}}^{4,\times}$ is proved correct and complete, and some complexity results are provided. Such procedure extends the one introduced in [7] as it handles HO $\mathcal{DL}_{\mathbf{D}}^{4,\times}$-conjunctive queries.

We are currently implementing Procedure HOCQA-$\mathcal{DL}_{\mathbf{D}}^{4,\times}$ and plan to increase its efficiency by providing a parallel model and enhancing the expansion rules. We also intend to allow data types reasoning.

Further, we plan to extend the fragment presented in [4] with a restricted form of composition operator, since this would allow one to represent various logics in set-theoretic terms. The KE-tableau based procedure will be adapted to the new set-theoretic fragments exploiting the techniques introduced in [5,6] in the area of relational dual tableaux.

References

1. Calvanese, D., De Giacomo, G., Lenzerini, M.: On the decidability of query containment under constraints. In: PODS, pp. 149–158 (1998)
2. Calvanese, D., De Giacomo, G., Lenzerini, M.: Conjunctive query containment and answering under description logic constraints. ACM Trans. Comput. Log. **9**(3), 22:1–31 (2008)
3. Cantone, D., Longo, C., Nicolosi-Asmundo, M., Santamaria, D.F.: Web ontology representation and reasoning via fragments of set theory. In: Cate, B., Mileo, A. (eds.) RR 2015. LNCS, vol. 9209, pp. 61–76. Springer, Cham (2015). doi:10.1007/978-3-319-22002-4_6
4. Cantone, D., Nicolosi-Asmundo, M.: On the satisfiability problem for a 4-level quantified syllogistic and some applications to modal logic. Fundamenta Informaticae **124**(4), 427–448 (2013)
5. Cantone, D., Nicolosi-Asmundo, M., Orłowska, E.: Dual tableau-based decision procedures for some relational logics. In: Proceedings of the 25th Italian Conference on Computational Logic, CEUR-WS, vol. 598, Rende, Italy, 7–9 July 2010 (2010)
6. Cantone, D., Nicolosi-Asmundo, M., Orłowska, E.: Dual tableau-based decision procedures for relational logics with restricted composition operator. J. Appl. Non-Classical Logics **21**(2), 177–200 (2011)
7. Cantone, D., Nicolosi-Asmundo, M., Santamaria, D.F.: Conjunctive query answering via a fragment of set theory. In: Proceedings of ICTCS 2016, CEUR-WS, Lecce, 7–9 September, vol. 1720, pp. 23–35 (2016)
8. Cantone, D., Nicolosi-Asmundo, M., Santamaria, D.F.: A set-theoretic approach to ABox reasoning services. CoRR, 1702.03096 (2017). Extended version
9. Cantone, D., Nicolosi-Asmundo, M., Santamaria, D.F., Trapani, F.: Ontoceramic: an OWL ontology for ceramics classification. In Proceedings of CILC 2015, CEUR-WS, vol. 1459, pp. 122–127, Genova, 1–3 July 2015
10. D'Agostino, M.: Tableau methods for classical propositional logic. In: D'Agostino, M., Gabbay, D.M., Hähnle, R., Posegga, J. (eds.) Handbook of Tableau Methods, pp. 45–123. Springer (1999)
11. Horrocks, I., Kutz, O., Sattler, U.: The even more irresistible $\mathcal{SROIQ}$. In: Proceedings of the 10th International Conference on Principles of Knowledge Representation and Reasoning, pp. 57–67. AAAI Press (2006)
12. Motik, B., Horrocks, I.: OWL datatypes: design and implementation. In: Sheth, A., Staab, S., Dean, M., Paolucci, M., Maynard, D., Finin, T., Thirunarayan, K. (eds.) ISWC 2008. LNCS, vol. 5318, pp. 307–322. Springer, Heidelberg (2008). doi:10.1007/978-3-540-88564-1_20
13. Ortiz, M., Sebastian, R., Šimkus, M.: Query answering in the Horn fragments of the description logics $\mathcal{SHOIQ}$ and $\mathcal{SROIQ}$. In: Proceedings of the 22th International Joint Conference on Artificial Intelligence, IJCAI 2011, vol. 2, pp. 1039–1044. AAAI Press (2011)
14. Smullyan, R.M.: First-Order Logic. Springer, Heidelberg (1968)

Verifying Controllability of Time-Aware Business Processes

Emanuele De Angelis[1]([⊠]), Fabio Fioravanti[1], Maria Chiara Meo[1],
Alberto Pettorossi[2], and Maurizio Proietti[3]([⊠])

[1] DEC, University 'G. D'Annunzio', Pescara, Italy
{emanuele.deangelis,fabio.fioravanti,cmeo}@unich.it
[2] DICII, University of Rome Tor Vergata, Rome, Italy
pettorossi@disp.uniroma2.it
[3] IASI-CNR, Rome, Italy
maurizio.proietti@iasi.cnr.it

Abstract. We present an operational semantics for *time-aware* business processes, that is, processes modeling the execution of business activities, whose durations are subject to linear constraints over the integers. We assume that some of the durations are *controllable*, that is, they can be determined by the organization that enacts the process, while others are *uncontrollable*, that is, they are determined by the external world.

Then, we consider *controllability* properties, which guarantee the completion of the enactment of the process, satisfying the given duration constraints, independently of the values of the uncontrollable durations. Controllability properties are encoded by *quantified* reachability formulas, where the reachability predicate is recursively defined by a set of Constrained Horn Clauses (CHCs). These clauses are automatically derived from the operational semantics of the process.

Finally, we present two algorithms for solving the so called *weak* and *strong* controllability problems. Our algorithms reduce these problems to the verification of a set of quantified integer constraints, which are simpler than the original quantified reachability formulas, and can effectively be handled by state-of-the-art CHC solvers.

1 Introduction

A business process model is a procedural, semi-formal specification of the order of execution of the activities in a business process (or BP, for short) and of the way these activities must coordinate to achieve a goal [18,35]. Many notations for BP modeling, and in particular the popular BPMN [26], allow the modeler to express time constraints, such as deadlines and activity durations. However, time related aspects are neglected when the semantics of a BP model is given through the standard Petri Net formalization [18], which focuses on the control

---

This work has been partially funded by INdAM-GNCS (Italy). E. De Angelis, F. Fioravanti, and A. Pettorossi are research associates at IASI-CNR, Rome, Italy.

S. Costantini et al. (Eds.): RuleML+RR 2017, LNCS 10364, pp. 103–118, 2017.
DOI: 10.1007/978-3-319-61252-2_8

flow only. Thus, formal reasoning about time related properties, which may be very important in many analysis tasks, is not possible in that context.

In order to overcome this difficulty, various approaches to BP modeling with time constraints have been proposed in the literature (see [5] for a recent survey). Some of these approaches define the semantics of *time-aware* BP models by means of formalisms such as *time Petri nets* [24], *timed automata* [33], and *process algebras* [36]. Properties of these models can then be verified by using very effective reasoning tools available for those formalisms [3,17,23].

In this paper we address the problem of verifying the *controllability* of time-aware business processes. This notion has been introduced in the context of scheduling and planning problems over *Temporal Networks* [32], but it has not received much attention in the more complex case of time-aware BP models. We assume that some of the durations are *controllable*, that is, they can be determined by the organization that enacts the process, while others are *uncontrollable*, that is, they are determined by the external world. Properties like *strong controllability* and *weak controllability* guarantee, in different senses, that the process can be completed, satisfying the given duration constraints, for all possible values of the uncontrollable durations. Controllability properties are particularly relevant in scenarios (e.g., healthcare applications [9]) where the completion of a process within a certain deadline must be guaranteed even if the durations of some activities cannot be fully determined in advance.

We propose a method for solving controllability problems by extending a logic-based approach that has been recently proposed for modeling and verifying time-aware business processes [11]. This approach represents both the BP structure and the BP behavior in terms of *Constrained Horn Clauses* (CHCs) [4], also known as *Constraint Logic Programs* [19], over Linear Integer Arithmetics. (Here we will use the 'Constrained Horn Clauses' term, which is more common in the area of verification.) In our setting, controllability properties can be defined by *quantified reachability formulas*.

An advantage of the logic-based approach over other approaches is that it allows a seamless integration of the various reasoning tasks needed to analyze business processes from different perspectives. For instance, logic-based techniques can easily perform ontology-related reasoning about the business domain where processes are enacted [29,34] and reasoning on the manipulation of data objects of an infinite type, such as databases or integers [2,10,28]. Moreover, for the various logic-based reasoning tasks, we can make use of very effective tools such as CHC solvers [15] and Constraint Logic Programming systems.

For reasons of simplicity, in this paper we consider business process models where the only time-related elements are constraints over task durations. However, other notions can be modeled by following a similar approach.

The main contributions of this paper are the following. (1) We define an operational semantics of time-aware BP models, which modifies the semantics presented in [11] by formalizing the synchronization of activities at parallel merge gateways and we prove some properties of this new semantics (see Sect. 3). Our semantics is defined under the assumption that the process is *safe*, that is, during its enactment there are no multiple, concurrent executions of the same task [1]. (2) We provide formal definitions of strong and weak controllability properties as quantified reachability formulas (see Sect. 4). (3) We present a transformation technique for automatically deriving the CHC representation of the reachability relation starting from the CHC encoding of the semantics of time-aware processes, and of the process and property under consideration (see Sect. 4). (4) Finally, we propose two algorithms that solve strong and weak controllability problems for time-aware BPs. These algorithms avoid the direct verification of quantified reachability formulas, which often cannot be handled by state-of-the-art CHC solvers, and they verify, instead, a set of simpler Linear Integer Arithmetic formulas, whose satisfiability can effectively be worked out by the Z3 constraint solver [15] (see Sect. 5). Detailed proofs of the results presented here can be found in a technical report [12].

2 Preliminaries

In this section we recall some basic notions about the constrained Horn clauses (CHCs) and the Business Process Model and Notation (BPMN).

Let $RelOp$ be the set $\{=, \neq, \leq, \geq, <, >\}$ of predicate symbols denoting the familiar relational operators over the integers. If p_1 and p_2 are linear polynomials with integer variables and integer coefficients, then $p_1 R p_2$, with $R \in RelOp$, is an *atomic constraint*. A *constraint* c is either *true* or *false* or an atomic constraint or a conjunction or a disjunction of constraints. Thus, constraints are formulas of Linear Integer Arithmetics (LIA). An *atom* is a formula of the form $p(t_1, \ldots, t_m)$, where p is a predicate symbol not in $RelOp$ and $t_1, \ldots, t_m$ are terms constructed as usual from variables, constants, and function symbols. A *constrained Horn clause* (or simply, a *clause*, or a CHC) is an implication of the form $A \leftarrow c, G$ (comma denotes conjunction), where the conclusion (or *head*) A is either an atom or *false*, the premise (or *body*) is the conjunction of a constraint c and a (possibly empty) conjunction G of atoms. The empty conjunction is identified with *true*. A *constrained fact* is a clause of the form $A \leftarrow c$, and a *fact* is a clause whose premise is *true*. We will write $A \leftarrow true$ also as $A \leftarrow$. A clause is *ground* if no variable occurs in it. A clause $A \leftarrow c, G$ is said to be *function-free* if no function symbol occurs in (A, G), while arithmetic function symbols may occur in c. For clauses we will use a Prolog-like syntax (in particular, '_' stands for an anonymous variable).

A set S of CHCs is said to be *satisfiable* if $S \cup LIA$ has a model, or equivalently, $S \cup LIA \not\models false$. Given two constraints c and d, we write $c \sqsubseteq d$ if $LIA \models \forall(c \rightarrow d)$, where $\forall(F)$ denotes the universal closure of formula F. The *projection* of a constraint c onto a set X of variables is a new constraint c', with variables in X, which is equivalent, in the domain of *rational* numbers, to $\exists Y.c$, where Y is the set of variables occurring in c and not in X. Clearly, $c \sqsubseteq c'$.

A BPMN model of a business process consists of a diagram drawn by using graphical notations representing: (i) *flow objects* and (ii) *sequence flows* (also called *flows*, for short).

A flow object is: either (i.1) a *task*, depicted as a rounded rectangle, or (i.2) an *event*, depicted as a circle, or (i.3) a *gateway*, depicted as a diamond. A sequence flow is depicted as an arrow connecting a source flow object to a target flow object (see Fig. 1).

Tasks are atomic units of work performed during the enactment (or execution) of the business process. An events is either a *start* event or an *end* event, which denote the beginning and the completion, respectively, of the activities of the process. Gateways denote the branching or the merging of activities. In this paper we consider the following four kinds of gateways: (a) the *parallel branch*, that simultaneously activates all the outgoing flows, if its single incoming flow is activated (see $g1$ in Fig. 1), (b) the *exclusive branch*, that (non-deterministically) activates exactly one out of its outgoing flows, if its single incoming flow is activated (see $g3$ in Fig. 1), (c) the *parallel merge*, that activates the single outgoing flow, if all the incoming flows are simultaneously activated (see $g4$ in Fig. 1), and (d) the *exclusive merge*, that activates the single outgoing flow, if any one of the incoming flows is activated (see $g2$ in Fig. 1). The diamonds representing parallel gateways and exclusive gateways are labeled by '+' and 'X', respectively. Branch and merge gateways are also called *split* and *join* gateways, respectively.

A sequence flow denotes that the execution of the process can pass from the source object to the target object. If there is a sequence flow from a_1 to a_2, then a_1 is a *predecessor* of a_2, and symmetrically, a_2 is a *successor* of a_1. A *path* is a sequence of flow objects such that every pair of consecutive objects in the sequence is connected by a sequence flow.

We will consider models of business processes that are *well-formed*, in the sense that they satisfy the following properties: (1) every business process contains a single start event and a single end event, (2) the start event has exactly one successor and no predecessors, and the end event has exactly one predecessor and no successors, (3) every flow object occurs on a path from the start event to the end event, (4) (parallel or exclusive) branch gateways have exactly one predecessor and at least one successor, while (parallel or exclusive) merge gateways have at least one predecessor and exactly one successor, (5) tasks have exactly one predecessor and one successor, and (6) no cycles through gateways only are allowed. Note that we do not require BP models to be block-structured.

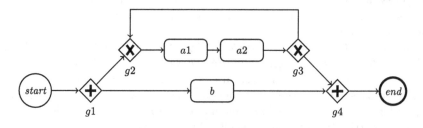

Fig. 1. A business process *Proc.*

In Fig. 1 we show the BPMN model of a business process, called *Proc*. After the *start* event, the parallel branch $g1$ simultaneously activates the two flow objects $g2$ and b. The exclusive merge $g2$ activates the sequential execution of the task $a1$ which in turn activates the execution of the task $a2$ which is followed by the exclusive branch $g3$. After $g3$, the execution can either return to $g2$ or proceed to $g4$. If $g3$ and b both complete their executions simultaneously, then the parallel merge $g4$ is executed, the *end* event occurs, and the process *Proc* terminates.

3   Specification and Semantics of Business Processes

In this section we introduce the notion of a *Business Process Specification* (BPS), which formally represents a business process by means of CHCs. Then we define the operational semantics of a BPS.

Business Process Specification via CHCs. A BPS contains: (i) a set of ground facts that specify the flow objects and the sequence flows between them, and (ii) a set of clauses that specify the duration of each flow object and the controllability (or uncontrollability) of that duration.

For the flow objects we will use of the following predicates: $task(X)$, $event(X)$, $gateway(X)$, $par\_branch(X)$, $par\_merge(X)$, $exc\_branch(X)$, $exc\_merge(X)$ with the expected meaning. For the sequence flows we will use the predicate $seq(X, Y)$ meaning that there is a sequence flow from X to Y. For every task X we specify its duration by the constrained fact $duration(X, D) \leftarrow d_{min} \leq D \leq d_{max}$, where d_{min} and d_{max} are positive integer constants representing the minimal and the maximal duration of X, respectively. Events and gateways, being instantaneous, have duration 0. For every task X and its duration, we also specify that they are controllable, or uncontrollable, by the fact $controllable(X) \leftarrow$, or $uncontrollable(X) \leftarrow$, respectively.

In Fig. 2 we show the BPS of process *Proc* of Fig. 1. For reasons of space, in that specification we did not list all the facts for the tasks, events, gateways, and sequence flows of the diagram of *Proc*.

$task(a1) \leftarrow$ $event(start) \leftarrow$ $gateway(g1) \leftarrow$ $\ldots$
$par\_branch(g1) \leftarrow$ $seq(start, g1) \leftarrow$ $seq(g1, b) \leftarrow$ $\ldots$
$uncontrollable(a1) \leftarrow$ $controllable(a2) \leftarrow$ $controllable(b) \leftarrow$
$duration(a1, D) \leftarrow 2 \leq D \leq 4$ $duration(a2, D) \leftarrow 1 \leq D \leq 2$ $duration(b, D) \leftarrow 5 \leq D \leq 6$
$duration(X, D) \leftarrow event(X), D = 0$ $duration(X, D) \leftarrow gateway(X), D = 0$

Fig. 2. The CHCs of the Business Process Specification of process *Proc* of Fig. 1.

Operational Semantics. We define the operational semantics of a business process under the assumption that the process is *safe*, that is, during its enactment there are no multiple, concurrent executions of the same flow object [1].

By using this assumption, we represent the *state* of a process enactment as a set of properties, called *fluents* holding at a time instant. We borrow the notion of fluent from *action languages* such as the *Situation Calculus* [25], the *Event Calculus* [20], or the *Fluent Calculus* [30], but we will present our semantics by following the *structural operational* approach often adopted in the field of programming languages.

Formally, a state $s \in States$ is a pair $\langle F, t \rangle$, where F is a set of fluents and t is a time instant, that is, a non-negative integer. A fluent is a term of the form: (i) $begins(x)$, which represents the beginning of the enactment of the flow object x, (ii) $completes(x)$, which represents the completion of the enactment of x, (iii) $enables(x, y)$, which represents that the flow object x has completed its enactment and it enables the enactment of its successor y, and (iv) $enacting(x, r)$, which represents that the enactment of x requires r units of time to complete (for this reason r is called the *residual time* of x). We have that $begins(x)$ is equivalent to $enacting(x, r)$, where r is the duration of x, and $completes(x)$ is equivalent to $enacting(x, 0)$. (This redundant representation allows us to write simpler rules for the operational semantics below.)

The operational semantics is defined by a rewriting relation $\longrightarrow$ which is a subset of $States \times States$. This relation is specified by rules S_1–S_7 below, where we use the following predicates, besides the ones introduced in Sect. 3 for defining the BPS: (i) $not\_par\_branch(x)$, which holds if x is *not* a parallel branch, and (ii) $not\_par\_merge(x)$, which holds if x is *not* a parallel merge.

$$(S_1) \quad \frac{begins(x) \in F \qquad duration(x, d)}{\langle F, t \rangle \longrightarrow \langle (F \setminus \{begins(x)\}) \cup \{enacting(x, d)\}, \ t \rangle}$$

$$(S_2) \quad \frac{completes(x) \in F \qquad par\_branch(x)}{\langle F, t \rangle \longrightarrow \langle (F \setminus \{completes(x)\}) \cup \{enables(x, s) \mid seq(x, s)\}, \ t \rangle}$$

$$(S_3) \quad \frac{completes(x) \in F \qquad not\_par\_branch(x) \qquad seq(x, s)}{\langle F, t \rangle \longrightarrow \langle (F \setminus \{completes(x)\}) \cup \{enables(x, s)\}, \ t \rangle}$$

$$(S_4) \quad \frac{\forall p \ seq(p, x) \rightarrow enables(p, x) \in F \qquad par\_merge(x)}{\langle F, t \rangle \longrightarrow \langle (F \setminus \{enables(p, x) \mid enables(p, x) \in F\}) \cup \{begins(x)\}, \ t \rangle}$$

$$(S_5) \quad \frac{enables(p, x) \in F \qquad not\_par\_merge(x)}{\langle F, t \rangle \longrightarrow \langle (F \setminus \{enables(p, x)\}) \cup \{begins(x)\}, \ t \rangle}$$

$$(S_6) \quad \frac{enacting(x, 0) \in F}{\langle F, t \rangle \longrightarrow \langle (F \setminus \{enacting(x, 0)\}) \cup \{completes(x)\}, \ t \rangle}$$

$$(S_7) \quad \frac{no\_other\_premises(F) \qquad \exists x \ \exists r \ enacting(x, r) \in F \qquad m > 0}{\langle F, t \rangle \longrightarrow \langle F \ominus m \setminus Enbls, \ t + m \rangle}$$

where: (i) *no_other_premises*(F) holds iff none of the premises of rules S_1–S_6 holds, (ii) $m = min\{r \mid enacting(x,r) \in F\}$, (iii) $F \ominus m$ is the set F of fluents where every *enacting*(x,r) is replaced by *enacting*$(x,r-m)$, and (iv) *Enbls* = $\{enables(p,s) \mid enables(p,s) \in F\}$.

We assume that, for every flow object x, there exists a *unique* value d of its duration, satisfying the given constraint, which is used for *every* application of rule S_1. Note that S_7 is the only rule that formalizes the passing of time, as it infers rewritings of the form $\langle F,t \rangle \longrightarrow \langle F',t+m \rangle$, with $m > 0$. In contrast, rules S_1–S_6 infer state rewritings of the form $\langle F,t \rangle \longrightarrow \langle F',t \rangle$, where time does not pass. Here is the explanation of rules S_1–S_7.

(S_1) If the execution of a flow object x begins at time t, then, at the same time t, x is enacting and its residual time is its duration d;

(S_2) If the execution of the parallel branch x completes at time t, then x enables *all its successors* at time t;

(S_3) If the execution of x completes at time t and x is not a parallel branch, then x enables *precisely one of its successors* at time t (in particular, this case occurs when x is a task);

(S_4) If *all* the predecessors of x enable the parallel merge x at time t, then the execution of x begins at time t;

(S_5) If *at least one* predecessor p of x enables x at time t and x is not a parallel merge, then the execution of x begins at time t (in particular, this case occurs when x is a task);

(S_6) If a flow object x is enacting at time t with residual time 0, then the execution of x completes at the same time t;

(S_7) Suppose that: (i) none of rules S_1–S_6 can be applied for computing a state rewriting $\langle F,t \rangle \longrightarrow \langle F',t' \rangle$, (ii) at time t at least one task is enacting with *positive* residual time (note that flow objects different from tasks cannot have positive residual time), and (iii) m is the least value among the residual times of all the tasks enacting at time t. Then, (i) every task x that is enacting at time t with residual time r, is enacting at time $t+m$ with residual time $r-m$ and (ii) all *enables*(p,s) fluents are removed.

Due to rules S_4 and S_5, if a fluent of the form *enables*(p,s) is removed by applying rule S_7, then s necessarily refers to a parallel merge that is not enabled at time t by some of its predecessors. Thus, a parallel merge is executed if and only if it gets *simultaneously* enabled by all its predecessors. For lack of space we omit to model the asynchronous version of the parallel merge [11], which does not require the simultaneity condition. Note also that, if desired, tasks can be added for modeling delays in an explicit way.

We say that state $\langle F',t' \rangle$ is *reachable* from state $\langle F,t \rangle$, if $\langle F,t \rangle \longrightarrow^* \langle F',t' \rangle$, where $\longrightarrow^*$ denotes the reflexive, transitive closure of the rewriting relation $\longrightarrow$.

The *initial state* is the state $\langle \{begins(start)\}, 0 \rangle$. The *final state* is the state of the form $\langle \{completes(end)\}, t \rangle$, for some time instant t.

Properties of the Operational Semantics. Now we first introduce the notions of: (i) a derivation, which is a sequence of states, and (ii) a selection function, which is a rule providing the order in which fluents are rewritten according to the relation $\longrightarrow$. In Theorem 1 below we will prove that the relation $\longrightarrow$ is independent of that order.

Definition 1 (Derivation). *A derivation from a state s_0 in a BPS is a (possibly infinite) sequence of states $s_0, s_1, s_2, \ldots$ such that for all $i \geq 0$, $s_i \longrightarrow s_{i+1}$.*

Let *States$_{sat}$* be the subset of *States* where *no_other_premises(F)* holds.

Definition 2 (Selection function). *Let δ be a finite derivation whose last state is $\langle F, t \rangle$, with $F \neq \emptyset$. A selection function $\mathcal{R}$ is a function that takes the derivation δ and returns: either (i) a subset of F whose elements satisfy the conditions in the premise of exactly one rule among S_1–S_6, or (ii) the union of the set of the 'enacting' fluents in F and the set of the 'enables' fluents in F, if $\langle F, t \rangle \in States_{sat}$ and at least one 'enacting' fluent belongs to F.*

The selection function is well-defined, because each fluent can be rewritten by at the most one rule and the rules S_1–S_6 are not overlapping, that is, the sets of fluents which can fire two distinct rules in S_1–S_6 (or two different instances of the same rule) are disjoint.

Definition 3 (Derivation via $\mathcal{R}$). *Given a selection function $\mathcal{R}$, we say that a derivation δ is via $\mathcal{R}$ iff for each proper prefix δ' of δ ending with a state s, if $s \longrightarrow s'$ and $(\delta' s')$ is a prefix of δ, then $\mathcal{R}(\delta')$ are the fluents of s that are rewritten when deriving s'.*

Theorem 1. *For every derivation δ from a state s_0, and selection function $\mathcal{R}$, there exists a derivation δ' from s_0 via $\mathcal{R}$ such that if $\langle F, t \rangle$ is a state in δ and f is a fluent in F, then there exists a state $\langle F', t \rangle$ in δ' such that f is a fluent in F'.*

4   Encoding Controllability Properties into CHCs

In this section we show how weak and strong controllability properties are formalized by defining a CHC *interpreter*, that is, a set of CHCs that encodes the operational semantics of business processes. Then, the interpreter is *specialized* with respect to the business process and property to be verified.

A CHC Interpreter for Time-Aware Business Processes. A state of the operational semantics is encoded by a term of the form $s(F, T)$, where F is a set of fluents and T is the time instant at which the fluents in F hold. The rewriting relation $\longrightarrow$ between states and its reflexive, transitive closure $\longrightarrow^*$ are encoded by the predicates *tr* and *reach*, respectively. The clauses defining these predicates are shown in Table 1. In the body of the clauses, the atoms that encode the premises of the rules of the operational semantics have been underlined.

The predicate $select(L, F)$ encodes a selection function (see Definition 2). We assume that $select(L, F)$ holds iff L is a subset of the set F of fluents such that: (i) there exists a clause in $\{C1, \ldots, C6\}$ that updates F by replacing the subset L of F by a new set of fluents, and (ii) among all such subsets of F, L is the one that contains the first fluent, in textual order (in this sense $select(L, F)$ is deterministic). The predicate $task\_duration(X, D, U, C)$ holds iff $duration(X, D)$ holds and D belongs to either the list U of durations of the uncontrollable tasks or the list C of durations of the controllable tasks. The predicate $update(F, R, A, FU)$ holds iff FU is the set obtained from the set F by removing all the elements of R and adding all the elements of A. The predicate $no\_other\_premises(F)$ holds iff the premise of every rule in $\{C1, \ldots, C6\}$ is unsatisfiable. The predicate $mintime(Enacts, M)$ holds iff $Enacts$ is a set of fluents of the form $enacting(X, R)$ and M is the minimum value of R for the elements of $Enacts$. The predicate $decrease\_residual\_times(Enacts, M, EnactsU)$ holds iff $EnactsU$ is the set of fluents obtained by replacing every element of $Enacts$, of the form $enacting(X, R)$, with the fluent $enacting(X, RU)$, where $RU = R - M$. The predicates $member(El, Set)$ and $set\_union(A, B, AB)$ are self-explanatory. The predicate $findall(X, G, L)$ holds iff X is a term whose variables occur in the conjunction G of atoms, and L is the set of instances of X such that $\exists Y. G$ holds, where Y is the tuple of variables occurring in G different from those in X.

We denote by Sem the set consisting of clauses $C1, \ldots, C7, R1, R2$, together with the clauses encoding the business process specification.

Theorem 2 (Correctness of Encoding). *Let init be the term that encodes the initial state $\langle \{begins(start)\}, 0 \rangle$, and fin(t) be the term that encodes the final state $\langle \{completes(end)\}, t \rangle$. Then, $\langle \{begins(start)\}, 0 \rangle \longrightarrow^* \langle \{completes(end)\}, t \rangle$ iff there exist tuples of integers x and y such that $Sem \cup LIA \models reach(init, fin(t), x, y)$.*

A *reachability property* is defined by a clause of the form:

$RP.\ reachProp(U, C) \leftarrow c(T, U, C),\ reach(init,\ fin(T),\ U,\ C)$

where: (i) U and C denote tuples of uncontrollable and controllable durations, respectively, and (ii) $c(T, U, C)$ is a constraint.

We say that the duration D of task X is *admissible* iff $duration(X, D)$ holds. The *strong controllability* problem for a BPS consists in checking whether or not there exist durations C such that, for all admissible durations U, the property $reachProp(U, C)$ holds. The *weak controllability* problem for a BPS consists in checking whether or not, for all admissible durations U, there exist durations C such that $reachProp(U, C)$ holds. Note that, if $reachProp(U, C)$ holds, then all durations used to reach the final state are admissible, and hence in the definition of controllability there is no need to require that the existentially quantified durations C are admissible. We denote by I the set $Sem \cup \{RP\}$.

Definition 4 (Strong and weak controllability). *Given a BPS $\mathcal{B}$,*

- *$\mathcal{B}$ is strongly controllable iff $I \cup LIA \models \exists C \forall U.\ adm(U) \rightarrow reachProp(U, C)$*

Table 1. The CHC interpreter for time-aware business processes.

$C1.\,tr(s(F,T),s(FU,T),U,C) \leftarrow \underline{select(\{begins(X)\},F)},\ task\_duration(X,D,U,C),$
$update(F,\{begins(X)\},\{enacting(X,D)\},FU)$

$C2.\,tr(s(F,T),s(FU,T),U,C) \leftarrow \underline{select(\{completes(X)\},F)},\ \underline{par\_branch(X)},$
$findall(enables(X,S),(seq(X,S)),Enbls),\ update(F,\{completes(X)\},Enbls,FU)$

$C3.\,tr(s(F,T),s(FU,T),U,C) \leftarrow \underline{select(\{completes(X)\},F)},\ \underline{not\_par\_branch(X)},\ seq(X,S),$
$update(F,\{completes(X)\},\{enables(X,S)\},FU)$

$C4.\,tr(s(F,T),s(FU,T),U,C) \leftarrow \underline{select(Enbls,F)},\ \underline{par\_merge(X)},$
$findall(enables(P,X),(seq(P,X)),Enbls),\ update(F,Enbls,\{begins(X)\},FU)$

$C5.\,tr(s(F,T),s(FU,T),U,C) \leftarrow \underline{select(\{enables(P,X)\},F)},\ \underline{not\_par\_merge(X)},$
$update(F,\{enables(P,X)\},\{begins(X)\},FU)$

$C6.\,tr(s(F,T),s(FU,T),U,C) \leftarrow \underline{select(\{enacting(X,R)\},F)},\ R{=}0,$
$update(F,\{enacting(X,R)\},\{completes(X)\},FU)$

$C7.\,tr(s(F,T),s(FU,TU),U,C) \leftarrow \underline{no\_other\_premises(F)},\ \underline{member(enacting(\_,\_),F)},$
$findall(Y,(Y{=}enacting(X,R),\ member(Y,F)),Enacts),$
$mintime(Enacts,M),\ \underline{M{>}0},\ decrease\_residual\_times(Enacts,M,EnactsU),$
$findall(Z,(Z{=}enables(P,S),member(Z,F)),Enbls),$
$set\_union(Enacts,Enbls,EnactsEnbls),\ update(F,EnactsEnbls,EnactsU,FU),$
$TU{=}T{+}M$

$R1.\,reach(S,S,U,C).$
$R2.\,reach(S,S2,U,C) \leftarrow tr(S,S1,U,C),\ reach(S1,S2,U,C)$

- $\mathcal{B}$ is weakly controllable iff $I \cup LIA \models \forall U.\,adm(U) \rightarrow \exists C\ reachProp(U,C)$
  where $adm(U)$ holds iff U is a tuple of admissible durations.

If a business process is weakly controllable, in order to determine the durations of the controllable tasks, we need to know in advance the actual durations of all the uncontrollable tasks. This might not be realistic in practice, as uncontrollable tasks may occur after controllable ones. Strong controllability implies weak controllability and guarantees that suitable durations of the controllable tasks can be computed, before the enactment of the process, by using the constraints on the uncontrollable durations, which are provided by the process specification.

Specializing the CHC Interpreter. The clauses in I make use of complex terms, and in particular lists of variable length, to represent states (see clauses $C1$–$C7$). However, I can be specialized to the particular BPS under consideration and transformed into an equivalent set I_{sp} of function-free CHCs, on which CHC solvers are much more effective. The specialization transformation is a variant of the ones for the so called *Removal of the Interpreter* proposed in the area of verification of imperative programs [14], and makes use of the following transformation rules: *unfolding, definition introduction,* and *folding* [16].

The specialization transformation (see [12] for details) starts off by unfolding clause RP, thereby performing a symbolic exploration of the space of the reachable states. The unfolding rule is defined as follows.

Unfolding Rule. Let C be a clause of the form $H \leftarrow c, L, A, R$, where A is an atom. Let $\{K_i \leftarrow c_i, B_i \mid i = 1, \ldots, m\}$ be the set of the (renamed apart) clauses in I such that, for $i = 1, \ldots, m$, A is unifiable with K_i via the most general unifier ϑ_i and $(c, c_i)\,\vartheta_i$ is satisfiable. Then, from C we derive the following set of clauses: $\{(H \leftarrow c, c_i, L, B_i, R)\,\vartheta_i \mid i = 1, \ldots, m\}$.

After unfolding, by applying the definition rule, for every *reach* atom occurring in the body of a clause, a new predicate is introduced by a clause of the form:

$$newr(Rs, T, Tf, U, C) \leftarrow f(Rs),\ reach(s(\mathit{fl}(Rs), T), \mathit{fin}(Tf), U, C)$$

where $f(Rs)$ is a constraint obtained by projecting the constraint occurring in the body of the clause where the *reach* atom occurs, onto the tuple Rs of variables representing the residual times, and $\mathit{fl}(Rs)$ denotes the set of fluents that hold at time T. Then, by applying the folding rule, *reach* atoms with complex arguments representing states (i.e., $reach(s(\mathit{fl}(Rs), T), \mathit{fin}(Tf), U, C)$), are replaced by function-free calls to the newly introduced predicates (i.e., $newr(Rs, T, Tf, U, C)$). The unfolding-definition-folding transformations are repeated until we derive a set I_{sp} of function-free CHCs. Since the unfolding, definition introduction, and folding rules preserve satisfiability [16], we have the following result.

Theorem 3 (Correctness of Specialization). *Every set I of CHCs encoding a reachability property of a BPS can be transformed into a set I_{sp} of CHCs such that: (i) I_{sp} is a set of function-free CHCs, and (ii) for all (tuples of) integer values x and y, $I \cup LIA \models reachProp(x, y)$ iff $I_{sp} \cup LIA \models reachProp(x, y)$.*

Example 1. Let I be the set of clauses defining the reachability property for the process *Proc* of Fig. 1, and let clause RP be:

$$reachProp(A1, A2, B) \leftarrow reach(init, \mathit{fin}(T), A1, (A2, B))$$

where $A1$ denotes the duration of the uncontrollable task $a1$ and $(A2, B)$ denotes the durations of the controllable tasks $a2$ and b. By applying the specialization transformation to I, we derive the following function-free clauses:

$reachProp(A1,A2,B) \leftarrow A=A1, B=B1, A1 \geq 2, A1 \leq 4, B \geq 5, B \leq 6,$
$\qquad new2(A, B1, F, G, A1, A2, B)$
$new2(A,B1,C,D,A1,A2,B) \leftarrow H=A+C, I=B1-A, J=0, A \geq 1, I \geq 0, A+I \geq 1,$
$\qquad new2(J, I, H, D, A1, A2, B)$
$new2(A,B1,C,D,A1,A2,B) \leftarrow H=B1+C, I=A-B1, J=0, A \geq 1, I \geq 0, A-I \geq 1,$
$\qquad new2(I,J,H,D,A1,A2,B)$
$new2(A,B1,C,D,A1,A2,B) \leftarrow H=A2, A=0, H \geq 1, H \leq 2,\ new5(H,B1,C,D,A1,A2,B)$
$new5(A,B1,C,C,A1,A2,B) \leftarrow A=0, B1=0$
$new5(A,B1,C,D,A1,A2,B) \leftarrow H=A+C, I=B1-A, J=0, A \geq 1, I \geq 0, A+I \geq 1,$
$\qquad new5(J,I,H,D,A1,A2,B)$
$new5(A,B1,C,D,A1,A2,B) \leftarrow H=B1+C, I=A-B1, J=0, A \geq 1, I \geq 0, A-I \geq 1,$
$\qquad new5(I,J,H,D,A1,A2,B)$
$new5(A,B1,C,D,A1,A2,B) \leftarrow H=A1, A=0, H \geq 2, H \leq 4,\ new2(H,B1,C,D,A1,A2,B)$

5   Solving Controllability Problems

State-of-the-art CHC solvers are often not effective in solving controllability problems defined by a direct encoding of the formulas in Definition 4, where nested universal and existential quantifiers occur. The main problem is that performing quantifier elimination on formulas defined by, possibly recursive, Constrained Horn Clauses is very expensive, and often unsuccessful. Thus, we propose an alternative method that is based on verifying a series of simpler properties, where quantification is restricted to LIA constraints.

We assume the existence of a solver that is sound and complete for Horn clauses with LIA constraints. The solver interface is a procedure $solve(P, Q)$ such that, for any set P of CHCs and for any *query* Q, which is a conjunction of atoms and LIA constraints, returns an *answer* A, that is, a satisfiable constraint A such that $P \models \forall(A \rightarrow Q)$, if such an answer exists, and *false* otherwise.

The method we propose solves controllability problems by looking for a satisfiable constraint $a(U, C)$, where U and C are tuples of variables denoting the durations of the uncontrollable and controllable tasks, respectively, such that $I \cup LIA \models \forall U \, \forall C. \, a(U, C) \rightarrow reachProp(U, C)$ and either
(†) $LIA \models \exists C \, \forall U. \, adm(U) \rightarrow a(U, C)$ (for strong controllability), or
(‡) $LIA \models \forall U. \, adm(U) \rightarrow \exists C. \, a(U, C)$ (for weak controllability).

In particular, we introduce the Strong and Weak Controllability algorithms (SC and WC for short, respectively) that, given a set of function-free CHCs defining $reachProp(U, C)$ (that is, a set of clauses generated by the specialization transformation of Sect. 4), produce a solution for the controllability problem by constructing $a(U, C)$ as a disjunction of the answer constraints provided by the solver until either condition (†) holds (respectively, condition (‡) holds) or there are no more answers (see Fig. 3). In order to avoid repeated answers, at each iteration of the *do-while* loop, the solver is invoked on a query containing the negation of the (disjunction of the) answers obtained so far.[1]

Since the durations of the tasks belong to finite integer intervals, the set of answers that can be returned by the *solve* procedure is finite. Hence the SC and WC algorithms always terminate. The following theorem states that SC and WC are sound and complete methods for solving strong and weak controllability problems, respectively.

Theorem 4 (Soundness and Completeness of SC and WC). *Let I be a set of CHCs defining a reachability property for a BPS $\mathcal{B}$. Then,*
(i) SC returns a satisfiable constraint if and only if $\mathcal{B}$ is strongly controllable
(ii) WC returns a satisfiable constraint if and only if $\mathcal{B}$ is weakly controllable.

We now illustrate how the WC algorithm works by applying it to the clauses obtained by specialization in Example 1. During the first iteration of the *do-while* loop the CHC solver is invoked by executing $solve(I, reachProp(A1, A2, B) \wedge \forall A2, B.\neg false)$, which returns the answer constraint $a1(A1, A2, B)$: $A1 \geq B - 2$,

---

[1] In WC we introduce a small optimization by using a query that avoids obtaining multiple answers with the same values of U.

Input: A set I of CHCs defining a reachability property.
Output: A satisfiable constraint $a(U, C)$, if the process is (strongly or weakly) controllable; *false* otherwise.

SC: *Strong Controllability*	WC: *Weak Controllability*
$a(U, C) := false$	$a(U, C) := false$
do {	*do* {
$\quad Q := (reachProp(U, C) \wedge \neg a(U, C));$	$\quad Q := (reachProp(U, C) \wedge \forall C. \neg a(U, C));$
$\quad$ *if* $(solve(I, Q) = false)$ *return false;*	$\quad$ *if* $(solve(I, Q) = false)$ *return false;*
$\quad a(U, C) := a(U, C) \vee solve(I, Q);$	$\quad a(U, C) := a(U, C) \vee solve(I, Q);$
} *while* $(LIA \not\models \exists C \, \forall U. \, adm(U) \to a(U, C))$	} *while* $(LIA \not\models \forall U. \, adm(U) \to \exists C. \, a(U, C))$
return $a(U, C);$	*return* $a(U, C);$

Fig. 3. The SC and WC algorithms for verifying strong and weak controllability.

$A1 \leq 4, A2 = B - A1, B \geq 5, B \leq 6$. In our example, the constraint $adm(A1)$ is $A1 \geq 2, A1 \leq 4$. Now we have that $LIA \not\models \forall A1. \, adm(A1) \to \exists A2, B. \, a1(A1, A2, B)$, and hence the algorithm executes the second iteration of the *do-while* loop. Next, the CHC solver is invoked by executing $solve(I, reachProp(A1, A2, B) \wedge \forall A2, B. \neg a1(A1, A2, B))$, which returns the answer constraint $a2(A1, A2, B)$: $A1 = 2, A2 = 1, B = 6$. Now the condition of the *do-while* loop is false, because $LIA \models \forall A1. \, adm(A1) \to \exists A2, B. \, (a1(A1, A2, B) \vee a2(A1, A2, B))$. Thus, the WC algorithm terminates and we can conclude that the considered weak controllability property holds.

We have used the VERIMAP transformation and verification system for CHCs [13] to implement the specialization transformation of Sect. 4, and SICStus Prolog and the Z3 solver to implement the SC and WC algorithms. We have applied our method to verify the weak controllability of the process *Proc*. The timings are as follows[2]: the execution of the specialization transformation requires 0.04 s and the execution of the WC algorithm requires 0.03 s.

We have also solved controllability problems for other small-sized processes, not shown here for reasons of space, whose reachability relation, like the one for process *Proc*, contains cycles that may generate an unbounded proof search, and hence may cause nontermination if not handled in an appropriate way. In particular, in all the examples we have considered, we noticed that Z3 is not able to provide a proof within a time limit of one hour for a direct encoding of the controllability properties as they are formulated in Definition 4.

6 Related Work and Conclusions

Controllability problems arise in all contexts where the duration of some tasks in a business process cannot be determined in advance by the process designer. We

---

[2] The experiments have been performed on an Intel Core Duo E7300 2.66 Ghz processor with 4GB of memory under GNU/Linux OS.

have presented a method for checking strong and weak controllability properties of business processes. The method is based upon well-established techniques and tools in the field of computational logic.

Modeling and reasoning about time in the field of business process management has been largely investigated in the recent years [5]. The notion of controllability, extensively studied in the context of scheduling and planning problems over temporal networks [6–8,27,31,32], has been considered as a useful concept for supporting decisions in business process management and design [9,21,22].

Algorithms for checking strong and weak controllability properties were first introduced for Simple Temporal Networks with Uncertainty [32]. Later, sound and complete algorithms were developed for both strong [27] and weak [31] controllability of Disjunctive Temporal Problems with Uncertainty (DTPU). More recently, a general and effective method for checking strong [7] and weak [8] controllability of DTPU's via SMT has been developed.

The task of verifying controllability of BP models we have addressed in this paper is similar to the task of checking controllability of temporal workflows addressed by Combi and Posenato [9]. These authors present a workflow conceptual framework that allows the designer to use temporal constructs to express duration, delays, relative, absolute, and periodic constraints. The durations of tasks are uncontrollable, while the delays between tasks are controllable. The controllability problem, which arises from relative constraints that limit the duration of two non-consecutive tasks, consists in checking whether or not the delays between tasks enforce the relative constraints for all possible durations of tasks. The special purpose algorithms for checking controllability presented in [9] enumerate all possible choices, and therefore are computationally expensive.

Our approach to controllability of BP models exhibits several differences with respect to the one considered by Combi and Posenato in [9]. In our approach the designer has the possibility of explicitly specifying controllable and uncontrollable durations. We also consider workflows with minimal restrictions on the control flow, and unlike the framework in [9], we admit loops. We automatically generate the clauses to be verified from the formal semantics of the BP model, thus making our framework easily extensible to other classes of processes and properties. Finally, we propose concrete algorithms for checking both strong and weak controllability, based on off-the-shelf CHC specializers and solvers.

As future work we plan to perform an extensive experimental evaluation of our method and to apply our approach to extensions of time-aware BP models, whose properties also depend on the manipulation of data objects.

References

1. van der Aalst, W.M.P.: The application of Petri nets to workflow management. J. Circ. Syst. Comput. **8**(1), 21–66 (1998)
2. Bagheri Hariri, B., Calvanese, D., De Giacomo, G., Deutsch, A., Montali, M.: Verification of relational data-centric dynamic systems with external services. In: Proceedings of the (PODS 2013), pp. 163–174. ACM (2013)

3. Berthomieu, B., Vernadat, F.: Time Petri nets analysis with TINA. In: Proceedings of QEST 2006, pp. 123–124. IEEE Computer Society (2006)

4. Bjørner, N., Gurfinkel, A., McMillan, K., Rybalchenko, A.: Horn clause solvers for program verification. In: Beklemishev, L.D., Blass, A., Dershowitz, N., Finkbeiner, B., Schulte, W. (eds.) Fields of Logic and Computation II. LNCS, vol. 9300, pp. 24–51. Springer, Cham (2015). doi:10.1007/978-3-319-23534-9_2

5. Cheikhrouhou, S., Kallel, S., Guermouche, N., Jmaiel, M.: The temporal perspective in business process modeling: a survey and research challenges. Serv. Oriented Comput. Appl. **9**(1), 75–85 (2015)

6. Cimatti, A., Hunsberger, L., Micheli, A., Posenato, R., Roveri, M.: Dynamic controllability via timed game automata. Acta Informatica **53**(6), 681–722 (2016)

7. Cimatti, A., Micheli, A., Roveri, M.: Solving strong controllability of temporal problems with uncertainty using SMT. Constraints **20**(1), 1–29 (2015)

8. Cimatti, A., Micheli, A., Roveri, M.: An SMT-based approach to weak controllability for disjunctive temporal problems with uncertainty. Artif. Intell. **224**, 1–27 (2015)

9. Combi, C., Posenato, R.: Controllability in temporal conceptual workflow schemata. In: Dayal, U., Eder, J., Koehler, J., Reijers, H.A. (eds.) BPM 2009. LNCS, vol. 5701, pp. 64–79. Springer, Heidelberg (2009). doi:10.1007/978-3-642-03848-8_6

10. Damaggio, E., Deutsch, A., Vianu, V.: Artifact systems with data dependencies and arithmetic. ACM Trans. Database Syst. **37**(3), 1–36 (2012)

11. De Angelis, E., Fioravanti, F., Meo, M.C., Pettorossi, A., Proietti, M.: Verification of time-aware business processes using Constrained Horn Clauses. In: Preliminary Proceedings of LOPSTR 2016, CoRR. http://arxiv.org/abs/1608.02807 (2016)

12. De Angelis, E., Fioravanti, F., Meo, M.C., Pettorossi, A., Proietti, M.: Verifying controllability of time-aware business processes. Technical report IASI-CNR 16-08 (2016)

13. Angelis, E., Fioravanti, F., Pettorossi, A., Proietti, M.: VeriMAP: a tool for verifying programs through transformations. In: Ábrahám, E., Havelund, K. (eds.) TACAS 2014. LNCS, vol. 8413, pp. 568–74. Springer, Heidelberg (2014). doi:10.1007/978-3-642-54862-8_47

14. De Angelis, E., Fioravanti, F., Pettorossi, A., Proietti, M.: Semantics-based generation of verification conditions by program specialization. In: Proceedings of the PPDP 2015, pp. 91–102. ACM (2015)

15. de Moura, L., Bjørner, N.: Z3: an efficient SMT solver. In: Ramakrishnan, C.R., Rehof, J. (eds.) TACAS 2008. LNCS, vol. 4963, pp. 337–340. Springer, Heidelberg (2008). doi:10.1007/978-3-540-78800-3_24

16. Etalle, S., Gabbrielli, M.: Transformations of CLP modules. Theor. Comput. Sci. **166**, 101–146 (1996)

17. Formal Systems (Europe) Ltd. Failures-Divergences Refinement, FDR2 User Manual (1998). http://www.fsel.com

18. ter Hofstede, A.M., van der Aalst, W.M.P., Adams, M., Russell, N. (eds.): Modern Business Process Automation: YAWL and its Support Environment. Springer, Heidelberg (2010)

19. Jaffar, J., Maher, M.: Constraint logic programming: a survey. J. Logic Program. **19**(20), 503–81 (1994)

20. Kowalski, R.A., Sergot, M.J.: A logic-based calculus of events. New Gener. Comput. **4**(1), 67–95 (1986)

21. Kumar, A., Sabbella, S.R., Barton, R.R.: Managing controlled violation of temporal process constraints. In: Motahari-Nezhad, H.R., Recker, J., Weidlich, M. (eds.) BPM 2015. LNCS, vol. 9253, pp. 280–96. Springer, Cham (2015). doi:10.1007/978-3-319-23063-4_20

22. Lanz, A., Posenato, R., Combi, C., Reichert, M.: Controlling time-awareness in modularized processes. In: Schmidt, R., Guédria, W., Bider, I., Guerreiro, S. (eds.) BPMDS/EMMSAD -2016. LNBIP, vol. 248, pp. 157–72. Springer, Cham (2016). doi:10.1007/978-3-319-39429-9_11

23. Larsen, K.G., Pettersson, P., Yi, W.: UPPAAL in a Nutshell. Int. J. Softw. Tools Technol. Transf. 1(1–2), 134–152 (1997)

24. Makni, M., Tata, S., Yeddes, M., Ben Hadj-Alouane, N.: Satisfaction and coherence of deadline constraints in inter-organizational workflows. In: Meersman, R., Dillon, T., Herrero, P. (eds.) OTM 2010. LNCS, vol. 6426, pp. 523–39. Springer, Heidelberg (2010). doi:10.1007/978-3-642-16934-2_39

25. McCarthy, J., Hayes, P.J.: Some philosophical problems from the standpoint of artificial intelligence. In: Meltzer, B., Michie, D. (eds.) Machine Intelligence 4, pp. 463–502. Edinburgh University Press (1969)

26. OMG. Business Process Model and Notation. http://www.omg.org/spec/BPMN/

27. Peintner, B., Venable, K.B., Yorke-Smith, N.: Strong controllability of disjunctive temporal problems with uncertainty. In: Bessière, C. (ed.) CP 2007. LNCS, vol. 4741, pp. 856–63. Springer, Heidelberg (2007). doi:10.1007/978-3-540-74970-7_64

28. Proietti, M., Smith, F.: Reasoning on data-aware business processes with constraint logic. In: Proceedings of the SIMPDA 2014. CEUR, vol. 1293, pp. 60–75 (2014)

29. Smith, F., Proietti, M.: Rule-based behavioral reasoning on semantic business processes. In: Proceedings of the ICAART 2013, vol. II, pp. 130–143. SciTePress (2013)

30. Thielscher, M.: From Situation Calculus to Fluent Calculus: State update axioms as a solution to the inferential frame problem. Artif. Intell. 111(1-2), 277–299 (1999)

31. Venable, K.B., Volpato, M., Peintner, B., Yorke-Smith, N.: Weak and dynamic controllability of temporal problems with disjunctions and uncertainty. In: Proceedings of the COPLAS 2010, pp. 50–59 (2010)

32. Vidal, T., Fargier, H.: Handling contingency in temporal constraint networks: from consistency to controllabilities. J. Exp. Theor. Artif. Intell. 11(1), 23-45 (1999)

33. Watahiki, K., Ishikawa, F., Hiraishi, K.: Formal verification of business processes with temporal and resource constraints. In: Proceedings of the SMC 2011, pp. 1173–1180. IEEE (2011)

34. Weber, I., Hoffmann, J., Mendling, J.: Beyond soundness: on the verification of semantic business process models. Distrib. Parallel Databases 27, 271–343 (2010)

35. Weske, M.: Business Process Management: Concepts, Languages, Architectures. Springer, Heidelberg (2007)

36. Wong, P.Y.H., Gibbons, J.: A relative timed semantics for BPMN. Electron. Notes Theor. Comput. Sci. 229(2), 59–75 (2009)

A Decidable Confluence Test for Cognitive Models in ACT-R

Daniel Gall$^{(\boxtimes)}$ and Thom Frühwirth

Institute of Software Engineering and Programming Languages, Ulm University,
89069 Ulm, Germany
{daniel.gall,thom.fruehwirth}@uni-ulm.de

Abstract. Computational cognitive modeling investigates human cognition by building detailed computational models for cognitive processes. Adaptive Control of Thought – Rational (ACT-R) is a rule-based cognitive architecture that offers a widely employed framework to build such models. There is a sound and complete embedding of ACT-R in Constraint Handling Rules (CHR). Therefore analysis techniques from CHR can be used to reason about computational properties of ACT-R models. For example, confluence is the property that a program yields the same result for the same input regardless of the rules that are applied.

In ACT-R models, there are often cognitive processes that should always yield the same result while others e.g. implement strategies to solve a problem that could yield different results. In this paper, a decidable confluence criterion for ACT-R is presented. It allows to identify ACT-R rules that are not confluent. Thereby, the modeler can check if his model has the desired behavior.

The sound and complete translation of ACT-R to CHR from prior work is used to come up with a suitable invariant-based confluence criterion from the CHR literature. Proper invariants for translated ACT-R models are identified and proven to be decidable. The presented method coincides with confluence of the original ACT-R models.

Keywords: Computational cognitive modeling · Confluence · Invariants · ACT-R · Constraint Handling Rules

1 Introduction

Computational cognitive modeling is a research field at the interface of cognitive sciences and computer science. It tries to explain human cognition by building detailed computational models of cognitive processes [15]. To support the modeling process, cognitive architectures like *Adaptive Control of Thought – Rational (ACT-R)* provide the ability to create models of specific cognitive tasks by offering representational formats together with reasoning and learning mechanisms to facilitate modeling [16].

ACT-R is widely employed in the field of computational cognitive modeling. It is defined as a production rule system that offers advanced conflict resolution mechanisms to model learning and competition of different strategies for

© Springer International Publishing AG 2017
S. Costantini et al. (Eds.): RuleML+RR 2017, LNCS 10364, pp. 119–134, 2017.
DOI: 10.1007/978-3-319-61252-2_9

problem solving. Therefore, many ACT-R models are highly non-deterministic to resemble the applicability of more than one strategy in many situations. The strategy is chosen depending on information learned from situations in the past.

Confluence is the property of a program that regardless of the order its rules are applied, they finally yield the same result. By identifying the rules that lead to non-confluence, model quality can be improved: It allows to check if the model has the desired behavior regarding competing strategies and e.g. identify rules that interfere with each other unintentionally.

In this paper, we present a *decidable confluence test for the abstract operational semantics of ACT-R* using confluence analysis tools for CHR. In prior work, we presented a sound and complete embedding of ACT-R in CHR [8,9]. An *invariant-based confluence test for CHR* [6,11] is used to decide confluence of the translated models with invariants on CHR states that come from the abstract operational semantics of ACT-R. The confluence test identifies the rules that lead to non-confluence supporting the decision if a model has the desired behavior regarding competing strategies.

First the preliminaries are recapitulated in Sect. 2. The main Sect. 3 describes the confluence criterion for ACT-R models. For this purpose, the invariant-based confluence test for CHR is introduced briefly (Sect. 3.1). Then, the ACT-R invariant is defined and a *decidable criterion* for the invariant is given (Sect. 3.2). It is shown that the ACT-R invariant is maintained in the translation. The theoretical foundations to apply the CHR invariant-based confluence test to ACT-R models are derived resulting in a *confluence criterion for terminating ACT-R models* (Sect. 3.3). An example is given in Sect. 3.4.

2   Preliminaries

2.1   Confluence

Confluence is the property of a state transition system that same inputs yield the same results regardless of which rules are applied.

Definition 1 (joinability and confluence [7]). *In a state transition system* $(\mathcal{S}, \mapsto)$ *with states* $\mathcal{S}$ *and a transition relation* $\mapsto: \mathcal{S} \times \mathcal{S}$ *with reflexive transitive closure* $\mapsto^*$, *two states* $\sigma_1, \sigma_2 \in \mathcal{S}$ *are* joinable, *denoted as* $\sigma_1 \downarrow \sigma_2$, *if there exists a state* σ' *such that* $\sigma_1 \mapsto^* \sigma'$ *and* $\sigma_2 \mapsto^* \sigma'$. *A state transition system is* confluent, *if for all states* $\sigma, \sigma_1, \sigma_2 : (\sigma \mapsto^* \sigma_1) \wedge (\sigma \mapsto^* \sigma_2) \rightarrow (\sigma_1 \downarrow \sigma_2)$.

Hence, a program is confluent if for all states that lead to different successor states, those states are joinable. A program is *locally confluent*, if $(\sigma \mapsto \sigma_1) \wedge (\sigma \mapsto \sigma_2)$ in one transition step and σ_1 and σ_2 are joinable. It can be shown that for all state transition systems local confluence and confluence are equivalent [7]. Figure 1 illustrates (local) confluence.

Fig. 1. Confluence and local confluence.

2.2 Adaptive Control of Thought – Rational (ACT-R)

In this section, ACT-R is introduced briefly. An extensive introduction to the theory can be found in [3,16]. ACT-R is a modular production rule system. Its data elements are so-called *chunks*. A chunk has a *type* and a set of *slots* (determined by the type) that are connected to other chunks. Hence, human declarative knowledge is represented in ACT-R as a network of chunks. Figure 2 shows an example chunk network that models the representation of an order over natural numbers.

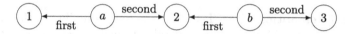

Fig. 2. A chunk network that represents the order of natural numbers 1, 2, 3. The chunks are represented by nodes, the slots by labeled edges. The labels of the nodes are chunk identifiers. Chunks 1, 2 and 3 are of type *number* that has no slots. Chunks *a* and *b* are of type *order* that has a *first* and a *second* slot.

ACT-R's modules are responsible for different cognitive features. For instance, the declarative knowledge (represented as a chunk network) can be found in the *declarative module*. Each module has a set of associated *buffers* that contain at most one chunk. The heart of ACT-R is the *procedural system* that consists of a set of *production rules*. Those rules only have access to the contents of the buffers. They match the contents of the buffer, i.e. they check if the chunks of particular buffers have certain values. If a rule is applicable, it can *modify* particular slots of the chunk in the buffer, *request* the module to put a whole new chunk in its buffer or *clear* a buffer. Modifications and clearings are available directly for the production rule system, whereas requests can take some time while the procedural system is continuing work in parallel.

Syntax of ACT-R. We use our simplified syntax in form of first-order terms that can be derived directly from the original syntax [8,9]. The syntax of ACT-R is defined over two disjoint sets of constant symbols $\mathcal{C}$ and variable symbols $\mathcal{V}$. An ACT-R model consists of a set of types $\mathbb{T}$ with type definitions and a set of rules Σ.

A production rule has the form $\mathcal{L} \Rightarrow R$ where $\mathcal{L}$ is a finite set of buffer tests. A buffer test is a first-order term of the form $=(b, t, P)$ where the buffer $b \in \mathcal{C}$, the type $t \in \mathcal{C}$ and $P \subseteq \mathcal{C} \times (\mathcal{C} \cup \mathcal{V})$ is a set of slot-value pairs (s, v) where $s \in \mathcal{C}$ and $v \in \mathcal{C} \cup \mathcal{V}$. This means that only the values in the slot-value pairs can consist of both constants and variables.

The right-hand side $R \subseteq \mathcal{A}$ of a rule is a finite set of actions where $\mathcal{A} = \{a(b, t, P) \mid a \in A, b \in \mathcal{C}, t \in \mathcal{C}$ and $P \subseteq \mathcal{C} \times (\mathcal{C} \cup \mathcal{V})\}$. Hence, an action is a term of the form $a(b, t, P)$ where the functor a of the action is in A, the set of action symbols, the first argument b is a constant (denoting a buffer), the second argument is a constant t denoting a type, and the last argument is a set of slot-value pairs, i.e. a pair of a constant and a constant or variable. Usually, the action symbols are defined as $A := \{=, +, -\}$ for modifications, requests and clearings respectively. Only one action per buffer is allowed, i.e. if $a(b, t, P) \in R$ and $a'(b', t', P') \in R$, then $b \neq b'$ [4].

We assume the rules to be in so-called *set normal form* that requires the slot tests of a rule to be total and unique with respect to the type of the test. This means that each slot defined by the type of the tested chunk must appear at most once in the set of slot-value pairs. Every rule can be transformed to set normal form [8].

Operational Semantics of ACT-R. For the understanding of this paper, it is sufficient to define ACT-R states and rules formally. The formal definition of the operational semantics can be found in [8,9]. We define the operational semantics of ACT-R through our CHR translation that has been first presented in [9] and in its most current form in [8]. Since the translation is sound and complete, we omit the formal definition of the ACT-R semantics here, since it would only distract from the contribution of this paper.

Definition 2 (chunk types, chunk stores). *A typing function* $\tau : \mathbb{T} \to 2^{\mathcal{C}}$ *maps each type from the set* $\mathbb{T} \subseteq \mathcal{C}$ *to a finite set of allowed slot names. A chunk store* Δ *is a multi-set of tuples* (t, val) *where* $t \in \mathbb{T}$ *is a chunk type and* $val : \tau(t) \to \Delta$ *is a function that maps each slot of the chunk (determined by the type* t*) to another chunk. Each chunk store* Δ *has a bijective identifier function* $id_\Delta : \Delta \to \mathcal{C}$ *that maps each chunk of the multi-set a unique identifier.*

Additional information represents the inner state of the modules and so-called sub-symbolic information used in ACT-R implementations to model cognitive features like forgetting, latencies and conflict resolution. The information is expressed as a conjunction of predicates from first-order logic. We now define ACT-R states as follows:

Definition 3 (cognitive state, ACT-R state). *A cognitive state* γ *is a function* $\mathbb{B} \to \Delta \times \mathbb{R}_0^+$ *that maps each buffer to a chunk and a delay. The delay decides at which point in time the chunk in the buffer is available to the production system. A delay* $d > 0$ *indicates that the chunk is not yet available to the production system. This implements delays of the processing of requests.*

An ACT-R state is a tuple $\langle \Delta; \gamma; \upsilon \rangle$ *where* γ *is a cognitive state and* υ *is a multi-set of ground, atomic first order predicates (called* additional information*).*

2.3   Constraint Handling Rules (CHR)

In this section, syntax and semantics of CHR are summarized briefly. For an extensive introduction to CHR, its semantics, analysis and applications, we refer to [7]. We use the latest definition of the state transition system of CHR that is based on state equivalence [12]. The definitions from those canonical sources are now reproduced.

The syntax of CHR is defined over a set of variables, a set of function symbols with arities and a set of predicate symbols with arities that is disjointly composed of *CHR constraint symbols* and *built-in constraint symbols*. The set of constraint symbols contains at least the symbols $= /2$, $\top/0$ and $\bot/0$. In this paper, we allow the terms to be sets of terms as they can be simply represented as lists in implementations. For a constraint symbol c/n and terms $t_1, \ldots, t_n$ over the variables and function symbols, $c(t_1, \ldots, t_n)$ is called a *CHR constraint* or a *built-in constraint*, depending on the constraint symbol. We now define the notion of CHR states.

Definition 4 (CHR state). *A CHR state is a tuple $\langle \mathbb{G}; \mathbb{C}; \mathbb{V} \rangle$ where the* goal $\mathbb{G}$ *is a multi-set of constraints, the* built-in constraint store $\mathbb{C}$ *is a conjunction of built-in constraints and $\mathbb{V}$ is a set of* global variables.

All variables occurring in a state that are not global are called local variables.

CHR states can be modified by rules that together form a CHR program. For the sake of brevity, we only consider simplification rules, as they are the only type of rules needed for the understanding of the paper.

Definition 5 (CHR program). *A CHR program is a finite set of rules of the form $r \ @ \ H \Leftrightarrow G \mid B_c, B_b$ where r is an optional rule name, the heads H are multi-sets of CHR constraints, the guard G is a conjunction of built-in constraints and the body is a multi-set of CHR constraints B_c and a conjunction of built-in constraints B_b. If G is empty, it is interpreted as the built-in constraint $\top$.*

Informally, a rule is applicable, if the head matches constraints from the store $\mathbb{G}$ and the guard holds, i.e. is a consequence of the built-in constraints $\mathbb{C}$. In that case, the constraints matching H are removed and the constraints from B_c, B_b and G are added.

In the context of the operational semantics, we assume a constraint theory $\mathcal{CT}$ for the interpretation of the built-in constraints. We define an equivalence relation over CHR states.

Definition 6 (CHR state equivalence [11,12]). *Let $\rho := \langle \mathbb{G}; \mathbb{C}; \mathbb{V} \rangle$ and $\rho' := \langle \mathbb{G}'; \mathbb{C}'; \mathbb{V}' \rangle$ be CHR states with local variables $\bar{y}, \bar{y}'$ that have been renamed apart. $\rho \equiv \rho'$ if and only if*

$$\mathcal{CT} \models \forall (\mathbb{C} \rightarrow \exists \bar{y}'.((\mathbb{G} = \mathbb{G}') \wedge \mathbb{C}')) \wedge \forall (\mathbb{C}' \rightarrow \exists \bar{y}.((\mathbb{G} = \mathbb{G}') \wedge \mathbb{C}))$$

where $\forall F$ denotes the universal closure of formula F.

The operational semantics is now defined by the following transition scheme over equivalence classes of CHR states i.e. $[\rho] := \{\rho' \mid \rho' \equiv \rho\}$

Definition 7 (operational semantics of CHR [11,12]). *For a CHR program the state transition system over CHR states and the rule transition relation $\mapsto$ is defined as the following transition scheme:*

$$\frac{r \ @ \ H \Leftrightarrow G \mid B_c, B_b}{[\langle H \uplus G; G \wedge \mathbb{C}; \mathbb{V}\rangle] \mapsto^r [\langle B_c \uplus G; G \wedge B_b \wedge \mathbb{C}; \mathbb{V}\rangle]}$$

Thereby, r is a variant of a rule in the program such that its local variables are disjoint from the variables occurring in the representative of the pre-transition state. We may just write $\mapsto$ instead of $\mapsto^r$ if the rule r is clear from the context.

2.4 Translation of ACT-R to CHR

We briefly summarize the translation of ACT-R models to CHR first presented in [8,9]. Since the translation is proven to be sound and complete [8], we explain the operational semantics of ACT-R with the help of the translation.

Definition 8 (translation of abstract states). *An abstract ACT-R state $\sigma := \langle \Delta; \gamma; \upsilon \rangle$ can be translated to the following CHR state:*

$$\langle \{ delta(\{ chunk(id_\Delta(c), t, [\![val]\!]) \mid c \in \Delta \wedge c = (t, val) \}) \}$$
$$\uplus \{ gamma(b, id_\Delta(c), d) \mid b \in \mathbb{B} \wedge \gamma(b) = (c, d) \wedge c = (t, val) \}; \upsilon; \emptyset \rangle$$

Thereby, $[\![val]\!]$ denotes the explicit relational notation of the function val as a set of tuples. We denote the translation of an ACT-R state σ by $chr(\sigma)$.

The chunk store is represented by a *delta* constraint that contains a set of *chunk*/3 terms representing the chunks with their identifiers, types and slot-value pairs.

For every buffer of the given architecture, there is a constraint *gamma* with buffer name, chunk identifier and delay. Since γ is a total function, every buffer has exactly one *gamma* constraint. Additional information is represented directly as built-in constraints.

Definition 9 (translation of rules). *Let $cogstate(\mathbb{B}) := \{(b, C_b) \mid b \in \mathbb{B}\}$ be the relation that connects each buffer with a variable C_b. An ACT-R rule in set-normal form $r := \mathcal{L} \Rightarrow \mathcal{R}$ can be translated to a CHR rule of the form:*

$$r \ @ \ delta(D) \uplus \{ gamma(b, C_b, E_b) \mid b \in \mathbb{B} \}$$

$$\Leftrightarrow$$

$$\bigwedge_{=(b,t,P) \in \mathcal{L}} (chunk(C_b, t, P) \ in \ D \wedge E_b{=}0) \mid$$

$$\{ delta(D^*) \} \uplus \{ gamma(b, C_b^{**}, resdelay(b)) \mid b \in \mathbb{B} \wedge a(b, t, P) \in \mathcal{R} \}$$
$$\uplus \{ gamma(b, C_b, E_b) \mid b \in \mathbb{B} \wedge a(b, t, P) \notin \mathcal{R} \},$$

$$\bigwedge_{\alpha=a(b,t,P)\in\mathcal{R}} action(\alpha, D, cogstate(\mathbb{B}), D_b^*, C_b^*, E_b^*)$$

$$\wedge \; merge([D_b^* : a(b,t,P) \in R], D')\} \wedge merge([D, D'], D^*) \; \uplus$$

$$\wedge \bigwedge_{a(b,t,P)\in R} map(D, D', C_b^*, C_b^{**}).$$

Note that ACT-R constants and variables from $\mathcal{C}$ and $\mathcal{V}$ are implicitly translated to corresponding CHR variables.

We denote the translation of a rule r by $chr(r)$ and the translation of an ACT-R model Σ that is a set of ACT-R rules by $chr(\Sigma)$. Thereby, $chr(\Sigma) :=$ $\{chr(r) \mid r \in \Sigma\}$.

The rule removes the *delta* and all *gamma* constraints from the store. It binds the translation of the chunk store Δ to the variable D. For all buffers b, each variable C_b is bound to the chunk identifier of the chunk in b, i.e. $C_b = id_\Delta(\gamma(b))$. The guard now performs all buffer tests $=(b, t, P)$ from the ACT-R rule by testing if a chunk term $chunk(C_b, t, P)$ is in the translated chunk store D that has type t and matches all slot-value pairs in P. The ACT-R variables in P are bound to the values in the state.

In the body, the built-in constraints *action* perform the actions of the ACT-R rule as defined by the architecture. An *action* constraint gets the action term α of the rule (with all variables bound through the matching), the original chunk store and a representation of the cognitive state. Since the C_b have been bound in the matching, it consists of tuples that connect each buffer b with the chunk identifier it holds.

The *action* built-in constraint returns a chunk store D_b^*, a chunk identifier C_b^* that represents the resulting chunk from the request and a result delay E_b^*. The *merge* constraints merge the chunk stores of all actions with the original store D to the store D^*. The result of merging two chunk stores can vary from implementation to implementation, but has to obey some rules defined in [8]. One can think of it as a multi-set union. As chunk identifiers might change in the merging process, the built-in *map* maps the chunk identifier of the results to the corresponding identifiers in the merged store.

Then, a new Δ constraint with the resulting chunk store D^* is added as well as the *gamma* constraints. If the buffer b has been part of an action, then it is altered such that it holds the resulting chunk identifier C_b^{**} after the merge and the resulting delay E_b^*. If it was not part of an action, its parameters C_b (the chunk identifier) and E_b (the delay) remain unchanged. This is possible, since the chunk merging guarantees that chunks in the original chunk store D the constraint *gamma* is referring to, are also part of the merged chunk store D^*.

Example 1 (counting). We now give an example ACT-R rule to explain its operational semantics. A classical example in ACT-R is counting by recalling count order facts. The model uses chunks of type *order* as illustrated in Fig. 2. An *order* chunk has a *first* and a *second* slot that link two chunks representing natural numbers in the right order. Additionally, we define a second chunk type g that memorizes the current number in the counting process. The main rule is defined as:

$$=(goal, g, \{(current, X)\}), =(retrieval, order, \{(first, X), (second, Y)\})$$
$$\Rightarrow =(goal, g, \{(current, Y)\}), +(retrieval, order, \{(first, Y)\})$$

The left-hand side tests if there is a chunk of type g in the *goal* buffer. The value of its *current* slot is bound to variable X by the matching. The second buffer test checks the *retrieval* buffer for a chunk of type *order* that has X in its *first* slot. The value of the *second* slot is bound to variable Y.

The right-hand side modifies the chunk in the *goal* buffer such that Y is written to the *current* slot. The second action requests the *retrieval* buffer for an *order* chunk that has Y in its *first* slot. As soon as the requested chunk is available, the program can apply the rule again. The head and guard of the CHR translation $H \Leftrightarrow G \mid B$ of the rule is

$$H := \{delta(D), gamma(g, C_g, 0), gamma(retrieval, C_r, 0)\},$$
$$G := chunk(C_g, g, \{(current, X)\}) \ in \ D \ \wedge$$
$$chunk(C_r, order, \{(first, X), (second, Y)\}) \ in \ D.$$

3 Confluence Criterion for ACT-R

This section is the main contribution of the paper. We gradually develop a decidable criterion for confluence of ACT-R using the CHR embedding.

Therefor, a brief introduction to invariant-based confluence analysis for CHR is given that extends the standard confluence criterion to handle invariants that must hold for the regarded states. We then define the ACT-R invariant $\mathcal{A}$ that is satisfied if a CHR state has been derived from an ACT-R state. Then a decidable criterion for the invariant is presented and it is shown that the invariant is maintained in translated ACT-R models. It is shown how invariant-based confluence analysis for CHR can be applied to decide ACT-R confluence.

3.1 Invariant-Based Confluence

We now give a brief introduction to invariant-based confluence analysis for CHR. The first results stem from [6]. We summarize the main theorem of the improved version that can be found in [11, Sect. 14].

The main idea of the confluence criterion is that heads and guards of the rules are overlapped to an overlap state. Then both overlapping rules are applied to this state forming a critical pair that is checked for joinability for all possible overlap states. An overlap is defined as follows:

Definition 10 (overlap and critical pairs [7,11]). *For any two (not necessarily different) rules of a CHR program with renamed apart variables of the form $r @ H \Leftrightarrow G \mid B_c, B_b$ and $r' @ H' \Leftrightarrow G' \mid B'_c, B'_b$, let $O \subseteq H, O' \subseteq H'$ such that for $B := (O = O') \wedge G \wedge G'$ it holds that $\mathcal{CT} \models \exists.B$ and $O \neq \emptyset$, then the state*

$$\sigma = \langle R \uplus R' \uplus O; B; \mathbb{V} \rangle$$

is called an overlap *of r and r' where $R := H \setminus O$, $R' := H' \setminus O'$ and $\mathbb{V}$ is the set of all variables occurring in heads and guards of both rules. The pair of states $\sigma_1 := \langle R' \uplus B_c; B \wedge B_b; \mathbb{V} \rangle$ and $\sigma_2 := \langle R \uplus B_c'; B \wedge B_b'; \mathbb{V} \rangle$ is a critical pair of the overlap σ.*

CHR has the monotonicity property. It states that all rules that are applicable in a state, are also applicable in any larger state. This idea can be exploited to reason from joinable overlap states about local confluence and therefore confluence of a CHR program. The problem with invariant-based confluence is that the idea of using monotonicity to reason about larger states does not work for states where the invariant does not hold. An overlap that does not satisfy the invariant makes all information about this state irrelevant [11, p. 79]. The idea of the invariant-based confluence theorem for CHR is to extend all states where the invariant does not hold such that the invariant is repaired and include the extended states in the confluence test. Since in general there are infinitely many extensions that maintain the invariant, only minimal extensions according to a partial order defined in [11] have to be considered. Then, monotonicity can be applied again.

Theorem 1 (invariant-based confluence for CHR [11]). *For an invariant $\mathcal{I}$, let $\Sigma^{\mathcal{I}}([\rho]) := \{ [\rho'] \mid [\rho'] \text{ is an extension of } [\rho] \text{ such that } \mathcal{I} \text{ holds } \}$ be the set of satisfying extensions of $[\rho]$. The set $\mathcal{M}^{\mathcal{I}}([\rho])$ is the set of minimal elements of $\Sigma^{\mathcal{I}}([\rho])$ w.r.t. the partial order on states defined in [11].*

Let $\mathcal{P}$ be a CHR program and $\mathcal{M}^{\mathcal{I}}([\rho])$ be well-defined for all overlaps ρ. $\mathcal{P}$ is locally confluent with respect to $\mathcal{I}$ if and only if for all overlaps ρ with critical pairs (ρ_1, ρ_2) and all $[\rho_m] \in \mathcal{M}^{\mathcal{I}}([\rho])$ holds that $[\rho_1]$ extended by $[\rho_m]$ and $[\rho_2]$ extended by $[\rho_m]$ are joinable. We then say that $\mathcal{P}$ is $\mathcal{I}$-(locally) confluent.

There are two problems with this result making it possibly undecidable: The invariant could be undecidable and the set of minimal elements can be infinitely large. We will show that in the case of the ACT-R invariant that we use for our confluence test, the set of satisfying extensions is empty and the invariant is decidable. Hence, it is not necessary for the understanding of this paper how the partial order on states and therefore the set of minimal elements is defined formally, since the set of satisfying extensions is already empty for the ACT-R invariant. The ACT-R invariant is defined in the following section.

3.2   ACT-R Invariant

To reason about confluence of ACT-R models in CHR, we need an invariant that restricts the CHR state space to states that stem from a valid ACT-R state. In the following example, we show how overlapping translated ACT-R rules can lead to overlap states that do not describe a valid ACT-R state.

Example 2. Let $\{delta(D), gamma(B, C, 0)\} \Leftrightarrow chunk(C, T, P)$ in $D \mid \ldots$ be a CHR rule that has been obtained from an ACT-R rule. By overlapping the rule with itself, we could get

$$\sigma := \langle delta(D), gamma(B, C, 0), gamma(B, C', 0);$$
$$chunk(C, T, P) \text{ in } D \wedge chunk(C', T', P') \text{ in } D; \mathbb{V} \rangle.$$

However, this state does not stem from a valid ACT-R state, since γ is a function with only one value for each buffer and therefore the translation of an ACT-R state can never contain two *gamma* constraints for the same buffer B.

In the following, we define the ACT-R invariant $\mathcal{A}$ on CHR states that limits the state space to states that stem from valid ACT-R states. We show that the invariant is decidable by breaking it down to five fine grained invariants. We also show that it actually defines an invariant for translated ACT-R models.

Definition 11 (ACT-R invariant). *Let $[\rho]$ be a CHR state. The ACT-R invariant $\mathcal{A}$ holds if and only if there is an ACT-R state σ such that $\rho \equiv chr(\sigma)$.*

Basically, this means that $\mathcal{A}([\rho])$ holds if $[\rho]$ is the valid translation of an ACT-R state. However, by this definition it is hard to decide if a CHR state satisfies the invariant.

We now show some decidable sub-invariants on CHR states and prove that their conjunction is equivalent to $\mathcal{A}$. For this purpose, we define an auxiliary function *ids* that returns the set of chunk identifiers for a set of *chunk*/3 terms.

Definition 12 (chunk identifiers). *Let d be a set. Then*

$$ids(d) := \{c \mid chunk(c, t, p) \in d\}$$

is the set of chunk identifiers *of the set d.*

The sub-invariants mainly consist of *uniqueness* invariants, i.e. they require that there is only one constraint of a certain kind for a class of arguments, and *functional dependency* invariants, i.e. that certain sets that represent relations appearing in constraints are functions. Eventually, the constraints that can be be used in a state are restricted.

Theorem 2 (ACT-R invariants). *Let $\rho \equiv \langle \mathbb{G}; \mathbb{C}; \mathbb{V} \rangle$ be a CHR state. We define the following sub-invariants:*

1. *unique chunk store*
   $\mathcal{A}_1([\rho]) \leftrightarrow$ There is exactly one constraint $delta(d) \in \mathbb{G}$ for some ground set d. For all elements $e \in d$, it holds that there exist $c \in \mathcal{C}, t \in \mathbb{T}, p \in \mathcal{C} \times \mathcal{C}, s \in \tau(t), v \in \mathcal{C}$ such that $e = chunk(c, t, p)$ and $p = \{(s, v) \mid s \in \tau(t) \wedge v \in ids(d)\}$.
2. *functional dependency of cognitive state*
   $\mathcal{A}_2([\rho]) \leftrightarrow$ For all buffers $b \in \mathbb{B}$ there is exactly one $gamma(b, c, e) \in \mathbb{G}$ where $c \in ids(d)$ for some $delta(d) \in \mathbb{G}$ and $e \in \mathbb{R}_0^+$.

3. *unique chunk identifiers*
   $\mathcal{A}_3([\rho]) \leftrightarrow$ *For all chunk identifiers $c \in \mathcal{C}$ and constraints $delta(d) \in \mathbb{G}$, if $chunk(c, t, p) \in d$, then there is no other term $chunk(c, t', p') \in d$.*
4. *functional dependency of slot-value pairs*
   $\mathcal{A}_4([\rho]) \leftrightarrow$ *For all constraints $delta(d) \in \mathbb{G}$, terms $chunk(c, t, p)$ in set d and (s, v) in set p, there is no other term (s, v') in p.*
5. *allowed constraints*
   $\mathcal{A}_5([\rho]) \leftrightarrow$ *In $\mathbb{G}$ there are only delta/1 and gamma/3 constraints, only syntactic equality $= /2$ and the allowed constraints defined by the ACT-R architectures appear in $\mathbb{C}$ and $[\rho]$ is ground.*

For all CHR states $[\rho]$ it holds that $\mathcal{A}([\rho]) \leftrightarrow \bigwedge_{i=1}^{5} \mathcal{A}_i([\rho])$.

Proof. **if direction** If $\mathcal{A}([\rho])$, then $[\rho]$ is the product of the translation of an ACT-R state. It follows directly from Definition 8 that in that case, $\mathcal{A}_1([\rho])$, $\mathcal{A}_2([\rho])$, $\mathcal{A}_3([\rho])$, $\mathcal{A}_4([\rho])$ and $\mathcal{A}_5([\rho])$ hold.

only-if direction We have to show that for all CHR states $[\rho]$ where the invariants $\mathcal{A}_1([\rho])$, $\mathcal{A}_2([\rho])$, $\mathcal{A}_3([\rho])$, $\mathcal{A}_4([\rho])$ and $\mathcal{A}_5([\rho])$ hold, there is an ACT-R state σ such that $\rho \equiv chr(\sigma)$. Let $[\rho] := [\langle \mathbb{G}; \mathbb{C}; \mathbb{V} \rangle]$.

We construct the ACT-R state $\sigma := \langle \Delta; \gamma; \upsilon \rangle$. Since $\mathcal{A}_1([\rho])$, there is exactly one $delta(d)$ constraint for a set d and all elements in d are of the form $chunk(c, t, p)$ where $c \in \mathcal{C}, t \in \mathbb{T}$ and p is a set of elements (s, v) with $s \in \tau(t)$ and $v \in ids(d)$. The set p is total with respect to s and the v are chunk identifiers that appear in d. Due to $\mathcal{A}_4$, there is exactly one $(s, v) \in p$ for each $s \in \tau(t)$, hence p is the relational representation of a value function. The invariant $\mathcal{A}_3$ guarantees that the chunk identifiers are unique.

We define $\Delta := \{(t, p) \mid chunk(c, t, p) \in d\}$ with the identifier function $id_\Delta := \{((t, p), c) \mid chunk(c, t, p)\}$.

Due to invariant $\mathcal{A}_2$, the cognitive state can then be defined for all $b \in \mathbb{B}$ such that $\gamma(b) := (id_\Delta^{-1}(c), e)$ for each $gamma(b, c, e) \in \mathbb{G}$.

Since $\mathcal{A}_5([\rho])$, $[\rho]$ is ground. Hence, we can find another representative of the state with $\rho \equiv \langle \mathbb{G}'; \mathbb{C}'; \emptyset \rangle$, that applies all equality constraints $X{=}t$ in $\mathbb{C}$ such that only constants appear in $\mathbb{G}'$ and $\mathbb{C}'$ and $\mathbb{C}'$ only consists of allowed predicates defined by the ACT-R architecture. Therefore, we can set $\upsilon := \mathbb{C}'$.

From the construction of σ it is clear that $\rho \equiv chr(\sigma)$.

The invariants $\mathcal{A}_1, \ldots, \mathcal{A}_5$ are obviously decidable. Since they are equivalent to the ACT-R invariant $\mathcal{A}$, Theorem 2 gives us a decidable criterion for the ACT-R invariant $\mathcal{A}$.

In the next step, we show that the ACT-R invariant $\mathcal{A}$ is maintained by transitions that come from a translated ACT-R program, i.e. that it really is an invariant.

Lemma 1. *Let $\mapsto$ be the state transition relation derived from the translation of an ACT-R model and $[\rho]$ a CHR state with $\mathcal{A}([\rho])$. If $[\rho] \mapsto [\rho']$, then $\mathcal{A}([\rho'])$.*

Proof. We are going to use soundness and completeness [8] to prove this.

Let $[\rho]$ be a CHR state with $\mathcal{A}([\rho])$. Since $\mathcal{A}([\rho])$, there is an ACT-R state σ with $\rho \equiv chr(\sigma)$. Due to the sound and complete embedding of ACT-R in CHR, there is an ACT-R state σ' with $\rho' \equiv chr(\sigma')$. Hence, $\mathcal{A}([\rho'])$ holds.

3.3   Invariant-Based Confluence Test

We want to use Theorem 1 [11, p. 83, Theorem 6] to prove confluence of all states $[\rho]$ that satisfy the ACT-R invariant, i.e. where $\mathcal{A}([\rho])$. Therefore, we have to construct the set $\Sigma^{\mathcal{A}}([\rho])$ for each state $[\rho]$ that does not satisfy $\mathcal{A}$. It contains all states that can be merged to $[\rho]$ such that they satisfy $\mathcal{A}$ (see Theorem 1). The minimal elements in this set have to be considered in the confluence test.

We will see that for all states $[\rho]$ that do not satisfy $\mathcal{A}$, the set of minimal elements is empty. Intuitively, this means that there are no states that can extend $[\rho]$ such that it satisfies $\mathcal{A}$.

Lemma 2 (minimal elements for $\mathcal{A}$). *Let $\mathcal{A}$ be the ACT-R invariant as defined in definition Theorem 2. For all states $[\rho]$ such that $\mathcal{A}([\rho])$ does not hold, $\Sigma^{\mathcal{A}}([\rho]) = \emptyset$ and therefore $\mathcal{M}^{\mathcal{A}}([\rho]) = \emptyset$.*

Proof. Let $[\rho] := [\langle \mathbb{G}; \mathbb{C}; \mathbb{V} \rangle]$. We use Theorem 2 that allows us to analyze the individual sub-invariants:

1. If $\mathcal{A}_1$ is violated, there are the following cases:
   - There are two constraints $delta(d), delta(d') \in \mathbb{G}$. We cannot extend $[\rho]$ (i.e. add constraints) to satisfy $\mathcal{A}_1$.
   - There is only one unique $delta(d) \in \mathbb{G}$, with elements that do not have the required form. Again, no constraints can be added to satisfy $\mathcal{A}_1$.
2. If $\mathcal{A}_2$ is violated, there are two constraints $gamma(b, c, e), gamma(b', c', e') \in \mathbb{G}$. We cannot satisfy $\mathcal{A}_2$ for such a state.
3. The proof is analogous for $\mathcal{A}_3$ and $\mathcal{A}_4$.
4. If $\mathcal{A}_5$ is violated, there are other constraints then $delta$ or $gamma$ in $\mathbb{G}$ or other than the allowed constraints defined by the architecture in $\mathbb{C}$. This cannot be repaired by extending $\mathbb{G}$ or $\mathbb{C}$.

We can directly apply Theorem 1: For all overlaps ρ where $\mathcal{A}([\rho])$ holds, the set of minimal elements is $\mathcal{M}^{\mathcal{A}}([\rho]) = \{[\rho_\emptyset]\}$ [11, p. 80, Lemma 13.13] where $\rho_\emptyset := \langle \emptyset; \top; \emptyset \rangle$ is the empty CHR state. Hence, for overlaps where $\mathcal{A}$ holds, we only have to show joinability of the critical pairs that stem from the overlap itself. This coincides with the regular confluence test of CHR as defined in [7].

For all overlaps ρ where $\mathcal{A}([\rho])$ does not hold, the set of minimal elements is $\mathcal{M}^{\mathcal{A}}([\rho]) = \emptyset$ by Lemma 2. Therefore, no critical pairs have to be tested. We summarize this in the following theorem.

Theorem 3 ($\mathcal{A}$-local confluence). *A CHR program is $\mathcal{A}$-local confluent if and only if for all critical pairs (ρ_1, ρ_2) with overlap ρ for which $\mathcal{A}(\rho)$, it is $\rho_1 \downarrow \rho_2$.*

Proof. This follows directly from Theorem 1 and Lemma 2 for overlaps where $\mathcal{A}([\rho])$ does not hold. For overlaps with $\mathcal{A}([\rho])$, the unique minimal element is the empty state $[\rho_\emptyset] := [\langle\emptyset; \top; \emptyset\rangle]$ which is the neutral element for state merging [11, Lemma 13.13, p. 80]. Therefore, if $\mathcal{A}([\rho])$ holds, it suffices to test the critical pairs that stem from $[\rho]$ by Theorem 1.

We now have a criterion to decide $\mathcal{A}$-confluence of $\mathcal{A}$-terminating CHR programs that have been translated from an ACT-R model. In the next theorem, we show that $\mathcal{A}$-confluence of such CHR programs coincides with ACT-R confluence. Therefore, the confluence criterion is applicable to decide confluence of ACT-R models.

Theorem 4 (confluence in ACT-R). *Let M be an ACT-R model. Then M is terminating and confluent if and only if $chr(M)$ is $\mathcal{A}$-terminating and $\mathcal{A}$-confluent.*

Proof. $\mathcal{A}$-termination is maintained through soundness and completeness. We now show that confluence for terminating models and their CHR counterparts coincides. Confluence is defined as $(\sigma \mapsto^* \sigma_1) \wedge (\sigma \mapsto^* \sigma_2) \rightarrow (\sigma_1 \downarrow \sigma_2)$ for all states $\sigma, \sigma_1, \sigma_2$. It remains to show that joinability in ACT-R and CHR are equivalent, i.e. $(\sigma_1 \downarrow \sigma_2) \leftrightarrow ([chr(\sigma_1)] \downarrow [chr(\sigma_2)])$.

If-direction If $(\sigma_1 \downarrow \sigma_2)$, there is a state σ' such that $\sigma_1 \mapsto^* \sigma'$ and $\sigma_2 \mapsto^* \sigma'$. Due to soundness and completeness of the embedding, we have that $[chr(\sigma_1)] \mapsto^* [chr(\sigma')]$ and $[chr(\sigma_2)] \mapsto^* [chr(\sigma')]$.

Only-if-direction This is analogous. We just have to construct the ACT-R state from the joined CHR state $[\rho']$. Since $\mathcal{A}([\rho'])$ holds by Lemma 1, this state exists.

3.4 Example: Counting

We continue our Example 1. We assume that each number chunk only appears in at most one *order* chunk at *first* or *second* position. This means that the model has learned a stable order on the numbers and hence requests to the declarative module are deterministic. It is clear that this example model terminates for finite declarative memories. Therefore, we can apply our confluence criterion.

The rule can overlap with itself, e.g. $\langle delta(D), delta(D'), \ldots; \ldots; \ldots\rangle$. This state invalidates invariant $\mathcal{A}_1$ and hence is not part of the confluence test. Another overlap is $\langle delta(D), gamma(g, C_g, 0), gamma(g, C'_g, 0), \ldots; \ldots; \ldots\rangle$. It violates invariant $\mathcal{A}_2$, because it has two *gamma* constraints for the same buffer.

All overlaps consist of the following built-in store:

$$\langle delta(D), \ldots; chunk(C_g, g, \{(current, X)\}) \text{ in } D$$
$$\wedge \ chunk(C_g, g, \{(current, X')\}) \text{ in } D, \ldots; \{D, X, X', \ldots\}\rangle.$$

By invariant $\mathcal{A}_3$ it must be $X = X'$, because otherwise there were two different *chunk* terms in the same chunk store with the same chunk identifier.

The overlap $\langle H; G; \mathbb{V} \rangle$ that only consists of the head and guard of the rule where $\mathbb{V}$ contains all variables of H and G is joinable, because we assumed determinism of requests, i.e. there is only one possible result chunk for each request. It can be seen that all possible overlaps in this small example invalidate the ACT-R invariant $\mathcal{A}$ or are joinable. Therefore, the model consisting only of this one counting rule is confluent. If we would assume an agent that has not learned a stable order of numbers, yet, i.e. there are numbers with different successors, the model would not be confluent. The confluence test constructs minimal representations of the states that are not joinable, i.e. giving an insight to the reason why a model is not confluent. This allows to decide whether the model has the desired behavior when it comes to different available strategies.

4   Related Work

There exist CHR embeddings of other rule-based approaches. The results on invariant-based confluence analysis have been used successfully to the embedding of graph transformation systems in CHR [10,13].

In the context of ACT-R, there are – to the best of our knowledge – no other approaches that deal with confluence so far. There have been other approaches to formalize the architecture with the aim to reason about cognitive models. For instance, F-ACT-R [1,2] formalizes the architecture of ACT-R to simplify comparison of different models or to use model checking techniques. In [14] mathematical reformulations of ACT-R models are used for parameter optimization by mathematical optimization techniques.

5   Conclusion

In this paper, we have shown a decidable confluence test for the abstract operational semantics of ACT-R. A confluence test can help to improve ACT-R models by identifying the rules that inhibit confluence. This enables the modeler to decide about the correct behavior of the model regarding competing strategies. In our approach, we use the sound and complete embedding of ACT-R in CHR to apply the invariant-based confluence criterion for CHR to reason about ACT-R confluence, since standard CHR confluence is too strict.

We have defined the ACT-R invariant $\mathcal{A}$ on CHR states such that it is satisfied for all states that stem from a valid ACT-R state. The first main result is a decidable criterion for the ACT-R invariant (Theorem 2).

Furthermore, the theoretical foundations for applicability of CHR invariant-based confluence for the ACT-R invariant $\mathcal{A}$ are established. This leads to the second main result: an invariant-based CHR $\mathcal{A}$-confluence test (Theorem 3).

Eventually, it is shown that $\mathcal{A}$-confluence coincides with ACT-R confluence (Theorem 4). This makes our CHR approach applicable to decide ACT-R confluence. The criterion is decidable as long as the constraint theories behind the actions are decidable, because the invariant is decidable and the preconditions for the invariant-based confluence test are satisfied in the context of ACT-R.

For the future, we want to investigate how the approach can be extended to confluence modulo equivalence [5], since ACT-R confluence can be too strict due to possibly differing chunk identifiers in the processing of the production rules. An equivalence relation on chunk networks that is defined as a special form of graph isomorphism could abstract from chunk identifiers making a chunk store more declarative. By summarizing possible outcomes of a model in equivalence classes, confluence modulo equivalence can also help to reason about correctness of a model. Confluence modulo this equivalence relation would then guarantee that the model always gives a result of a certain kind defined by the equivalence class. For instance, it would be possible to check if a model always yields a chunk of a certain type, e.g. a number or an order chunk.

Reasoning about requests to modules that appear in a confluence proof can be extended by specific constraint theories on the modules that integrate domain-specific knowledge about the model. This idea can be extended by allowing for model-specific constraint theories. For instance, the integration of domain-specific knowledge on chunk types in the context of a particular cognitive model could improve reasoning about module requests in such models.

References

1. Albrecht, R., Westphal, B.: Analysing psychological theories with F-ACT-R. In: Proceedings of the 12th Biannual conference of the German cognitive science society (Gesellschaft für Kognitionswissenschaft). Cognitive Processing, vol. 15(Suppl. 1), pp. 27–28. Springer (2014)
2. Albrecht, R., Westphal, B.: F-ACT-R: defining the ACT-R architectural space. In: Proceedings of the 12th Biannual conference of the German cognitive science society (Gesellschaft für Kognitionswissenschaft). Cognitive Processing, vol. 15(Suppl. 1), pp. 79–81. Springer (2014)
3. Anderson, J.R., Bothell, D., Byrne, M.D., Douglass, S., Lebiere, C., Qin, Y.: An integrated theory of the mind. Psychol. Rev. 111(4), 1036–1060 (2004)
4. Bothell, D.: ACT-R 6.0 Reference Manual - Working Draft. Department of Psychology, Carnegie Mellon University, Pittsburgh, PA
5. Christiansen, H., Kirkeby, M.H.: On proving confluence modulo equivalence for Constraint Handling Rules. Formal Aspects Comput. 29(1), 57–95 (2017). http://dx.doi.org/10.1007/s00165-016-0396-9
6. Duck, G.J., Stuckey, P.J., Sulzmann, M.: Observable confluence for Constraint Handling Rules. In: Dahl, V., Niemelä, I. (eds.) ICLP 2007. LNCS, vol. 4670, pp. 224–239. Springer, Heidelberg (2007). doi:10.1007/978-3-540-74610-2_16
7. Frühwirth, T.: Constraint Handling Rules. Cambridge University Press, New York (2009)
8. Gall, D., Frühwirth, T.: An Operational Semantics for the Cognitive Architecture ACT-R and its Translation to Constraint Handling Rules. ArXiv e-prints, February 2017. http://arxiv.org/abs/1702.01606
9. Gall, D., Frühwirth, T.: Translation of cognitive models from ACT-R to Constraint Handling Rules. In: Alferes, J.J.J., Bertossi, L., Governatori, G., Fodor, P., Roman, D. (eds.) RuleML 2016. LNCS, vol. 9718, pp. 223–237. Springer, Cham (2016). doi:10.1007/978-3-319-42019-6_15

10. Raiser, F.: Graph transformation systems in CHR. In: Dahl, V., Niemelä, I. (eds.) ICLP 2007. LNCS, vol. 4670, pp. 240–254. Springer, Heidelberg (2007). doi:10. 1007/978-3-540-74610-2_17
11. Raiser, F.: Graph Transformation Systems in Constraint Handling Rules: Improved Methods for Program Analysis. Ph.D. thesis, Ulm University, Germany (2010). http://dx.doi.org/10.18725/OPARU-1742
12. Raiser, F., Betz, H., Frühwirth, T.: Equivalence of CHR states revisited. In: Raiser, F., Sneyers, J. (eds.) 6th International Workshop on Constraint Handling Rules (CHR), pp. 33–48. KULCW, Technical report CW 555, July 2009
13. Raiser, F., Frühwirth, T.: Analysing graph transformation systems through Constraint Handling Rules. Theory Pract. Logic Program. **11**(1), 65–109 (2011)
14. Said, N., Engelhart, M., Kirches, C., Körkel, S., Holt, D.V.: Applying mathematical optimization methods to an ACT-R instance-based learning model. PLoS ONE **11**(7), e0158832 (2016)
15. Sun, R.: Introduction to computational cognitive modeling. In: Sun, R. (ed.) The Cambridge Handbook of Computational Psychology, pp. 3–19. Cambridge University Press, New York (2008)
16. Taatgen, N.A., Lebiere, C., Anderson, J.: Modeling paradigms in ACT-R. In: Cognition and Multi-Agent Interaction: From Cognitive Modeling to Social Simulation, pp. 29–52. Cambridge University Press (2006)

On the Chase for All Provenance Paths with Existential Rules

Abdelraouf Hecham[1(✉)], Pierre Bisquert[2], and Madalina Croitoru[1]

[1] GraphIK Inria, University of Montpellier, Montpellier, France
hecham@lirmm.fr
[2] GraphIK Inria, French Institute of Research in Agronomy (INRA), Paris, France

Abstract. In this paper we focus on the problem of *how lineage* for existential rules knowledge bases. Given a knowledge base and an atomic ground query, we want to output all minimal provenance paths of the query (i.e. the sequence of rule applications that generates an atom from a given set of facts). Obtaining all minimal provenance paths of a query using forward chaining can be challenging due to the simplifications done during the rule applications of different chase mechanisms. We build upon the notion of Graph of Atoms Dependency (GAD) and use it to solve the problem of provenance path loss in the context of forward chaining with existential rules. We study the properties of this structure and investigate how different chase mechanisms impact its construction.

1 Introduction

Provenance is used in many information management systems [3,16,17] and describes where data came from, how it was derived and how it was updated over time [12]. In this paper we focus on the problem of *how lineage* [12] that, given a knowledge base and a ground query, outputs the provenance paths of the query (i.e. the sequences of rule applications that generate a query from a given set of facts). Given that in a provenance path certain rule applications are unnecessary for provenance justification, it is usually assumed that one is interested in minimal provenance paths. Unlike existing work that focuses on obtaining only one provenance path, the novelty of this work consists in obtaining all provenance paths to a ground query. This problem is relevant in many practical applications such as explanation [9], abduction [13], debugging [4] and notably, defeasible reasoning. In [11], the authors have stumbled upon this problem as query answering in defeasible reasoning with existential rules became unsound due to provenance path loss (not all provenance paths could be extracted). This unexpected behavior as we will show in this paper is due to the *order in which rules are applied* and to the *type of forward chaining mechanism* used.

Forward chaining (a.k.a. *chase*) is the exhaustive application of a set of rules on a set of facts. In this paper we focus on classes of existential rules where forward chaining is finite while backward chaining might be infinite. Different types of chases have been defined in the literature (Oblivious [5], Skolem [14],

© Springer International Publishing AG 2017
S. Costantini et al. (Eds.): RuleML+RR 2017, LNCS 10364, pp. 135–150, 2017.
DOI: 10.1007/978-3-319-61252-2_10

Restricted [8], etc.), each chase provides a more powerful restriction test for detecting when to stop. While these tests are crucial for the chase to stop, they might induce a loss of rule applications depending on the order in which the rules are applied. This loss is not picked up by existing work on provenance path extraction which only addressed the problem of obtaining one path, as it was implicitly assumed that obtaining all provenance paths is not a difficult task but a mere enumeration of the first. Unfortunately this is not the case as shown in the following example:

Example 1. *Consider a knowledge base* $KB = (\mathcal{F}, \mathcal{R})$ *and a query* $q = t(b)$ *where the set of facts* $\mathcal{F} = \{p(a), q(b), s(b)\}$, *and the set of rules* $\mathcal{R} = \{R_1 : p(X) \rightarrow r(X,Y), R_2 : \{p(X) \wedge s(Y) \rightarrow p(Y), R_3 : q(X) \rightarrow r(X,Y), R_4 : r(X,Y) \rightarrow t(X)\}$.

Extracting the provenance paths for the query q using backward chaining [4] is not possible as it is infinite. To extract provenance paths using forward chaining the state of the art uses a chase graph [6] (also called derivation tree [1]). A chase graph is a directed graph consisting of a set of nodes representing the facts of the chase and having an arrow from a fact u to v iff v is obtained from u (possibly with other atoms) by the application of a rule in $\mathcal{R}$.

The saturated set of facts $\mathcal{F}^* = \mathcal{F} \cup \{r(a, Y_1), p(b), r(b, Y_2), r(b, Y_3), t(a), t(b)\}$ is obtained using an Oblivious chase. This is represented by the chase graph in Fig. 1. From the chase graph we can find that there is only one provenance path for $t(b)$ which is applying R_3 on $q(b)$ then R_4 on the resulting $r(b, Y_2)$. However, we can see that by applying $R4$ on the atom $r(b, Y_3)$ we get $t(b)$, which gives us another provenance path that does not show in the chase graph. This loss of provenance path is due to the order in which rules are applied. When the chase applies the rule R_4 on $r(b, Y_3)$ it generates the atom $t(b)$ but this atom is considered redundant as $t(b)$ already exists. This rule application is hence considered not useful and the resulting atoms are not added to the chase graph.

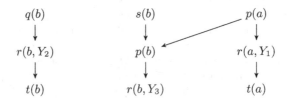

Fig. 1. Chase graph for $\mathcal{F}$ w.r.t. $\mathcal{R}$ of Example 1

In [11], a solution to the provenance path loss problem limited to the restricted chase has been proposed by defining a combinatorial structure called Graph of Atom Dependency (GAD). In this paper we build upon that work and extend the GAD for other types of chase, define its construction algorithms in Sect. 3, define the provenance path extraction algorithm, study its properties and prove its soundness and completeness in Sect. 4.

2   Preliminaries

Existential rules extend the Datalog language [7] with existential variables in the conclusion of the rules (also called tuple generating dependencies – TGDs) and generalise certain fragments of Description Logics by allowing n-ary predicates as well as cyclic structures [6]. We consider a first-order logical (FOL) language with constants but no other function symbol based on a vocabulary V composed of an infinite set of predicates, an infinite set of constants, an infinite set of variables and an infinite set of existential 'fresh' variables (called 'nulls', which act as placeholders for unknown constants). Different constants represent different values (unique name assumption) while *different fresh variables may represent the same value*. An atomic formula (or atom) is of the form $p(t_1 \ldots t_k)$, where p is a predicate and t_i are variables or constants in V. $\top$ and $\bot$ are also allowed and considered themselves atoms. For a formula Φ, we note $terms(\Phi)$ and $vars(\Phi)$ respectively the terms and variables occurring in Φ. We denote variables by uppercase letters $X, Y, Z, \ldots$, constants by lowercase letters $a, b, c, \ldots$, nulls with numbered uppercase letter $Y_1, Y_2, \ldots$, and predicate symbols by lowercase letters p, q, r, s, etc. We use FOL classical entailment and equivalence, noted $\models$ and $\equiv$ respectively.

A fact F is a ground atom (an atom with only constants and nulls). An existential rule (or a tuple generating dependency) R is a closed formula of the form $\forall \boldsymbol{X}, \boldsymbol{Y} \big(\mathcal{H}(\boldsymbol{X}, \boldsymbol{Y}) \rightarrow \exists \boldsymbol{Z}\, C(\boldsymbol{X}, \boldsymbol{Z}) \big)$ where $\boldsymbol{X}, \boldsymbol{Y}$ are tuples of variables, $\boldsymbol{Z}$ is a tuple of existential variables, and $\mathcal{H}, C$ are finite non empty conjunctions of atoms respectively called *premise* and *conclusion* of R. We omit quantifiers when there is no ambiguity, and we use the form $R = (\mathcal{H}, C)$ to represent a rule. The frontier of $R = (\mathcal{H}, C)$ noted $fr(R)$ is the set of variables occurring in both $\mathcal{H}$ and C: $fr(R) = vars(\mathcal{H}) \cap vars(C)$. Given a set of variables $\boldsymbol{X}$ and a set of terms T, a substitution of $\boldsymbol{X}$ by T is a mapping from $\boldsymbol{X}$ to T. Let $\pi : \boldsymbol{X} \rightarrow T$ be a substitution, and Φ be a formula, $\pi(\Phi)$ denotes the set of atoms obtained from Φ by replacing each occurrence of $X \in \boldsymbol{X} \cap terms(\Phi)$ by $\pi(X)$. A homomorphism from a set of atoms S to a set of atoms S' is a substitution of $vars(S)$ by $terms(S')$ such that $\pi(S) \subseteq S'$ (S maps to S' by π).

A rule $R = (\mathcal{H}, C)$ is said to be applicable to a set of facts $\mathcal{F}$ if there is a homomorphism π from $\mathcal{H}$ to $\mathcal{F}$. In that case, the application of R to $\mathcal{F}$ according to π adds to the set $\mathcal{F}$ the conclusion C with constants and possibly new fresh existential variables. More precisely, the application produces a set of facts $\alpha(\mathcal{F}, R, \pi) = \mathcal{F} \cup \pi^{safe}(C)$, where $\pi^{safe}(X) = \pi(X)$ if X belongs to the frontier, and is a fresh variable otherwise. This rule application is said to be redundant if $\alpha(\mathcal{F}, R, \pi) \equiv \mathcal{F}$. The application of R to $\mathcal{F}$, $\alpha(\mathcal{F}, R, \pi)$ w.r.t to π, is also denoted by $R_\pi(\mathcal{F})$. Given a set of facts $\mathcal{F}$ and a set of rules $\mathcal{R}$ the application of all rules $\mathcal{R}$ on the facts $\mathcal{F}$ is denoted $\mathcal{R}(\mathcal{F})$. Please note that we denote by Π the set of homomorphisms. A knowledge base $\mathcal{KB} = (\mathcal{F}, \mathcal{R})$ is composed of a set of facts $\mathcal{F}$ and a set of rules $\mathcal{R}$. A query q is an *atom* without fresh or free variables. We consider the boolean query answering problem for atomic ground queries that checks whether $\mathcal{KB} \models q$ (i.e. if $\mathcal{R}(\mathcal{F}) \models q$).

The approach in this paper relies on the notion of hypergraphs and hyperpaths. We use the classical definitions of hyperedges and hypergraphs [10,15]: a *directed hyperedge* $e \in \mathcal{E}$ is an ordered pair $e = (U, W)$ of non empty disjoint subsets of vertices $U, W \in 2^{\mathcal{V}}$; U is the tail of e while W is its head noted $tail(e)$ and $head(e)$ respectively. A *directed edge-labeled hypergraph* is a tuple $\mathcal{H} = (\mathcal{V}, \mathcal{E}, \mathcal{L})$ where $\mathcal{V}$ is a set of vertices (or nodes), $\mathcal{E} \subseteq 2^{\mathcal{V}} \times 2^{\mathcal{V}}$ is a set of directed *hyperedges* (or edges) and $\mathcal{L} : \mathcal{E} \to L$ is a labeling function that maps each edge $e \in \mathcal{E}$ with an element of the labeling set L.

We define a path $P_{s/t}$ of length k in a hypergraph $\mathcal{H} = (\mathcal{V}, \mathcal{E})$ from a node $s \in \mathcal{V}$ to a node $t \in \mathcal{V}$ as a sequence of hyperedges $\langle e_1, \ldots, e_k \rangle$ such that: $s \in tail(e_1)$, $t \in head(e_k)$, and $\forall 1 < i \leq k, head(e_{i-1}) \cap tail(e_i) \neq \emptyset$. We say that two nodes $v_i, v_j \in \mathcal{V}$ are connected if there is a path P_{v_i/v_j} from v_i to v_j. In a hypergraph $\mathcal{H} = (\mathcal{V}, \mathcal{E})$, a hyperpath $\Theta_{S/t}$ from $S \subseteq \mathcal{V}$ to $t \in \mathcal{V}$ is a hypergraph $\mathcal{H}_p = (\mathcal{V}_p, \mathcal{E}_p)$ satisfying the following conditions: (1) $\mathcal{E}_p \subseteq \mathcal{E}$, (2) $S \cup \{t\} \subseteq \mathcal{V}_p = \bigcup_{e \in \mathcal{E}_p}(tail(e) \cup head(e))$, and (3) $\forall v \in \mathcal{V}_p$, v is connected to t. A hyperpath $\Theta_{S/t} = (\mathcal{V}_p, \mathcal{E}_p)$ from $S \subseteq \mathcal{V}$ to $t \in \mathcal{V}$ is said to be *minimal* w.r.t. to $\mathcal{V}_p$ and $\mathcal{E}_p$ if no other hyperpath $\Theta'_{S/t} = (\mathcal{V}'_p, \mathcal{E}'_p)$ from S to t exits s.t.: $\mathcal{V}'_p \subset \mathcal{V}_p$ and $\mathcal{E}'_p \subset \mathcal{E}_p$. We denote by $BS(v) = \{e \in \mathcal{E} | v \in head(e)\}$ the backward star (incoming edges) of a node $v \in \mathcal{V}$.

In order to clearly define hypergraphs and how we draw them in this paper, let us consider the following Example 2 that illustrates the notion of hypergraph and hyperedge. In Fig. 3 we give the equivalent bipartite depiction of the hypergraph in Fig. 2. For clarity reasons we will use the bipartite depiction throughout the paper.

Example 2. *Consider a hypergraph* $\mathcal{H} = (\mathcal{V}, \mathcal{E}, \mathcal{L})$ *with* $\mathcal{V} = \{v_1, v_2, v_3, v_4, v_5\}$, $\mathcal{E} = \{\varepsilon_1, \varepsilon_2\}$ *such that* $\varepsilon_1 = (\{v_1\}, \{v_3, v_4, v_5\})$ *and* $\varepsilon_2 = (\{v_1, v_2\}, \{v_3\})$, *and* $\mathcal{L} = \{(\varepsilon_1, label_{\varepsilon_1}), (\varepsilon_2, label_{\varepsilon_2})\}$. *In this hypergraph we have* $tail(\varepsilon_2) = \{v_1, v_2\}$ *(please note that* $tail(\varepsilon_2)$ *is depicted in the upper half of the hyperedge* ε_2 *in Fig. 3). A path from* v_1 *to* v_4 *is a sequence of hyperedges* $P_{v_1/v_4} = \langle \varepsilon_2 \rangle$. *A hyperpath from* $\{v_1\}$ *to* v_4 *is the hypergraph* $\Theta_{\{v_1\}/v_4} = (\mathcal{V}_\Theta, \mathcal{E}_\Theta)$ *s.t.* $\mathcal{V}_\Theta = \{v_1, v_3, v_4, v_5\}$ *and* $\mathcal{E}_\Theta = \{\varepsilon_1\}$.

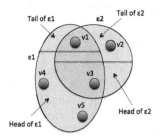

Fig. 2. Hypergraph in Example 2

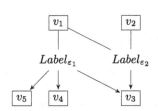

Fig. 3. Bipartite depiction of the hypergraph in Example 2

3   Constructing the Graph of Atom Dependency

In this section we present the notion of Graph of Atom Dependency (GAD), then we define the algorithms that can be used to construct it, and finally we explain how chase variants can impact its construction. This hypergraph structure will be used in order to construct all provenance paths as detailed in Sect. 4.

3.1   Provenance Paths

In order to define the notion of provenance path we first need to define the notion of derivation of a set of facts with respect to a set of rules.

Definition 1 (Derivation of $\mathcal{F}$ with respect to $\mathcal{R}$). *Given a set of facts $\mathcal{F}$, and a set of rules $\mathcal{R}$, a **derivation of $\mathcal{F}$ with respect to $\mathcal{R}$** is a (potentially infinite) sequence $\mathcal{D}$ of D_i s.t. D_i is a tuple $(\mathcal{F}_i, R_i, \pi_i)$ composed of a set of facts $\mathcal{F}_i$, a rule $R_i = (\mathcal{H}_i, C_i)$ and a homomorphism π_i from $\mathcal{H}_i$ to $\mathcal{F}_i$ where: $D_0 = (\mathcal{F}, \emptyset, \emptyset)$, and $\mathcal{F}_i = \alpha(\mathcal{F}_{i-1}, R_i, \pi_i)$.*

In a tuple $D_i = (\mathcal{F}_i, R_i, \pi_i)$ we denote by $fact(D_i) = \mathcal{F}_i$, $rule(D_i) = R_i$ and $homorph(D_i) = \pi_i$ the facts, rule and homomorphism of D_i respectively.

In this paper we are interested in the notion of provenance path of a query. Given a query q and a set of facts $\mathcal{F}$, the provenance of the query q from the facts $\mathcal{F}$ with respect to a set of rules $\mathcal{R}$ is a finite derivation of $\mathcal{F}$ with respect to $\mathcal{R}$ that ends with a set of atoms containing q.

Definition 2 (Provenance path from $\mathcal{F}$ to an atom F w.r.t. $\mathcal{R}$). *A provenance path $\mathcal{PP}$ from the set of facts $\mathcal{F}$ to the atom F with respect to a set of rules $\mathcal{R}$ is a finite derivation of $\mathcal{F}$ with respect to $\mathcal{R}$ s.t.: $\mathcal{PP} = \langle D_0, \ldots, D_n \rangle$ and $F \in fact(D_n)$.*

Example 3. *Let us consider a simple knowledge base $KB = (\mathcal{F}, \mathcal{R})$ where $\mathcal{F} = \{p(a), r(a)\}$, $\mathcal{R} = \{R_1 : p(X) \wedge r(X) \to s(X) \wedge t(X),\ R_2 : t(X) \to q(X),\ R_3 : p(X) \to u(X)\}$. A possible derivation of $\mathcal{F}$ w.r.t. $\mathcal{R}$ is:*
$\langle (\mathcal{F}, \emptyset, \emptyset), (\mathcal{F}_1 = \mathcal{F} \cup \{s(a), t(a)\}, R_1, \pi_1 = \{X \to a\}),$
$(\mathcal{F}_2 = \mathcal{F}_1 \cup \{u(a)\}, R_3, \pi_2 = \{X \to a\}),$
$(\mathcal{F}_3 = \mathcal{F}_2 \cup \{q(a)\}, R_2, \pi_3 = \{X \to a\}) \rangle.$
The provenance path from $\mathcal{F}$ to $q(a)$ is the sequence
$\mathcal{PP}_{KB} = \langle (\mathcal{F}, \emptyset, \emptyset), (\mathcal{F}_1 = \mathcal{F} \cup \{s(a), t(a)\}, R_1, \pi_1), (\mathcal{F}_1 \cup \{q(a)\}, R_2, \pi_3) \rangle.$

3.2   Graph of Atom Dependency (GAD)

A Graph of Atom Dependency (GAD) [11] is a hypergraph where the set of nodes corresponds to the set of atoms and the set of labeled edges corresponds to rule applications labeled by the rule and the corresponding homomorphisms.

Definition 3 (Graph of Atom Dependency). *Given a knowledge base $KB = (\mathcal{F}, \mathcal{R})$, a Graph of Atom Dependency of KB is a directed edge-labeled hypergraph that allows repeated edges $\mathcal{H}_{KB} = (\mathcal{V}_{KB}, \mathcal{E}_{KB}, \mathcal{L}_{KB})$ where:*

- $\mathcal{V}_{\mathcal{KB}}$ is a set of **ground atoms** s.t. $\mathcal{F} \subseteq \mathcal{V}_{\mathcal{KB}}$ ($\mathcal{V}_{\mathcal{KB}}$ contains $\mathcal{F}$ and all generated atoms from $\mathcal{F}$ using $\mathcal{R}$).
- $\mathcal{E}_{\mathcal{KB}} \subseteq 2^{\mathcal{V}_{\mathcal{KB}}} \times 2^{\mathcal{V}_{\mathcal{KB}}}$ is a set of hyperedges.
- $\mathcal{L} : \mathcal{E}_{\mathcal{KB}} \to \mathcal{R} \times \Pi$ is a labeling function that maps each edge $e \in \mathcal{E}_{\mathcal{KB}}$ to a tuple (R, π) where $R \in \mathcal{R}$ and $\pi \in \Pi$, s.t. $head(e) = \alpha(tail(e), R, \pi)$.

Example 4. Let us consider the knowledge base in Example 3, $KB = (\mathcal{F}, \mathcal{R})$ where $\mathcal{F} = \{p(a), r(a)\}$, $\mathcal{R} = \{R_1 : p(X) \wedge r(X) \to s(X) \wedge t(X), R_2 : t(X) \to q(X), R_3 : p(X) \to u(X)\}$. Figure 4 describes the Graph of Atom Dependency of the derivation in Example 3, that is $GAD_{\mathcal{KB}}(\mathcal{F}, \mathcal{R}) = (\mathcal{V}_{\mathcal{KB}}, \mathcal{E}_{\mathcal{KB}}, \mathcal{L}_{\mathcal{KB}})$:

- $\mathcal{V}_{\mathcal{KB}} = \{p(a), r(a), s(a), t(a), u(a), q(a)\}$
- $\mathcal{E}_{\mathcal{KB}} = \{e_1 = (\{p(a), r(a)\}, \{s(a), t(a)\}), e_2 = (\{p(a)\}, \{u(a)\}), e_3 = (\{t(a)\}, \{q(a)\})\}$
- $\mathcal{L}_{\mathcal{KB}} = \{(e_1, (R_1, \pi_1)), (e_2, (R_3, \pi_2)), (e_3, (R_2, \pi_3))\}$

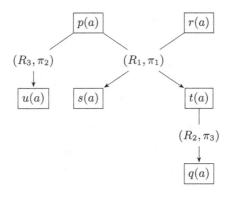

Fig. 4. Graph of Atom Dependency $GAD_{\mathcal{KB}}$ (Example 3)

3.3   Chase Variants for GAD

In this section we will describe how to build the Graph of Atom Dependency using a breadth-first forward chaining algorithm (chase) [5]. We describe the effects of different variants of the chase on the resulting GAD.

Different kinds of chase can be defined by using different derivation reducers. A derivation reducer σ is a function that, given a derivation $\mathcal{D}$ of $\mathcal{F}$ w.r.t. $\mathcal{R}$ returns a sequence of sets of facts such that $\forall D_i \in \mathcal{D}, \sigma(D_i) \subseteq fact(D_i)$. We call $\sigma - chase$ a chase relying on some derivation reducer σ. It generates a possibly infinite derivation $\sigma - chase(\mathcal{F}, \mathcal{R})$ of $D'_i = (\sigma(D_i), R_i, \pi)$. We say that a (possibly infinite) derivation obtained by a $\sigma - chase$ is complete when any further rule application on that derivation would produce the same set of facts. Since we place ourselves in a context where the chase is finite (for example, concrete Finite Expansion Set classes for Skolem and Restricted chases [2]), then we can extract all provenance paths without loss. This will be detailed below.

The algorithm to construct the $GAD = (\mathcal{V}, \mathcal{E})$ using a chase $\sigma-chase(\mathcal{F}, \mathcal{R})$ is straightforward (as described by Algorithm 1): for each rule application, if it generates new facts (according to the chase derivation reducer), then a hyper-edge between the involved atoms and the generated ones is added. If, on the other hand, the generated facts are not considered new according to the chase derivation reducer (these atoms already exists) then a procedure that handles atoms that are considered the same is called. This procedure is specific to the type of chase as each chase defines same atoms differently. The algorithm is polynomial in the size of the saturated knowledge base. The call to the procedure $HandleSameAtoms$ is what differentiates a Graph of Atom Dependency from a chase graph.

Algorithm 1. GAD construction with chase

Function ChaseGAD $(\sigma-chase(\mathcal{F}, \mathcal{R}))$
   input : $\sigma-chase(\mathcal{F}, \mathcal{R})$: the chase
   output: $GAD = (\mathcal{V}, \mathcal{E})$: Graph of Atom dependency w.r.t. $\mathcal{F}$ and $\mathcal{R}$
   $\mathcal{V} \leftarrow \mathcal{F}$; $\mathcal{E} \leftarrow \emptyset$; $GAD \leftarrow (\mathcal{V}, \mathcal{E})$;
   foreach $D_i = (\mathcal{F}_i, R_i = (H_i, C_i), \pi_i) \in \sigma-chase(\mathcal{F}, \mathcal{R})$ **do**
      if $\sigma(D_i) \neq (\mathcal{F}_{i-1})$ **then**
         foreach $v \in \pi_i(C_i)$ and $v \notin (\mathcal{F}_{i-1})$ **do**
          | Add v to $\mathcal{V}$;
         end
      end
      $HandleSameAtoms(F_{i-1}, D_i, GAD)$;
   end
   return GAD;

In a chase graph, if the atom v has been generated before the atom w and w is considered the same as v then w is removed along with the subtree rooted in w. This is problematic as it removes some provenance paths as detailed in Example 5. In what follows we define the $HandleSameAtoms$ algorithm for each different kind of chase: oblivious, skolem and restricted.

Oblivious Chase. The oblivious chase $\sigma_{obl} - chase$ (also called naive chase) [5] relies on the oblivious derivation reducer denoted by σ_{obl} and is defined as follows: for any derivation $\mathcal{D}$, $\sigma_{obl}(D_1) = \mathcal{F}_1$ and $\forall D_i = (\mathcal{F}_i, R_i, \pi_i) \in \mathcal{D}$:

$$\sigma_{obl}(D_i) = \begin{cases} \mathcal{F}_{i-1} \cup \pi_i^{safe}(C_i) & \text{if } \forall j < i, \pi_j \neq \pi_j \text{ or } R_j \neq R_i \\ \mathcal{F}_{i-1} & \text{otherwise} \end{cases}$$

Essentially, the oblivious chase ensures that a rule R is applied according to a homomorphism π only if it has not already been applied according to the same homomorphism. For this chase, two atoms are considered the same if they are exactly the same (i.e. redundant). Due to the simplicity of the test performed by the oblivious chase, the $HandleSameAtoms$ procedure (defined in Algorithm 2) for this chase simply ensures that for any rule application, if an edge representing it has not already been created, then it creates it. This algorithm is polynomial in the size of $\mathcal{F}_{i-1}$.

Algorithm 2. Handle same atoms for Oblivious chase

Procedure HandleSameAtoms $(\mathcal{F}_{i-1}, D_i, GAD)$
  input : F_{i-1} : set of facts, $D_i(\mathcal{F}_i, \mathcal{R}_i = (H_i, C_i), \pi_i)$: element of the chase, $GAD =$
         $(\mathcal{V}, \mathcal{E})$: graph of atom dependency
  if $e = (\pi_i(H_i), \pi_i(C_i)) \notin \mathcal{E}$ **then**
    if e *does not create a cycle* **then**
      | Add e to $\mathcal{E}$;
    end
  end

Example 5. *Let us consider* $\mathcal{KB} = (\mathcal{F}, \mathcal{R})$ *from Example 1. A possible derivation for the oblivious chase of* $\mathcal{F}$ *w.r.t.* $\mathcal{R}$ *is:*
$\sigma_{obl} - chase(\mathcal{F}, \mathcal{R}) = < (\mathcal{F}, \emptyset, \emptyset),$
$(\mathcal{F}_1 = \mathcal{F} \cup \{r(a, Y_1)\}, R_1, \pi_1 = \{X \to a\}),$
$(\mathcal{F}_2 = \mathcal{F}_1 \cup \{p(b)\}, R_2, \pi_2 = \{X \to a, X \to b\}),$
$(\mathcal{F}_3 = \mathcal{F}_2 \cup \{r(b, Y_2)\}, R_3, \pi_3 = \{X \to b\}),$
$(\mathcal{F}_4 = \mathcal{F}_3 \cup \{t(a)\}, R_4, \pi_4 = \{X \to a, Y \to Y_1\}),$
$(\mathcal{F}_5 = \mathcal{F}_4 \cup \{t(b)\}, R_4, \pi_5 = \{X \to b, Y \to Y_2\}),$
$(\mathcal{F}_6 = \mathcal{F}_5 \cup \{r(b, Y_3)\}, R_1, \pi_6\{X \to b\}),$
$(\mathcal{F}_7 = \mathcal{F}_6, R_4, \pi_7 = \{X \to b, Y \to Y_3\}) >$
     The chase graph and GAD resulting from the oblivious chase $\sigma_{obl} - chase(\mathcal{F}, \mathcal{R})$ *are shown in Figs. 1 and 5 respectively. As described before, the chase graph can only find one minimal provenance path* $\mathcal{PP}_1$ *for* $t(b)$ *whereas the GAD can find another minimal provenance path* $\mathcal{PP}_2$ *that the chase graph lost due to the fact that the application of* R_4 *on* $r(b, Y_3)$ *generates what the oblivious chase considers a redundant atom:*

- $\mathcal{PP}_1 = < (\mathcal{F}, \emptyset, \emptyset), (\mathcal{F}_1 = \mathcal{F} \cup \{r(b, Y_2)\}, R_3, \pi_3), (\mathcal{F}_2 = \mathcal{F}_1 \cup \{t(b)\}, R_4, \pi_5) >$
- $\mathcal{PP}_2 = < (\mathcal{F}, \emptyset, \emptyset), (\mathcal{F}_1 = \mathcal{F} \cup \{p(b)\}, R_2, \pi_2), (\mathcal{F}_2 = \mathcal{F}_1 \cup \{r(b, Y_3)\}, R_3, \pi_6),$
  $(\mathcal{F}_3 = \mathcal{F}_2 \cup \{t(b)\}, R_4, \pi_7) >.$

The following proposition states that for any rule application generated by an oblivious chase, there exists an edge representing it in the generated GAD using Algorithm 2, meaning that no rule application is lost.

Proposition 1 (GAD $\sigma_{obl} - chase(\mathcal{F}, \mathcal{R})$ **Completeness).** *Given a knowledge base* $\mathcal{KB} = (\mathcal{F}, \mathcal{R})$ *and* $GAD = (\mathcal{V}, \mathcal{E})$ *generated by an oblivious chase,* $\forall D_i = (\mathcal{F}_i, R_i = (\mathcal{H}_i, C_i), \pi_i) \in \sigma_{obl} - chase(\mathcal{F}, \mathcal{R}), \exists e \in \mathcal{E}$ *such that* $e = (\pi_i(\mathcal{H}_i), \pi_i(C_i)).$

Proof (Sketch). We prove this by construction, since for any $D_i = (\mathcal{F}_i, R_i = (\mathcal{H}_i, C_i), \pi_i) \in \sigma_{obl} - chase(\mathcal{F}, \mathcal{R})$, $HandleSameAtoms$ is called (as per Algorithm 1), if $e = (\pi_i(H_i), \pi_i(C_i)) \notin \mathcal{E}$ then it is added, otherwise, it already exists.

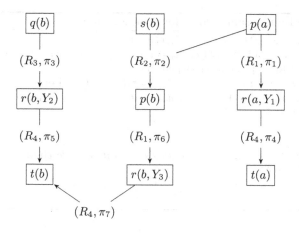

Fig. 5. Graph of atom dependency generated for Example 1

Skolem/Frontier Chase. In the frontier chase $\sigma_{fr}-chase$ two applications $\alpha(\mathcal{F}, R, \pi)$ and $\alpha(\mathcal{F}, R, \pi')$ of the same rule add the same atoms if they map frontier variables identically ($\forall X \in fr(R), \pi(X) = \pi'(X)$). The frontier derivation reducer denoted by σ_{fr} is defined as follows: for any derivation $\mathcal{D}$, $\sigma_{fr}(D_1) = \mathcal{F}_1$ and $\forall D_i = (\mathcal{F}_i, R_i, \pi_i) \in \mathcal{D}$:

$$\sigma_{fr}(D_i) = \begin{cases} \mathcal{F}_{i-1} \cup \pi_i^{safe}(C_i) & \text{if } \forall j < i, \pi_j|_{fr(R_j)}(C_j) \neq \pi_i|_{fr(R_i)}(C_i) \\ & \text{and } R_j \neq R_i \\ \mathcal{F}_{i-1} & \text{otherwise} \end{cases}$$

The frontier chase is equivalent to the skolem chase [14] that relies on a skolemisation of the rules by replacing each occurrence of an existential variable Y with a functional term $f_Y^R(\boldsymbol{X})$, where $\boldsymbol{X} = fr(R)$ are the frontier variables of R; the oblivious chase is then run on skolemized rules. Frontier chase and skolem chase yield isomorphic results [2], in the sense that they generate exactly the same atoms, up to a bijective renaming of variables by skolem terms.

The oblivious chase is strictly 'weaker' than the frontier chase [2] meaning that if $\sigma_{obl}-chase(\mathcal{F}, \mathcal{R})$ is finite then $\sigma_{fr}-chase(\mathcal{F}, \mathcal{R})$ is also finite. In the frontier chase, two atoms are considered the same if they have the same constants (and possibly different freshly generated constants). The $HandleSameAtoms$ procedure (defined in Algorithm 3) for the frontier chase is more general than the one for the oblivious chase and might result in different GADs. This algorithm is polynomial in the size of the $\mathcal{F}_{i-1}$.

Algorithm 3. Handle same atoms for Frontier chase

Procedure HandleSameAtoms $(\mathcal{F}_{i-1}, D_i, GAD)$
   input : F_{i-1} : set of facts, $D_i(\mathcal{F}_i, \mathcal{R}_i = (H_i, C_i), \pi_i)$: element of the chase, $GAD = $
       $(\mathcal{V}, \mathcal{E})$: graph of atom dependency
   if $\exists j, \pi_j, R_j$ s.t. $j < i$ and $\pi_j|_{fr(R_j)}(C_j) = \pi_i|_{fr(R_i)}(C_i)$ **then**
      if $e = (\pi_i(H_i), \pi_j(C_i)) \notin \mathcal{E}$ and does not create a cycle **then**
        | Add e to $\mathcal{E}$;
      end
   else
      if $e = (\pi_i(H_i), \pi_i(C_i)) \notin \mathcal{E}$ and does not create a cycle **then**
        | Add e to $\mathcal{E}$;
      end
   end

Similarly to Propositions 1 and 2 states that no rule application is lost, even if it does not generate new atoms, it is still added to the edges of the GAD.

Proposition 2 (GAD $\sigma_{fr}-chase(\mathcal{F}, \mathcal{R})$ Completeness). *Given a knowledge base $\mathcal{KB} = (\mathcal{F}, \mathcal{R})$ and $GAD = (\mathcal{V}, \mathcal{E})$ generated by a frontier chase, $\forall D_i = (\mathcal{F}_i, R_i = (\mathcal{H}_i, C_i), \pi_i) \in \sigma_{fr}-chase(\mathcal{F}, \mathcal{R}), \exists e \in \mathcal{E}$ such that $e = (\pi_i(\mathcal{H}_i), \pi_i(C_i))$ or $e = (\pi_i(\mathcal{H}_i), \pi_j(C_i))$ where π_j and π_i map frontier variables of R identically.*

Proposition 3 expresses the structural link between GADs obtained thanks to oblivious and frontier chases.

Proposition 3. *Let $GAD_{\sigma_{obl}} = (\mathcal{V}_{\sigma_{obl}}, \mathcal{E}_{\sigma_{obl}})$ and $GAD_{\sigma_{fr}} = (\mathcal{V}_{\sigma_{fr}}, \mathcal{E}_{\sigma_{fr}})$ be two Graphs of Atom Dependency for $(\mathcal{F}, \mathcal{R})$ generated by a complete oblivious chase and a complete frontier chase. If $GAD_{\sigma_{obl}}$ and $GAD_{\sigma_{fr}}$ are finite, then $|\mathcal{V}_{\sigma_{fr}}| \leq |\mathcal{V}_{\sigma_{obl}}|$ and $|\mathcal{E}_{\sigma_{obl}}| = |\mathcal{E}_{\sigma_{fr}}|$.*

Proof (Sketch). Given that frontier is stronger than the oblivious chase [2], some generated atoms are judged redundant by the frontier chase while considered new by the oblivious one, thus $|\mathcal{V}_{\sigma_{fr}}| \leq |\mathcal{V}_{\sigma_{obl}}|$. Furthermore, since rule applications are not lost given Propositions 1 and 2, then $|\mathcal{E}_{\sigma_{obl}}| = |\mathcal{E}_{\sigma_{fr}}|$.

Restricted Chase. The restricted chase $\sigma_{res} - chase$ (also called standard chase) [8] uses the restricted derivation reducer denoted by σ_{res} and defined as follows: for any derivation $\mathcal{D}$, $\sigma_{res}(D_1) = \mathcal{F}_1$ and $\forall D_i = (\mathcal{F}_i, R_i, \pi_i) \in \mathcal{D}$:

$$\sigma_{res}(D_i) = \begin{cases} \mathcal{F}_{i-1} \cup \pi_i^{safe}(C_i) & \text{if } \mathcal{F}_{i-1} \nvDash \pi_i^{safe}(C_i) \\ \mathcal{F}_{i-1} & \text{otherwise} \end{cases}$$

The restricted chase relies on the notion of useful homomorphism. For a rule $R = (\mathcal{H}, C)$ and a set of facts $\mathcal{F}$, a homomorphism π from $\mathcal{H}$ to $\mathcal{F}$ is said to be useful if it cannot be extended to a homomorphism from $\mathcal{H} \cup C$ to $\mathcal{F}$, meaning that $\pi^{safe}(H \cup C)$ does not exist in $\mathcal{F}$. The frontier chase is strictly weaker than the restricted chase, thus, the *HandleSameAtoms* procedure (defined in Algorithm 4) for the restricted chase is more general than the one for the frontier chase and might result in different GADs (as described in Example 6). Furthermore, the restricted chase checks only for local redundancy, meaning that the order in which rules are applied affects the resulting set of atoms as described in Example 6. This algorithm is polynomial in the size of the $\mathcal{F}_{i-1}$.

Algorithm 4. Handle same atoms for Restricted chase

Procedure HandleSameAtoms $(\mathcal{F}_{i-1}, D_i, GAD)$
    input : F_{i-1} : set of facts, $D_i(\mathcal{F}_i, \mathcal{R}_i = (\mathcal{H}_i, C_i), \pi_i)$: element of the chase, $GAD =$
           $(\mathcal{V}, \mathcal{E})$: graph of atom dependency
    if $\exists \pi'$ *s.t.* $\pi'(\mathcal{H}_i \cup C_i) \subseteq \mathcal{F}_{i-1}$ **then**
        if $e = (\pi'(\mathcal{H}_i), \pi'(C_i)) \notin \mathcal{E}$ *and does not create a cycle* **then**
           | Add e to $\mathcal{E}$;
        end
    else
        if $e = (\pi_i(\mathcal{H}_i), \pi_i(C_i))$ *does not create a cycle* **then**
           | Add e to $\mathcal{E}$;
        end
    end

Similarly to Proposition 1 and 2, no rule application is lost for the restricted chase.

Proposition 4 (GAD $\sigma_{res}-chase(\mathcal{F}, \mathcal{R})$ **Completeness).** *Given a knowledge base* $\mathcal{KB} = (\mathcal{F}, \mathcal{R})$ *and* $GAD = (\mathcal{V}, \mathcal{E})$ *generated by a restricted chase,* $\forall D_i = (\mathcal{F}_i, R_i = (\mathcal{H}_i, C_i), \pi_i) \in \sigma_{res}-chase(\mathcal{F}, \mathcal{R}), \exists e \in \mathcal{E}$ *such that* $e = (\pi_i(\mathcal{H}_i), \pi_i(C_i))$ *or* $e = (\pi'(\mathcal{H}_i), \pi'(C_i))$ *where* π' *is a homomorphism such that* $\pi'(\mathcal{H}_i \cup C_i) \subseteq \mathcal{F}_{i-1}$.

Example 6. *We will consider the knowledge base* $\mathcal{KB} = (\mathcal{F}, \mathcal{R})$ *such that* $\mathcal{F} = \{p(a)\}$ *and the set of rules* $\mathcal{R} = \{R_1 : p(X) \to r(X, Y) \wedge q(Y), R_2 : p(X) \to r(X, Y), R_3 : r(X, Y) \to q(Y)\}$. *The GAD generated by the frontier chase for this example is exactly the same as the one generated by the oblivious chase regardless of the order in which the rules are applied at each breadth-first derivation. On the other hand, the order of rule applications affects the GAD generated by a restricted chase as shown in Figs. 6 and 7.*

Let $GAD_{\sigma_{res}}$ *be the Graph of Atom Dependency generated by first applying the rule* R_1: $\alpha(\mathcal{F}, R_1, \pi_1)$ *gives* $\{r(a, Y_1), q(Y_1)\}$, *which are considered new as these atoms are not contained in* $\mathcal{F}$ ($\mathcal{F} \not\models \{r(a, Y_1), q(Y_1)\}$). *Hence* $\mathcal{F}_2 = \mathcal{F} \cup \{r(a, Y_1), q(Y_1)\}$.

Then R_2 *is applied:* $\alpha(\mathcal{F}_2, R_2, \pi_2)$ *generates* $\{r(a, Y_2)\}$, *which is considered redundant as the chase maps it to* $\{r(a, Y_1)\}$ *(the fresh variable* Y_2 *is mapped to the fresh variable* Y_1). *We have* $\mathcal{F} \models \{r(a, Y_2)\}$, *so it is not added and the chase continues.*

However, in $GAD'_{\sigma_{res}}$, the rule R_1 is applied after R_2. First applying R_2 $(\alpha(\mathcal{F}, R_2, \pi_1))$ gives $r(a, Y_1)$ which is new as $F \not\models \{r(a, Y_1)\}$. So $\mathcal{F}_2 = \mathcal{F} \cup \{r(a, Y_1)\}$.

Then R_1 is applied $(\alpha(\mathcal{F}_2, R_1, \pi_2))$, generating $\{r(a, Y_2), q(Y_2)\}$ which are considered new as this set of atoms cannot be mapped to any existing atoms (Y_2 cannot be mapped to Y_1 as there is no $q(Y_1)$). We have $\mathcal{F}_2 \not\models \{r(a, Y_2), q(Y_2)\}$, so $\mathcal{F}_3 = \mathcal{F}_2 \cup \{r(a, Y_2), q(Y_2)\}$.

4 Obtaining Provenance Paths

The intuition behind the use of the GAD is that, for a given GAD and a given query, there is a one-to-one mapping, up to provenance path equivalence, between the set of hyperpaths to q and the set of provenance paths to q. Therefore, once the GAD constructed (by considering the different chase mechanisms) the problem of obtaining all provenance paths can be transformed into the problem of generating all hyperpaths of q in the GAD.

Let us first define the notion of provenance path minimality and equivalence. We recall that a provenance path is a sequence $\mathcal{PP}$ of D_i such that D_i is a tuple $(\mathcal{F}_i, R_i, \pi_i)$. We say that two provenance paths $\mathcal{PP}$ and $\mathcal{PP}'$ from a set of facts $\mathcal{F}$ to q are **equivalent** iff they have the same set of atoms and the same set of applied rules (along with their respective homomorphisms) i.e. $\bigcup_{D \in \mathcal{PP}} fact(D) = \bigcup_{D' \in \mathcal{PP}'} fact(D')$ and $\bigcup_{D \in \mathcal{PP}}(rule(D), homorph(D)) = \bigcup_{D' \in \mathcal{PP}'}(rule(D'), homorph(D'))$. We denote that $\mathcal{PP}$ and $\mathcal{PP}'$ are equivalent by $\mathcal{PP} \simeq \mathcal{PP}'$. Please note that $\simeq$ is an equivalence relation (as it is obviously reflexive, symmetric and transitive). Therefore it induces a partition of the set of all provenance paths. A provenance path $\mathcal{PP}$ from a set of facts F to q is said to be **minimal** w.r.t. a set of rules $\mathcal{R}$ and homomorphisms Π if no other provenance path $\mathcal{PP}'$ from F to q exits s.t. $\bigcup_{D' \in \mathcal{PP}'} fact(D') \subset \bigcup_{D \in \mathcal{PP}} fact(D)$

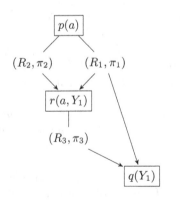

Fig. 6. $GAD_{\sigma_{res}}$ (Example 6) where R_1 is applied before R_2

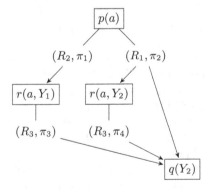

Fig. 7. $GAD'_{\sigma_{res}}$ (Example 6) where R_2 is applied before R_1

and $\bigcup_{D' \in \mathcal{PP'}}(rule(D'), homorph(D')) \subset \bigcup_{D \in \mathcal{PP}}(rule(D), homorph(D))$. The following property trivially holds.

Proposition 5. *If a provenance path $\mathcal{PP}$ is equivalent to another minimal provenance path $\mathcal{PP'}$ then $\mathcal{PP}$ is minimal.*

Provenance paths are constructed from the hyperpaths of the GAD. The following proposition shows that for every hyperpath of the GAD we can construct an equivalent provenance path. This will ensure the soundness of the hyperpath generation with respect to the problem of generating all provenance paths.

Proposition 6 (Hyperpath Soundness w.r.t. a Provenance Path). *Let GAD be a Graph of Atom Dependency generated by applying a $\sigma-chase(\mathcal{F}, \mathcal{R})$ on a set of facts $\mathcal{F}$ w.r.t. a set of rules $\mathcal{R}$. If there exists a hyperpath $\Theta_{\mathcal{F}/t}$ in GAD from $\mathcal{F}$ to a fact $t \in fact(D)$ s.t. $D \in \sigma-chase(\mathcal{F}, \mathcal{R})$, then there exist a provenance path $\mathcal{PP}$ from $\mathcal{F}$ to t.*

Proof (Sketch). Since GAD is acyclic by definition, then $\Theta_{\mathcal{F}/t}$ is acyclic. If $\Theta_{\mathcal{F}/t}$ is acyclic then a valid ordering of its hyperedges is possible [10]. Based on this valid ordering we can then generate the sequence in the provenance path.

Please note that for a given GAD and for a given hyperpath the provenance paths that can be constructed from $\Theta_{\mathcal{F}/t}$ are equivalent (i.e. they belong to the same class of $\simeq$).

Proposition 7 (Hyperpath Soundness). *Given the GAD for the knowledge base $\mathcal{KB} = (\mathcal{F}, \mathcal{R})$ and a hyperpath $\Theta_{\mathcal{F}/t}$ in GAD from $\mathcal{F}$ to a fact $t \in fact(D)$ s.t. $D \in \sigma-chase(\mathcal{F}, \mathcal{R})$, if two provenance paths $\mathcal{PP}_1$ and $\mathcal{PP}_2$ are generated from $\Theta_{\mathcal{F}/t}$ then $\mathcal{PP}_1 \simeq \mathcal{PP}_2$.*

Proof (Sketch). Since GAD is acyclic by definition, then $\Theta_{\mathcal{F}/t}$ is acyclic. If $\Theta_{\mathcal{F}/t}$ is acyclic then a valid ordering of its hyperedges is possible. In fact, $\Theta_{\mathcal{F}/t}$ can have different valid orderings of its hyperedges. Provenance paths generated from these valid orderings contain the same facts and rule applications since all ordering are for the same hyperedges. Thus, the generated provenance paths are equivalent.

Let us now show that the completeness holds. More precisely we can show that for a given knowledge base and a minimal provenance path there exists an equivalent hyperpath in the GAD associated to the knowledge base.

Proposition 8 (Hyperpath Completeness). *Given a knowledge base $\mathcal{KB} = (\mathcal{F}, \mathcal{R})$, a query q and $\mathcal{PP}$ a minimal provenance path for q in $\mathcal{KB}$, there exists a hyperpath $\Theta_{\mathcal{F}/q}$ in the GAD of $\mathcal{KB}$.*

Proof (Sketch). We prove this by contradiction. Let us suppose that there exists a minimal provenance path $\mathcal{PP}$ for q in $\mathcal{KB}$ such that no hyperpath $\Theta_{\mathcal{F}/q}$ can be constructed in the associated GAD. This means that a rule application in the provenance path is not present in the hyperpath. This means that in the construction of the GAD this rule application has not been considered. This is impossible given the results of the completeness of GAD construction using different chase variants (Propositions 1, 2 and 4).

Similar to above, for a given knowledge base and a class of $\simeq$ minimal provenance paths there exists a hyperpath in the associated GAD. The above propositions show the soundness and completeness of minimal provenance path generation with respect to hyperpath finding in a GAD.

Please note that the GAD construction is chase sensitive. For each chase (*oblivious*, *frontier* and *restricted*) a different GAD can be constructed, as shown in the previous section. For a given knowledge base the *oblivious*-generated GAD can be infinite, and for the same knowledge base the *frontier*-generated GAD is finite. The same result shows for *frontier* chase and restricted chase. Therefore if the GAD is finite then, for any of the above chase methods, for a given query we can generate all minimal provenance paths supporting this query.

Algorithm 5. Find Paths & Hyperpaths

Function FP *(S, t)*
   | **input** : S : source nodes, t: target node
   | **output:** paths: set of all paths between S and t
   | paths $\leftarrow \{\}$;
   | **if** $t \in S$ **then**
   | | return paths;
   | **end**
   | **if** $BS(t)$ *is equal to* $\emptyset$ **then**
   | | return null;
   | **end**
   | **foreach** $e \in BS(t)$ **do**
   | | path $\leftarrow \{e\}$;
   | | tmp $\leftarrow \{\}$;
   | | **foreach** $v \in tail(e)$ **do**
   | | | tmp $\leftarrow$ FP $(S, v) \times$ tmp;
   | | **end**
   | | paths $\leftarrow$ paths $\cup$ (path $\times$ tmp);
   | **end**
   | return paths;

Procedure FindAllHyperpaths *(S, t)*
   | **input** : S : source nodes, t: target node
   | **output:** hyperpaths: set of all hyperpaths between S and t
   | hyperpaths $\leftarrow \{\}$; paths $\leftarrow FP(S, t)$;
   | **foreach** *path* $\in$ paths **do**
   | | $\mathcal{V} \leftarrow S$;
   | | $\mathcal{E} \leftarrow path$;
   | | **foreach** $e \in \mathcal{E}$ **do**
   | | | Add $head(e)$ and $tail(e)$ to $\mathcal{V}$;
   | | **end**
   | | Add $\mathcal{H} = (\mathcal{V}, \mathcal{E})$ to hyperpaths;
   | **end**

To construct all non-equivalent minimal provenance paths from a set of facts S to a fact t we only need to find all minimal hyperpaths from S to t. For this we need to compute all paths (sequence of hyperedges) from S to t. The recursive function FP defined in Algorithm 5 computes all paths that connect a subset of $\mathcal{F}$ to an atom t using backward branching; we then use these paths in the procedure FindAllHyperpaths in order to construct the hyperpaths. Please note that Algorithm 5 is based on a modification of [15] to take into account hyperedges rather than hyperarcs. The modification does not affect its complexity which is polynomial in the size of the nodes of the hypergraph.

5 Discussion

In this paper we studied the problem of generating all minimal provenance paths for an atomic ground query in the context of a knowledge base expressed using existential rules. As we have shown, this problem can be tricky as it was implicitly assumed that obtaining all provenance paths can be reduced to obtaining one path. However, given the restriction test of different chase, provenance path loss can occur in certain cases depending on the order in which rules are applied. This provenance path loss can be critical in applications such as defeasible reasoning [11]. To resolve this problem, we extended the notion of a graph of atom dependency, and showed how the chase choice impacts its construction. We then used this graph to generate all minimal provenance paths for a given atom.

For future work directions we aim to define an optimized algorithm for *conjunctive* atomic queries. The ideas developed in this paper can be used to tackle this issue however performance can optimized when paths intersect. We also plan to consider the core chase, and investigate the use of the GAD in the backward chaining reasoning; more precisely, we plan to study if this could lead to a beneficial combination of backward and forward chaining.

References

1. Arora, T., Ramakrishnan, R., Roth, W.G., Seshadri, P., Srivastava, D.: Explaining program execution in deductive systems. In: Ceri, S., Tanaka, K., Tsur, S. (eds.) DOOD 1993. LNCS, vol. 760, pp. 101–119. Springer, Heidelberg (1993). doi:10. 1007/3-540-57530-8_7
2. Baget, J.-F., Garreau, F., Mugnier, M.-L., Rocher, S.: Extending acyclicity notions for existential rules. In: ECAI, pp. 39–44 (2014)
3. Buneman, P., Chapman, A., Cheney, J.: Provenance management in curated databases. In: Proceedings of the 2006 ACM SIGMOD international conference on Management of data, pp. 539–550. ACM (2006)
4. Caballero, R., García-Ruiz, Y., Sáenz-Pérez, F.: A theoretical framework for the declarative debugging of datalog programs. In: Schewe, K.-D., Thalheim, B. (eds.) SDKB 2008. LNCS, vol. 4925, pp. 143–159. Springer, Heidelberg (2008). doi:10. 1007/978-3-540-88594-8_8
5. Calì, A., Gottlob, G., Kifer, M.: Taming the infinite chase: query answering under expressive relational constraints. In: Proceeding of KR, pp. 70–80 (2008)

6. Calì, A., Gottlob, G., Lukasiewicz, T.: A general datalog-based framework for tractable query answering over ontologies. Web Semant. Sci. Serv. Agents World Wide Web **14**, 57–83 (2012)
7. Ceri, S., Gottlob, G., Tanca, L.: What you always wanted to know about datalog (and never dared to ask). IEEE Trans. Knowl. Data Eng. **1**(1), 146–166 (1989)
8. Fagin, R., Kolaitis, P.G., Miller, R.J., Popa, L.: Data exchange: semantics and query answering. Theoret. Comput. Sci. **336**(1), 89–124 (2005)
9. Frawley, W.J., Piatetsky-Shapiro, G., Matheus, C.J.: Knowledge discovery in databases: an overview. AI Mag. **13**(3), 57 (1992)
10. Gallo, G., Longo, G., Pallottino, S., Nguyen, S.: Directed hypergraphs and applications. Discrete Appl. Math. **42**(2), 177–201 (1993)
11. Hecham, A., Croitoru, M., Bisquert, P.: Argumentation-based defeasible reasoning for existential rules. In: Proceedings of AAMAS 2017 (2017, to appear)
12. Ikeda, R., Widom, J.: Data Lineage: A Survey (2009)
13. Kakas, A.C., Kowalski, R.A., Toni, F.: The role of abduction in logic programming. Handb. Logic Artif. Intell. Logic Program. **5**, 235–324 (1998)
14. Marnette, B.: Generalized schema-mappings: from termination to tractability. In: Proceedings of the Twenty-Eighth ACM SIGMOD-SIGACT-SIGART Symposium on Principles of Database Systems, pp. 13–22. ACM (2009)
15. Nguyen, S., Pallottino, S.: Hyperpaths and shortest hyperpaths. In: Simeone, B. (ed.) Combinatorial Optimization. LNM, vol. 1403, pp. 258–271. Springer, Heidelberg (1989). doi:10.1007/BFb0083470
16. Ré, C., Suciu, D.: Approximate lineage for probabilistic databases. Proc. VLDB Endowment **1**(1), 797–808 (2008)
17. Widom, J.: Trio: a system for data, uncertainty, and lineage. In: Aggarwa, C.C. (ed.) Managing and Mining Uncertain Data, vol. 35, pp. 1–35. Springer, New York (2008)

Rewriting Queries with Negated Atoms

Enrique Matos Alfonso and Giorgos Stamou[(✉)]

National Technical University of Athens (NTUA), Zografou, Greece
gardero@image.ntua.gr

Abstract. Query rewriting is a popular approach for ontology based data access and in general for first order rewritable knowledge bases. The algorithms defined in the field are based on conjunctive queries with no use of negation over the atoms that are part of them. Also, the constraints present in the knowledge base are ignored in the process of rewriting a query and they are only used to check the consistency of the data. In this paper, we study the problem of answering queries that allow negated atoms. Our approach uses a rewriting algorithm as a black box and the constraints in the system to find a set of conjunctive queries without negated atoms that is equivalent to the original query containing negated atoms. A system (COMPLETO) was implemented with the proposed method and compared to another system (REBSIR) that is able to rewrite negated concepts. In the experimental evaluation COMPLETO performed better than REBSIR for most of the datasets in the benchmark and it portrayed a more scalable performance i.e. describing a faster relative performance with respect to REBSIR's performance with the increase of the size of assertions in the dataset.

1 Introduction

The use of Description Logics (DLs) [1] and Existential Rules [4] has become a powerful tool to answer conjunctive queries over incomplete data. The rules we can express in those knowledge representation languages are used to infer assertions that could yield answers to the query and that are not present in the original data. Query rewriting [7,12] is a very popular reasoning approach that takes an input query and a set of rules and outputs an equivalent expression used to find the answers in the data without using the rules in the knowledge base.

The majority of the existing rewriting algorithms focus on rewriting conjunctive queries with non negated atoms. The use of negation in queries when combined even with very simple languages like $\mathsf{DL-Lite}_{core}^{\mathcal{H}}$ can make the problem of query answering undecidable [11]. On the other hand, the use of guarded negation in queries is proven to be decidable [5] over frontier-guarded existential rules. Yet, the only rewriting based approach we found in the literature [8] only focuses on answering negated concepts.

Our approach proposes the elimination of negated atoms in the query by applying resolution of controlled length with respect to the constraints existing

© Springer International Publishing AG 2017
S. Costantini et al. (Eds.): RuleML+RR 2017, LNCS 10364, pp. 151–167, 2017.
DOI: 10.1007/978-3-319-61252-2_11

in the knowledge base. After this process of elimination we obtain a set of queries containing answers of the initial query and classical rewriting algorithms can then be applied. Furthermore, we prove that the method yields a set of queries containing all the answers when the expressivity of the initial query is restricted. Additionally, some experiments were conduced to compare our approach to the existing one for rewriting negated concepts.

In this paper, the next section introduces some basic concepts related to First Order Logic Resolution, Existential Rules and Queries with Negation. Next, a rewriting approach to answer queries with negations is introduced. In Sect. 4, the experimental results are presented and discussed. We end with some conclusions derived from the results.

2   Preliminaries

We assume the reader is familiar with all the basic notions of first order logic formulas and the semantics associated with them.

2.1   First Order Logic Resolution

Resolution is a sound and complete algorithm that comes from propositional logic and it is extended to deal with first-order logic (FOL) formulas. The method considers FOL formulas F in *clausal form*, represented by a set

$$F = \{C_0, \ldots, C_n\}. \tag{1}$$

The formula F is *semantically equivalent* to the conjunction of the clauses in the set ($F \equiv C_0 \wedge \ldots \wedge C_n$). A *clause* is defined as a set of literals generally denoted with square brackets, semantically equivalent to the universal closure of the disjunction of all the literals in the clause:

$$C_i = [l_1, \ldots, l_k] \quad C_i \equiv \forall (l_1 \vee \ldots \vee l_k). \tag{2}$$

When $k = 0$ we have the *empty clause* $[] \equiv \bot$.

In case the original formula has existential variables the resolution algorithm needs to be applied to the corresponding *equisatisfiable* formula with the existential variables replaced by *Skolem* terms. The *complement* of a literal l is defined as the literal with the opposite polarity:

$$\bar{l} = \begin{cases} a(\mathbf{x}) & \text{for } l = \neg a(\mathbf{x}) \\ \neg a(\mathbf{x}) & \text{for } l = a(\mathbf{x}) \end{cases}$$

We say that a formula in clausal form is unsatisfiable if and only if the resolution algorithm reports that it is unsatisfiable i.e. reaches a formula that contains the empty clause $[] \in F$. For propositional logic, the algorithm can be used as a decision procedure for unsatisfiability because it always terminates. For FOL, resolution is still sound and complete, but the algorithm might not terminate.

A resolution rule can be applied to non-ground clauses (i.e. clauses containing literals with occurrence of variables in their arguments) by including *unification* as part of the resolution rule. A *substitution* is a set $\theta = \{x_1 \leftarrow t_1, \ldots, x_n \leftarrow t_n\}$ of variable x_i and term t_i pairs. The application of a substitution to a formula $F\theta$ is the result of replacing simultaneously the occurrences of x_i by t_i. Substitutions θ and σ can be *composed* $\theta\sigma$ yielding another substitution:

$$\theta\sigma = \{x_1 \leftarrow t_1\sigma, \ldots, x_n \leftarrow t_n\sigma\} \cup \{x_i' \leftarrow t_i' \mid x_i' \leftarrow t_i' \in \sigma \land \neg\exists t \; x_i' \leftarrow t \in \theta\}.$$

We say a substitution μ is *more general* than θ ($\mu \succeq \theta$) if there is another substitution σ such that $\theta = \mu\sigma$. The relation $\succeq$ defines a *partial order* on the set of substitutions. In a similar way when we can find a substitution such that $F\theta = G$ for two formulas, we can then say that F is more general than G ($F \succeq G$). Applying the composition of two substitutions to a formula is equivalent to applying first one and then the other to the result: $F(\theta\sigma) = (F\theta)\sigma$. A *unifier* for a set of atoms $A = \{A_1, \ldots, A_n\}$ is a substitution θ such that $A_1\theta = \ldots = A_i\theta = \ldots = A_n\theta$. The *most general unifier* $\theta = mgu(A)$ is a unifier that is more general than any other unifier for the same set of atoms.

Definition 1 (General Resolution Rule). *Let $C^{(1)}$ and $C^{(2)}$ be two clauses with no variables in common and let $L_1 \subseteq C^{(1)}$ and $L_2 \subseteq C^{(2)}$ be sets of complementary literals after applying the most general unifier $\sigma = mgu(L_1 \cup \overline{L_2})$. The resolvent of $C^{(1)}$ and $C^{(2)}$ with respect to the literals in L_1 and L_2 is the clause:*

$$Res(C^{(1)}, C^{(2)}) = (C^{(1)}\sigma \backslash L_1\sigma) \cup (C^{(2)}\sigma \backslash L_2\sigma).$$

$C^{(1)}$ and $C^{(2)}$ are said to be clashing *clauses.*

Since clauses are considered sets, all the set operations defined for them in the General Resolution Rule assume that identical literals will be collapsed. Sometimes this can be defined as an additional step called *factoring*. To ensure that clauses do not share variables they are always *standardized apart* i.e. all the variables are renamed before using them in the resolution rule.

Theorem 1 (Soundness). *Any model satisfying two clashing clauses will also satisfy their resolvent i.e. $C^{(1)}, C^{(2)} \models Res(C^{(1)}, C^{(2)})$.*

The resolution algorithm for FOL is based on the general resolution rule and it tries to reach the empty clause from an initial set of clauses that represent a FOL formula.

Definition 2. *A* resolution derivation *of a clause C from a set of clauses $\mathfrak{C}$ is a sequence of clauses $C^{(0)}, \ldots, C^{(n)}$, where (i) $C^{(n)} = C$ and (ii) for every $i \in \{0, \ldots, n-1\}$ we have that $C^{(i)} \in \mathfrak{C}$ or it is the resolvent of two previous clauses $C^{(j)}$ and $C^{(k)}$ on the derivation with $j < i$ and $k < i$.*

A resolution derivation can be seen as a tree rooted in $C^{(n)}$, with leaves being the clauses belonging to $\mathfrak{C}$ and the inner nodes are the resolvents of other two clauses. In this case, the resolvent clause is connected to the other two clauses used in the resolution step.

Considering the Soundness Theorem, we can affirm that the clause C will be a logical consequence of $\mathfrak{C}$ i.e. $\mathfrak{C} \models C$. A resolution derivation of the empty clause $\bot$ from $\mathfrak{C}$ is called a *resolution refutation* of $\mathfrak{C}$.

Theorem 2 (Completeness). *If $\mathfrak{C}$ is an unsatisfiable set of clauses then there exists a resolution refutation of $\mathfrak{C}$.*

A *Linear resolution derivation* is a sequence of clauses starting with a clause $C^{(0)}$ from $\mathfrak{C}$ and the rest of the clauses $C^{(i)}$ are obtained applying resolution with the previous clause $C^{(i-1)}$ and a clause from $\mathfrak{C}$. Any resolution derivation can be transformed to a linear resolution derivation.

Theorem 3. *Let $C^{(1)}$ and $C^{(2)}$ be two clashing clauses with resolvent C' and $C^{(3)}$ a clashing clause with C'. Lets assume that $C^{(3)}$ only clashes with one of the two other clauses and without loss of generality we can assume that clause will be $C^{(2)}$. Then we have that*

$$Res(Res(C^{(1)}, C^{(2)}), C^{(3)}) = Res(C^{(1)}, Res(C^{(2)}, C^{(3)})). \tag{3}$$

Proof. The proof of the theorem can be done by replacing the resolvents with the equivalent set expression as defined in the general resolution rule. See Appendix A[1] for a detailed proof. □

2.2   Existential Rules

An *existential rule* r is defined as a logical implication $B[\mathbf{x} \cup \mathbf{y}] \rightarrow H[\mathbf{x} \cup \mathbf{z}]$, where its body $B[\mathbf{s}]$ and the head $H[\mathbf{s}]$ are a conjunction of atoms $a_1(\mathbf{x_1}) \wedge \ldots \wedge a_m(\mathbf{x_m})$, with $\mathbf{s}$ to denote the set of all the variables in the arguments of the atoms. A positive (not negated) atom $a_i(\mathbf{x_i})$ is a *guard* for a set of variables $\mathbf{x}$ iff $\mathbf{x} \subseteq \mathbf{x_1}$. A set of variables $\mathbf{x}$ is *guarded* in a formula F (we could also limit it to a sub-formula) if there is a guard for $\mathbf{x}$ in F. The common variables $\mathbf{x}$ between B and H are called *frontier* variables of the rule and those variables in the head $\mathbf{z}$ which are not present in the body are called *existential* variables. Note that $\mathbf{z} \cap (\mathbf{x} \cup \mathbf{y}) = \emptyset$. An existential rule is equivalent to the following first order logic formula:

$$\forall \mathbf{x} \, \forall \mathbf{y} \, \exists \mathbf{z} \, (\mathbf{b_1}(\mathbf{x_1}) \wedge \ldots \wedge \mathbf{b_m}(\mathbf{x_m}) \rightarrow \mathbf{h_1}(\mathbf{y_1}) \wedge \ldots \wedge \mathbf{h_k}(\mathbf{y_k})) \, .$$

A rule is *guarded* iff there is a guard in the body of the rule for the set of all its variables. A *frontier-guarded* rule contains a guard in the body of the rule for the variables in the frontier of the rule. A *fact* $\mathcal{F}$, is defined as a set of atoms and is equivalent to the existential closure of a conjunction of the atoms in the set:

$$\mathcal{F} \equiv \exists \mathbf{x_1} \ldots \exists \mathbf{x_n} \, (\mathbf{a_1}(\mathbf{x_1}) \wedge \ldots \wedge \mathbf{a_m}(\mathbf{x_m})) \, .$$

A *database* $\mathcal{D}$ is a *grounded* fact i.e. without existential variables.

---

[1] http://image.ntua.gr/~gardero/completo-rr2017/Appendixes.pdf.

A *conjunctive query* $q(\mathbf{x}) = \mathbf{a_1}(\mathbf{x_1}), \ldots, \mathbf{a_n}(\mathbf{x_n})$ is a conjunction of the atoms $a_i(\mathbf{x_i})$ with $\mathbf{x}$ as free variables (called *answer variables*) and the remaining variables $(\mathbf{y} = (\cup_i^n \mathbf{x_1}) \backslash \mathbf{x})$ are existentially quantified:

$$q(\mathbf{x}) \equiv \exists \mathbf{y} \, (\mathbf{a_1}(\mathbf{x_1}) \wedge \ldots \wedge \mathbf{a_n}(\mathbf{x_n})).$$

A *union of conjunctive queries* (UCQ), denoted as a set $\{q_1(\mathbf{x}), \ldots, \mathbf{q_{n'}}(\mathbf{x})\}$ of conjunctive queries, represents a disjunction of conjunctive queries $q_1(\mathbf{x}) \vee \ldots \vee \mathbf{q_{n'}}(\mathbf{x})$.

Rules are often used to find the *answers* of conjunctive queries (or UCQ) over incomplete databases $\mathcal{D}$ i.e. find the set $ans(q(\mathbf{x}), \mathcal{R}, \mathcal{D})$ of tuples $\mathbf{t}$ such that $\mathcal{D}, \mathcal{R} \models q(\mathbf{t})$, where $q(\mathbf{t}) = \mathbf{q}(\mathbf{x})\theta$ and θ replaces all variables in $\mathbf{x}$ by the corresponding component in the tuple $\mathbf{t}$. The tuples contain only constants from $\mathcal{D}$. A *boolean* conjunctive query (BCQ) is a conjunctive query without free variables q. When $\mathcal{D}, \mathcal{R} \models q$ we say that the answer of q is the *empty tuple* $ans(q, \mathcal{R}, \mathcal{D}) = \{()\}$. A CQ $q(\mathbf{x})$ can be associated to a BCQ $q = q(\mathbf{x})$ and we can say that a tuple $\mathbf{t}$ is an answer to $q(\mathbf{x})$ if there is substitution θ to the variables in q is such that $\mathbf{x}\theta = \mathbf{t}$ and

$$\mathcal{D}, \mathcal{R} \models q\theta. \tag{4}$$

A way to reduce a CQ to a BCQ is by introducing a predicate (ans) that is not present in the knowledge base and building a BCQ by adding an atom built with that predicate and the answer variables ($q = ans(\mathbf{x}), \mathbf{a_1}(\mathbf{x_1}), \ldots, \mathbf{a_n}(\mathbf{x_n})$). Yet, we need to remember that the special predicate ans is only there as a *place holder* so that the answer variables $\mathbf{x}$ get modified by the unifiers we apply to the query but no reasoning step would modify the atom directly.

From now on, we focus on the problem of answering BCQs, since CQs can be transformed to BCQs. Therefore, the term conjunctive query (union of conjunctive queries) will actually refer to a boolean conjunctive query (union of boolean conjunctive queries).

In a *rule system* used for query answering we can have also *constraints* i.e. rules with a *false* head denoted by $\bot$, a symbol always interpreted as the empty set:

$$(\mathcal{R}, \mathcal{C}) = (\{R_1, \ldots, R_n\} \cup \{C_1, \ldots, C_k\}),$$

where $C_i = B_i^c[\mathbf{x_i}] \rightarrow \bot$.

The only way the constraints are fulfilled is by allowing only interpretations of $\mathcal{D}$ in which the body of the constraints is always evaluated to false. Therefore, constraints are not normally used to answer queries. Instead, they are used to check consistency of the rules system and the database before the process of query answering [8]. Constraints can be associated to queries $q_c = B_i^c[\mathbf{x_i}]$ to detect when they are violated. In case one of the constraints is violated ($\exists i \, ans(B_i^c[\mathbf{x_i}], \mathcal{R}, \mathcal{D}) \neq \emptyset$), the answers of the original query will not make much sense because every possible answer would be correct. For this reason, they do not add extra complexity to the system of rules. Obviously, more operations need to be performed when we consider the constraints but not enough to change the complexity class of the problem that does not consider them. Indeed, adding a constant number k of constraints to a system would only increase the number of times we answer queries by k times and we know that $O(k \cdot f)$ is still $O(f)$ for a constant k.

According to the definition of existential rule, a system could have existential rules with more than one atom in the head. Nevertheless, such a system can be transformed in polynomial time to an equivalent one where the rules have only one atom in the head e.g. [4]. Thus, from now on we focus on existential rules with one atom in the head.

The rewriting approach [7,12] can be considered in order to find an equivalent expression to the query with a much simpler expressivity i.e. a datalog program or a union of conjunctive queries. For a given set of rules $\mathcal{R}$, a set of *UCQ-rewritings* of a conjunctive query (or UCQ) q is defined as a UCQ $\mathcal{R}_q^*$ such that for all databases $\mathcal{D}$:

$$\exists i \; q_i \in \mathcal{R}_q^* \text{ such that } \mathcal{D} \models q_i \text{ implies that } \mathcal{R}, \mathcal{D} \models q. \tag{5}$$

If the converse of (5) holds i.e.

$$\mathcal{R}, \mathcal{D} \models q \text{ implies that } \exists i \; q_i \in \mathcal{R}_q^* \text{ such that } \mathcal{D} \models q_i,$$

the set $\mathcal{R}_q^*$ is a *complete* UCQ-rewriting of q with respect to $\mathcal{R}$. Each element of a UCQ-rewriting set is called a *rewriting* of the original query with respect to $\mathcal{R}$.

Rewriting algorithms allow us to reduce the problem of reasoning with respect to a set of rules $\mathcal{R}$ and a database $\mathcal{D}$, to the problem of query answering with respect to $\mathcal{D}$. A set of rules $\mathcal{R}$ is called a *finite unification set* (*fus*) if for any query $q(\mathbf{x})$ there exists a sound and complete UCQ-rewriting of $q(\mathbf{x})$ with respect to $\mathcal{R}$. Finding if there exists a UCQ rewriting with respect to an arbitrary set of rules $\mathcal{R}$ is undecidable [4] yet several classes of rules ensure the existence of that property [3].

2.3   Queries with Negated Atoms

Lets study the problem of answering conjunctive queries with negated atoms (CQ⁻):

$$q = a_1(\mathbf{x_1}), \ldots, a_n(\mathbf{x_n}), \neg p_1(\mathbf{y_1}), \ldots, \neg p_m(\mathbf{y_m}),$$

for a *knowledge base* composed by $\mathcal{D}$ and $(\mathcal{R}, \mathcal{C})$. If the system does not have constraints ($\mathcal{C} = \emptyset$), when we have an interpretation I of $\mathcal{D}, \mathcal{R}$ adding $p_i(\mathbf{t_i})$ to I will eventually take us to another interpretation I' such that $\{p_i(\mathbf{t_i})\} \cup \mathbf{I} \subseteq \mathbf{I'}$ and also $I' \models \mathcal{D}, \mathcal{R}$. Notice that $p_i(\mathbf{t_i})$ together with some other facts in I, might have consequences that need to be materialized in order to have a proper interpretation I' of all the rules in $\mathcal{R}$. If we do that for all the elements $\mathbf{t_i}$ of the domain we can clearly say that

$$I' \not\models a_1(\mathbf{x_1}), \ldots, a_n(\mathbf{x_n}), \neg p_1(\mathbf{y_1}), \ldots, \neg p_i(\mathbf{y_i}), \ldots, \neg p_m(\mathbf{y_m}),$$

because $p_i(\mathbf{y_i})$ is true in I' for all possible tuples. Therefore, for all possible interpretations I we cannot ensure that $I \models \mathcal{D}, \mathcal{R}$ implies that $I \models q$. Consequently, $ans(q, \mathcal{R}, \mathcal{D}) = \emptyset$ when the knowledge base has no constraints.

When we have constraints, we can transform the decision problem $\mathcal{D},(\mathcal{R},\mathcal{C}) \models q$ into checking the consistency of $\mathcal{D},(\mathcal{R},\mathcal{C}),\neg q$. Hence, we have that:

$$\mathcal{D},(\mathcal{R},\mathcal{C}) \models q \text{ iff } \mathcal{D},(\mathcal{R},\mathcal{C}),\neg q \text{ is inconsistent.} \qquad (6)$$

A conjunctive query with negated atoms is based on *safe* negation ($\mathsf{CQ}^{\neg s}$) if all the variables in negated atoms are also present in positive atoms of the query. The Problem (6) is undecidable for $\mathsf{CQ}^{\neg s}$ even for a $\mathsf{DL-Lite}_{core}^{\mathcal{H}}$ knowledge base [11]. Conjunctive queries with *guarded* negated atoms ($\mathsf{CQ}^{\neg g}$) have guards for the variables that appear in every negated atom. For a $\mathsf{UCQ}^{\neg g}$ with a set of frontier-guarded rules the consistency of our system (6) is in the $coNP$ complexity class [5].

The consistency check approach (6) is useful to study the decidability of the problem yet finding answers for a query in this way is too inefficient. Basically, one would need to solve problem (6) for all possible tuples that can be built using the constants in $\mathcal{D}$.

3 Rewriting Approach for Queries with Negation

To the best of our knowledge, all the rewriting algorithms defined up to now in the field of existential rules consider only queries with positive atoms and queries with negated atoms could also be rewritten.

3.1 Constraint Saturation

Example 1. Lets consider the following system and the corresponding clauses $C^{(i)}$ corresponding to the rules, constraints, and the query:

$$\mathcal{R} = \{a(x) \rightarrow r(x,y)\} \qquad C^{(1)} = [\neg a(x), r(x, f(x))],$$
$$\mathcal{C} = \{b(x), r(x,y) \rightarrow \bot\} \qquad C^{(2)} = [\neg b(x), \neg r(x,y)],$$

and a query

$$q = s(x,y), \neg a(x) \qquad C^{(3)} = [\neg s(x,y), a(x)].$$

With the initial clauses we can do the following resolution derivation:

$$C^{(1)}, \ C^{(2)}, \ C^{(3)},$$
$$C^{(4)} = [\neg s(x,y), r(x, f(x))] \quad res(C^{(1)}, C^{(3)}),$$
$$C^{(5)} = [\neg s(x,y), \neg b(x)] \quad res(C^{(4)}, C^{(2)}),$$

which basically means that the last clause is a consequence of the initial clauses (Theorem (1)). i.e.

$$\mathcal{R},\mathcal{C} \models \exists x \exists y \ s(x,y), b(x) \rightarrow \exists x \exists y \ s(x,y), \neg a(x),$$

for any $\mathcal{D}$. In other words:

$$ans(q',(\mathcal{R},\mathcal{C}),\mathcal{D}) \subseteq ans(q,(\mathcal{R},\mathcal{C}),\mathcal{D}),$$

where $q' = s(x,y), b(x)$.

Therefore, we can say that q' is a rewriting of our initial query. Yet, it cannot be obtained applying a classical rewriting algorithm on the initial query because it contains a negated atom. On the other hand, it is well known that resolution for FOL is semi-decidable and arbitrary length resolution derivations should be avoided. However, if we rewrite the constraint of our example we get that:

$$b(x), r(x,y) \rightarrow \bot$$

$$b(x), a(x) \rightarrow \bot \qquad C^{(6)} = [\neg b(x), \neg a(x)].$$

Now we can apply one step resolution between the clause corresponding to q ($C^{(3)}$) and $C^{(6)}$ and we obtain again the clause corresponding to q'. Note that at this point if we have more rules in our system, the query q' could be rewritten using a classical algorithm and all the rewritings of q' will also be rewritings of q.

Generalizing the process described in the previous example, we could define the *constraint saturation* as the process of eliminating negative atoms from the queries by using constraints to make resolution derivations of controlled length. We can achieve that by only allowing resolution steps using clauses corresponding to constraints.

Definition 3. *For a* CQ⁻ *q and a set of constraints C, the* constraint saturation *C_q is the most general set of conjunctive queries $\{\ldots, q_i, \ldots\}$ with no negative atoms that can be obtained from a linear resolution derivation $C^{(0)}, C^{(1)}, \ldots, C^{(k)}$, where (i) $C^{(0)}$ is the clause corresponding to $\neg q$, (ii) $C^{(k)}$ is the clause corresponding to $\neg q_i$ and (iii) The set of clauses used are the ones corresponding to the constraints $C_1, \ldots, C_{|C|}$ in C together with $C^{(0)}$.*

Lemma 1. *The answers of the elements q_i of the constraint saturation of a query C_q are also answers of the original query q i.e. $\forall i \; ans(q_i, (\mathcal{R}, C), \mathcal{D}) \subseteq ans(q, (\mathcal{R}, C), \mathcal{D})$.*

Clearly since the elements q_i were built using a linear resolution derivation starting with a clause corresponding to $\neg q$ and using as side clauses the clauses corresponding to the constraints C of our system, we can affirm that $C \models q_i \rightarrow q$. Therefore, whenever we have that $() \in ans(q_i, (\mathcal{R}, C), \mathcal{D})$ then we it will also be the case that $() \in ans(q, (\mathcal{R}, C), \mathcal{D})$.

When the rules of our system form a *fus*, we can ensure that the constraint saturation of a query C_q covers all the answers of q if C contains all the possible rewritings of the queries associated to the constraints in it i.e. if $\mathcal{R}, \mathcal{D} \models C$ iff $\mathcal{D} \models C$ holds for all $\mathcal{D}$.

In Example 1, the shape of the initial query is also important. To ensure the termination of the resolution involving the set of clauses corresponding to the rewritten constraints and the query we need to avoid cases in which the query clause clashes with itself and produces a resolvent that could contain different answers.

Example 2. Lets consider the query

$$q = B(x), s(x,y), \neg B(y) \qquad C^{(0)} = [\neg B(x), \neg s(x,y), B(y)],$$

and the constraint:

$$\mathcal{C} = \{B(x), W(x) \to \bot\} \qquad C^{(1)} = [\neg B(x), \neg W(x)].$$

Here since $C^{(0)}$ clashes with itself one can end up in a resolution derivation of unbounded length when trying to remove the negative atoms in q. Particularly, every query of the form $q_n = B(x), s(x,x_1), \ldots, s(x,x_n), W(x_n)$ is a rewriting of the initial query.

A CQ⁻ is *disconnected* if the corresponding clause to $C = \neg q$ does not clash with itself or if the query q' corresponding to the resolvent $\neg Res(C,C)$ is less general i.e. $q \succeq q'$. Disconnected queries will prevent generating new answers based on applying resolution involving the clause corresponding to $\neg q$ and itself.

Even if at the beginning our query is disconnected a rewriting of it could end up resolving with itself and such cases should also be avoided. In general, we say a CQ⁻ q is *strongly disconnected* with respect to a knowledge base $(\mathcal{R}, \mathcal{C})$ if it is disconnected and all the queries corresponding to a clause resulting from a resolution derivation of $\neg q$ using clauses of $(\mathcal{R}, \mathcal{C})$ are also disconnected.

Clearly, the resolution derivations in Definition 3 have a bounded length for strongly disconnected queries.

Lemma 2. *In Definition 3 the length of the resolution derivation is bounded by m for a strongly disconnected query with m negative atoms.*

Indeed, every resolution step is performing resolution using a clause corresponding to a constraint, with all the atoms negated on it. Therefore, each of those steps removes one or more positive atoms on the clause corresponding to the negated query, but those positive atoms in $C^{(0)}$ correspond to the negated atoms in q and there are only m of them. Moreover, since the query is strongly disconnected possible steps applying resolution of the query with itself are discarded.

Theorem 4. *For a knowledge base $(\mathcal{R}, \mathcal{C})$ and a strongly disconnected query q with respect to the knowledge base, if $\mathcal{C}$ contains all the possible rewritings of the queries corresponding to the constraints in it then the constraints saturation $\mathcal{C}_q$ contains all the answers of q:*

$$ans(q, (\mathcal{R}, \mathcal{C}), \mathcal{D}) = ans(\mathcal{C}_q, (\mathcal{R}, \mathcal{C}), \mathcal{D}) \text{ for all } \mathcal{D}.$$

Proof. Lemma 1 ensures $ans(\mathcal{C}_q, (\mathcal{R}, \mathcal{C}), \mathcal{D}) \subseteq ans(q, (\mathcal{R}, \mathcal{C}), \mathcal{D})$. Then, we need to focus on proving $ans(q, (\mathcal{R}, \mathcal{C}), \mathcal{D}) \subseteq ans(\mathcal{C}_q, (\mathcal{R}, \mathcal{C}), \mathcal{D})$.

The proof is based on showing that a resolution derivation starting in $\neg q$ and ending in the empty clause can be rearranged using Theorem 3 so that the first resolution steps are applied using constraints from $\mathcal{C}$. After those steps we can affirm that the clause will correspond to a query in the constraint saturation of q, so there will also be a resolution derivation starting from a clause corresponding to a query in $\mathcal{C}_q$ and ending in the empty clause i.e. () $\in ans(q, (\mathcal{R}, \mathcal{C}), \mathcal{D}) \rightarrow$ () $\in ans(\mathcal{C}_q, (\mathcal{R}, \mathcal{C}), \mathcal{D})$.

For a more detailed proof see Appendix B[2]. $\square$

Theorem (4) allow us to find a set of CQ that will contain all the answers of the original query q and then we can apply rewriting algorithms to them in order to find a complete UCQ rewriting of q with respect to $\mathcal{R}$.

To check whether a query is strongly disconnected or not would involve performing resolution therefore it is not an easy condition to check before starting the rewriting of the query. Furthermore, if we use a rewriting algorithm as a black box it will be impossible to check while rewriting the query. Yet, if we implement the rewriting algorithm using the method proposed in [9] we could focus on checking if the atoms introduced in every rewriting step could at some point clash with some of the negated atoms that the query had originally. At the end of the process, if we find out that the query is strongly disconnected, we will know for sure that the resulting UCQ is equivalent to the initial query.

Depending on the rules we have, there are maybe some atoms that when negated are not strongly disconnected (Example 3) and so any other query containing them in negated form will neither be.

Example 3. Lets consider the simple query

$$q = \neg P(x) \qquad C^{(0)} = [P(x)],$$

and the knowledge base:

$$
\begin{aligned}
P(x), B(x) &\rightarrow P'(x) & C^{(1)} &= [\neg P(x), \neg B(x), P'(x)], \\
P'(x), s(x, y) &\rightarrow B(y) & C^{(2)} &= [\neg P'(x), \neg s(x, y), B(y)], \\
\mathcal{C} &= \{B(x), W(x) \rightarrow \bot\} & C^{(3)} &= [\neg B(x), \neg W(x)].
\end{aligned}
$$

After computing $res(res(C^{(0)}, C^{(1)}), C^{(2)})$ we will reach again the clause equivalent to the query in Example 2:

$$
\begin{aligned}
q' &= B(x), \neg P'(x) & C^{(4)} &= res(C^{(0)}, C^{(1)}) = [\neg B(x), P'(x)], \\
q'' &= B(x), s(x, y), \neg B(y) & res(C^{(4)}, C^{(2)}) &= [\neg B(x), \neg s(x, y), B(y)],
\end{aligned}
$$

and we end up again in a resolution derivation of unbounded length when trying to remove the negative atoms. Therefore, no query that contains $\neg P(x)$ will be strongly disconnected with respect to this knowledge base.

A negated atom $\neg p(\mathbf{x})$ is *self disconnected* with respect to $\mathcal{R}$ if the query $q = \neg p(\mathbf{x})$ is strongly disconnected w.r.t. $\mathcal{R}$. Notice that the only resolution steps that would probably produce non disconnected queries are those that make resolution with a clause corresponding to a rule and the head of the rule unifies

---

[2] http://image.ntua.gr/~gardero/completo-rr2017/Appendixes.pdf.

with another atom belonging to the body of another rule (or the same one) used previously in the resolution derivation. In case our rules contain only one atom in the body (known as *Atomic-hypothesis* or *linear* rules [3]), resolution steps with rules will not introduce other body atoms.

Property 1. Negated atoms are self disconnected with respect to an Atomic-hypothesis set of rules.

Proof. Indeed, the initial clause corresponding to $q = \neg p(\mathbf{x})$ cannot yield another clause with more than one atom by applying resolution with clauses corresponding to rules. □

3.2 Algorithm for Rewriting Conjunctive Queries with Negation

For the design of the algorithm to rewrite negative conjunctive queries we use the help of another algorithm that rewrites conjunctive queries into UCQs. We can refer to it as `rewrite-ext` : $R \times CQ \to UCQ$ and it can be any of the state of the art rewriters (RAPID[13], SYSNAME[9], GRAAL [2]) compatible with the theory we support for finding the constraints saturation of a conjunctive query with negation.

To illustrate better the general idea of the algorithms presented, we treat data structures in the most simple way. We assume the $+/2$ operator is the *set union* when overloaded for sets, likewise the $-/2$ operator refers to the *set difference*. The method `pop` when applied to a set, returns one of its elements and also removes it from the set. The function `cover/1` computes the set of most general conjunctive queries given a set of conjunctive queries.

Preprocessing. For a fixed Knowledge base $(\mathcal{R}, \mathcal{C})$ we initially perform the computation of the rewritings of each one of the initial constraints (Fig. 1). Then, as long as the rules or constraints do not change, the same computed rewritings of the constraints can be used to perform the constraint saturation for different queries.

```
function computeConstraints(R, C)
    expand := C
    while expand.size > 0 do
        c := expand.pop
        C := C + rewrite-ext(R,c)
    end for
    return cover(C)
end function
```

Fig. 1. Function to rewrite the initial set of constraints

```
function rewrite-completo(R, C, q)
    C := computeConstraints(R, C)
    qCsat := Csaturation(C,q)
    ucq := {}
    while qCsat.size > 0 do
        qi := qCsat.pop
        ucq := ucq + rewrite-ext(R,qi)
    end for
    return cover(ucq)
end function
```

Fig. 2. Main algorithm to rewrite queries with negated atoms

The Algorithm. Figure 2 shows the main algorithm for rewriting queries with negated atoms. It computes the rewriting of the constraints (if it is not already computed for that knowledge base). The function `Csaturation` (Fig. 3) takes the clause corresponding to $\neg q$ and performs linear resolution with respect to the clauses corresponding to the constraints in $\mathcal{C}$ to obtain the constraint saturation $\mathcal{C}_q$. The derivations on each step remove at least one of the negated atoms in q by performing a resolution step (`resolve/3`) with a derivation of the original query q'' and a constraint c from $\mathcal{C}$. For each constraint, we check all possible clashing sets with the queries in order to explore all possible linear derivations starting in $\neg q$ and ending in a clause representing a query without negative atoms. The initial query is transformed to a clause (`queryToClause/1`) by creating a set with the complement of each of the atoms in the query. In the resolution derivation, when the clause generated has no positive atoms we can affirm that it represents a query with only positive atoms therefore we convert it back to a query (`clauseToQuery/1`), by taking the complement of the atoms in the clause.

With each of the queries in the UCQ resulting from the main algorithm we can perform query answering, by trying to unify the atoms of the query with atoms in the database $\mathcal{D}$. In case the original query had some answer variables the atom $ans(\mathbf{x})$ would be part of each of the queries in the rewriting, but it will not unify with atoms in $\mathcal{D}$. As a result of the unification of the atoms in the query and the atoms in $\mathcal{D}$ (if possible and in all possible ways), the variables in the ans predicate will be replaced by constants and we will end up with tuples t that will be part of the answers of our query. For each query, finding an answer tuple is an NP-Complete process, yet there are potentially an exponential number of tuples that can be answers of the query.

In the process of constraints saturation, we have to avoid the queries that remove answer variables from the atoms of the query in the process of resolution to avoid ending up in domain dependent queries with answer variables that do not belong to the atoms of the query. Yet we only need to pay attention to it when we try to answer queries without safe negation.

```
function Csaturation(C, q)
    ucq := {}
    cq := queryToClause(q)
    expand := {cq}
    while expand.size > 0 do
      q' := expand.pop
      foreach c in C do
        foreach l clashing set in c and q' do
          q'' := resolve(l,c,q')
          if (q'' has no positive atom)
              ucq := ucq + clauseToQuery(q'')
          else
              expand := expand + q''
          end if
        end for
      end for
    end while
    return cover(ucq)
end function
```

Fig. 3. Function to compute the constraints saturation of a query

4   Experiments

Negated concepts are strongly disconnected queries with respect to a DL − Lite ontology because DL − Lite axioms are a set of linear of rules (Property 1). Therefore, the constraint saturation for negated concepts will contain all the possible answers. In this paper, we focus on comparing the performance of the proposed approach with another approach by Jianfeng Du and Jeff Z. Pan that is able to rewrite negated concepts [8].

Our system COMPLETO was implemented using RAPID as an external rewriter and a connection to a MySQL database for efficient instance retrieval. A TBox is used to obtain a rewriting of the initial constraints in the system. Then, the assertions that could be encoded initially in OWL format are translated to a MySQL database. Finally, the rewriting and instance retrieval processes can be carried out by using the constraints rewriting, the database of assertions and the queries that need to be rewritten and answered. Appendix C[3] shows a description of the system and how it can be installed and used.

The experiments were carried out on an Intel® Core™ i7-3612QM CPU @ 2.10 GHz x 8, with 8 Gb of RAM memory and a SSD running Ubuntu 17.04 64-bit. The benchmark used consists of two groups of ontologies used in [8]. One of the groups was from the Lehigh University Benchmark (LUBM) [10] and the other from DBPedia (version 2014) [6]. Some axioms were removed from the original versions of the ontologies in order to make them compatible with the RAPID system. Also constraints stating that sibling atomic concepts are disjoint

---

[3] http://image.ntua.gr/~gardero/completo-rr2017/Appendixes.pdf.

were added to the LUMB ontologies. The group of LUMB ontologies consists of the same set of axioms and different number of assertions associated to different number of universities (1, 5, 10, 50 and 100) given as a parameter to the LUMB generator [10]. The second group of DBPedia ontologies, was built with basic assertions about atomic concepts and abstract roles from DBPedia-as-Tables[4] to construct the ABox. Each version of the ontology uses the same axioms and a percentage of the assertions (1, 5, 10, 50 and 100%). The queries to rewrite and to answer using the assertions were built by negating each of the concepts present in the TBox. For the LUBM ontologies they were 43 concepts and for the DBPedia ontologies 783.

Figure 4 shows the comparison of the average runtime taken to answer each query of the dataset. The performance of COMPLETO is better than the performance of REBSIR for the LUBM group of ontologies. On the other hand, for the DBPedia datasets COMPLETO on average takes longer than REBSIR to answer a query for small ontologies. Yet, when the ontologies grow in size the performance of COMPLETO gets closer to the performance of REBSIR eventually becoming better than it.

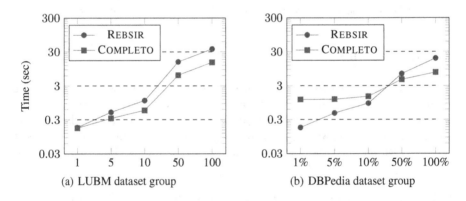

(a) LUBM dataset group   (b) DBPedia dataset group

Fig. 4. Comparison of the average runtime per query for the benchmarks

The relative runtime can be seen in Fig. 5 where the coordinates of the dots plotted represent the average times taken by each system in each of the datasets. Both axes of the graph are in logarithmic scale and points over the $y = x$ line represent datasets where the COMPLETO system takes on average less time than REBSIR to answer a query. We can clearly see that for the LUBM group COMPLETO is always faster and it takes on average 59% of the time taken by REBSIR to answer a query. For the DBPedia group of ontologies, COMPLETO on average takes 238% of the time that REBSIR takes to answer a query. Yet, for both cases we can see that the COMPLETO system is more scalable i.e. with the increase of the size of the ABox the COMPLETO system improves the relative runtime difference.

---

[4] http://web.informatik.uni-mannheim.de/DBpediaAsTables/.

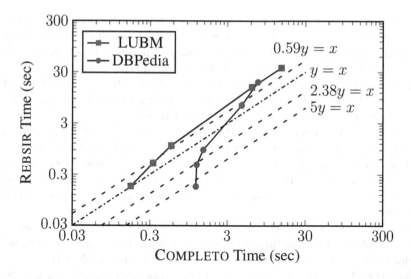

Fig. 5. Relative average runtime per query for the benchmark

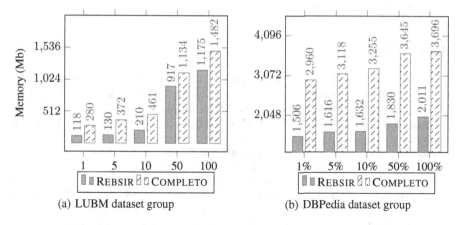

(a) LUBM dataset group   (b) DBPedia dataset group

Fig. 6. Comparison of the maximum RSS used to answer all the queries of the benchmark

Figure 6 shows a comparison of the maximum *resident set size* (RSS) of the systems during the process of answering all the queries of the benchmark. REBSIR uses in all the cases less memory than COMPLETO. Considering the relative memory difference for each case, on average, REBSIR uses 54% of the memory used by COMPLETO.

5 Conclusions

In this paper, we proposed a method to rewrite conjunctive queries with negated atoms. The constraints in the knowledge base are rewritten using the rules in order to express the inconsistencies without the need of the rules. The expanded set of constraints is used to build a constraint saturation of the initial query by eliminating the negated atoms using resolution. Finally, conventional rewriting algorithms are used in the resulting union of conjunctive queries.

The method was implemented in the system COMPLETO. The RAPID system was used as an external rewriter and a connection to a MySQL database allowed efficient instance retrieval for the obtained rewriting.

COMPLETO was compared to REBSIR for rewriting negated concepts. The experimental results showed that COMPLETO is generally faster than REBSIR, specially when the number of assertions in the knowledge base grows. The relative performance of COMPLETO with respect to REBSIR is always improved when the number of assertions grows. On the other hand, REBSIR used less memory resources.

Finally, despite the satisfactory performance of COMPLETO we believe that the principal result in this investigation is the definition of query answering for queries with negated atoms based on the classical rewriting algorithms.

As future directions we will perform an experimental evaluation of the system with other strongly disconnected queries. We are also interested in being able to rewrite more expressive queries.

References

1. Baader, F., Calvanese, D., McGuinness, D.L., Nardi, D., Patel-Schneider, P.F. (eds.): The Description Logic Handbook: Theory, Implementation, and Applications. Cambridge University Press, New York (2003)
2. Baget, J.-F., Leclère, M., Mugnier, M.-L., Rocher, S., Sipieter, C.: Graal: a toolkit for query answering with existential rules. In: Bassiliades, N., Gottlob, G., Sadri, F., Paschke, A., Roman, D. (eds.) RuleML 2015. LNCS, vol. 9202, pp. 328–344. Springer, Cham (2015). doi:10.1007/978-3-319-21542-6_21
3. Baget, J.F., Leclère, M., Mugnier, M.L., Salvat, E.: DL-SR: a lite DL with expressive rules: preliminary results. In: Baader, F., Lutz, C., Motik, B. (eds.) Description Logics, vol. 353. CEUR Workshop Proceedings (2008). CEUR-WS.org
4. Baget, J.F., Leclere, M., Mugnier, M.L., Salvat, E.: On rules with existential variables: walking the decidability line. Artif. Intell. **175**(9), 1620–1654 (2011)
5. Bárány, V., Cate, B.T., Otto, M.: Queries with guarded negation (full version). CoRR, abs/1203.0077 (2012)
6. Bizer, C., Lehmann, J., Kobilarov, G., Auer, S., Becker, C., Cyganiak, R., Hellmann, S.: Dbpedia - a crystallization point for the web of data. Web Semant. **7**(3), 154–165 (2009)
7. Calvanese, D., Giacomo, G., Lembo, D., Lenzerini, M., Rosati, R.: Tractable reasoning and efficient query answering in description logics: the DL-Lite family. J. Autom. Reason. **39**(3), 385–429 (2007)
8. Du, J., Pan, J.Z.: Rewriting-based instance retrieval for negated concepts in description logic ontologies. In: Arenas, M., et al. (eds.) ISWC 2015. LNCS, vol. 9366, pp. 339–355. Springer, Cham (2015). doi:10.1007/978-3-319-25007-6_20
9. Gottlob, G., Orsi, G., Pieris, A.: Query rewriting and optimization for ontological databases. ACM Trans. Database Syst. **39**(3), 25:1–25:46 (2014)

10. Guo, Y., Pan, Z., Heflin, J.: LUBM: a benchmark for OWL knowledge base systems. Web Semant. **3**(2–3), 158–182 (2005)
11. Gutiérrez-Basulto, V., Ibañez-García, Y., Kontchakov, R., Kostylev, E.V.: Conjunctive queries with negation over DL-Lite: a closer look. In: Faber, W., Lembo, D. (eds.) RR 2013. LNCS, vol. 7994, pp. 109–122. Springer, Heidelberg (2013). doi:10.1007/978-3-642-39666-3_9
12. König, M., Leclère, M., Mugnier, M.-L., Thomazo, M.: Sound, complete and minimal ucq-rewriting for existential rules. Semant. Web **6**(5), 451–475 (2015)
13. Trivela, D., Stoilos, G., Chortaras, A., Stamou, G.: Optimising resolution-based rewriting algorithms for owl ontologies. Web Semant. Sci. Serv. Agents World Wide Web **33**, 30–49 (2015)

Fast ABox Consistency Checking
Using Incomplete Reasoning and Caching

Christian Meilicke[1], Daniel Ruffinelli[1(✉)], Andreas Nolle[2], Heiko Paulheim[1], and Heiner Stuckenschmidt[1]

[1] Research Group Data and Web Science,
University of Mannheim, Mannheim, Germany
{christian,daniel,heiko,heiner}@informatik.uni-mannheim.de
[2] Data Science, Department of Business and Computer Science,
Albstadt-Sigmaringen University, Albstadt, Germany
nolle@hs-albsig.de

Abstract. Reasoning with complex ontologies can be a resource-intensive task, which can be an obstacle, e.g., for real-time applications. Hence, weakening the constraints of soundness and/or completeness is often an approach to practical solutions. In this paper, we propose an extension of incomplete reasoning methods for checking the consistency of a large number of ABoxes against a given TBox. In particular, we use and extend the clash queries proposed by Lembo et al. [9] for *DL-Lite* to compute inconsistent patterns of ABox assertions. By caching instantiations of these patterns, we are able to reduce the amount of reasoning required to determine the inconsistency of an ABox with every previously processed ABox. We present experimental results of our approach in terms of runtime and accuracy and compare it against complete reasoning techniques, the reasoning approach for *DL-Lite$_A$*, and an approximate reasoning approach based on machine learning proposed in [15].

1 Introduction

Ontologies, and the reasoning with ontologies, are well established techniques for capturing and processing knowledge. In the past decades, a large body of research has been conducted on optimizing reasoning systems for ontology languages of different expressiveness. So far, the major part of research on ontology reasoning focuses on developing reasoning systems that are both sound and complete. However, as already argued in [15], reasoning results that are 100% accurate are not required in many use cases for which ontology reasoning has been proposed and/or applied in the past, e.g., information retrieval, recommender systems, or activity recognition. On the other hand, many of those use cases have very strict performance requirements, as they are usually applied in real time settings.

These considerations led to the development of reasoning systems that weaken the constraint of soundness or completeness for the sake of better performance. In this paper, we propose an approach for checking the consistency of many ABoxes against the same TBox, a task to which many real world reasoning tasks can be reduced. Our approach is sound but not complete for detecting

© Springer International Publishing AG 2017
S. Costantini et al. (Eds.): RuleML+RR 2017, LNCS 10364, pp. 168–183, 2017.
DOI: 10.1007/978-3-319-61252-2_12

inconsistencies in OWL 2 ontologies. It builds upon *DL-Lite*$_\mathcal{A}$ clash queries [10] and extends them in order to detect inconsistencies beyond the scope of *DL-Lite*$_\mathcal{A}$. Furthermore, we propose a caching method to avoid costly calls to a reasoner, which becomes more effective with every processed ABox.

We conduct comprehensive experiments on two real life datasets and compare our method against three different types of reasoning approaches: First, we apply complete reasoning techniques using HermiT [6]. Second, we apply the reasoning approach for inconsistency detection in *DL-Lite*$_\mathcal{A}$ as proposed by Lembo et al. [9]. Third, we have reimplemented the approximate reasoning approach based on machine learning, proposed by Paulheim and Stuckenschmidt [15]. The results indicate that our approach is highly efficient and capable of detecting significantly more inconsistencies than other incomplete methods. We analyze the results of our experiments and explain under which conditions a method that is based on caching (parts of) explanations is a better choice than a method that is based on learning from previously seen examples and vice versa.

The rest of this paper is structured as follows. Section 2 introduces some basic concepts, the preliminaries on checking consistency in *DL-Lite*$_\mathcal{A}$, and the basic idea of using machine learning techniques as proposed in [15] to solve the given problem. Section 3 introduces our approach, which is based on the extension of the techniques proposed for *DL-Lite*$_\mathcal{A}$ combined with a caching technique. Section 4 discusses experimental results both w.r.t. result quality and runtime performance. We conclude with a summary and an outlook on future work.

2   Preliminaries and Related Work

Within this section we first recall the notion of inconsistency and explanation. We also argue why explanations are useful for our problem (Sect. 2.1). Then we introduce the description logics *DL-Lite*$_\mathcal{A}$ (Sect. 2.2) before we finally explain how inconsistencies can be detected in *DL-Lite*$_\mathcal{A}$ (Sect. 2.3). Later on we use the *DL-Lite*$_\mathcal{A}$ query expansion techniques as a baseline in our experiments and extend this approach to detect inconsistencies within ontologies that are beyond *DL-Lite*$_\mathcal{A}$. In Sect. 2.4 we present and discuss the idea of using machine learning for detecting inconsistencies.

2.1   Inconsistencies and Explanations

In the following we use $\mathcal{T}$ to refer to a TBox that defines the vocabulary used in a set of ABoxes $\mathcal{A}_1$ to $\mathcal{A}_n$. In description logics, an interpretation $\mathcal{I}$ that satisfies all axioms in $\mathcal{T}$ and all assertions in $\mathcal{A}$ is called a model of $\mathcal{T} \cup \mathcal{A}$. If such a model exists, $\mathcal{T} \cup \mathcal{A}$ is called consistent. Otherwise, $\mathcal{T} \cup \mathcal{A}$ is called inconsistent [1,3]. The inconsistency of an ontology is usually a sign for an error, i.e., a sign for a faulty axiom or assertions. In our setting we assume that the TBox $\mathcal{T}$ is not causing the problem, but helps to reveal a mistake in (at least) one of the assertions in an ABox.

According to Kalyanpur et al. [7], an *explanation* (or justification) for an assertion or an axiom ϕ is a subset $\mathcal{O}'$ of $\mathcal{O} = \mathcal{T} \cup \mathcal{A}$ such that $\mathcal{O}' \models \phi$ while $\mathcal{O}'' \not\models \phi$ for all $\mathcal{O}'' \subset \mathcal{O}'$. An explanation can be understood as a minimal reason that explains why ϕ follows from $\mathcal{O}$. Analogously, given an inconsistent ontology $\mathcal{O}$, we are interested in explanations for the inconsistency, i.e., minimal subsets $\mathcal{O}'$ of $\mathcal{O}$ such that there exists no model for $\mathcal{O}'$. More precisely, a minimal inconsistent subset $\mathcal{O}'$ (also referred to as MIS) is a subset of $\mathcal{O}$ such that $\mathcal{O}'$ is inconsistent while $\mathcal{O}''$ is consistent for all $\mathcal{O}'' \subset \mathcal{O}'$. An example for a MIS is shown as Example 1.

Example 1. This example shows a simplified inconsistency explanation for one of the ABoxes from the experiments with DBpedia and DOLCE. The inconsistency is related to the fact that *clintonMorrison11* is implicitly typed as a *Person*, but at the same time as a time span in the life of a person via the concept *Situation*.

$$team(clintonMorrison11, irelandFootballTeam) \tag{1}$$

$$PhysicalObject \sqsubseteq \neg SocialObject \tag{2}$$

$$PhysicalAgent \sqsubseteq PhysicalObject \tag{3}$$

$$Person \sqsubseteq PhysicalAgent \tag{4}$$

$$Situation(clintonMorrison11) \tag{5}$$

$$\exists team \sqsubseteq Athlete \tag{6}$$

$$Athlete \sqsubseteq Person \tag{7}$$

$$Situation \sqsubseteq SocialObject \tag{8}$$

The example shows that the explanations for an inconsistency are not trivial and that mistakes in the ABox can only be detected via chains of relevant axioms. With respect to our setting, we are only interested in the ABox elements, since we trust in the correctness of the TBox axioms. For that reason, the relevant assertions are (1) and (5). It is important to understand that we can replace the concrete instances in (1) and (5) by any other pair of instances. This means that any instantiation of $team(x, y) \wedge Situation(x)$ will be inconsistent. The computation and caching of the relevant information that corresponds to such a partial explanation will be an important element of our approach. In particular, we focus only on a specific type of partial explanations, which correspond to the clash types in *DL-Lite$_\mathcal{A}$*.

2.2   *DL-Lite$_\mathcal{A}$*

DL-Lite is a family of lightweight description logics proposed by Calvanese et al. [2] with the aim to find a trade-off between expressiveness and reasoning complexity. This resulted in a family of languages where terminological reasoning can be done in PTIME in the size of the TBox and query answering in AC^0 in the size of the ABox. In *DL-Lite$_\mathcal{A}$*, which is a concrete member of the *DL-Lite* family, concept, role, value-domain, and attribute expressions are formed according to the following syntax:

$$B \ ::= \ \perp_C \mid A \mid \exists Q \mid \delta(U) \qquad\qquad E \ ::= \ \rho(U)$$
$$C \ ::= \ \top_C \mid B \mid \neg B \mid \exists Q.C \qquad F \ ::= \ \top_D \mid T_1 \mid \ldots \mid T_n$$
$$Q \ ::= \ P \mid P^- \qquad\qquad\qquad\qquad V \ ::= \ U \mid \neg U$$
$$R \ ::= \ Q \mid \neg Q$$

where $\top_C$ denotes the *top* or *universal concept*, $\perp_C$ the *bottom* or *empty concept*, A an *atomic concept*, B a *basic concept* and C a *general concept*. Similar to that, we have *atomic roles* denoted by P, *basic roles* by Q and *general roles* by R. *Atomic attributes* are represented by U and *general attributes* by V whereas E denotes a *basic value-domain* and F a *value-domain expression*. Furthermore, $\exists Q$ (*unqualified existential restrictions*) represent objects that are related by role Q to some objects, $\exists Q.C$ (*qualified existential restrictions*) denote objects that are related by Q to objects denoted by concept C, $\neg$ denotes the negation of concepts, roles or attributes and P^- is used to represent the inverse of role P. Concerning an attribute U its *domain* is denoted by $\delta(U)$ and its *range* (set of values) by $\rho(U)$. *Value domains* are represented by $T_1 \mid \ldots \mid T_n$, where each T_i denotes a pairwise disjoint data type of values and $\top_D$ the *universal value-domain* [2,16]. In *DL-Lite$_A$* a knowledge base $\mathcal{K} = \langle \mathcal{T}, \mathcal{A} \rangle$ consists of a TBox $\mathcal{T}$ also known as schema, and an ABox $\mathcal{A}$, the extensional knowledge part which represents a data source.

The defined expressions can be used in TBox axioms in the following way. Axioms of the form $B \sqsubseteq C$ denote *concept inclusions*, $Q \sqsubseteq R$ *role inclusions*, $E \sqsubseteq F$ *value-domain inclusions* and $U \sqsubseteq V$ *attribute inclusions*. *Functionality assertions* on roles and attributes in $\mathcal{T}$ are denoted by funct Q and funct U. TBox axioms of the form $B_1 \sqsubseteq B_2$ and $Q_1 \sqsubseteq Q_2$ are called *positive inclusions* (*PI*) whereas $B_1 \sqsubseteq \neg B_2$ and $Q_1 \sqsubseteq \neg Q_2$ *negative inclusions* (*NI*). For ABox assertions a and b represent object constants and v represents a value constant. We refer the reader to [2,16] for a discussion of the semantics of *DL-Lite$_A$*, which we omit here due to the lack of space.

An example of an axiom that is not within the scope of *DL-Lite* is an axiom of the form $\exists partOf.Event \sqsubseteq Event$. If such an axiom is part of a MIS, the approach based on clash query expansion, which is shortly presented in the following section, will not be able to detect the respective inconsistency.

2.3 Inconsistency Detection in *DL-Lite$_A$*

Lembo et al. [9] identified a collection of six different patterns that cause clashes in *DL-Lite$_A$* knowledge bases listed as follows. This collection is complete for *DL-Lite$_A$*. This means that any inconsistency in $\mathcal{O} = \mathcal{T} \cup \mathcal{A}$, as long as the axioms and assertions are within the *DL-Lite$_A$* profile, can be detected by checking the following patterns. With respect to the following listing let a, b and c be individuals, let A and A' be named concepts, P and P' be roles, and let U be an attribute in accordance with the naming conventions of the previous section.

(1) Instantiation of an unsatisfiable named concept, role, attribute
    (a) $\mathcal{T} \models A \sqsubseteq \neg A$ and $A(a) \in \mathcal{A}$
    (b) $\mathcal{T} \models P \sqsubseteq \neg P$ and $P(a,b) \in \mathcal{A}$
    (c) $\mathcal{T} \models U \sqsubseteq \neg U$ and $U(a,v) \in \mathcal{A}$
(2) Assertions contradicting axioms that prohibit self-interrelations
    (a) $\mathcal{T} \models P \sqsubseteq \neg P^-$ and $P(a,a) \in \mathcal{A}$
(3) Incorrect data types
    (a) $\mathcal{T} \models \rho(U) \sqsubseteq T$ and $U(a,v) \in \mathcal{A}$ and $v^{\mathcal{I}} \notin T^{\mathcal{I}}$
(4) Assertions contradicting negative inclusions
    (a) $\mathcal{T} \models A \sqsubseteq \neg A'$ and $A(a), A'(a) \in \mathcal{A}$
    (b) $\mathcal{T} \models A \sqsubseteq \neg \exists P$ and $A(a), P(a,b) \in \mathcal{A}$
    (c) $\mathcal{T} \models A \sqsubseteq \neg \exists U$ and $A(a), U(a,v) \in \mathcal{A}$
    (d) $\mathcal{T} \models A \sqsubseteq \neg \exists P^-$ and $A(b), P(a,b) \in \mathcal{A}$
    (e) $\mathcal{T} \models P \sqsubseteq \neg P'$ and $P(a,b), P'(a,b) \in \mathcal{A}$
    (f) $\mathcal{T} \models \exists P \sqsubseteq \neg \exists P'$ and $P(a,b), P'(a,c) \in \mathcal{A}$
    (g) $\mathcal{T} \models \exists P \sqsubseteq \neg \exists P'^-$ and $P(a,b), P'(c,a) \in \mathcal{A}$
    (h) $\mathcal{T} \models \exists P^- \sqsubseteq \neg \exists P'^-$ and $P(a,b), P'(c,b) \in \mathcal{A}$
(5) Assertions contradicting role functionality
    (a) (funct P) $\in \mathcal{T}$ and $P(a,b), P(a,c) \in \mathcal{A}$ and $b \neq c$
    (b) (funct P^-) $\in \mathcal{T}$ and $P(a,c), P(b,c) \in \mathcal{A}$ and $a \neq b$
(6) ABox assertions contradicting attribute functionality
    (a) (funct U) $\in \mathcal{T}$ and $U(a,v_1), P(a,v_2) \in \mathcal{A}$ and $v_1 \neq v_2$

In the context of *DL-Lite$_\mathcal{A}$* it is sufficient to implement the $\models$ operator in terms of the *DL-Lite$_\mathcal{A}$* expansion rules. All clashes related to clash type (4)(a) can, for example, be detected by applying the *DL-Lite$_\mathcal{A}$* expansion rules recursively on each directly stated disjointness axiom $B \sqsubseteq \neg C$. As a result, all relevant clashes of the type $\mathcal{T} \models A \sqsubseteq \neg A'$ are collected and the ABox can be checked against these inconsistency patterns. If we apply the approach on the axiom *PhysicalObject* $\sqsubseteq \neg SocialObject$ given a TBox that contains amongst others all of the axioms listed in Example 1, the expansion rules will entail *Situation* $\sqsubseteq \neg \exists team$. This means that every ABox is inconsistent that instantiates $team(x,y) \wedge Situation(x)$.

2.4   Learning vs Computing Explanations

It has been a trend over the last years to train statistical models on large knowledge graphs in order to predict new facts about the world. An overview is given in [12]. These works are mainly concerned with the prediction of a fact that cannot be entailed by deductive reasoning. Opposed to that, in [15] the authors propose to mimic a reasoner for checking consistency by training a machine learning model. To this end, the authors propose to translate an ABox to a binary feature representation. On top of this representation a TBox specific classifier is learned that is able to distinguish between consistent and inconsistent ABoxes. The approach requires the usage of a reasoner to annotate the training examples, which are ABoxes translated to the feature representation, as consistent or inconsistent. Once the classifier has been trained, it mimics the behavior of the reasoner. Results presented in [15] have shown that the approach is highly efficient once the training phase has been finished.

A crucial aspect of the method is the chosen feature representation. In [15] the authors propose the use of path kernels introduced in [11] for generating the features. Without recalling the details, we point out that the generated features for Example 1 contain a feature for $team(x, y)$, a feature for $Situation(z)$, and another feature for the conjunction $team(x, y) \wedge Situation(x)$. This means that the classifier can also learn that each instantiation of $team(x, y) \wedge Situation(x)$ is inconsistent. In order to successfully learn that this pattern causes inconsistency, the training examples have to cover at least one inconsistent ABox $\mathcal{A}^*$ that makes use of this pattern. Moreover, there need to be some consistent training examples that use $team(x, y)$ only and some that use $Situation(x)$ only without the conjunction to avoid over-fitting. For the same purpose, the training examples must also cover consistent ABoxes that make use of the other concepts and roles in $\mathcal{A}^*$ that are not causing the inconsistency.

Contrary to an approach based on machine learning, we compute a partial explanation for the inconsistency of $\mathcal{A}^*$. By projecting the explanatory entailment to its corresponding assertional pattern, we are able to directly achieve the goal of the learning process without the need for annotating a sufficient number of samples with a standard reasoner. However, the computation of an explanation is known to be rather costly and several approaches have been proposed for this purpose [5,7]. We base our work on the *DL-Lite* clash patterns. We will argue in the following section that we can use the *DL-Lite* techniques or a standard reasoner to check for $\mathcal{A}^*$ if a certain pattern, which might be part of a complex explanation, results in an inconsistency. By storing inconsistent patterns we can directly decide that each ABox that instantiates this pattern is inconsistent.

3   Our Approach

We describe two approaches for checking a sequence of ABoxes $\mathcal{A}_1, \ldots, \mathcal{A}_n$ against a given TBox $\mathcal{T}$. The first approach (Sect. 3.1) is a straightforward application of the inconsistency reasoning techniques of *DL-Lite*$_\mathcal{A}$ that are based on the clash types of Lembo et al. [9]. Our approach (Sect. 3.2) extends and modifies this approach by using a reasoner that is fully compliant with the OWL 2 semantics.

3.1   Precompiling *DL-Lite*$_\mathcal{A}$ Clash Types

At the end of Sect. 2.3 we explained how the expansion rules of *DL-Lite*$_\mathcal{A}$ can be used to compute all combinations of concepts, roles and attributes resulting in inconsistencies in an *DL-Lite*$_\mathcal{A}$ ontology. Given a TBox $\mathcal{T}$ we apply this procedure for all clash types storing the results in an efficient index structure. We have to distinguish between clash types that are related to the use of

(a) a single concept, role, or attribute (Type 1 and 2),
(b) two concepts, two roles, concept and role, or concept and attribute (Type 4),
(c) an attribute and a value from a datatype (Type 3),
(d) a role or an attribute and the inequality of two instances or values (Type 5 and 6).

For each of these four cases we use a dedicated hash structure (referred to as $\mathbb{H}_a^\perp$ to $\mathbb{H}_d^\perp$), which allows to check if, e.g., the relevant combination of signature elements (concepts, roles, attributes), is contained. We sometimes refer to these data structures in an more general way by omitting the subscript. Once $\mathbb{H}_a^\perp$ to $\mathbb{H}_d^\perp$ have been computed, checking an ABox for consistency breaks down to checking for each single assertion or each pair of assertions if the used signature elements are stored in the respective data structures. We refer to this approach as CQ in the following. This approach has proven itself in practice and was successfully applied in Nolle et al. [13].

3.2   On Demand Reasoning

Our approach, which is a modified extension of CQ, omits the up-front computation of clash queries. Instead, we invoke a reasoner on the fly if we cannot decide the consistency based on clash queries already observed. We refer to that approach as CQ+. CQ+ differs from CQ in three aspects.

First, instead of using the expansion rules, we use a standard OWL 2 reasoner to compute the signature combinations that correspond to instantiations of the clash types. This does not guarantee completeness. There are still possible signature combinations resulting in inconsistencies that are not captured by one of the clash types, e.g., inconsistent combinations of more than two type assertions like $A(a), B(a), C(a)$ with $A \sqcap B \sqsubseteq D$ and $D \sqsubseteq \neg C$. Nevertheless, we will be able to detect inconsistencies that cannot be detected by expanding the stated axioms via the DL-Lite$_\mathcal{A}$ expansion rules, because sometimes relevant entailments are based on axioms that are beyond the DL-Lite$_\mathcal{A}$ expressivity.

Second, we do not compute inconsistent combinations of signature elements in advance, but on the fly during checking combinations of ABox assertions from the given set of ABoxes. We store every detected clash type instantiation in one of the $\mathbb{H}^\perp$ caches. Note that these caches are empty when we apply the approach to check the consistency of the first ABox. This differs from the CQ approach, where we compute all inconsistent signature combinations in advance. To minimize the calls to the reasoner, we check prior to any reasoning if the currently used combination of signature elements is already stored in one of the $\mathbb{H}^\perp$ caches (or in one of the $\mathbb{H}^\top$ caches, which will be explained in the following paragraph). This will obviously be more effective the more ABoxes are already processed.

Third, we do not only store inconsistent signature combinations, but also consistent combinations. Without this extension we cannot leverage the knowledge about the inconsistencies we detected so far. In the CQ approach we first computed the assertional patterns resulting in inconsistencies, then we started processing the ABoxes checking each assertion or combination of assertions against the pattern stored in $\mathbb{H}^{\perp}$. If this check is negative, we conclude that the checked combination is consistent. We cannot apply this procedure in the current approach, because $\mathbb{H}^{\perp}$ will be empty at the beginning and highly incomplete in the initial phase until a significant number of inconsistencies has been observed. For that reason we have to store inconsistent combinations in $\mathbb{H}^{\perp}$ and consistent combinations in $\mathbb{H}^{\top}$. For each combination of axioms within an ABox that can found in one of these caches, we decide upon the consistency of this ABox fragment without calling a reasoner.

The algorithm for checking the consistency of an ABox $\mathcal{A}$ against a TBox $\mathcal{T}$ is shown in Algorithm 1. This algorithm is called for each of the ABoxes that need to be checked. The different variants of $\mathbb{H}^{\perp}$ and $\mathbb{H}^{\top}$ are referenced via global variables pointing to data structures for which the operations of adding and containment checking run in constant time. We have depicted the algorithm only for Case (4)(b). In our actual implementation, we extended the algorithm by a comprehensive set of case distinctions covering the remaining clash types using all four caches.

Algorithm 1. CHECKCONSISTENCY$(\mathcal{A}, \mathcal{T})$

1: **for all** $a \in instances(\mathcal{A})$ **do**
2:     **for all** $\phi(a) \in class\text{-}assertions(\mathcal{A})$ **do**
3:         **for all** $\psi(a, b) \in role\text{-}assertions(\mathcal{A})$ **do**
4:             **if** $\langle \phi, \exists \psi \rangle \in \mathbb{H}_b^{\perp}$ **then**
5:                 **return** false
6:             **end if**
7:             **if** $\langle \phi, \exists \psi \rangle \in \mathbb{H}_b^{\top}$ **then**
8:                 **continue** // ... with next loop cycle
9:             **end if**
10:            **if** $\mathcal{T} \models \phi \sqsubseteq \neg \exists \psi$ **then**
11:                $\langle \phi, \exists \psi \rangle \xrightarrow{add} \mathbb{H}_b^{\perp}$
12:                **return** false
13:            **else**
14:                $\langle \phi, \exists \psi \rangle \xrightarrow{add} \mathbb{H}_b^{\top}$
15:            **end if**
16:        **end for**
17:    **end for**
18: **end for**
19: **return** true

For the CQ+ approach, every processed ABox increases the probability that a certain combination of signature elements has already been observed to be consistent or inconsistent, which means that no reasoning activities are required for that combination. In terms of Algorithm 1, this means that line 10 to 15 will be executed less often the more often the procedure is called. However, this depends both on the size of the TBox and on the distribution of factually used combinations of signature elements, which will be discussed in the following section.

4   Experiments

In Sect. 4.1 we first describe the datasets used in our experiments and give an overview on the reasoning methods that we evaluate. We present and discuss the most important results of our experiments in Sect. 4.2.

4.1   Setting

We use two datasets in our experiments[1]. These datasets have also been used in [15] to demonstrate how machine learning can be applied efficiently to mimic a reasoner. We rebuild larger versions of these datasets according to the descriptions in [15]. The first dataset, that we refer to as the DBpedia+ dataset, uses the DBpedia TBox that consists of all mapping-based roles and types in DBpedia [8]. This TBox is extended with the top-level ontology DOLCE-Zero [4]. The reason for this extension is related to the fact that DBpedia contains only few disjointness axioms, while DOLCE-Zero introduces disjointness on the top level [14]. We generated 100k ABoxes where each ABox consists of a randomly chosen role assertion and all class assertions related to its subject and object. Thus, all of the ABoxes have a very simple structure and most of the reasoning task is related to checking the asserted types against the domain and range restrictions of the role. However, the explanations for an inconsistency can nevertheless be quite complex. This is illustrated by Example 1, which is an (already slightly simplified) explanation for one of the generated ABoxes. Note also that an ABox usually contains more assertions than shown in Example 1.

The second dataset uses the GoodRelations ontology as TBox. GoodRelations [4] is a vocabulary designed for e-commerce, which is used as RDFa to describe products and offers. We have used a sample of documents from the WebData-Commons 2014 Microdata corpus, and extracted 5k randomly chosen documents (= ABoxes) that make use of the GoodRelations vocabulary. In doing so we encountered syntactic errors and related parsing problems, which required a semi-automated extraction process. For that reason, we were able to extract only 5000 ABoxes. Opposed to the ABoxes from the DBpedia+ dataset, these ABoxes do not share a common structure and are larger compared to the ABoxes from the DBpedia+ dataset. The characteristics of the two datasets are presented in Table 1.

We have not used the schema.org and the YAGO dataset used in [15] because they pose less complex reasoning tasks. According to our inspection of the schema.org dataset, many mistakes are based on roles that have been used as

---

[1] All the datasets created for this paper are available online at http://web.informatik. uni-mannheim.de/rr2017.

Table 1. Characteristics of the DBpedia+ and GoodRelations dataset in terms of number of generated ABoxes, percentage of inconsistent ABoxes, average size of ABoxes; the description logic of the TBox, and number of logical axioms in the TBox.

	ABoxes	Inconsistent	Average Size	DL	Logical Axioms
DBpedia+	100000	24.07%	58.1	$\mathcal{SHIN}(\mathcal{D})$	7436
GoodRelations	5000	28.54%	13.9	$\mathcal{SHI}(\mathcal{D})$	450

attributes (or vice versa). The remaining inconsistencies seem to be only clashes related to attributes using data values that are incompatible with the explicitly stated data type. Each of the ABoxes in the YAGO dataset is describing a single instance by all of its concept assertions. This means that each ABox is of the form $C_1(a), \ldots, C_2(a)$. Moreover, these assertions are extended in a preprocessing step by adding the transitive closure on the stated class assertions, in order to support the machine learning.

In our experiments we analyze the following reasoning techniques with respect to their performance on the two datasets we introduced above.

CQ refers to the technique that uses the *DL-Lite$_\mathcal{A}$* expansion rules. We apply this technique to compute inconsistent patterns of assertions in a preprocessing step. Checking an ABox boils down to checking the ABox against these precompiled clash patterns.

CQ+ refers to the method that uses the *DL-Lite$_\mathcal{A}$* clash patterns. However, instead of using expansion rules in a preprocessing step it uses a complete reasoner to check the relevant entailments on the fly when the corresponding combinations appear in the currently processed ABox. We will also report about experiments, where we turn off the reasoning components after n ABoxes have been processed and the results are than solely based on the cache.

ML refers to the machine learning approach that has been described in [15]. For the feature transformation of the ABoxes, we used all paths up to length 3 for the GoodRelations dataset, while the ABoxes from the DBpedia dataset naturally have a path length of at most 2. All experiments were conducted with RapidMiner Studio.[2] In particular, we report about results using Decision Trees which has turned out to achieve good and stable results.

HermiT is a well-known OWL 2 reasoner [6], which we also used to annotate the training examples for the ML approach.

4.2 Results

The main results of our experiments are depicted in Table 2. The first column is relevant only for CQ+ and ML. For CQ+ it shows the number of ABoxes that have been processed to set up the cache. For ML the same number refers to the

---

[2] http://www.rapidminer.com.

Table 2. Runtime and accuracy of CQ, CQ+, CQ+ turning off reasoning, ML and HermiT for the DBpedia+ and GoodRelations dataset averaged over ten runs for each setting. For settings that depend on previously processed ABoxes ("Training"), we randomly selected the set of these ABoxes in each of the runs.

		Training	Runtimes		Accuracy
			Preprocessing (s)	Checking Inc. (ms)	
DBpedia+	CQ	–	746	0.046	98.59%
	CQ+	–	-	77 to ≤0.5	100%
	CQ+ (cache only)	1000	77	0.041	98.6%
		10000	172	0.043	99.59%
		50000	253	0.04	99.84%
	ML	1000	98 + 1	0.356	97.62%
		10000	984 + 22	0.383	98.46%
		50000	4919 + 183	0.525	98.52%
	HermiT	–	10	98.38	100%
GoodRelations	CQ	–	20	0.311	100%
	CQ+	–	-	4.5 to ≤0.33	100%
	CQ+ (cache only)	50	0	0.318	99.89%
		500	1	0.315	99.92%
		2500	2	0.321	100%
	ML	50	1 + 0	1.483	95.60%
		500	12 + 0	1.589	99.87%
		2500	61 + 1	1.757	99.9%
	HermiT	–	2	24.48	100%

number of training examples. The second column shows to the preprocessing time in seconds. In the preprocessing phase the CQ approach computes the expanded clash queries, the ML method trains a classifier which includes also the labeling of the samples with a reasoner (HermiT in our setting), the CQ+ (cache only) method requires processing some ABoxes in order to observe and store clashes (explanations) in the cash, HermiT requires loading the TBox. The third column shows the average time for checking the consistency of an ABox in milliseconds. While we know that all reasoning based methods are sound, i.e., a consistent ABox will never be labeled as inconsistent, an approach based on ML cannot guarantee soundness. For that reason we compare the results in terms of accuracy in the fourth column informing about the fraction of correct answers for each of the methods.

HermiT achieves an accuracy of 100% on both datasets. However, the runtimes are ≈25 ms and ≈100 ms for checking a single ABox. This shows that it is problematic to apply standard reasoning techniques if we want to check a very high number of ABoxes, without resorting to parallelization.

The CQ method reaches an accuracy of 98.59% on DBpedia+ and 100% on Good- Relations. An accuracy of 98.59% corresponds, with respect to the

DBpedia+ dataset, to 5.44% inconsistent ABoxes that have not been detected to be inconsistent. The runtimes of the CQ approach are about 0.05 ms for a DBpedia+ ABox and 0.3 ms for a GoodRelations ABox. The differences can be explained by the different size of the ABoxes. Comparing these runtimes to the runtimes of HermiT, the CQ method is about 2000 times faster. The method requires relatively high preprocessing runtimes for the preprocessing step due to the fact that all possible *DL-Lite$_A$* clashes are computed even though most of them will never be instantiated.

The CQ+ approach is capable of detecting all inconsistencies for both datasets. The improvement for DBpedia+ from 98.59% (CQ) to 100% (CQ+) is caused by the use of full-fledged reasoning when checking such patterns as $\mathcal{T} \models A \sqsubseteq \neg \exists P$, while the patterns themselves cover all factually existing inconsistencies. The runtimes of the CQ+ approach cannot be presented in terms of an average number, but require presenting the runtime depending on the number of previously checked ABoxes. Remember that with every processed ABox more information is stored in the $\mathbb{H}^\perp$ and $\mathbb{H}^\top$ caches. To measure the impact of the cache, we apply our algorithm on consecutive blocks of 1000 ABoxes w.r.t DBpedia+ (100 ABoxes w.r.t GoodRelations) measuring the average runtime for a single ABox within such a block.

The resulting runtimes are shown in Fig. 1 on a logarithmic scale. We start with a runtime of ≈ 80 ms for DBpedia. After processing 10 k ABoxes the runtime for an ABox is ≈ 5 ms. After 50 k ABoxes have been processed less than 1 ms is required. The runtime behavior is similar for GoodRelations. However, significantly less processed ABoxes are required to reduce the initial runtimes. After having processed 1000 ABoxes, the runtimes for CQ and CQ+ are roughly the same. The differences between DBpedia+ and GoodRelations are related to the significantly smaller TBox of GoodRelations. Since there are less concepts, roles and attributes in GoodRelations, there are also less (frequently used) inconsistent and consistent vocabulary combinations.

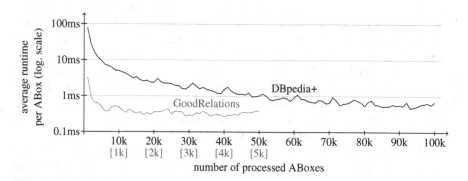

Fig. 1. Runtime of CQ+ for processing a single ABox with respect to the number of already processed ABoxes for DBpedia+ [GoodRelations].

The CQ method is about 80 times (GoodRelations) to 2000 times (DBpedia+) faster compared to HermiT. This means that by applying the CQ method we are losing completeness, as described above, but gain a significant improvement in runtime. The CQ+ method detects all inconsistencies in both datasets. Its runtimes are at the beginning similar to the runtimes of HermiT. However, after processing a large number of ABoxes, CQ+ is between 80 and 200 times faster compared to HermiT.

One of the most important features of the CQ+ method is the option to turn off reasoning and to rely solely on the cache after a reasonable number of ABoxes have been processed. Table 2 shows the runtimes after turning off reasoning as soon as n ABoxes have been processed. The time required to process the first n ABoxes is counted as preprocessing time in this setting. n is specified in the column entitled "Training". For the ML approach we use exactly this number of ABoxes as training examples. The CQ+ runtimes, after turning off the reasoning component, are approximately the same runtimes that we measured for the CQ approach. However, the accuracy is surprisingly high after processing a relatively small number of ABoxes. After processing 1 k ABoxes of DBpedia+, the accuracy is similar to the accuracy of the CQ method; after 10 k ABoxes we are already reaching an accuracy of 99.59% which is increased to 99.84% when processing 50 k ABoxes. For GoodRelations we achieve an accuracy of 100% after having processed 2500 ABoxes. This shows that the CQ+ method is highly flexible and can be configured for the needs of a given application scenario (runtime vs. accuracy).

We have also applied the ML approach of Paulheim and Stuckenschmidt [15]. The runtimes are slightly worse compared to the runtimes of the CQ method. Note that most of the runtimes are related to generating the feature representation of an ABox, while the classification itself is extremely fast. The high runtimes for preprocessing are caused by the need to annotate the training examples with the help of HermiT, while the runtimes for learning the classifier are of little significance. The accuracy of the approach is rather high. However, the ML results that are based on learning from n examples are worse than comparable results of the CQ+ approach relying solely on the cache after n ABoxes have been processed with an active reasoning component. This becomes more evident when we present the results in terms of the error rate $(1 - accuracy)$. The error rate on DBpedia+ with $n = 10000$ is 1.54% for ML and 0.41% for CQ+, the error rate on GoodRelations with $n = 2500$ is 0.13% for ML and 0.08% for CQ+. This illustrates the theoretical considerations that we presented in Sect. 2.4. Moreover, the accuracy of the learned classifier is in none of the settings higher than the well known CQ method.

In Table 3 we present numbers relevant to the memory usage. For CQ and CQ+ we show the number of stored combinations in the $\mathbb{H}_b^\top$ (consistent usage) and $\mathbb{H}_b^\perp$ (inconsistent usage). Note that the $\mathbb{H}_b$ caches are the only ones that can increase up to the square of the concepts, roles and attributes defined in the TBox, while the other caches will only grow linearly. For ML we show the dimension of the feature vector that describes a single ABox. First, we compare

Table 3. Characteristics related to memory consumption for CQ, CQ+ and ML.

	DBpedia		GoodRelations	
# processed/training examples	10 k	100 k	500	5000
CQ ($\mathbb{H}_b^\top / \mathbb{H}_b^\perp$)	-/8810234		-/11184	
CQ+ ($\mathbb{H}_b^\top / \mathbb{H}_b^\perp$)	17057/480	27580/1460	804/7	1722/12
ML (number of features)	4211.6	8261	1781.4	2427

the clash patterns stored by CQ and CQ+. While there are more than 8 million instantiations of clashes, there occur only 1460 of these clashes in a set of 100k ABoxes. This is less then 0.02%. For GoodRelations we measured only 12 different inconsistency patterns.[3] The fact that only very specific errors occur in the dataset is also a reason why learning works in the given setting. The fact that DBpedia results in more than 8 million inconsistent combinations shows that the CQ approach is only applicable to larger TBoxes if extensive memory resources are available. While the number of consistent combinations clearly dominates the inconsistent combinations for CQ+, the overall cache size is still acceptable and seems to grow linearly with respect to the size of the TBox. The number of features in the ML approach is less for DBpedia+ and more for GoodRelations compared to the sum of the entries in the CQ+ caches. Overall, the numbers are in the same order of magnitude. The differences are mainly based on the fact that the maximal path length in the DBpedia+ ABoxes is two, while the GoodRelations dataset has ABoxes that correspond to graphs with longer paths.

5   Conclusion and Future Work

In this work, we have studied different methods to solve the problem of efficiently checking the consistency of a large set of ABoxes against a given TBox. Our results indicate that the approach proposed in [10], which is complete for *DL-Lite$_A$*, can also be applied successfully to scenarios where the given TBox is more expressive. While such an approach, referred to as CQ, is incomplete in theory, our experiments indicted that only few inconsistencies remain undetected. Moreover, the CQ approach clearly outperforms an approach based on machine learning, which has been proposed more recently [15].

We extended the CQ resulting in an approach referred to as CQ+. This approach is based on the use of a complete reasoner to check on the fly the entailment that results in an instantiation of a clash pattern. Spotted inconsistent and consistent combinations of vocabulary usage are stored in a cache, which is used prior to any calls to the reasoner. This extension resulted in an accuracy of 100% for both datasets used in our experiments. Moreover, we could show that the runtimes decrease with every processed ABox resulting in a highly efficient procedure for checking consistency.

---

[3] Note that the $\mathbb{H}_b$ caches do not contain errors related to wrong datatypes. However, these errors are less important from a reasoning perspective since all of them have been detected by comparing the stated datatype against the type of the given value.

Even though we measured in our experiments an accuracy of 100%, we are aware that this is only an empirical observation related to the datasets we used in our experiments. Even within the simple structure of the DBpedia ABoxes, there is no guarantee that the CQ+ method finds all inconsistencies. One can easily define sets of axioms that would result, in combination with an ABox that has the same structure as the ABoxes of the DBpedia+ dataset, in an inconsistency. An example are the following axioms and assertions.

$$\exists P.B \sqsubseteq A, A \sqsubseteq \neg C, P(a,b), C(a), B(b)$$

Both CQ and CQ+ are not capable of detecting this inconsistency, due to the fact that the involved assertions do not instantiate one of the clash types. A machine learning based approach is in principle capable of learning a classifier that will work for such cases. This will happen if instantiations of $P(x,y)$, $C(x)$, $B(y)$ appear sufficiently often within the training examples, while proper subsets of these instantiations, that are marked as consistent, will also appear sufficiently often within the training examples. Other inconsistencies that are beyond the scope of CQ+ involve, for example, role transitivity and role irreflexivity.

In general, an approach that is based on learning can pay-off only for datasets where two conditions hold:

- Some inconsistencies in the dataset cannot be detected with incomplete but efficient reasoning techniques.
- These inconsistencies are instantiations of the same pattern that appears rather frequently in the dataset.

In such a setting it might make sense to use (additionally) an approach that leverages machine learning techniques to learn patterns that are not covered by CQ, CQ+ or any alternative inference method. This requires the development of an appropriate feature representation without introducing a huge feature space that cannot be handled efficiently. However, unless such a method based on machine learning is available, it seems to be the best choice to rely on the CQ method, the CQ+ method, or another elementary inference method.

As a first step in our future work, we plan to use the reasoner Konclude [17] in our experiments.

References

1. Baader, F.: The Description Logic Handbook: Theory, Implementation, and Applications. Cambridge University Press, Cambridge (2003)
2. Calvanese, D., De Giacomo, G., Lembo, D., Lenzerini, M., Rosati, R.: Tractable reasoning and efficient query answering in description logics: the DL-Lite family. J. Autom. Reasoning **39**(3), 385–429 (2007)
3. Flouris, G., Huang, Z., Pan, J.Z., Plexousakis, D., Wache, H.: Inconsistencies, negations and changes in ontologies. In: Proceedings of the National Conference on Artificial Intelligence, vol. 21, no. 2, p. 1295 (2006)

4. Gangemi, A., Mika, P.: Understanding the semantic web through descriptions and situations. In: Meersman, R., Tari, Z., Schmidt, D.C. (eds.) OTM 2003. LNCS, vol. 2888, pp. 689–706. Springer, Heidelberg (2003). doi:10.1007/978-3-540-39964-3_44

5. Horridge, M., Parsia, B., Sattler, U.: Explaining inconsistencies in OWL ontologies. In: Godo, L., Pugliese, A. (eds.) SUM 2009. LNCS (LNAI), vol. 5785, pp. 124–137. Springer, Heidelberg (2009). doi:10.1007/978-3-642-04388-8_11

6. Horrocks, I., Motik, B., Wang, Z.: The HermiT OWL reasoner. In: Proceedings of the 1st International Workshop on OWL Reasoner Evaluation (ORE-2012), Manchester, UK (2012)

7. Kalyanpur, A., Parsia, B., Horridge, M., Sirin, E.: Finding all justifications of OWL DL entailments. In: Aberer, K., Choi, K.-S., Noy, N., Allemang, D., Lee, K.-I., Nixon, L., Golbeck, J., Mika, P., Maynard, D., Mizoguchi, R., Schreiber, G., Cudré-Mauroux, P. (eds.) ASWC/ISWC -2007. LNCS, vol. 4825, pp. 267–280. Springer, Heidelberg (2007). doi:10.1007/978-3-540-76298-0_20

8. Lehmann, J., Isele, R., Jakob, M., Jentzsch, A., Kontokostas, D., Mendes, P.N., Hellmann, S., Morsey, M., Van Kleef, P., Auer, S., et al.: DBpedia-a large-scale, multilingual knowledge base extracted from wikipedia. Semant. Web **6**(2), 167–195 (2015)

9. Lembo, D., Lenzerini, M., Rosati, R., Ruzzi, M., Savo, D.F.: Query rewriting for inconsistent DL-Lite ontologies. In: Rudolph, S., Gutierrez, C. (eds.) RR 2011. LNCS, vol. 6902, pp. 155–169. Springer, Heidelberg (2011). doi:10.1007/978-3-642-23580-1_12

10. Lembo, D., Lenzerini, M., Rosati, R., Ruzzi, M., Savo, D.F.: Inconsistency-tolerant first-order rewritability of DL-Lite with identification and denial assertions. In: Proceedings of the 25th International Workshop on Description Logics (2012)

11. Lösch, U., Bloehdorn, S., Rettinger, A.: Graph kernels for RDF data. In: Simperl, E., Cimiano, P., Polleres, A., Corcho, O., Presutti, V. (eds.) ESWC 2012. LNCS, vol. 7295, pp. 134–148. Springer, Heidelberg (2012). doi:10.1007/978-3-642-30284-8_16

12. Nickel, M., Murphy, K., Tresp, V., Gabrilovich, E.: A review of relational machine learning for knowledge graphs. Proc. IEEE **104**(1), 11–33 (2016). http://dx.doi.org/10.1109/JPROC.2015.2483592

13. Nolle, A., Meilicke, C., Chekol, M., Nemirovski, G., Stuckenschmidt, H.: Schema-based debugging of federated data sources. In: Proceedings of the 22nd European Conference on Artificial Intelligence (ECAI2016). IOS Press (2016)

14. Paulheim, H., Gangemi, A.: Serving DBpedia with DOLCE – more than just adding a cherry on top. In: Arenas, M., et al. (eds.) ISWC 2015. LNCS, vol. 9366, pp. 180–196. Springer, Cham (2015). doi:10.1007/978-3-319-25007-6_11

15. Paulheim, H., Stuckenschmidt, H.: Fast approximate A-Box consistency checking using machine learning. In: Sack, H., Blomqvist, E., d'Aquin, M., Ghidini, C., Ponzetto, S.P., Lange, C. (eds.) ESWC 2016. LNCS, vol. 9678, pp. 135–150. Springer, Cham (2016). doi:10.1007/978-3-319-34129-3_9

16. Poggi, A., Lembo, D., Calvanese, D., Giacomo, G., Lenzerini, M., Rosati, R.: Linking data to ontologies. In: Spaccapietra, S. (ed.) Journal on Data Semantics X. LNCS, vol. 4900, pp. 133–173. Springer, Heidelberg (2008). doi:10.1007/978-3-540-77688-8_5

17. Steigmiller, A., Liebig, T., Glimm, B.: Konclude: system description. J. Web Sem. **27**, 78–85 (2014). http://dx.doi.org/10.1016/j.websem.2014.06.003

An Online Tool for Tuning Fuzzy Logic Programs

Ginés Moreno[(✉)] and José A. Riaza

Department of Computing System, University of Castilla-La Mancha,
02071 Albacete, Spain
{Gines.Moreno,JoseAntonio.Riaza}@uclm.es

Abstract. In this paper we are concerned with a fuzzy logic language where program rules extend the classical notion of clause by adding fuzzy connectives and truth degrees on their bodies. In this work we describe an efficient online tool which helps to select such operators and weights in an automatic way, accomplishing with our recent technique for tuning this kind of fuzzy programs. The system offers a comfortable interaction with users for introducing test cases and also provides useful information about the choices that better fit their preferences.

Keywords: Fuzzy logic programming · Symbolic execution · Tuning

1 Introduction

Logic Programming [14] has been widely used as a formal method for problem solving and knowledge representation. Nevertheless, traditional logic programming languages do not incorporate techniques or constructs to explicitly deal with uncertainty and approximated reasoning. In order to fill this gap, *fuzzy logic programming* has emerged as an interesting—and still growing—research area which aims to consolidate the efforts for introducing fuzzy logic into logic programming.

During the last decades, several fuzzy logic programming systems have been developed. Here, essentially, the classical SLD resolution principle of logic programming has been replaced by a fuzzy variant with the aim of dealing with partial truth and reasoning with uncertainty in a natural way. Most of these systems implement (extended versions of) the resolution principle introduced by Lee [12], such as Elf-Prolog [7], F-Prolog [13], generalized annotated logic programming [10], Fril [2], MALP [15], R-fuzzy [3], FASILL [5], the QLP scheme of [18] and the many-valued logic programming language of [19].

In this paper we focus on the so-called *multi-adjoint logic programming* approach MALP [15], a powerful and promising approach in the area of fuzzy

---

This work has been partially supported by the EU (FEDER), the State Research Agency (AEI) and the Spanish *Ministerio de Economía y Competitividad* under grant TIN2016-76843-C4-2-R (AEI/FEDER, UE).

S. Costantini et al. (Eds.): RuleML+RR 2017, LNCS 10364, pp. 184–198, 2017.
DOI: 10.1007/978-3-319-61252-2_13

$\&_P(x, y) \triangleq x * y$	$\leftarrow_P (x, y) \triangleq \begin{cases} 1 & \text{if } y \leq x \\ x/y & \text{if } 0 < x < y \end{cases}$	*Product logic*
$\&_G(x, y) \triangleq \min(x, y)$	$\leftarrow_G (x, y) \triangleq \begin{cases} 1 & \text{if } y \leq x \\ x & \text{otherwise} \end{cases}$	*Gödel logic*
$\&_L(x, y) \triangleq \max(0, x + y - 1)$	$\leftarrow_L (x, y) \triangleq \min(x - y + 1, 1)$	*Łukasiewicz logic*

Fig. 1. Adjoint pairs of three different fuzzy logics over $\langle [0, 1], \leq \rangle$.

logic programming. Intuitively speaking, logic programming is extended with a *multi-adjoint lattice* L of truth values (typically, a real number between 0 and 1), equipped with a collection of *adjoint pairs* $\langle \&_i, \leftarrow_i \rangle$ and connectives: implications, conjunctions, disjunctions, and other operators called aggregators, which are interpreted on this lattice. Consider, for instance, the following MALP rule: "$good(X) \leftarrow_P @_{aver}(nice(X), cheap(X))$ *with* 0.8", where the adjoint pair $\langle \&_P, \leftarrow_P \rangle$ is defined as shown in the first line of Fig. 1, and the aggregator $@_{aver}$ is typically defined as $@_{aver}(x_1, x_2) \triangleq (x_1 + x_2)/2$. Therefore, the rule specifies that X is good—with a truth degree of 0.8—if X is nice and cheap. Assuming that X is nice and cheap with, e.g., truth degrees n and c, respectively, then X is good with a truth degree of $0.8 * ((n + c)/2)$.

When specifying a MALP program, it might sometimes be difficult to assign weights—truth degrees—to program rules, as well as to determine the right connectives.[1] This is a common problem with fuzzy control system design, where some trial-and-error is often necessary. In our context, a programmer can develop a prototype and repeatedly execute it until the set of answers is the intended one. Unfortunately, this is a tedious and time consuming operation. Actually, it might be impractical when the program should correctly model a large number of test cases provided by the user.

In order to overcome this drawback, in [16] we have recently introduced a symbolic extension of MALP programs called *symbolic multi-adjoint logic programming* (sMALP). Here, we can write rules containing *symbolic* truth degrees and *symbolic* connectives, i.e., connectives which are not defined on its associated multi-adjoint lattice. In order to evaluate these programs, we introduce a symbolic operational semantics that delays the evaluation of symbolic expressions. Therefore, a *symbolic answer* could now include symbolic (unknown) truth values and connectives. The approach is correct in the sense that using the symbolic semantics and then replacing the unknown values and connectives by concrete ones gives the same result as replacing these values and connectives in the original sMALP program and, then, applying the concrete semantics on the resulting MALP program. Furthermore, in [16] it is showed how sMALP programs can

---

[1] For instance, we have typically several adjoint pairs as shown in Fig. 1: *Łukasiewicz logic* $\langle \&_L, \leftarrow_L \rangle$, *Gödel logic* $\langle \&_G, \leftarrow_G \rangle$ and *product logic* $\langle \&_P, \leftarrow_P \rangle$, which might be used for modeling *pessimist*, *optimist* and *realistic scenarios*, respectively.

be used to tune a program w.r.t. a given set of test cases, thus easing what is considered the most difficult part of the process: the specification of the right weights and connectives for each rule. The main goal of the present paper is to describe the online implementation of this technique which is freely available from http://dectau.uclm.es/tuning/.

The structure of this paper is as follows. Sections 2 and 3 focus on the syntax and operational semantics of the framework of symbolic multi-adjoint logic programming by showing how such kind of programs can be loaded and executed into the online tool. Then, in Sect. 4, we describe the capability of the tool for tuning several parameters of symbolic programs so that a concrete program is obtained. Finally, Sect. 5 concludes and points out some directions for further research.

2   Symbolic Multi-adjoint Logic Programs

We assume the existence of a multi-adjoint lattice $\langle L, \preceq, \&_1, \leftarrow_1, \ldots, \&_n, \leftarrow_n \rangle$, equipped with a collection of *adjoint pairs* $\langle \&_i, \leftarrow_i \rangle$—where each $\&_i$ is a conjunctor which is intended to be used for the evaluation of *modus ponens* [15]—. In addition, on each program rule, we can have a different adjoint implication ($\leftarrow_i$), conjunctions (denoted by $\wedge_1, \wedge_2, \ldots$), adjoint conjunctions ($\&_1, \&_2, \ldots$), disjunctions ($|_1, |_2, \ldots$), and other operators called aggregators (usually denoted by $@_1, @_2, \ldots$); see [17] for more details. More exactly, a multi-adjoint lattice fulfill the following properties:

- $\langle L, \preceq \rangle$ is a (bounded) complete lattice.[2]
- For each truth function of $\&_i$, an increase in any of the arguments results in an increase of the result (they are *increasing*).
- For each truth function of $\leftarrow_i$, the result increases as the first argument increases, but it decreases as the second argument increases (they are *increasing* in the consequent and *decreasing* in the antecedent).
- $\langle \&_i, \leftarrow_i \rangle$ is an *adjoint pair* in $\langle L, \preceq \rangle$, namely, for any $x, y, z \in L$, we have that: $x \preceq (y \leftarrow_i z)$ if and only if $(x \ \&_i \ z) \preceq y$.

Aggregation operators are useful to describe or specify user preferences. An aggregation operator, when interpreted as a truth function, may be an arithmetic mean, a weighted sum or in general any monotone function whose arguments are values of a multi-adjoint lattice L. Although, formally, these connectives are binary operators, we often use them as n-ary functions so that $@(x_1, \ldots, @(x_{n-1}, x_n), \ldots)$ is denoted by $@(x_1, \ldots, x_n)$. By abuse, in these cases, we consider $@$ an n-ary operator. The truth function of an n-ary connective ς is denoted by $[\![\varsigma]\!] : L^n \mapsto L$ and is required to be monotonic and fulfill the following conditions: $[\![\varsigma]\!](\top, \ldots, \top) = \top$ and $[\![\varsigma]\!](\bot, \ldots, \bot) = \bot$.

---

[2] A complete lattice is a (partially) ordered set $\langle L, \preceq \rangle$ such that every subset S of L has infimum and supremum elements. It is bounded if it has bottom and top elements, denoted by $\bot$ and $\top$, respectively. L is said to be the *carrier set* of the lattice, and $\preceq$ its ordering relation.

Program

```
popularity(X) #<s1 facilities(X) #|s2 @aver(location(X),rates(X)) with 0.9.    symbolic.fpl

facilities(sun) with #s3.    location(sun) with 0.4.    rates(sun) with 0.7.
facilities(sweet) with 0.5.  location(sweet) with 0.3.  rates(sweet).
facilities(lux) with 0.9.    location(lux) with 0.8.    rates(lux) with 0.2.
```

Lattice

```
% Elements
member(X) :- number(X), 0 =< X, X =< 1.   members([0.3, 0.5, 0.7]).     bool.lat.pl  num.lat.pl

% Ordering relation      % Supremum and infimum
leq(X,Y) :- X =< Y.        bot(0).  top(1).

% Binary operations
and_prod(X,Y,Z) :- Z is X*Y.                or_prod(X,Y,Z) :- Z is X+Y-X-Y.
and_godel(X,Y,Z) :- (X=<Y,Z=X;X>Y,Z=Y).     or_godel(X,Y,Z) :- (X=<Y,Z=Y;X>Y,Z=X).

% Aggregators
agr_aver(X,Y,Z) :- Z is (X+Y)/2.    agr_very(X,Y) :- Y is X*X.
```

Fig. 2. Screenshot of the online tool showing a loaded program and lattice.

Example 1. In the down window of Fig. 2, we show the shape of the lattice of truth degrees $([0,1], \leq)$ loaded by default in our tool. In general, lattices are described by means of a set of **Prolog** clauses where the definition of the following predicates is mandatory: `member/1`, that identifies the elements of the lattice; `members/1`, that highlights into a list a subset of truth degrees to be used at tuning time as we will see in Sect. 4; `bot/1` and `top/1` stand for the infimum and supremum elements of the lattice; and finally `leq/2`, that implements the ordering relation. Connectives are defined as predicates whose meaning is given by a number of clauses. The name of a predicate has the form **and_label**, **or_label** or **agr_label** depending on whether it implements a conjunction, a disjunction or an aggregator, where *label* is an identifier of that particular connective. The arity of the predicate is $n + 1$, where n is the arity of the connective that it implements, so its last parameter is a variable to be unified with the truth value resulting of its evaluation.

In this work, given a multi-adjoint lattice L, we consider a first order language $\mathcal{L}_L$ built upon a signature Σ_L, that contains the elements of a countably infinite set of variables $\mathcal{V}$, function and predicate symbols (denoted by $\mathcal{F}$ and Π, respectively) with an associated arity—usually expressed as pairs f/n or p/n, respectively, where n represents its arity—, and the truth degree literals Σ_L^T and connectives Σ_L^C from L. Therefore, a well-formed formula in $\mathcal{L}_L$ can be either:

- A *value* $v \in \Sigma_L^T$, which will be interpreted as itself, i.e., as the truth degree $v \in L$.
- $p(t_1, \ldots, t_n)$, if $t_1, \ldots, t_n$ are terms over $\mathcal{V} \cup \mathcal{F}$ and p/n is an n-ary predicate. This formula is called *atomic* (or just an *atom*).

- $\varsigma(e_1, \ldots, e_n)$, if $e_1, \ldots, e_n$ are well-formed formulas and ς is an n-ary connective with truth function $[\![\varsigma]\!] : L^n \mapsto L$.

As usual, a *substitution* σ is a mapping from variables from $\mathcal{V}$ to terms over $\mathcal{V} \cup \mathcal{F}$ such that $Dom(\sigma) = \{x \in \mathcal{V} \mid x \neq \sigma(x)\}$ is its domain. Substitutions are usually denoted by sets of mappings like, e.g., $\{x_1/t_1, \ldots, x_n/t_n\}$. Substitutions are extended to morphisms from terms to terms in the natural way. The identity substitution is denoted by id. The composition of substitutions is denoted by juxtaposition, i.e., $\sigma\theta$ denotes a substitution δ such that $\delta(x) = \theta(\sigma(x))$ for all $x \in \mathcal{V}$.

A MALP *rule* over a multi-adjoint lattice L is a formula $H \leftarrow_i \mathcal{B}$, where H is an *atomic formula* (usually called the *head* of the rule), $\leftarrow_i$ is an implication symbol belonging to some adjoint pair of L, and $\mathcal{B}$ (which is called the *body* of the rule) is a well-formed formula over L without implications. A *goal* is a body submitted as a query to the system. A MALP program is a set of expressions R *with* v, where R is a rule and v is a *truth degree* (a value of L) expressing the confidence of a programmer in the truth of rule R. By abuse of the language, we often refer to R *with* v as a rule (see, e.g., [15] for a complete formulation of the MALP framework).

We are now ready for summarizing the *symbolic* extension of multi-adjoint logic programming initially presented in [16] where, in essence, we allow some undefined values (truth degrees) and connectives in the program rules, so that these elements can be systematically computed afterwards. In the following, we will use the abbreviation sMALP to refer to programs belonging to this setting.

Here, given a multi-adjoint lattice L, we consider an augmented language $\mathcal{L}_L^s \supseteq \mathcal{L}_L$ which may also include a number of symbolic values, symbolic adjoint pairs and symbolic connectives which do not belong to L. Symbolic objects are usually denoted as o^s with a superscript s and, in our online tool, their identifiers always start with #.

Definition 1 (sMALP program). *Let L be a multi-adjoint lattice. An sMALP program over L is a set of symbolic rules, where each symbolic rule is a formula $(H \leftarrow_i \mathcal{B}$ with $v)$, where the following conditions hold:*

- *H is an atomic formula of $\mathcal{L}_L$ (the head of the rule);*
- *$\leftarrow_i$ is a (possibly symbolic) implication from either a symbolic adjoint pair $\langle \&^s, \leftarrow^s \rangle$ or from an adjoint pair of L;*
- *$\mathcal{B}$ (the body of the rule) is a symbolic goal, i.e., a well-formed formula of $\mathcal{L}_L^s$;*
- *v is either a truth degree (a value of L) or a symbolic value.*

Example 2. At the top of Fig. 2, we can see a sMALP program loaded into our online tool. Here, we consider a travel agency that offers booking services on three hotels, named *sun*, *sweet* and *lux*, where each one of them is featured by three factors: the hotel facilities, the convenience of its location, and the rates, denoted by predicates *facilities*, *location* and *rates*, respectively. Here, we assume that all weights can be easily obtained except for the weight of the fact *facilities(sun)*, which is unknown, so we introduce a symbolic weight #s3.

Also, the programmer has some doubts on the connectives used in the first rule, so she introduces two symbolic connectives, i.e., the implication and disjunction symbols $\# < s1$ and $\#|s2$.

3   Running Symbolic Programs

The procedural semantics of sMALP is defined in a stepwise manner as follows. First, an *operational* stage is introduced which proceeds similarly to SLD resolution in pure logic programming. In contrast to standard logic programming, though, our operational stage returns an expression still containing a number of (possibly symbolic) values and connectives. Then, an *interpretive* stage evaluates these connectives and produces a final answer (possibly containing symbolic values and connectives). The procedural semantics of both MALP and sMALP programs is based on a similar scheme. The main difference is that, for MALP programs, the interpretive stage always returns a value, while for sMALP programs we might get an expression containing symbolic values and connectives that should be first instantiated in order to compute a value.

In the following, $C[A]$ denotes a formula where A is a sub-expression which occurs in the—possibly empty—context $C[]$. Moreover, $C[A/A']$ means the replacement of A by A' in context $C[]$, whereas $Var(s)$ refers to the set of distinct variables occurring in the syntactic object s, and $\theta[Var(s)]$ denotes the substitution obtained from θ by restricting its domain to $Var(s)$. An sMALP *state* has the form $\langle Q; \sigma \rangle$ where Q is a symbolic goal and σ is a substitution. We let $\mathcal{E}^s$ denote the set of all possible sMALP states.

Definition 2 (admissible step). *Let L be a multi-adjoint lattice and $\mathcal{P}$ an sMALP program over L. An admissible step is formalized as a state transition system, whose transition relation $\to_{AS} \subseteq (\mathcal{E}^s \times \mathcal{E}^s)$ is the smallest relation satisfying the following transition rules:[3]*

1. $\langle Q[A]; \sigma \rangle \to_{AS} \langle (Q[A/v \&_i B])\theta; \sigma\theta \rangle$,
   if $\theta = mgu(\{H = A\}) \neq fail$, $(H \leftarrow_i B$ with $v) \ll \mathcal{P}$ and B is not empty.[4]
2. $\langle Q[A]; \sigma \rangle \to_{AS} \langle (Q[A/\bot]); \sigma \rangle$,
   if there is no rule $(H \leftarrow_i B$ with $v) \ll \mathcal{P}$ such that $mgu(\{H = A\}) \neq fail$.

Here, $(H \leftarrow_i B$ with $v) \ll \mathcal{P}$ denotes that $(H \leftarrow_i B$ with $v)$ is a renamed apart variant of a rule in $\mathcal{P}$ (i.e., all its variables are fresh). Note that symbolic values and connectives are not renamed.

Observe that the second rule is needed to cope with expressions like $@_{aver}(p(a), 0.8)$, which can be evaluated successfully even when there is no rule

---

[3] Here, we assume that A in $Q[A]$ is the selected atom. Furthermore, as it is common practice, $mgu(E)$ denotes the *most general unifier* of the set of equations E [11].

[4] For simplicity, we consider that facts $(H$ with $v)$ are seen as rules of the form $(H \leftarrow_i \top$ with $v)$ for some implication $\leftarrow_i$. Furthermore, in this case, we directly derive the state $\langle (Q[A/v])\theta; \sigma\theta \rangle$ since $v \&_i \top = v$ for all $\&_i$.

matching $p(a)$ since $@_{aver}(0, 0.8) = 0.4$. We sometimes call *failure steps* to this kind of admissible steps.

In the following, given a relation $\rightarrow$, we let $\rightarrow^*$ denote its reflexive and transitive closure. Also, an L^s-*expression* is now a well-formed formula of $\mathcal{L}_L^s$ which is composed by values and connectives from L as well as by symbolic values and connectives.

Definition 3 (admissible derivation). *Let L be a multi-adjoint lattice and $\mathcal{P}$ be an sMALP program over L. Given a goal $\mathcal{Q}$, an admissible derivation is a sequence $\langle \mathcal{Q}; id \rangle \rightarrow^*_{AS} \langle \mathcal{Q}'; \theta \rangle$. When $\mathcal{Q}'$ is an L^s-expression, the derivation is called* final *and the pair $\langle \mathcal{Q}'; \sigma \rangle$, where $\sigma = \theta[Var(\mathcal{Q})]$, is called a symbolic admissible computed answer (saca, for short) for goal $\mathcal{Q}$ in $\mathcal{P}$.*

Example 3. Consider again the multi-adjoint lattice L and the sMALP program $\mathcal{P}$ of Example 2. Here, we have the following final admissible derivation for goal $popularity(X)$ in $\mathcal{P}$ (the selected atom is underlined):

$$\langle popularity(X);\ id \rangle \qquad\qquad\qquad\qquad\qquad\qquad\qquad\qquad\rightarrow_{AS}$$
$$\langle \#\&s1(0.9, \#|s2(facilities(X), @aver(location(X), rates(X))));\ \{X_1/X\} \rangle \quad \rightarrow_{AS}$$
$$\langle \#\&s1(0.9, \#|s2(\#s3, @aver(location(sun), rates(sun))));\ \{X/sun, X_1/sun\} \rangle \rightarrow_{AS}$$
$$\langle \#\&s1(0.9, \#|s2(\#s3, @aver(0.4, rates(sun))));\ \{X/sun, X_1/sun\} \rangle \qquad \rightarrow_{AS}$$
$$\langle \#\&s1(0.9, \#|s2(\#s3, @aver(0.4, 0.7)));\ \{X/sun, X_1/sun\} \rangle$$

Hence, the associated saca is $\langle \#\&s1(0.9, \#|s2(\#s3, @aver(0.4, 0.7)));\ \{X/sun\} \rangle$.

Given a goal $\mathcal{Q}$ and a final admissible derivation $\langle \mathcal{Q}; id \rangle \rightarrow^*_{AS} \langle \mathcal{Q}'; \sigma \rangle$, we have that $\mathcal{Q}'$ does not contain atomic formulas. Now, $\mathcal{Q}'$ can be *solved* by using the following interpretive stage:

Definition 4 (interpretive step). *Let L be a multi-adjoint lattice and $\mathcal{P}$ be an sMALP program over L. Given a saca $\langle Q; \sigma \rangle$, the interpretive stage is formalized by means of the following transition relation $\rightarrow_{IS} \subseteq (\mathcal{E}^s \times \mathcal{E}^s)$, which is defined as the least transition relation satisfying:*

$$\langle \mathcal{Q}[\varsigma(r_1, \ldots, r_n)]; \sigma \rangle \ \rightarrow_{IS} \ \langle \mathcal{Q}[\varsigma(r_1, \ldots, r_n)/r_{n+1}]; \sigma \rangle$$

where ς denotes a connective defined on L and $[\![\varsigma]\!](r_1, \ldots, r_n) = r_{n+1}$.

An interpretive derivation of the form $\langle \mathcal{Q}; \sigma \rangle \rightarrow^*_{IS} \langle \mathcal{Q}'; \theta \rangle$ such that $\langle \mathcal{Q}'; \theta \rangle$ cannot be further reduced, is called a final *interpretive derivation. In this case, $\langle \mathcal{Q}'; \theta \rangle$ is called a symbolic fuzzy computed answer (sfca, for short). Also, if $\mathcal{Q}'$ is a value of L, we say that $\langle \mathcal{Q}'; \theta \rangle$ is a fuzzy computed answer (fca, for short).*

Example 4. Given the saca of Example 3, we have the following final interpretive derivation (the connective reduced is underlined):

$$\langle \#\&s1(0.9, \#|s2(\#s3, @aver(0.4, 0.7)));\ \{X/sun\} \rangle \rightarrow_{IS}$$
$$\langle \#\&s1(0.9, \#|s2(\#s3, 0.55));\ \{X/sun\} \rangle$$

with $[\![@_{aver}]\!](0.4, 0.7) = 0.55$. Therefore, $\langle \#\&s1(0.9, \#|s2(\#s3, 0.55));\ \{X/sun\} \rangle$ is a sfca of $popularity(X)$ in $\mathcal{P}$ since it cannot be further reduced.

In Fig. 3, we can see the run area of our online tool. After introducing a goal and clicking on the Answers & Tree button, the system executes the goal and generates both the whole set of its sfca's as well as its associated derivation tree (in plain text and also graphically), as seen in Fig. 4. Each sfca appears on a different leaf of the tree, where each state contains its corresponding goal and

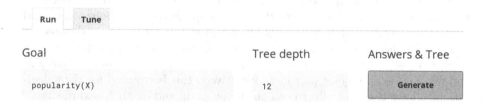

Run	Tune

Goal   Tree depth   Answers & Tree

`popularity(X)`   12   **Generate**

Fig. 3. Screenshot of the online tool showing the run input area.

Answers

Computed answers

```
< #&s1(0.9,#|s2(#s3,0.55)), {X/sun} >

< #&s1(0.9,#|s2(0.5,0.65)), {X/sweet} >

< #&s1(0.9,#|s2(0.9,0.5)), {X/lux} >
```

Derivation tree

```
R0 < popularity(X), {} >
   R1 < #&s1(0.9,#|s2(facilities(X),@aver(location(X),rates(X)))), {X1/X} >
      R2 < #&s1(0.9,#|s2(#s3,@aver(location(sun),rates(sun)))), {X/sun,X1/sun} >
         R3 < #&s1(0.9,#|s2(#s3,@aver(0.4,rates(sun)))), {X/sun,X1/sun} >
            R4 < #&s1(0.9,#|s2(#s3,@aver(0.4,0.7))), {X/sun,X1/sun} >
```

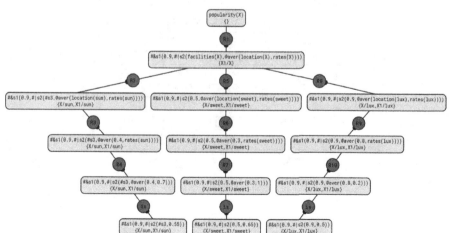

Fig. 4. Screenshot of the symbolic derivation tree generated by the online tool.

substitution components and they are drawn inside yellow ovals. Computational steps, colored in blue, are labeled with the program rule they exploit in the case of *admissible* steps or with the word "is", corresponding to *interpretive* steps. In our particular example, note that the leftmost branch in the tree of Fig. 4, contains the sequence of computational steps performed on the admissible and interpretive derivations shown in Examples 3 and 4, respectively.

Given a multi-adjoint lattice L and a symbolic language $\mathcal{L}_L^s$, in the following we consider *symbolic substitutions* that are mappings from symbolic values and connectives to expressions over $\Sigma_L^T \cup \Sigma_L^C$. Symbolic substitutions are denoted by $\Theta, \Gamma, \dots$ Furthermore, for all symbolic substitution Θ, we require the following condition: $\leftarrow^s / \leftarrow_i \in \Theta$ iff $\&^s / \&_i \in \Theta$, where $\langle \&^s, \leftarrow^s \rangle$ is a symbolic adjoint pair and $\langle \&_i, \leftarrow_i \rangle$ is an adjoint pair in L. Intuitively, this is required for the substitution to have the same effect both on the program and on an L^s-expression.

Answers

Computed answers

```
< 0.6165, {X/sun} >

< 0.7425, {X/sweet} >

< 0.855, {X/lux} >
```

Derivation tree

```
R0 < popularity(X), {} >
    R1 < &prod(0.9,|prod(facilities(X),@aver(location(X),rates(X)))), {X1/X} >
        R2 < &prod(0.9,|prod(0.3,@aver(location(sun),rates(sun)))), {X/sun,X1/sun} >
            R3 < &prod(0.9,|prod(0.3,@aver(0.4,rates(sun)))), {X/sun,X1/sun} >
                R4 < &prod(0.9,|prod(0.3,@aver(0.4,0.7))), {X/sun,X1/sun} >
```

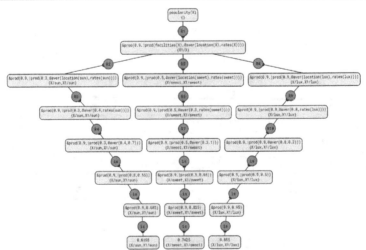

Fig. 5. Fuzzy computed answers and derivation tree generated for a MALP program.

Given an sMALP program $\mathcal{P}$ over L, we let $\mathsf{sym}(\mathcal{P})$ denote the symbolic values and connectives in $\mathcal{P}$. Given a symbolic substitution Θ for $\mathsf{sym}(\mathcal{P})$, we denote by $\mathcal{P}\Theta$ the program that results from $\mathcal{P}$ by replacing every symbolic symbol e^s by $e^s\Theta$. Trivially, $\mathcal{P}\Theta$ is now a MALP program.

The following theorem formally proved in [16] is a key result in order to use sMALP programs for tuning the components of a MALP program:

Theorem 1. *Let L be a multi-adjoint lattice and $\mathcal{P}$ be an sMALP program over L. Let Q be a goal. Then, for any symbolic substitution Θ for $\mathsf{sym}(\mathcal{P})$, we have that $\langle v; \theta \rangle$ is a fca for Q in $\mathcal{P}\Theta$ iff there exists a sfca $\langle Q'; \theta' \rangle$ for Q in $\mathcal{P}$ and $\langle Q'\Theta; \theta' \rangle \rightarrow_{IS}^* \langle v; \theta' \rangle$, where θ' is a renaming of θ.*

Example 5. Consider again the multi-adjoint lattice L and the sMALP program $\mathcal{P}$ in Fig. 2. Let $\Theta = \{\#\&s_1/\leftarrow_{\mathrm{prod}}, \&s_1/\&_{\mathrm{prod}}, \#|s_2/|_{\mathrm{prod}}, \#s_3/0.3\}$ be a symbolic substitution. Given the sfca from Example 4, we have:

$$\langle \#\&s_1(0.9, \#|s_2(\#s_3, 0.55))\rangle\Theta; \{X/sun\}\rangle \equiv \langle \&_{\mathrm{prod}}(0.9, |_{\mathrm{prod}}(0.3, 0.55)), \{X/sun\}\rangle$$

So, we have the following interpretive final derivation for the instantiated sfca:

$$\langle \&_{\mathrm{prod}}(0.9, |_{\mathrm{prod}}(0.3, 0.55)), \{X/sun\}\rangle \rightarrow_{IS}$$
$$\langle \&_{\mathrm{prod}}(0.9, 0.685), \{X/sun\}\rangle \rightarrow_{IS}$$
$$\langle 0.6165; \{X/sun\}\rangle$$

By Theorem 1, we have that $\langle 0.6165; \{X/sun\}\rangle$ is also a fca for $popularity(X)$ in $\mathcal{P}\Theta$, as confirmed in Fig. 5, where we can see the result of running the MALP program obtained after instantiating the original sMALP program in Example 2 with the proposed symbolic substitution Θ.

4   Tuning Multi-adjoint Logic Programs

In this section, we summarize the automated technique for tuning multi-adjoint logic programs using sMALP programs initially presented in [16] and recently implemented in our online tool (see Fig. 6) as we are going to explain.

Consider a typical Prolog clause "$H : -B_1, \ldots, B_n$". It can be fuzzified in order to become a MALP rule "$H \leftarrow_{label} \mathcal{B}$ with v" by performing the following actions:

1. weighting it with a truth degree v,
2. connecting its head and body with a fuzzy implication symbol $\leftarrow_{label}$ (belonging to a concrete adjoint pair $\langle \leftarrow_{label}, \&_{label} \rangle$) and,
3. linking the set of atoms $B_1, \ldots, B_n$ on its body $\mathcal{B}$ by means of a set of fuzzy connectives (i.e., conjunctions $\&_i$, disjunctions $|_j$ or aggregators $@_k$).

Introducing changes on each one of the three fuzzy components just described above may affect—sometimes in an unexpected way—the set of fuzzy computed answers for a given goal.

Fig. 6. Screenshot of the online tool for starting the tuning process.

Typically, a programmer has a model in mind where some parameters have a clear value. For instance, the truth value of a rule might be statistically determined and, thus, its value is easy to obtain. In other cases, though, the most appropriate values and/or connectives depend on subjective notions and, thus, programmers do not know how to obtain these values. In a typical scenario, we have an extensive set of *expected* computed answers (i.e., *test cases*), so the programmer can follow a "try and test" strategy. Unfortunately, this is a tedious and time consuming operation. Actually, it might even be impractical when the program should correctly model a large number of test cases.

The first action for initializing the tuning process in the online tool obviously consists in introducing a set of test cases as shown in Fig. 6. Each test case appears in a different line with syntax: $r \; -> \; Q$, where r is the desired truth degree for the fca associated to query Q (which obviously does not contain symbolic constants). Before directly using the test cases introduced in the input box, the system firstly tries to refine them by automatically instantiating the variable symbols as much as possible. So, in our particular example, after introducing the test case 0.6-> popularity(X), the tool generates the three sfca's shown in Fig. 4 and then uses their substitution components for instantiating the original query, thus changing the original test case by the following three ones: 0.6-> popularity(sun), 0.6-> popularity(sweet), and 0.6-> popularity(lux). Next, the user can manually update the truth degrees of some refined test cases, as done in the top box of Fig. 7, where we observe that the three final test cases to be used at tuning time are: 0.6-> popularity(sun), 0.77-> popularity(sweet), and 0.85-> popularity(lux).

Once the set of test cases has been appropriately customized, users simply need to click on the Generate substitution button for proceeding with the tuning process. The precision of the technique depends on the set of symbolic substitutions considered at tuning time. So, for assigning values to the symbolic constant (starting with #), our tool takes into account all the truth values defined on the members/1 predicate (which in our case is defined as members([0.3,0.5,0.8])) as well as the set of connectives defined in the lattice of Fig. 2, which in our running example coincides with the three conjunction and disjunction connectives

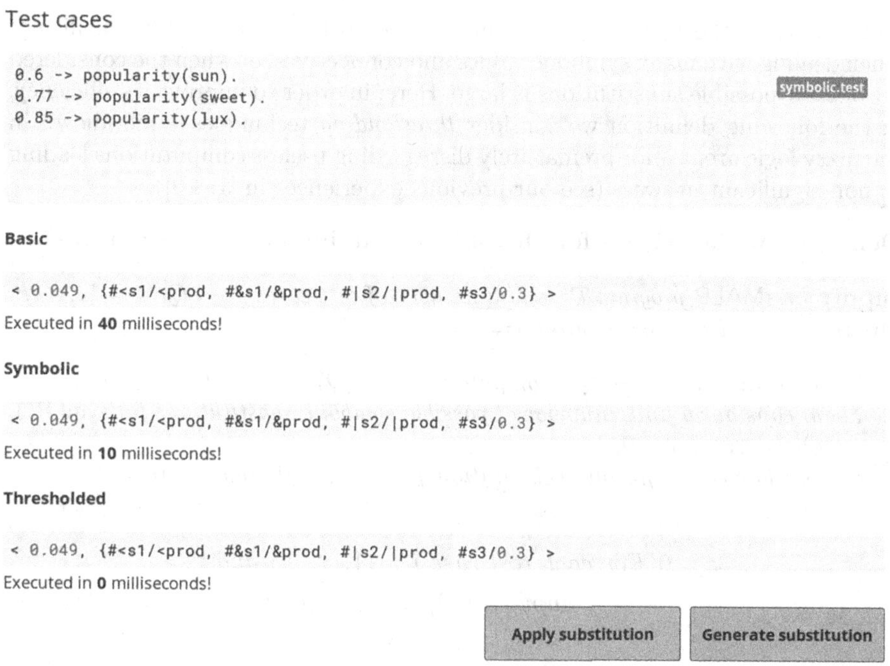

Test cases

```
0.6  -> popularity(sun).
0.77 -> popularity(sweet).                              symbolic.test
0.85 -> popularity(lux).
```

Basic

```
< 0.049, {#<s1/<prod, #&s1/&prod, #|s2/|prod, #s3/0.3} >
```
Executed in **40** milliseconds!

Symbolic

```
< 0.049, {#<s1/<prod, #&s1/&prod, #|s2/|prod, #s3/0.3} >
```
Executed in **10** milliseconds!

Thresholded

```
< 0.049, {#<s1/<prod, #&s1/&prod, #|s2/|prod, #s3/0.3} >
```
Executed in **0** milliseconds!

> [Apply substitution]   [Generate substitution]

Fig. 7. Screenshot of the online tool showing the output of a tuning process.

based on the so-called *Product, Gödel* and *Łukasiewicz* logics, as shown in Fig. 8. Obviously, the larger the domain of values and connectives is, the more precise the results are (but the algorithm is more expensive, of course).

$$\&_P(x, y) = x * y \qquad |_P(x, y) = x + y - x * y \qquad \textit{Product logic}$$
$$\&_G(x, y) = \min(x, y) \qquad |_G(x, y) = \max(x, y) \qquad \textit{Gödel logic}$$
$$\&_L(x, y) = \max(x + y - 1, 0) \qquad |_L(x, y) = \min(x + y, 1) \qquad \textit{Łukasiewicz logic}$$

Fig. 8. Conjunctions and disjunctions of three different fuzzy logics over $\langle [0, 1], \leq \rangle$.

The following definition resumes the tuning algorithm described in [16]:

Definition 5 (algorithm for symbolic tuning of MALP programs).

Input: *an sMALP program $\mathcal{P}^s$ and a number of test cases $v_i \to Q_i$, $i = 1, \ldots, k$.*
Output: *a symbolic substitution Θ.*

1. *For each test case $v_i \to Q_i$, compute the sfca $\langle Q_i', \theta_i \rangle$ of $\langle Q_i, id \rangle$ in $\mathcal{P}^s$.*
2. *Then, consider a finite number of possible symbolic substitutions for sym($\mathcal{P}^s$), say $\Theta_1, \ldots, \Theta_n$, $n > 0$.*
3. *For each $j \in \{1, \ldots, n\}$, compute $\langle Q_i' \Theta_j, \theta_i \rangle \to_{IS}^* \langle v_{i,j}; \theta_i \rangle$, for $i = 1, \ldots, k$. Let $d_{i,j} = |v_{i,j} - v_i|$, where $|\_|$ denotes the absolute value.*
4. *Finally, return the symbolic substitution Θ_j that minimizes $z = \sum_{i=1}^{k} d_{i,j}$.*

Unfortunately, the naive algorithm introduced so far might be very inefficient when dealing with many symbolic values and connectives, or when the considered set of their possible substitutions is large. Here, in order to improve its efficiency, in the following definition we consider *thresholding* techniques—well-known in the fuzzy logic arena—for prematurely disregarding useless computations leading to non-significant answers (see our previous experiences in [1,8,9]).

Definition 6 (algorithm for thresholded tuning of MALP programs).

Input: *an* sMALP *program* $\mathcal{P}^s$ *and a number of test cases* $v_i \rightarrow Q_i$, $i = 1, \ldots, k$.
Output: *a symbolic substitution* Θ_τ.

1. *For each test case* $v_i \rightarrow Q_i$, *compute the* sfca $\langle Q'_i, \theta_i \rangle$ *of* $\langle Q_i, id \rangle$ *in* $\mathcal{P}^s$.
2. *Then, consider a finite number of possible symbolic substitutions for* sym$(\mathcal{P}^s)$, *say* $\Theta_1, \ldots, \Theta_n$, $n > 0$.
3. $\tau = \infty$; *For each symbolic substitution* $j \in \{1, \ldots, n\}$ *and* $\tau \neq 0$

$$z = 0; For\ each\ test\ case\ i = \{1, \ldots, k\}\ and\ \tau > z$$
$$compute \langle Q'_i \Theta_j, \theta_i \rangle \rightarrow^*_{IS} \langle v_{i,j}; \theta_i \rangle$$
$$let z = z + |v_{i,j} - v_i|.$$
$$if\ z < \tau\ then\{\tau = z; \quad \Theta_\tau = \Theta_j\}.$$

4. *Finally, return the best symbolic substitution* Θ_τ.

The improved algorithm of Definition 6 is perfectly analogous to the algorithm in Definition 5, but makes use of a threshold τ for determining when a *partial* solution is acceptable. The value of τ is initialized to ∞ (in practice, a very large number). Then, this threshold dynamically decreases whenever we find a symbolic substitution with an associated deviation which is lower that the actual value of τ. Moreover, a partial solution is discarded as soon as the cumulative deviation computed so far is greater than τ. In general, the number of discarded solutions grows as the value of τ decreases, thus improving the pruning power of thesholding.

For tuning an sMALP program, we have implemented the three methods just commented before (which exhibit different run-times for obviously producing the same outputs as shown in Fig. 7, where number 0.049 refers to the accumulated deviation z computed in the algorithms of Definitions 5 and 6):

Basic: The basic method is based on applying each symbolic substitution to the original sMALP program and then fully executing the resulting instantiated MALP programs (both the operational and the admissible stages).

Symbolic: This version refers to the algorithm introduced in Definition 5, where symbolic substitutions are
directly applied to sfca's (thus only the interpretive stage is repeatedly executed).

Thresholded: In this case, we consider the symbolic algorithm improved with thresholding techniques detailed in Definition 6.

The system also reports the processing time required by each method and offers an option for applying the best symbolic substitution to the original sMALP program in order to show the final, tuned MALP program. In our case, by clicking the Apply substitution button, the first two rules of our tuned program become:

```
popularity(X) <prod facilities(X) |prod
                         @aver(location(X),rates(X)) with 0.9.
facilities(sun) with 0.3.
```

And the result of executing goal `popularity(X)` is shown in Fig. 5.

5   Conclusions and Future Work

In this paper, we have been concerned with fuzzy programs belonging to the so-called *multi-adjoint logic programming* approach. More exactly, we have described an online tool implementing the following two main results achieved in [16]:

- On one side, we have extended the MALP syntax for allowing the presence of symbolic weights and connectives on program rules, which very often prevents the full evaluations of goals. As a consequence, we have also relaxed the operational principle for producing what we call *symbolic fuzzy computed answers*, where all atoms have been exploited and the maximum number of expressions involving connectives of the underlaying lattice of truth degrees have been solved too.
- On the other hand, we have implemented three versions of a tuning process for MALP programs that takes as inputs a set of expected test cases and an sMALP program where some connectives and/or truth degrees are unknown. The efficiency of the method has been largely improved by combining it with thresholding techniques, as it can be checked online via the URL http://dectau.uclm.es/tuning/.

Since in [4–6], we have defined a new fuzzy language dealing with *similarity relations* that cohabit with lattices of truth degrees, as future work we plan to extend the implementation of the tuning method to cope with such similarity relations.

References

1. Almendros-Jiménez, J.M., Luna, A., Moreno, G.: Fuzzy xpath through fuzzy logic programming. New Generation Comput. **33**(2), 173–209 (2015)
2. Baldwin, J.F., Martin, T.P., Pilsworth, B.W.: Fril- Fuzzy and Evidential Reasoning in Artificial Intelligence. Wiley, New York (1995)

3. Guadarrama, S., Muñoz, S., Vaucheret, C.: Fuzzy Prolog: a new approach using soft constraints propagation. Fuzzy Sets Syst. **144**(1), 127–150 (2004)
4. Julián Iranzo, P., Moreno, G., Penabad, J., Vázquez, C.: A fuzzy logic programming environment for managing similarity and truth degrees. In: Escobar, S. (ed.), Proceeding of XIV Jornadas sobre Programación y Lenguajes, PROLE 2014, Cádiz, Spain, vol. 173. EPTCS, pp. 71–86 (2015). doi:10.4204/EPTCS.173.6
5. Julián-Iranzo, P., Moreno, G., Penabad, J., Vázquez, C.: A declarative semantics for a fuzzy logic language managing similarities and truth degrees. In: Alferes, J.J.J., Bertossi, L., Governatori, G., Fodor, P., Roman, D. (eds.) RuleML 2016. LNCS, vol. 9718, pp. 68–82. Springer, Cham (2016). doi:10.1007/978-3-319-42019-6_5
6. Julián-Iranzo, P., Moreno, G., Vázquez, C.: Similarity-based strict equality in a fully integrated fuzzy logic language. In: Bassiliades, N., Gottlob, G., Sadri, F., Paschke, A., Roman, D. (eds.) RuleML 2015. LNCS, vol. 9202, pp. 193–207. Springer, Cham (2015). doi:10.1007/978-3-319-21542-6_13
7. Ishizuka, M., Kanai, N.: Prolog-ELF incorporating fuzzy logic. In: Proceeding of the 9th International Joint Conference on Artificial Intelligence, IJCAI 1985, pp. 701–703. Morgan Kaufmann (1985)
8. Julián, P., Medina, J., Moreno, G., Ojeda, M.: Efficient thresholded tabulation for fuzzy query answering. In: Bouchon-Meunier, B., Magdalena, L., Ojeda-Aciego, M., Verdegay, J.-L., Yager, R.R. (eds.) Foundations of Reasoning under Uncertainty. STUDFUZZ, vol. 249, pp. 125–141. Springer, Heidelberg (2010). doi:10.1007/978-3-642-10728-3_7
9. Julián, P., Moreno, G., Penabad, J.: An improved reductant calculus using fuzzy partial evaluation techniques. Fuzzy Sets Syst. **160**, 162–181 (2009). doi:10.1016/j.fss.2008.05.006
10. Kifer, M., Subrahmanian, V.S.: Theory of generalized annotated logic programming and its applications. J. Logic Programm. **12**, 335–367 (1992)
11. Lassez, J.L., Maher, M.J., Marriott, K.: Unification revisited. In: Foundations of Deductive Databases and Logic Programming, pp. 587–625. Morgan Kaufmann, Los Altos (1988)
12. Lee, R.C.T.: Fuzzy logic and the resolution principle. J. ACM **19**(1), 119–129 (1972)
13. Li, D., Liu, D.: A Fuzzy Prolog Database System. Wiley, New York (1990)
14. Lloyd, J.W.: Foundations of Logic Programming. Springer, Berlin (1987)
15. Medina, J., Ojeda-Aciego, M., Vojtáš, P.: Similarity-based unification: a multi-adjoint approach. Fuzzy Sets Syst. **146**, 43–62 (2004)
16. Moreno, G., Penabad, J., Vidal, G.: Tuning fuzzy logic programs with symbolic execution. CoRR, abs/1608.04688 (2016)
17. Nguyen, H.T., Walker, E.A.: A First Course in Fuzzy Logic. Chapman & Hall, Boca Ratón (2006)
18. Rodríguez-Artalejo, M., Romero-Díaz, C.A.: Quantitative logic programming revisited. In: Garrigue, J., Hermenegildo, M.V. (eds.) FLOPS 2008. LNCS, vol. 4989, pp. 272–288. Springer, Heidelberg (2008). doi:10.1007/978-3-540-78969-7_20
19. Straccia, U.: Managing uncertainty and vagueness in description logics, logic programs and description logic programs. In: Baroglio, C., Bonatti, P.A., Maluszynski, J., Marchiori, M., Polleres, A., Schaffert, S. (eds.) Reasoning Web. LNCS, vol. 5224, pp. 54–103. Springer, Heidelberg (2008). doi:10.1007/978-3-540-85658-0_2

Hybrid ASP-Based Approach to Pattern Mining

Sergey Paramonov[1]($\boxtimes$), Daria Stepanova[2], and Pauli Miettinen[2]

[1] Department of Computer Science, KU Leuven, Leuven, Belgium
sergey.paramonov@kuleuven.be
[2] Max Planck Institute of Informatics, Saarbrücken, Germany
{dstepano,pmiettin}@mpi-inf.mpg.de

Abstract. Detecting small sets of relevant patterns from a given dataset is a central challenge in data mining. The relevance of a pattern is based on user-provided criteria; typically, all patterns that satisfy certain criteria are considered relevant. Rule-based languages like Answer Set Programming (ASP) seem well-suited for specifying such criteria in a form of constraints. Although progress has been made, on the one hand, on solving individual mining problems and, on the other hand, developing generic mining systems, the existing methods either focus on scalability or on generality. In this paper we make steps towards combining local (frequency, size, cost) and global (various condensed representations like maximal, closed, skyline) constraints in a generic and efficient way. We present a hybrid approach for itemset and sequence mining which exploits dedicated highly optimized mining systems to detect frequent patterns and then filters the results using declarative ASP. Experiments on real-world datasets show the effectiveness of the proposed method and computational gains both for itemset and sequence mining.

1 Introduction

Motivation. Availability of vast amounts of data from different domains has led to an increasing interest in the development of scalable and flexible methods for data analysis. A key feature of flexible data analysis methods is their ability to incorporate users' background knowledge and different criteria of interest. They are often provided in the form of *constraints* to the valid set of answers, the most common of which is the frequency threshold: a pattern is only considered interesting if it appears often enough. Mining all frequent (and otherwise interesting) patterns is a very general problem in data analysis, with applications in medical treatments, customer shopping sequences, Weblog click streams and text analysis, to name but a few examples.

Most data analysis methods consider only one (or few) types of constraints, limiting their applicability. Constraint Programming (CP) has been proposed as a general approach for (sequential) mining of frequent patterns [1], and Answer Set Programming (ASP) [6] has been proved to be well-suited for defining the constraints conveniently thanks to its expressive and intuitive modelling language and the availability of optimized ASP solvers (see e.g., [5,9,13] for existing approaches).

This work has been partially funded by the ERC AdG SYNTH grant (Synthesising inductive data models).

© Springer International Publishing AG 2017
S. Costantini et al. (Eds.): RuleML+RR 2017, LNCS 10364, pp. 199–214, 2017.
DOI: 10.1007/978-3-319-61252-2_14

In general, all constraints can be classified into *local constraints*, that can be validated by the pattern candidate alone, and *global constraints*, that can only be validated via an exhaustive comparison of the pattern candidate against all other candidates. Combining local and global constraints in a generic way is an important and challenging problem, which has been widely acknowledged in the constraint-based mining community. Although progress has been made, on the one hand, on solving individual mining problems and, on the other hand, on developing generic mining systems, the existing methods either focus on scalability or on generality, but rarely address both of these aspects. This naturally limits the practical applicability of the existing approaches.

State of the art and its limitations. Purely declarative ASP encodings for frequent and maximal itemset mining were proposed in [13]. In this approach, first every item's inclusion into the candidate itemset is guessed, and the guessed candidate pattern is checked against frequency and maximality constraints. While natural, this encoding is not truly generic, as adding extra local constraints requires significant changes in it. Indeed, for a database, where all available items form a frequent (and hence maximal) itemset, the maximal ASP encoding has a single model. The latter is, however, eliminated once restriction on the length of allowed itemsets is added to the program. This is undesired, as being maximal is not a property of an itemset on its own, but rather in the context of a collection of other itemsets [3]. Thus, ideally one would be willing to first apply all local constraints and only afterwards construct a condensed representation of them, which is not possible in [13].

This shortcoming has been addressed in the recent work [5] on ASP-based sequential pattern mining, which exploits ASP preference-handling capacities to extract patterns of interest and supports the combination of local and global constraints. However, both [5, 13] present purely declarative encodings, which suffer from scalability issues caused by the exhaustive exploration of the huge search space of candidate patterns. The subsequence check amounts to testing whether an embedding exists (matching of the individual symbols) between sequences. In sequence mining, a pattern of size m can be embedded into a sequence of size n in $O(n^m)$ different ways, therefore, clearly a direct pattern enumeration is unfeasible in practice.

While a number of individual methods tackling selective constraint-based mining tasks exist (see Table 1 for comparison) there is no uniform ASP-based framework that is capable of effectively combining constraints both on the global and local level and is suitable for itemsets and sequences alike.

Contributions. The goal of our work is to make steps towards building a generic framework that supports mining of condensed (sequential) patterns, which (1) effectively combines dedicated algorithms and declarative means for pattern mining and (2) is easily extendable to incorporation of various constraints. More specifically, the salient contributions of our work can be summarized as follows:

- We present a general extensible pattern mining framework for mining patterns of different types using ASP.
- We introduce a feature comparison, such as closedness under solutions, between different ASP mining models and dominance programming, which is a generic itemset mining language and solver.

Table 1. Feature comparison between various ASP mining models and dominance programming ("–": "not designed for this datatype", ✓*: only maximal is supported)

Datatype	Task	[13]	[5]	[16]	Our work
Itemset	Frequent pattern mining	✓	–	✓	✓
	Condensed (closed, max, etc.)	✓*	–	✓	✓
	Condensed under constraints	–	–	✓	✓
Sequence	Frequent pattern mining	–	✓	–	✓
	Condensed (closed, max, etc.)	–	✓	–	✓
	Condensed under constraints	–	✓	–	✓

– We demonstrate the feasibility of our approach with an experimental evaluation across multiple itemset and sequence datasets.

2 Preliminaries

In this section we briefly recap the necessary background both from the fields of pattern mining and Answer Set Programming (ASP).

Let D be a dataset, $\mathcal{L}$ a language for expressing pattern properties or defining subgroups of the data, and q a selection predicate. The task of pattern mining is to find $Th(\mathcal{L}, D, q) = \{\phi \in \mathcal{L} \mid q(D, \phi) \text{ is true}\}$ (see the seminal work [14]).

Pattern mining has been mainly studied for itemsets, sequences and graphs. These settings are determined by the language of $\mathcal{L}$. We focus on the first two categories.

2.1 Patterns

Itemsets. *Itemsets* represent the most simple setting of frequent pattern mining. Let $\mathcal{I}$ be a set of items $\{o_1, o_2, \ldots, o_n\}$. Then a nonempty subset of $\mathcal{I}$ is called an *itemset*. A *transaction dataset* D is a collection of itemsets, $D = \{t_1, \ldots, t_m\}$, where $t_i \subseteq \mathcal{I}$. For any itemset α, we denote the set of transactions that contain α as $D_\alpha = \{i \mid \alpha \subseteq t_i, t_i \in D\}$ and we refer to $|D_\alpha|$ as the *support (frequency)* of α in D, written $sup(\alpha)$. The *relative frequency* of α in D refers to the ratio between $sup(\alpha)$ and $|D|$. The *cardinality* (or *size*) $|\alpha|$ of an itemset α is the number of items contained in it.

Definition 1 (Frequent Itemset). *For a transaction dataset D and a frequency threshold $\sigma \geq 0$, an itemset α is* frequent *in D if $sup(\alpha) \geq \sigma$.*[1]

Example 1. Consider a transaction dataset D from Table 2. We have $\mathcal{I} = \{a, b, c, d, e\}$ and $|D| = 3$. For $\sigma = 2$, the following itemsets are frequent: $\alpha_1 = \{a\}$, $\alpha_2 = \{b\}$, $\alpha_3 = \{e\}$, $\alpha_4 = \{a, e\}$ and $\alpha_5 = \{b, e\}$. □

---

[1] In *frequent pattern mining*, often, a *relative threshold*, i.e., $\dfrac{\sigma}{|D|}$ is specified by the user.

Table 2. Transaction database

ID	a	b	c	d	e
1	✓	✓		✓	✓
2		✓	✓		✓
3	✓				✓

Table 3. Sequence database

ID	Sequence
1	$\langle a\,b\,c\,d\,a\,e\,b \rangle$
2	$\langle b\,c\,e\,b \rangle$
3	$\langle a\,a\,e \rangle$

Sequences. A *sequence* is an ordered set of items $\langle s_1, \ldots, s_n \rangle$. The setting of *sequence mining* includes two related yet different cases: frequent substrings and frequent subsequences. In this work we focus on the latter.

Definition 2 (Embedding in a Sequence). *Let* $S = \langle s_1, \ldots, s_m \rangle$ *and* $S' = \langle s'_1, \ldots, s'_n \rangle$ *be two sequences of size* m *and* n *respectively with* $m \leq n$. *The tuple of integers* $e = (e_1, \ldots, e_m)$ *is an* embedding *of* S *in* S' *(denoted* $S \sqsubseteq_e S'$*) if and only if* $e_1 < \ldots < e_m$ *and for any* $i \in \{1, \ldots, m\}$ *it holds that* $s_i = s'_{e_i}$.

Example 2. For a dataset in Table 3 we have that $\langle b\,c\,e\,b \rangle \sqsubseteq_{e_1} \langle a\,b\,c\,d\,a\,e\,b \rangle$ for $e_1 = (2, 3, 6, 7)$ and analogously, $\langle a\,a\,e \rangle \sqsubseteq_{e_2} \langle a\,b\,c\,d\,a\,e\,b \rangle$ with $e_2 = (1, 5, 6)$.

We are now ready to define an inclusion relation for sequences.

Definition 3 (Sequence Inclusion). *Given two sequences* $S = \langle s_1, \ldots, s_n \rangle$ *and* $S' = \langle s'_1, \ldots, s'_m \rangle$, *of size* m *and* n *resp. with* $n \leq m$, *we say that* S *is* included *in* S' *or* S *is a* subsequence *of* S' *denoted by* $S \sqsubseteq S'$ *iff an embedding* e *of* S *in* S' *exists, i.e.*

$$S \sqsubseteq S' \leftrightarrow \exists e_1 < \ldots < e_m \text{ and } \forall i \in 1 \ldots m : s_i = s'_{e_i}. \tag{1}$$

Example 3. In Example 2 we have $\langle b\,c\,e\,b \rangle \sqsubseteq \langle a\,b\,c\,d\,a\,e\,b \rangle$ but $\langle a\,a\,e \rangle \not\sqsubseteq \langle b\,c\,e\,b \rangle$. □

For a given sequence S and a sequential dataset $D = \{S_1, \ldots, S_n\}$ we denote by D_S the subset of D s.t. $S \sqsubseteq S'$ for all $S' \in D_S$. The support of S is $sup(S) = |D_S|$.

Definition 4 (Frequent Sequence). *For a sequential dataset* $D = \{S_1, \ldots, S_n\}$ *and a frequency threshold* $\sigma \geq 0$, *a sequence* S *is* frequent *in* D *if* $sup(S) \geq \sigma$.

Example 4. For a dataset in Table 3 and $\sigma = 2$, it holds that $\langle b\,c\,e\,b \rangle$ and $\langle a\,a\,e \rangle$ are frequent, while $\langle b\,d\,b \rangle$ is not. □

Note that $\sqsubseteq$ and $\subseteq$ are incomparable relations. Indeed, consider two sequences $s_1 = \langle a\,b \rangle$ and $s_2 = \langle b\,a\,a \rangle$. While $s_1 \subset s_2$, we clearly have that $s_1 \not\sqsubseteq s_2$.

2.2 Condensed Pattern Representations Under Constraints

In data mining, constraints are typically specified by the user to encode domain background knowledge. In [17] four types of constraints are distinguished: constraints (1) over the pattern (e.g., restriction on its size), (2) over the cover set (e.g., minimal frequency), (3) over the inclusion relation (e.g., maximal allowed gap in sequential patterns) and (4) over the solution set (e.g., condensed representations).

Orthogonally, constraints can be classified into *local* and *global* ones. A constraint is *local* if deciding whether a given pattern satisfies it is possible without looking at other patterns. For example, minimal frequency or maximal pattern size are local constraints. On the contrary, deciding whether a pattern satisfies a *global* constraint requires comparing it to other patterns. All constraints from the 4th group are global ones. We are interested in global constraints related to condensed representations.

As argued in Sect. 1, the order in which constraints are applied influences the solution set [3]. As in [3] in this work we apply global constraints only after local ones.

We now present the notions required in our pattern mining framework. Here, the definitions are given for itemsets; for sequences they are identical up to substitution of $\subset$ with $\sqsubset$ (subsequence relation). First, to rule out patterns that do not satisfy some of the local constraints, we introduce the notion of validity.

Definition 5 (Valid Pattern Under Constraints). *Let C be a constraint function from $\mathcal{L}$ to $\{\top, \bot\}$ and let p be a pattern in $\mathcal{L}$, then the pattern p is called* valid *iff $C(p) = \top$, otherwise it is referred as* invalid.

Example 5. Let C be a constraint function checking whether a given pattern is of size at least 2. Then for Example 1, we have $C(\alpha_i) = \bot, i = 1..3$ and $C(\alpha_j) = \top, j = 4..5$. □

For detecting patterns that satisfy a given global constraint, the notion of *dominance* is of crucial importance. Intuitively, a dominance relation reflects pairwise preference ($<^*$) between patterns and it is specific for each mining setting. In this work we primarily focus on global constraints related to maximal, closed, free and skyline condensed representations, for which $<^*$ is defined as follows:

(i) **Maximal.** For itemsets $p, q, p <^* q$ holds iff $p \subset q$
(ii) **Closed.** For itemsets $p, q, p <^* q$ holds iff $p \subset q \land sup(p) = sup(q)$
(iii) **Free.** For itemsets $p, q, p <^* q$ holds iff $q \subset p \land sup(p) = sup(q)$
(iv) **Skyline.** For itemsets $p, q, p <^* q$ holds iff
  (a) $sup(p) \le sup(q)$ and $size(p) < size(q)$ or
  (b) $sup(p) < sup(q)$ and $size(p) \le size(q)$

Dominated patterns under constraints are now formally defined.

Definition 6 (Dominated Pattern Under Constraints). *Let C be a constraint function, and let p be a pattern, then p is called* dominated *iff there exists a pattern $p' \in \mathcal{L}$ such that $p <^* p'$ and p' is valid under C.*

Example 6. In Example 1 for the maximality constraint we have that α_1 is dominated by α_4, α_2 by α_5, while α_3 both by α_4 and α_5. □

Exploiting the above definitions we obtain condensed patterns under constraints.

Definition 7 (Condensed Pattern Under Constraints). *Let p be a pattern from $\mathcal{L}$, and let C be a constraint function, then a pattern p is called* condensed *under constraints iff it is valid and not dominated under C.*

Example 7. For the constraint function selecting maximal itemsets of size at most 2 and size at least 2, α_4 and α_5 from Example 1 are condensed patterns.   □

2.3 Answer Set Programming

Answer Set Programming (ASP) [6] is a declarative problem solving paradigm oriented towards difficult search problems. ASP has its roots in Logic Programming and Non-monotonic Reasoning. An *ASP program* Π is a set of rules of the form

$$\texttt{a\_0} \quad \texttt{:-} \quad \texttt{b\_1,} \quad \texttt{...,} \quad \texttt{b\_k,} \quad \texttt{not} \quad \texttt{b\_k+1,...,} \quad \texttt{not b\_m,} \quad (2)$$

where $1 \leq k \leq m$, and $\texttt{a\_0}$, $\texttt{b\_1}$, $\ldots$, $\texttt{b\_m}$ are classical literals, and *not* is default negation. The right-hand side of r is its body, $Body(r)$, while the left-hand side is the head, $Head(r)$. $Body^+(r)$ and $Body^-(r)$ stand for the positive and negative parts of $Body(r)$ respectively. A rule r of the form (2) is a *fact* if $m = 0$. We omit the symbol :- when referring to facts. A rule without head literals is a *constraint*. A rule is *positive* if $k = m$.

An ASP program Π is *ground* if it consists of only ground rules, i.e. rules without variables. Ground instantiation $Gr(\Pi)$ of a nonground program Π is obtained by substituting variables with constants in all possible ways. The *Herbrand universe* $HU(\Pi)$ (resp. *Herbrand base* $HB(\Pi)$) of Π, is the set of all constants occurring in Π, (resp. the set of all possible ground atoms that can be formed with predicates and constants occurring in Π). Any subset of $HB(P)$ is a *Herbrand interpretation*. $MM(\Pi)$ denotes the subset-minimal Herbrand interpretation (*model*) of a ground positive program Π.

The semantics of an ASP program is given in terms of its answer sets. An interpretation A of Π is an *answer set* (or *stable model*) of Π iff $A = MM(\Pi^A)$, where Π^A is the *Gelfond–Lifschitz (GL) reduct* [6] of Π, obtained from $Gr(\Pi)$ by removing (i) each rule r such that $Body^-(r) \cap A \neq \emptyset$, and (ii) all the negative atoms from the remaining rules. The set of answer sets of a program Π is denoted by $AS(\Pi)$.

Example 8. Consider the program Π given as follows:

```
(1) pattern(1);  (2) pattern(2);  (3) item(1,a);
(4) item(1,b);   (5) item(2,a);
(6) not_subset(I,J)  :- pattern(I), item(I,V), I != J,
                        pattern(J), not item(J,V).
```

The grounding $Gr(\Pi)$ of Π is obtained from Π by substituting I,J with 1,2 and V with b resp. The GL-reduct $\Pi^{A'}(\Pi)$ for the interpretation A' containing facts of Π and not_subset(1,2) differs from $Gr(\Pi)$ only in that not item(2,b) is not in the body of the rule. A' is the minimal model of $\Pi^{A'}(\Pi)$, and thus it is in $AS(\Pi)$.   □

Other relevant language constructs include conditional literals and cardinality constraints [22]. The former are of the form $\texttt{a:b\_1,} \ldots \texttt{,b\_m}$, the latter can be written as

$1\{c\_1, \ldots, c\_n\}t$, where a and b_i are possibly default negated literals and each c_j is a conditional literal; 1 and t provide lower and upper bounds on the number of satisfied literals in a cardinality constraint. For instance, $1\{a(X):b(X)\}3$ holds, whenever between 1 and 3 instances of $a(X)$ (subject to $b(X)$) are true. Furthermore, aggregates are of the form #sum{K: cost(I,K)}>N. This atom is true, whenever the sum of all K, such that cost(I,K) is true, exceeds N.

3   Hybrid ASP-Based Mining Approach

In this section we present our hybrid method for frequent pattern mining. Unlike previous ASP-based mining methods, our approach combines highly optimized algorithms for frequent pattern discovery with the declarative ASP means for their convenient post-processing. Here, we focus on itemset and sequence mining; however our approach can be also applied to subgraph discovery (details are left for future work).

Given a frequency threshold σ, a (sequential) dataset D and a set of constraints $C = C_l \cup C_g$, where C_l and C_g are respectively local and global constraints, we proceed in two steps as follows.

Step 1. First, we launch a dedicated optimized algorithm to extract all (sequential) frequent patterns from a given dataset, satisfying the minimal frequency threshold σ. Here, any frequent pattern mining algorithm can be invoked. We use Eclat [24] for itemsets and PPIC [2] for sequences.

Step 2. Second, the computed patterns are post-processed using the declarative means to select a set of *valid* patterns (i.e., those satisfying constraints in C_l). For that the frequent patterns obtained in Step 1 are encoded as facts item(i, j) for itemsets and seq(i, j, p) for sequences where i is the pattern's ID, j is an item contained in it and p is its position. The local constraints in C_l are represented as ASP rules, which collect IDs of patterns satisfying constraints from C_l into the dedicated predicate valid, while the rest of the IDs are put into the not_valid predicate.

Finally, from all valid patterns a desired condensed representation is constructed by storing patterns i in the selected predicate if they are not dominated by other valid patterns based on constraints from C_g. Following the principle of [13], in our work every answer set represents a single desired pattern, which satisfies both local and global constraints. The set of all such patterns forms a condensed representation. In what follows we discuss our encodings of local and global constraints in details.

3.1   Encoding Local Constraints

In our declarative program we specify local constraints by the predicate valid, which reflects the conditions given in Definition 5. For every constraint in C_l we have a set of dedicated rules, stating when a pattern is not valid. For instance, a constraint checking whether the cost of items in a pattern exceeds a given threshold N is encoded as

$$\text{not\_valid(I)} :- \#\text{sum}\{C : \text{item(I, J), cost(J, C)}\} > N, \text{pattern(I)}.$$

A similar rule for sequences can be defined as follows:

$$\text{not\_valid}(I) :- \#\text{sum}\{C : \text{seq}(I, J, P), \text{cost}(J, C)\} > N, \text{pattern}(I).$$

Analogously, one can specify arbitrary domain constraints on patterns.

Example 9. Consider a dataset storing moving habits of young people during their studies. Let the dedicated frequent sequence mining algorithm return the following patterns: $S_1 = \langle bG\ mF\ ba\ mG\ ma \rangle$; $S_2 = \langle bF\ mG\ ba\ mF\ ma \rangle$; $S_3 = \langle bA\ ba\ ma \rangle$, where bG, bF, bA stand for born in Germany, France and America, ba, ma stand for bachelors and masters and the predicates mG, mF reflect that a person moved to Germany and France, respectively. Suppose, we are only interested in moving habits of Europeans, who got their masters degree from a German university. The local domain constraint expressing this would state that (1) bA should not be in the pattern, while (2) either both bG and ma should be in it without any mF in between or mG should precede ma. These constraints are encoded in the program in Listing 1.1. From the answer set of this program we get that both S_2 and S_3 are not valid, while S_1 is.   □

```
 1 time(1..5).
 2 % people born in Germany or France are Europeans
 3 eu(I) :- seq(I,bG,P).
 4 eu(I) :- seq(I,bF,P).
 5 % collect those who moved to France before P
 6 moved_before(X,P) :- seq(X,mF,P1), P>P1, time(P), time(P1).
 7 % collect those who moved to France after P and before masters
 8 moved_after(X,P) :- seq(X,mF,P1), seq(X,ma,P2), P<P1,
 9                     p1<P2, time(P), time(P1), time(P2).
10 % keep Europeans who moved to Germany straight before masters
11 keep(X) :- seq(X,ma,P+1), seq(X,mG,P), eu(X).
12 % keep Germans who did not move before masters
13 keep(X) :- seq(X,bG,P1), seq(X,ma,P), not moved_before(X,P).
14 % keep Europeans whose last move before masterswas to Germany
15 keep(X) :- seq(X,mG,P1), seq(X,ma,P2), P1<P2,
16                eu(X), not moved_after(X,P1).
17 % a pattern is not valid, if it should not bekept
18 not_valid(X) :- pattern(X), not keep(X)
```

Listing 1.1. Moving habits of people during studies

To combine all local constraints from $\mathcal{C}_l$ we add to a program a generic rule specifying that a pattern I is valid whenever not_valid(I) cannot be inferred.

$$\text{valid}(I) :- \text{pattern}(I), \text{not not\_valid}(I)$$

Patterns i, for which valid(i) is deduced are then further analyzed to construct a condensed representation based on global constraints from $\mathcal{C}_g$.

3.2 Encoding Global Constraints

The key for encoding global constraints is the declarative formalization of the dominance relation (Definition 6). For example, for itemsets the maximality constraint boils down to pairwise checking of subset inclusion between patterns. For sequences this requires a check of embedding existence between sequences.

Regardless of a pattern type from $\mathcal{L}$ and a constraint from $\mathcal{C}_g$ every encoding presented in this section is supplied with a rule, which guesses (selected/1 predicate) a single valid pattern to be a candidate for inclusion in the condensed representation, and a constraint that rules out dominated patterns thus enforcing a different guess.

```
1  % I is not a subset of J if I has items that arenot in J
2  not_subset(J) :- selected(I), item(I,V), not item(J,V),
3                   valid(J), I != J.
4  % derive dominated whenever I is subset of J
5  dominated :- selected(I), valid(J),
6               I != J, not not_subset(J).
```

Listing 1.2. Maximal itemsets encoding

$$1 \ \{selected(I) \ : \ valid(I)\} \ 1.$$

$$: - \ dominated.$$

In what follows, we discuss concrete realizations of the dominance relation both for itemsets and sequences for various global constraints, i.e., we present specific rules related to the derivation of the dominated/0 predicate.

Itemset Mining. We first provide an encoding for maximal itemset mining in Listing 1.2. To recall, a pattern is *maximal* if none of its supersets is frequent. An itemset I is included in J iff for every item $i \in I$ we have $i \in J$. We encode the violation of this condition in lines (1)–(3). The second rule presents the dominance criteria.

For closed itemset mining a simple modification of Listing 1.2 is required. An itemset is *closed* if none of its supersets has the same support. Thus to both of the rules from Listing 1.2 we need to add atoms support(I, X), support(J, X), which store the support sets of I and J respectively (extracted from the output of Step 1).

For free itemset mining the rules of the maximal encoding are changed as follows:

```
4  not_superset(J) :- selected(I), item(J,V), not item(I,V),
5                     valid(J), I != J.
6  dominated :- selected(I), valid(J), support(I,X),
7               I != J, not not_superset(J), support(J,X).
```

```
1  % support and size comparison among patterns
2  g_size_geq_fr(J) :- selected(I), valid(J), support(I,X),
3                      support(J,Y), size(I,Si), size(J, Sj),
4                      Si < Sj, X <= Y.
5  geq_size_g_fr(J) :- selected(I), valid(J), support(I,X),
6                      support(J,Y), size(I,Si), size(J, Sj),
7                      Si <= Sj, X < Y.
8  % derivation of the domination condition
9  dominated :- valid(J), g_size_geq_fr(J).
10 dominated :- valid(J), geq_size_g_fr(J).
```

Listing 1.3. Skyline itemsets encoding

Finally, the skyline itemset/sequence encoding is given in Listing 1.3, where the first two rules specify the conditions (a) and (b) for skyline itemsets as specified in Sect. 2.

```
1  % if V appears in a valid pattern I, derive in(V,I)
2  in(V,I) :- seq(I,V,P), valid(I).
3  % I is not a subset of J if I has V that J does not have
4  not_subset(J) :- selected(I), valid(J), I != J,
5                   seq(I,V,P), not in(V,J).
6  % if for a subseq <V,W> in I there is V followed
7  % by W in J then deduce domcand(V,J)
8  domcand(V,J,P) :- selected(I), seq(I,V,P), seq(I,W,P+1), I != J
9                    valid(J), seq(J,V,Q), seq(J,W,Q'), Q'>Q.
10 % if domcand(V,J) does not hold for some V in I
11 % and a pattern J then derive not_dominated_by(J)
12 not_dominated_by(J) :- selected(I), seq(I,V,P), seq(I,W,P+1),
13                    I != J, valid(J), not domcand(V,P,J).
14 % if neither not_dominated_by(J) nor not_subset_of(J)
15 % are derived for some J, then I is dominated
16 dominated :- selected(I), valid(J), I != J,
17           not not_subset_of(J), not not_dominated_by(J).
```

Listing 1.4. Maximal sequence encoding

Sequence Mining. The subpattern relation for sequences is slightly more involved, than for itemsets, as it preserves the order of elements in a pattern. To recall, a sequence S is included in S' iff an embedding e exists, such that $S \sqsubseteq_e S'$.

In Listing 1.4 we present the encoding for maximal sequence mining. A selected pattern is not maximal if it has at least one valid superpattern. We rule out patterns that are for sure not superpatterns of a selected sequence. First, obviously J is not a superpattern of I if I is not a subset of J (lines (4)–(5)), i.e., if not_subset(J) is derived, then J does not dominate I. If J is a superset of I then to ensure that I is not dominated by J, the embedding existence has to be checked (lines (6)–(9)). I is not dominated by J if an item exists in I, which together with its sequential neighbor cannot be embedded in J. This condition is checked in lines (10)–(13), where domcand(V, J, P) is derived if for an item V at position P and its follower, embedding in J can be found.

The encoding for closed sequence mining is obtained from the maximal sequence encoding analogously as it is done for itemsets. The rules for free sequence mining are constructed by substituting lines (4)–(13) of Listing 1.4 with the following ones:

```
4  not_superset(J) :- selected(I), in(V,J),
5                 not in(V,I), I != J.
6  domcand(V,J) :- selected(I), seq(J,V,P), item(J,P+1,W),
7              item(I,V,Q), seq(I,W,Q'),Q'>Q, I != J.
8  not_dominated_by(J) :- selected(I), valid(J), I != J,
9                     seq(J,V,P), seq(J,W,P+1),
10                 not domcand(V,J).
```

Finally, the encoding for mining skyline sequences coincides with the skyline itemsets encoding, which is provided in Listing 1.3.

4   Evaluation

In this section we evaluate the proposed hybrid approach by comparing it to the existing declarative pattern mining methods: ASP model for sequences from [5] and Dominance Programming (DP) from [16]. We do not consider the itemset mining ASP model [13], since it focuses only on frequent itemset mining and is not applicable to the construction of condensed representations under constraints as in [16]. Moreover, we do not perform comparison with dedicated algorithms designed for a specific problem type; these are known to be more efficient than declarative mining approaches [17].

More specifically, we investigate the following experimental questions.

- Q_1: how does the runtime of our method compare to the existing ASP-based sequence mining models?
- Q_2: what is the runtime gap between the specialized mining languages such as dominance programming and our method?
- Q_3: what is the influence of local constraints on the runtime of our method?

In Q_1 we compare our work with the ASP-based model from [5]. In Q_2 we measure the runtime difference between specialized itemset mining languages [16] and our ASP-based model. Finally, in Q_3 we estimate the runtime effect of adding local constraints.

We report evaluation on 2 transaction datasets,[2] *Mushrooms* (8124 transactions/119 items) and *Vote* (435/48), and on 3 sequence datasets (full),[3] *JMLR* (788 sequences/3847 distinct symbols), *Unix Users* (9099/4093), and *iPRG* (8628/21). All experiments have been performed on a desktop with Ubuntu 14.04, 64-bit environment, Intel Core i5-3570 4xCPU 3.40 GHz and 8 GB memory using clingo 4.5.4[4] and C++14 for the wrapper. The timeout was set to one hour. Free pattern mining demonstrates the same runtime behavior as closed, due to the symmetric encoding, and is thus omitted.

To investigate Q_1, in Fig. 1a, we compare the ASP model [5] with our method on the default 200 sequence sample, generated by the tool[5] from [5]. We performed the comparison on the synthetic data, as the sequence-mining model [5] failed to compute condensed representations on any of the standard sequence datasets for any support threshold value within the timeout. One can observe that our method consistently outperforms the purely declarative approach [5] and the advantage naturally becomes more apparent for smaller frequency threshold values.

In Figs. 1b, c and d (the point 0.05 for JMLR is a timeout), we present the runtimes of our method for *maximal, closed* and *skyline* sequential pattern mining settings on JMRL, Unix Users and iPRG datasets. In contrast to [5], our method managed to produce results on all of these datasets for reasonable threshold values within a couple of minutes.

To investigate Q_2, we compare out-of-the-box performance of DP [16] with our approach on maximal, closed and skyline itemset mining problems using standard

---

[2] From https://dtai.cs.kuleuven.be/CP4IM/datasets/.

[3] From https://dtai.cs.kuleuven.be/CP4IM/cpsm/datasets.html.

[4] http://potassco.sourceforge.net.

[5] https://sites.google.com/site/aspseqmining.

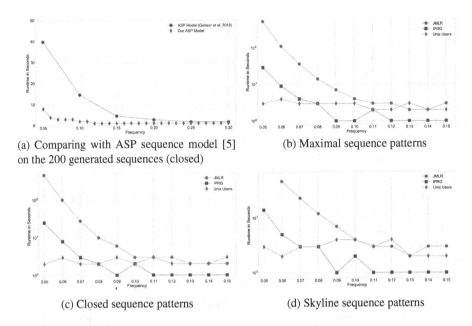

(a) Comparing with ASP sequence model [5] on the 200 generated sequences (closed)

(b) Maximal sequence patterns

(c) Closed sequence patterns

(d) Skyline sequence patterns

Fig. 1. Investigating Q_1: comparison with pure ASP model (a) and maximal (b), closed (c), and skyline (d) sequence mining on JMLR, Unix Users, and iPRG datasets.

datasets Vote and Mushrooms. As we see in Figs. 2a and b, on average, DP is one-to-two orders of magnitude faster; this gap is, however, diminishing as the minimum frequency increases. Surprisingly, our approach is significantly faster than DP out-of-the-box for skyline patterns (Fig. 2c); this holds also for the Mushrooms dataset, not presented here.

Fine-tuning parameters of DP by changing the order in which operators are applied within the system (skyline+ option) allowed to close this gap. With this adaptation DP demonstrates one-to-two orders of magnitude better performance, as can be seen in Fig. 2c. However, fine-tuning such a system requires the understanding of its inner mechanisms or exhaustive application of all available options.

To address Q_3 we introduced three simple local constraints for the itemset mining setting from Q_2: two size constraints $size(I) > 2$ and $size(I) < 7$ and a cost constraint: each item gets weight equal to its value with the maximal budget of n, which is set to 20 in the experiments.

In Fig. 2d, we present the results for closed itemset mining with and without local constraints (experiments with other global constraints demonstrate a similar runtime pattern and are not depicted here for space reasons). Local constraints ensure better propagation and speed up the search. One of the key design features of our encoding is the filtering technique used to select candidate patterns among only valid patterns. Its effect can be clearly seen, e.g., for the Vote dataset in Fig. 2d, where for certain frequencies the runtime gap is close to an order of magnitude.

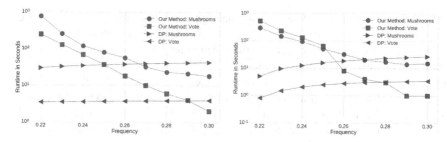

(a) Maximal itemset mining: comparing with DP on Vote and Mushrooms

(b) Closed itemset mining: comparing with DP on Vote and Mushrooms

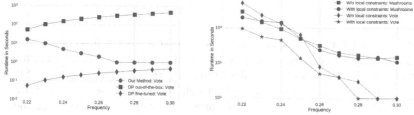

(c) Skyline itemset mining: comparing with out-of-the-box and fine-tuned DP on Vote

(d) Closed itemset mining: our method with (w/o) local constraints on Vote and Mushrooms

Fig. 2. Investigating Q_2: comparison with DP [16] (a, b, c); and Q_3: the effect of local constraints on runtime (d)

In all experiments, Step 1 of our method contributes to less than 5% of runtime. Overall, our approach can handle real world datasets for sequential pattern mining as demonstrated in Q_1. In many cases its performance is close to the specialized mining languages, as shown in Q_2. Finally, as demonstrated in Q_3 various local constraints can be effectively incorporated into our encoding bringing additional performance benefits.

5   Related Work

The problem of enhancing pattern mining by injecting various user-specified constraints has recently gained increasing attention. On the one hand, optimized dedicated approaches exist, in which some of the constraints are deeply integrated into the mining algorithm, e.g., [19]. On the other hand, declarative methods based on Constraint Programming [15, 17, 21], SAT solving [11, 12] and ASP [5, 9, 13] have been proposed.

Techniques from the last group are the closest to our work. However, in contrast to our method, they typically focus only on one particular pattern type and consider local constraints and condensed representations in isolation [20, 23]. The works [7, 16] focused on CP-based rather than ASP-based itemset mining and did not take into account sequences unlike we do. The authors of [5] studied declarative sequence mining with ASP, but in contrast to our approach, optimized algorithms for frequent pattern discovery are not exploited in their method. A theoretical framework for structured pattern mining was proposed in [8], whose main goal was to formally define the core components of the main mining tasks and compare dedicated mining algorithms to their declarative versions. While generic, this work did not take into account local and global constraints and neither has it been implemented.

In [5, 13], purely declarative ASP methods have been considered; unlike our approach, they do not admit integration of optimized mining algorithms and thus lack practicality. In fact, the need for such an integration in the context of complex structured mining was even explicitly stated in [18] and in [10], which study formalizations of graph mining problems using logical means.

6   Conclusion

We have presented a hybrid approach for condensed itemset and sequence mining, which uses the optimized dedicated algorithms to determine the frequent patterns and post-filters them using a declarative ASP program. The idea of exploiting ASP for pattern mining is not new; it was studied for both itemsets and sequences. However, unlike previous methods we made steps towards optimizing the declarative techniques by making use of the existing specialized methods and also integrated the dominance programming machinery in our implementation to allow for combining local and global constraints on a generic level.

One of the possible future directions is to generalize the proposed approach into an iterative technique, where dedicated data mining and declarative methods are interlinked and applied in an iterative fashion. More specifically, all constraints can be split into two parts: those that can be effectively handled using declarative means and those for which specialized algorithms are much more scalable. Answer set programs with external computations [4] possibly could be exploited in this mining context.

Another promising but challenging research stream concerns the integration of data *decomposition* techniques into our approach. Here, one can divide a given dataset into several parts, such that the frequent patterns are identified in these parts separately, and then the results are combined.

Orthogonal to this, materialization of the presented ideas on other pattern types including graphs and sequences of itemsets instead of sequences of individual symbols is an interesting future direction.

References

1. Agrawal, R., Mannila, H., Srikant, R., Toivonen, H., Verkamo, A.I.: Fast discovery of association rules. In: Advances in Knowledge Discovery and Data Mining, pp. 307–328 (1996)
2. Aoga, J.O.R., Guns, T., Schaus, P.: An efficient algorithm for mining frequent sequence with constraint programming. In: Frasconi, P., Landwehr, N., Manco, G., Vreeken, J. (eds.) ECML PKDD 2016. LNCS, vol. 9852, pp. 315–330. Springer, Cham (2016). doi:10.1007/978-3-319-46227-1_20
3. Bonchi, F., Lucchese, C.: On condensed representations of constrained frequent patterns. Knowl. Inf. Syst. 9(2), 180–201 (2006)

4. Eiter, T., Brewka, G., Dao-Tran, M., Fink, M., Ianni, G., Krennwallner, T.: Combining non-monotonic knowledge bases with external sources. In: Ghilardi, S., Sebastiani, R. (eds.) FroCoS 2009. LNCS (LNAI), vol. 5749, pp. 18–42. Springer, Heidelberg (2009). doi:10.1007/978-3-642-04222-5_2

5. Gebser, M., Guyet, T., Quiniou, R., Romero, J., Schaub, T.: Knowledge-based sequence mining with ASP. In: Proceedings of 25th International Joint Conference on Artificial Intelligence, IJCAI (2016)

6. Gelfond, M., Lifschitz, V.: The stable model semantics for logic programming. In: Proceedings of ICLP/SLP, pp. 1070–1080 (1988)

7. Guns, T., Dries, A., Nijssen, S., Tack, G., De Raedt, L.: MiningZinc: a declarative framework for constraint-based mining. Artif. Intell. **244**, 6–29 (2017)

8. Guns, T., Paramonov, S., Négrevergne, B.: On declarative modeling of structured pattern mining. In: Declarative Learning Based Programming, AAAI Workshop (2016)

9. Guyet, T., Moinard, Y., Quiniou, R.: Using answer set programming for pattern mining. CoRR abs/1409.7777 (2014)

10. van der Hallen, M., Paramonov, S., Leuschel, M., Janssens, G.: Knowledge representation analysis of graph mining. CoRR abs/1608.08956 (2016)

11. Jabbour, S., Sais, L., Salhi, Y.: Boolean satisfiability for sequence mining. In: Proceedings of 22nd ACM International Conference on Information and Knowledge Management (CIKM), pp. 649–658 (2013)

12. Jabbour, S., Sais, L., Salhi, Y.: Decomposition based SAT encodings for itemset mining problems. In: Cao, T., Lim, E.-P., Zhou, Z.-H., Ho, T.-B., Cheung, D., Motoda, H. (eds.) PAKDD 2015. LNCS (LNAI), vol. 9078, pp. 662–674. Springer, Cham (2015). doi:10.1007/978-3-319-18032-8_52

13. Järvisalo, M.: Itemset mining as a challenge application for answer set enumeration. In: Delgrande, J.P., Faber, W. (eds.) LPNMR 2011. LNCS (LNAI), vol. 6645, pp. 304–310. Springer, Heidelberg (2011). doi:10.1007/978-3-642-20895-9_35

14. Mannila, H., Toivonen, H.: Levelwise search and borders of theories in knowledge discovery. Data Min. Knowl. Discov. **1**(3), 241–258 (1997)

15. Métivier, J., Loudni, S., Charnois, T.: A constraint programming approach for mining sequential patterns in a sequence database. CoRR abs/1311.6907 (2013)

16. Négrevergne, B., Dries, A., Guns, T., Nijssen, S.: Dominance programming for itemset mining. In: 2013 IEEE 13th International Conference on Data Mining, pp. 557–566 (2013)

17. Negrevergne, B., Guns, T.: Constraint-based sequence mining using constraint programming. In: Michel, L. (ed.) CPAIOR 2015. LNCS, vol. 9075, pp. 288–305. Springer, Cham (2015). doi:10.1007/978-3-319-18008-3_20

18. Paramonov, S., Leeuwen, M., Denecker, M., Raedt, L.: An exercise in declarative modeling for relational query mining. In: Inoue, K., Ohwada, H., Yamamoto, A. (eds.) ILP 2015. LNCS (LNAI), vol. 9575, pp. 166–182. Springer, Cham (2016). doi:10.1007/978-3-319-40566-7_12

19. Pei, J., Han, J.: Can we push more constraints into frequent pattern mining? In: ACM SIGKDD, pp. 350–354 (2000)

20. Pei, J., Han, J., Mao, R.: CLOSET: an efficient algorithm for mining frequent closed itemsets. In: ACM SIGMOD Workshop on Research Issues on Data Mining and Knowledge Discovery, pp. 21–30 (2000)

21. Ugarte Rojas, W., Boizumault, P., Loudni, S., Crémilleux, B., Lepailleur, A.: Mining (soft-) skypatterns using dynamic CSP. In: Simonis, H. (ed.) CPAIOR 2014. LNCS, vol. 8451, pp. 71–87. Springer, Cham (2014). doi:10.1007/978-3-319-07046-9_6

22. Simons, P., Niemelä, I., Soininen, T.: Extending and implementing the stable model semantics. Artif. Intell. **138**(1–2), 181–234 (2002)
23. Yan, X., Han, J., Afshar, R.: CloSpan: mining closed sequential patterns in large datasets. In:
SDM, pp. 166–177 (2003)
24. Zaki, M.J., Parthasarathy, S., Ogihara, M., Li, W.: New algorithms for fast discovery of
association rules. Technical report, Rochester, NY, USA (1997)

Inconsistency-Tolerant Instance Checking in Tractable Description Logics

Rafael Peñaloza[(⊠)]

KRDB Research Centre, Free University of Bozen-Bolzano, Bolzano, Italy
`penaloza@inf.unibz.it`

Abstract. Research on inconsistency-tolerant query answering usually assumes that the terminological knowledge is correct, and only the facts (ABox) need to be repaired. In this paper we study the problem of answering instance queries over inconsistent ontologies, by repairing the whole knowledge base (KB). Contrary to ABox repairs, when KB repairs are considered, instance checking in $DL\text{-}Lite_{Horn}$ w.r.t. the brave semantics remains tractable, and the intersection semantics allow for an anytime algorithm. We also show that inconsistency-tolerant instance checking w.r.t. ABox repairs is intractable even if only polynomially many ABox repairs exist.

1 Introduction

Inconsistent-tolerant reasoning arose as a means of obtaining meaningful information from an inconsistent knowledge base (KB). The main idea behind this reasoning task is to consider the different ways in which the KB can be repaired to avoid the inconsistency—or, more generally, any other observed error. The most natural approach is to consider only consequences that follow from *all* such repairs. This approach, which is at the root of the original consistent query answering in databases [1], provides many logical guarantees. Most importantly, it only yields answers that are certain in the sense that they will remain the same, regardless of how the inconsistency is removed. However, providing these answers tends to be computationally hard. In order to regain tractability, several different semantics have been proposed [8,20]. Two notable examples are the *brave* semantics that require the consequence to follow from at least one repair, and the *intersection* semantics that limit reasoning to the intersection of all repairs.

The computational complexity of dealing with all these semantics has been thoroughly studied for a wide variety of description logics, which have the capability of expressing terminological knowledge along with facts [6,24,35]. A running assumption in all this previous work is that the terminological knowledge is always correct, and hence repairs are only made on the data (ABox repairs). However, this assumption is not always valid, since ontology engineering is a very error-prone task.

In this work, we consider the problem of inconsistent-tolerant query answering where repairs allow also parts of the terminological knowledge to be removed,

© Springer International Publishing AG 2017
S. Costantini et al. (Eds.): RuleML+RR 2017, LNCS 10364, pp. 215–229, 2017.
DOI: 10.1007/978-3-319-61252-2_15

which we call KB repairs. To the best of our knowledge, the only work where a similar problem has been considered before is [12]. In that work, they consider the problem of inconsistency-tolerant query answering over KB repairs, in a different logic. To guide our complexity analysis, we focus on instance checking in the light-weight description logic $DL\text{-}Lite_{Horn}$. This choice is motivated by $DL\text{-}Lite_{Horn}$ being the largest member of the $DL\text{-}Lite$ family where instance checking remains tractable (w.r.t. so-called KB complexity). For the scope of this paper, we focus only on instance checking as a first step towards dealing with conjunctive queries. Moreover, we do not analyse the data complexity since the problem depends strongly on the input terminological knowledge.

We show that under KB repairs, brave instance checking remains tractable. Although cautious and IR semantics become coNP-complete, we provide an any-time algorithm for the latter, based on methods for enumerating minimal inconsistent subKBs. Afterwards, we revisit the case of ABox repairs. We show that hardness of this problem goes deeper than previously implied, as brave and cautious instance checking cannot be solved in polynomial time even if only polynomially many ABox repairs exist.

2   Preliminaries

We start by introducing the description logic $DL\text{-}Lite_{Horn}$ [4], along with the main reasoning problems that we consider in this paper. The importance of looking at $DL\text{-}Lite_{Horn}$ is that it is one of the largest members of the $DL\text{-}Lite$ family that remains tractable w.r.t. combined complexity.

Let N_C, N_R, and N_I be mutually disjoint sets of *concept*, *role*, and *individual* names, respectively. The classes of $DL\text{-}Lite$ concepts B, and *roles* R are defined, respectivley, by the syntax rules:

$$B ::= A \mid \exists R \mid \bot$$
$$R ::= P \mid P^-$$

where $A \in N_C$ and $P \in N_R$. A $DL\text{-}Lite_{Horn}$ TBox is a finite set of *concept inclusions* (CIs) of the form $B_1 \sqcap \cdots \sqcap B_n \sqsubseteq B$, $n \geq 1$, where each B, B_i is a concept, and *role inclusions* (RIs) $R_1 \sqsubseteq R_2$, where R_1, R_2 are roles. An *ABox* is a finite set of *assertions* of the form $A(a)$ or $P(a,b)$ with $A \in N_C, P \in N_R$, and $a, b \in N_I$. A *knowledge base* (KB) is a pair $(\mathcal{T}, \mathcal{A})$, where $\mathcal{T}$ is a TBox and $\mathcal{A}$ an ABox.

The semantics of this logic is based on interpretations. An *interpretation* is a pair $\mathcal{I} = (\Delta^{\mathcal{I}}, \cdot^{\mathcal{I}})$, where $\Delta^{\mathcal{I}}$ is a non-empty set called the *domain* and $\cdot^{\mathcal{I}}$ is the *interpretation function* that maps every $a \in N_I$ to an element $a^{\mathcal{I}} \in \Delta^{\mathcal{I}}$, every $A \in N_C$ to a set $A^{\mathcal{I}} \subseteq \Delta^{\mathcal{I}}$, and every $P \in N_R$ to a binary relation $R^{\mathcal{I}} \subseteq \Delta^{\mathcal{I}} \times \Delta^{\mathcal{I}}$. This interpretation function is extended to concepts and roles by setting $(P^-)^{\mathcal{I}} := \{(y,x) \mid (x,y) \in P^{\mathcal{I}}\}$, $\exists R^{\mathcal{I}} := \{x \in \Delta^{\mathcal{I}} \mid \exists y.(x,y) \in R^{\mathcal{I}}\}$, and $\bot^{\mathcal{I}} := \emptyset$. The interpretation $\mathcal{I}$ *satisfies* the CI $B_1 \sqcap \cdots \sqcap B_n \sqsubseteq B$ if $\bigcap_{i=1}^{n} B_i^{\mathcal{I}} \subseteq B^{\mathcal{I}}$. It *satisfies* the assertions $A(a)$ and $P(a,b)$ if $a^{\mathcal{I}} \in A^{\mathcal{I}}$ and $(a^{\mathcal{I}}, b^{\mathcal{I}}) \in P^{\mathcal{I}}$, respectively. This interpretation is a *model* of the TBox $\mathcal{T}$ (ABox $\mathcal{A}$, respectively), if it satisfies all the CIs in $\mathcal{T}$ (all the assertions in $\mathcal{A}$, respectively). It is a *model* of the KB $(\mathcal{T}, \mathcal{A})$ if it is a model of both, $\mathcal{T}$ and $\mathcal{A}$.

To simplify the notation, throughout this paper we will often speak of KBs as finite sets of CIs and assertions, unless the distinction between ABox and TBox is relevant. Set operations between KBs are defined in the obvious manner, by operating over each component. For example, if $\mathcal{K} = (\mathcal{T}, \mathcal{A})$ and $\mathcal{K}' = (\mathcal{T}', \mathcal{A}')$, then $\mathcal{K} \cap \mathcal{K}' := (\mathcal{T} \cap \mathcal{T}', \mathcal{A} \cap \mathcal{A}')$ and $\mathcal{K} \cup \mathcal{K}' := (\mathcal{T} \cup \mathcal{T}', \mathcal{A} \cup \mathcal{A}')$.

Two of the most basic reasoning problems in description logics are deciding consistency of a KB and instance checking. A KB is *consistent* if it has a model. The individual name a is an *instance* of the concept B w.r.t. the KB $\mathcal{K}$ (denoted by $\mathcal{K} \models B(a)$) if $a^{\mathcal{I}} \in B^{\mathcal{I}}$ holds for all models $\mathcal{I}$ of $\mathcal{K}$. It is known that deciding consistency and instance checking in $DL\text{-}Lite_{Horn}$ is polynomial on the size of the KB, which is usually known as the *KB complexity* in the query answering literature.

When a KB is inconsistent, its lack of models means that all logical consequences follow trivially. In particular, every individual is an instance of every concept w.r.t. an inconsistent KB. Thus, instance checking is uninformative in this case. Inconsistency-tolerant semantics have been introduced as a way to extract meaningful information from inconsistent KBs by considering some or all the ways in which the inconsistency can be avoided through a repair.

Definition 1. *Let $\mathcal{K} = (\mathcal{T}, \mathcal{A})$ be an inconsistent KB. A KB repair of $\mathcal{K}$ is a consistent KB $\mathcal{K}' = (\mathcal{T}', \mathcal{A}')$ with $\mathcal{T}' \subseteq \mathcal{T}, \mathcal{A}' \subseteq \mathcal{A}$ such that for all $\mathcal{T}' \subseteq \mathcal{T}'' \subseteq \mathcal{T}$ and all $\mathcal{A}' \subseteq \mathcal{A}'' \subseteq \mathcal{A}$ it holds that $(\mathcal{T}', \mathcal{A}'')$ and $(\mathcal{T}'', \mathcal{A}')$ are inconsistent.*

An ABox repair of $\mathcal{K}$ is a maximal (w.r.t. set inclusion) subset $\mathcal{A}' \subseteq \mathcal{A}$ such that $(\mathcal{T}, \mathcal{A}')$ is consistent.

Intuitively, a KB repair is obtained by removing the least amount of axioms from a KB to regain consistency. An ABox repair is similar, but assuming that the TBox is correct, thus removing only assertions from the ABox. This latter notion is the one most typically used in the literature of inconsistency-tolerant reasoning. For the rest of this paper, we will use the generic term *repair* to encompass both, KB- and ABox repairs.

It is easy to see that repairs are not unique in general. In fact, a single KB may contain exponentially many repairs (see e.g. [22]). We denote by $\mathsf{Rep}_{\mathcal{K}}$ the set of all repairs of $\mathcal{K}$. Depending on how these repairs are used, different inconsistency-tolerant semantics can be defined. We present the three most commonly studied, focusing on the case of instance checking.

Definition 2. *Let $\mathcal{K}$ be an inconsistent KB, $a \in N_I$ and B a concept. We say that a is a:*

- cautious *instance of B ($\mathcal{K} \models_c B(a)$) if $\mathcal{R} \models B(a)$ holds for every $\mathcal{R} \in \mathsf{Rep}_{\mathcal{K}}$;*
- brave *instance of B ($\mathcal{K} \models_b B(a)$) if $\mathcal{R} \models B(a)$ holds for some $\mathcal{R} \in \mathsf{Rep}_{\mathcal{K}}$;*
- intersection repair *(IR) instance of B ($\mathcal{K} \models_{IR} B(a)$) if $\bigcap_{\mathcal{R} \in \mathsf{Rep}_{\mathcal{K}}} \mathcal{R} \models B(a)$ holds.*

When it is relevant to distinguish the class of repairs under consideration, we will denote it through a superscript on the entailment relation. Thus, $\mathcal{K} \models_c^{KB} B(a)$ refers to cautious entailment w.r.t. the set of all KB repairs, while for $\mathcal{K} \models_b^A B(a)$ the inference is made w.r.t. ABox repairs only.

Notice that every IR instance is a cautious instance, and cautious instances themselves are always brave, as long as the input KB is inconsistent. Interest on IR semantics has arisen since they have been shown to provide some tractability guarantees for different scenarios.

The dual notion of a repair is that of a *MinA*—also known as *justification* [16, 18, 28] or MIPS [33, 34]— which is a minimal inconsistent sub-KB of $\mathcal{K}$. We will denote the set of all MinAs as $\mathsf{Min}_{\mathcal{K}}$. It is well known that repairs and MinAs are dual in the sense that the set of all MinAs can be obtained from all the justifications, and *vice versa*, through the complementation of all Hitting Sets [5, 31].[1] A simple consequence of this duality is that the union of MinAs complements the intersection of repairs; that is, $\bigcup_{\mathcal{M} \in \mathsf{Min}_{\mathcal{K}}} \mathcal{M} = \mathcal{K} \setminus \bigcap_{\mathcal{R} \in \mathsf{Rep}_{\mathcal{K}}} \mathcal{R}$. Notice that although the computation of Hitting Sets is an important problem with applications in many fields of computer science [15], its precise complexity remains unknown. It has been shown that this problem can be solved in a time bound below $n^{o(\log n)}$, which implies that it is most likely not coNP-hard [14]. It is conjectured that, together with several computationally equivalent problems, it forms a class properly contained between P and coNP [13].

An important property that will be useful in the following sections is that if $\mathcal{K}$ is an inconsistent KB, then every consistent sub-KB of $\mathcal{K}$ can be extended to a repair, by adding axioms that do not affect its consistency. Analogously, every inconsistent sub-KB of $\mathcal{K}$ can be reduced to a MinA, by removing all superfluous axioms. Thus, for instance, brave instance checking is equivalent to deciding the existence of a consistent sub-KB $\mathcal{R}$ (not necessarily maximal w.r.t. set inclusion) that entails the desired instance relation.

Finally, to simplify the presentation of the paper, we assume w.l.o.g. that the concept $\bot$ appears only in CIs of the form $B_1 \sqcap \cdots \sqcap B_n \sqsubseteq \bot$, where for every $i, 1 \leq i \leq n$, $B_i \neq \bot$. Notice that a CI that contains $\bot$ on its left-hand side is trivially satisfied by every interpretation, and would hence appear in every repair, and in no MinA.

3   Instance Checking Under KB Repairs

In this section, we study the case where KB repairs are taken into account. The case of ABox repairs will be the focus of the following section. As the result depends on the whole KB, including the TBox, it does not make much sense to consider the data complexity, in which only the size of the ABox is taken into account. Thus, in the following we focus on the KB complexity only, without mentioning it explicitly in every instance. In previous work [8] it has been shown that inconsistency-tolerant instance checking in *DL-Lite_{Horn}* w.r.t.

---

[1] A *hitting set* for e.g. $\mathsf{Rep}_{\mathcal{K}}$ is a set $\mathcal{S}$ that satisfies $\mathcal{S} \cap \mathcal{R} \neq \emptyset$ for every $\mathcal{R} \in \mathsf{Rep}_{\mathcal{K}}$.

ABox repairs is hard in general, even if one focuses on the simpler brave and intersection semantics. We show that the same does not hold if KB repairs are taken into account. Indeed, as we show next, brave instance checking remains tractable in this case.

Theorem 3. *Brave instance checking w.r.t. KB repairs can be decided in polynomial time.*

Proof. Given a KB $\mathcal{K} = (\mathcal{T}, \mathcal{A})$ and an individual $a \in N_I$, let $\mathcal{A}_a$ be the sub-ABox of $\mathcal{A}$ that contains only the assertions that refer to a; that is, $\mathcal{A}_a$ contains all axioms $A(a), P(a, b)$, and $P(b, a)$ appearing in $\mathcal{A}$ with $A \in N_C, P \in N_R$, and $b \in N_I$. Define $\mathcal{T}_\top := \mathcal{T} \setminus \{B_1 \sqcap \cdots \sqcap B_n \sqsubseteq \bot \in \mathcal{T}\}$, to be the sub-TBox of $\mathcal{T}$ that does not use $\bot$. Clearly, a is a brave instance of the concept B iff $(\mathcal{T}_\top, \mathcal{A}_a) \models B(a)$. Since (standard) instance checking in *DL-Lite$_{Horn}$* is polynomial, we obtain the desired upper bound.   □

Unfortunately, tractability does not extend to the other two semantics. As we show next, hardness for cautious and IR instance checking is a consequence of the intractability of finding simple paths in a graph that cross through a given edge.

Theorem 4. *Cautious and IR instance checking are coNP-complete.*

Proof. The upper bounds are obvious, so we focus only on showing hardness through a reduction from the following NP-hard problem: given a directed graph $\mathcal{G} = (\mathcal{V}, \mathcal{E})$, two nodes $v, v' \in \mathcal{V}$ and an edge $e \in \mathcal{E}$, decide whether there is a simple path from v to v' in $\mathcal{G}$ that passes through e.

Let $\mathcal{G} = (\mathcal{V}, \mathcal{E})$, $v, v' \in \mathcal{V}$, and $e = (u, u') \in \mathcal{E}$, be an instance of this decision problem. We assume w.l.o.g. that the edge (v, v') does not appear in $\mathcal{E}$, and that u, u' are both different from v and v'. These cases can be dealt with easily. For every $w \in \mathcal{V} \setminus \{v, v'\}$ create a concept name B_w, and additionally create two individual names a, b. Then, we construct the *DL-Lite$_{Horn}$* KB $\mathcal{K}_\mathcal{G} = (\mathcal{T}, \mathcal{A})$, where

$$\mathcal{T} := \{B_w \sqsubseteq B_{w'} \mid (w, w') \in \mathcal{E}, v, v' \notin \{w, w'\}\} \cup \{B_w \sqsubseteq \bot \mid (w, v') \in \mathcal{E}\},$$
$$\mathcal{A} := \{B_w(a) \mid (v, w) \in \mathcal{E}\} \cup \{B_u(b)\}.$$

It is easy to see that there is a simple path from v to v' passing through (u, u') iff there is a repair for $\mathcal{K}_\mathcal{G}$ that does not contain the axiom $B_u \sqsubseteq B_{u'}$. Thus, such a path exists iff b is *not* a cautious instance *nor* an IR instance of $B_{u'}$.   □

Interestingly, despite this hardness result, the duality between MinAs and repairs can be exploited to produce an any-time algorithm for deciding intersection repair instances. The main idea of this algorithm consists on enumerating all the possible MinAs for inconsistency of the KB. Since the union of all MinAs and the intersection of all repairs are complements of each other, any set of MinAs provides an approximation of the intersection of all repairs. If it is possible to enumerate all MinAs with only a polynomial (on the size of the KB) delay between each new output, then we can efficiently improve this approximation in polynomial time steps.

A first step towards developing this algorithm is to show that MinAs can be enumerated in polynomial delay. It was previously shown that this holds for $DL\text{-}Lite_{Horn}$ TBoxes, but the case in which an ABox considered was left open [29,30]. We build on those previous ideas and provide an algorithm capable of handling ABoxes too.

First, we make a small simplifying assumption. For the following approach, we assume that the TBox contains no role inclusions $R_1 \sqsubseteq R_2$. Notice that, in the case of $DL\text{-}Lite_{Horn}$, this assumption is without loss of generality since the role inclusion $R_1 \sqsubseteq R_2$ can be equivalently expressed through the CI $\exists R_1 \sqsubseteq \exists R_2$.

Our algorithm is based on the notion of a hypergraph. Formally, a (directed) *hypergraph* is a pair $\mathcal{H} = (\mathcal{V}, \mathcal{E})$, where $\mathcal{V}$ is a finite set of *vertices* and $\mathcal{E}$ is a set of *edges* of the form $V \rightarrow v$, where $V \subseteq \mathcal{V}$ and $v \in \mathcal{V}$. Given two vertices $v, w \in \mathcal{V}$, a *path* from v to w in $\mathcal{H}$ is a sequence of edges $\mathcal{P} = V_1 \rightarrow v_1, \ldots, V_n \rightarrow v_n$ such that for every $i, 1 \leq i \leq n$, $V_i \subseteq \{v\} \cup \bigcup_{j=1}^{i-1}\{v_j\}$ and $v_n = w$. Such a path is called *simple* if no subsequence of $\mathcal{P}$ is also a path from v to w.

Given a KB $\mathcal{K} = (\mathcal{T}, \mathcal{A})$, we construct a directed hypergraph $\mathcal{H}_\mathcal{K}$ as follows. The set of vertices $\mathcal{V}_\mathcal{K}$ of $\mathcal{H}_\mathcal{K}$ contains one element v_a for each individual name a appearing in the ABox $\mathcal{A}$, and an element w_B for every concept B appearing in the KB $\mathcal{K}$; that is, either in the TBox or in the ABox. We call the vertices of the form v_a *individual nodes*. The set of hyperedges of this hypergraph is defined by $\mathcal{E}_\mathcal{K} := \mathcal{E}_\mathcal{T} \cup \mathcal{E}_\mathcal{A}$, where

$$\mathcal{E}_\mathcal{A} := \{v_a \rightarrow w_B \mid B(a) \in \mathcal{A}\} \cup \{v_a \rightarrow w_{\exists R}, v_b \rightarrow w_{\exists R^-} \mid R(a,b) \in \mathcal{A}\},$$
$$\mathcal{E}_\mathcal{T} := \{\{w_{B_1}, \ldots, w_{B_n}\} \rightarrow w_B \mid B_1 \sqcap \cdots \sqcap B_n \sqsubseteq B \in \mathcal{T}\}.$$

It is easy to see that $\mathcal{K}$ is inconsistent iff there is a path from some v_a to $w_\perp$ in $\mathcal{H}_\mathcal{K}$. More interestingly, every simple path of this kind corresponds to a MinA for the inconsistency of $\mathcal{K}$. Unfortunately, this relationship between simple paths and MinAs is not bijective. As the following example shows, two simple paths may correspond to the same MinA.

Example 5. Consider the $DL\text{-}Lite_{Horn}$ KB $\mathcal{K}_{\text{exa}} = (\mathcal{T}_{\text{exa}}, \mathcal{A}_{\text{exa}})$ defined by

$$\mathcal{A}_{\text{exa}} := \{P(a,b), P(b,a), C(a)\}$$
$$\mathcal{T}_{\text{exa}} := \{\exists P \sqcap \exists P^- \sqsubseteq B, \ B \sqsubseteq \perp, \ C \sqcap \exists P \sqsubseteq \perp\}.$$

The hypergraph $\mathcal{H}_{\mathcal{K}_{\text{exa}}}$ is depicted in Fig. 1(a). Two simple paths from an individual node to $w_\perp$ are shown below (Figs. 1(b) and (c)). Clearly, both paths correspond to the same MinA $\mathcal{M} = (\mathcal{T}_1, \mathcal{A}_1)$ with $\mathcal{A}_1 := \{P(a,b), P(b,a)\}$ and $\mathcal{T}_1 := \{\exists P \sqcap \exists P^- \sqsubseteq B, B \sqsubseteq \perp, \}$.

In order to enumerate all MinAs with polynomial delay, we thus try to enumerate all the simple paths leading from an individual node to $w_\perp$, but taking care of removing all those paths that would yield a repeated MinA. The idea behind the enumeration of all simple paths in a hypergraph is, given one such

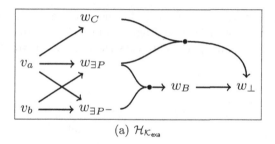

(a) $\mathcal{H}_{\mathcal{K}_{exa}}$

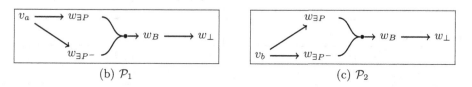

(b) $\mathcal{P}_1$ (c) $\mathcal{P}_2$

Fig. 1. The hypergraph $\mathcal{H}_{\mathcal{K}_{exa}}$ from Example 5, and two simple paths.

path, construct a set of sub-hypergraphs that partition the set of all remaining simple paths from an individual node to $w_\perp$, in the sense that each such path exists in exactly one of the generated sub-hypergraphs. The main insight needed for dealing with the repetition of MinAs is that role assertions $R(a, b)$ generate two hyperedges in $\mathcal{H}_{\mathcal{K}}$, even though they correspond to the same ABox axiom. Thus, these two hyperedges need to be always considered simultaneously: either they are both included, or both excluded in the search of a new simple path.

One (arbitrary) simple path from an individual node to $w_\perp$ can be found in polynomial time using standard techniques [25,27]. Given such a path $\mathcal{P}$, let v_a be the (unique) individual node appearing in it. Then, by definition $\mathcal{P}$ is of the form $L_1 \rightarrow r_1, \ldots, L_n \rightarrow r_n$, where n is the size of $\mathcal{P}$. Intuitively, the sequence defined by $\mathcal{P}$ provides an ordering of the edges in such a way that all the required nodes to traverse an edge are visited before the head is observed.

Given $\mathcal{P}$ and $n := |\mathcal{P}|$, we define n subgraphs of $\mathcal{H}_{\mathcal{K}}$ as follows. For each $i, 1 \leq i \leq n$, let

$$\mathcal{H}'_i := \mathcal{H}_{\mathcal{K}} \setminus \bigcup_{i < j \leq n} \{L \rightarrow r \in \mathcal{H}_{\mathcal{K}} \mid r = r_j, L \neq L_j\}.$$

Then we define

$$\mathcal{H}_i := \begin{cases} \mathcal{H}'_i \setminus \{v_a \rightarrow w_{\exists R}, v_b \rightarrow w_{\exists R^-}\} & \text{if } L_i \rightarrow r_i \text{ was created by } R(a, b) \in \mathcal{A}, \\ \mathcal{H}'_i \setminus \{L_i \rightarrow r_i\} & \text{otherwise.} \end{cases}$$

Example 6. Consider again the KB $\mathcal{K}_{exa}$ from Example 5, and the path $\mathcal{P}_1$ depicted in Fig. 1(b), which is defined by the sequence

$$v_a \rightarrow w_{\exists P}, \quad v_a \rightarrow w_{\exists P^-}, \quad \{w_{\exists P}, w_{\exists P^-}\} \rightarrow w_B, \quad w_B \rightarrow w_\perp$$

The four subgraphs $\mathcal{H}_1, \ldots, \mathcal{H}_4$ of $\mathcal{H}_{\mathcal{K}_{\text{exa}}}$ obtained through this path are depicted in Fig. 2. As it can be seen from the figure, only $\mathcal{H}_4$ contains a path from an individual node to $w_\perp$. This path represents the only other MinA for the inconsistency of $\mathcal{K}_{\text{exa}}$.

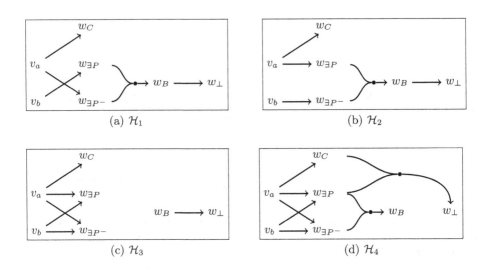

Fig. 2. The subgraphs $\mathcal{H}_1, \ldots, \mathcal{H}_4$ of $\mathcal{H}_{\mathcal{K}_{\text{exa}}}$ obtained from $\mathcal{P}_1$.

Intuitively, each hypergraph $\mathcal{H}_i$ can only contain paths reaching $w_\perp$ in which the last edges coincide with the last $n - i$ edges of the path $\mathcal{P}$. For that reason, in the previous example only $\mathcal{H}_4$ contains the edge $\{w_C, w_{\exists P}\} \rightarrow w_\perp$; in all other subgraphs, this edge is removed to guarantee that only paths ending with the edge $w_B \rightarrow w_\perp$ are considered. Taking this intuition into account, it is easy to see that the following result holds.

Lemma 7. *Let $\mathcal{P}$ be a simple path from some individual node v_a to $w_\perp$ in $\mathcal{H}_\mathcal{K}$, and $\mathcal{H}_i$, $1 \leq i \leq n := |\mathcal{P}|$ constructed as above. Then, for every MinA $\mathcal{M}$, if $\mathcal{P} \not\subseteq \mathcal{H}_\mathcal{M}$, then there exists exactly one $i, 1 \leq i \leq n$ such that $\mathcal{H}_\mathcal{M}$ contains a MinA for inconsistency in $\mathcal{H}_i$.*

Notice that the sets $\mathcal{H}_i$ can be all computed in polynomial time. Hence, Lemma 7 suggests an approach for enumerating all MinAs with only polynomial delay between answers. Recall here that our interest is not in enumerating these MinAs *per se*, but rather on finding their union to answer intersection repair instance queries in any-time. Algorithm 1 shows an approach for doing this. The algorithm iteratively updates the intersection of all repairs (stored in the set $\mathcal{U}$) and checks whether this KB still entails the instance query q. As soon as the answer is no, the algorithm stops and returns this answer. Otherwise, it answers yes. This

---

Algorithm 1. Any-time intersection repair instance query answering.

Procedure IC($\mathcal{K}$,q)   ($\mathcal{K}$ inconsistent *DL-Lite$_{Horn}$* KB, q instance query)

  1: $\mathcal{U} \leftarrow \mathcal{K}$
  2: ALL-MINAS($\mathcal{H}_{\mathcal{K}}$,$q$)
  3: **return** "yes"

Procedure ALL-MINAS($\mathcal{H}_{\mathcal{K}}$,$q$)

  1: $\mathcal{M} \leftarrow$ a MinA in $\mathcal{H}_{\mathcal{K}}$
  2: $\mathcal{U} \leftarrow \mathcal{U} \setminus \mathcal{M}$
  3: **if** $\mathcal{U} \not\models q$ **then return** "no"
  4: **for** $1 \leq i \leq |\mathcal{M}|$ **do**
  5:      compute $\mathcal{H}_i$ from $\mathcal{M}$
  6:      **if** there is a path from an individual node to $w_\perp$ in $\mathcal{H}_i$ **then**
  7:          ALL-MINAS($\mathcal{H}_i$,q)

---

algorithm can be stopped at any time, in which case, only an (upper) approximation of $\bigcap_{\mathcal{R} \in \mathsf{Rep}_{\mathcal{K}}} \mathcal{R}$ is computed. Although the answer (yes) in this case is not guaranteed to be correct, the approximation gets tighter in polynomial intervals.

We now turn our attention to inconsistency-tolerant instance query answering when repairs are limited to removing assertions from the ABox only.

4   Instance Checking Under ABox Repairs

Answering inconsistency-tolerant instance queries under ABox repairs has been shown to be harder, in terms of computational complexity, to standard instance query answering over KBs [6–8]. The blame for this increase in complexity is often laid on the exponential number of repairs available. We argue that the issue goes deeper than this argument suggests showing that brave and cautious instance checking are hard already for KBs having polynomially many ABox repairs. One reason behind this result is the fact that even knowing whether a set of repairs is equal to $\mathsf{Rep}_{\mathcal{K}}$ is computationally expensive.[2]

Definition 8. *Let $\mathcal{K}$ be a KB and $\mathfrak{R}$ a set of ABox repairs of $\mathcal{K}$. The problem* ALL-REPS *consists on deciding whether $\mathfrak{R} = \mathsf{Rep}_{\mathcal{K}}$.*

Theorem 9. ALL-REPS *is coNP-complete.*

Proof. We prove coNP-hardness through a reduction from the negation of the following NP-complete problem [31]: given a monotone Boolean formula φ (that is, a propositional formula without negations) and a set $\mathfrak{V}$ of valuations of the variables in φ, decide whether there exists a maximal valuation $\mathcal{V}$ of the variables in φ that *falsifies* φ and does not contain any valuation in $\mathfrak{V}$.[3]

---

[2] Throughout this section, $\mathsf{Rep}_{\mathcal{K}}$ denotes the set of all ABox repairs.
[3] For simplicity, we identify a propositional valuation $\mathcal{V}$ with the set of variables that it makes true.

Given an instance $\varphi, \mathfrak{V}$ of this problem, let sub be the set of all subformulas of φ, and csub the subset of sub not containing any propositional variable. For each $\psi \in$ sub, we create a concept name A_ψ, and for every $\psi \in$ csub define the TBox

$$\mathcal{T}_\psi := \begin{cases} \{A_{\xi_1} \sqcap A_{\xi_2} \sqsubseteq A_\psi\} & \text{if } \psi = \xi_1 \wedge \xi_2 \\ \{A_{\xi_1} \sqsubseteq A_\psi, A_{\xi_2} \sqsubseteq A_\psi\} & \text{if } \psi = \xi_1 \vee \xi_2. \end{cases}$$

Let now

$$\mathcal{T}_{\varphi,\mathfrak{V}} := \bigcup_{\psi \in \mathsf{csub}} \mathcal{T}_\psi \cup \{A_\varphi \sqsubseteq \bot\}$$

$$\mathcal{A}_{\varphi,\mathfrak{V}} := \{A_x(a) \mid x \text{ is a variable from } \varphi\}.$$

It is easy to see that $\mathfrak{R} := \{(\mathcal{T}_{\varphi,\mathfrak{V}}, \{A_x(a) \mid x \in \mathcal{W}\}) \mid \mathcal{W} \in \mathfrak{V}\}$ is the set of all ABox repairs of $(\mathcal{T}_{\varphi,\mathfrak{V}}, \mathcal{A}_{\varphi,\mathfrak{V}})$ iff every maximal valuation falsifying φ contains some $\mathcal{W} \in \mathfrak{V}$. $\qquad\square$

Since all repairs can be computed in exponential time, e.g. by testing all possible sub-KBs, this theorem intuitively means that there exist KBs that have polynomially many repairs, but finding them all requires super-polynomial time. In terms of enumeration complexity theory, the set of all repairs cannot be computed in *output polynomial time* [17].

Obviously, Theorem 9 does not imply that inconsistency-tolerant semantics are necessarily hard on the number of repairs. However, it does give an indication that efficient algorithms cannot rely on finding all repairs. We strengthen previous results by showing that these problems remain hard even in the number of ABox repairs. First, we recall the notion of *repair-polynomial* from [22].

Definition 10. *An inconsistency-tolerant decision problem w.r.t. a KB $\mathcal{K}$ is called* repair-polynomial *if it can be solved by an algorithm that runs in polynomial time on the size of both $\mathcal{K}$ and $\mathsf{Rep}_{\mathcal{K}}$.*

Theorem 11. *Cautious instance checking w.r.t. ABox repairs is not repair-polynomial, unless* P = NP.

Proof. We show this result through a reduction similar to the one presented in the proof of Theorem 9. Given φ and $\mathfrak{V}$, we construct the TBoxes $\mathcal{T}_\psi$ and the ABox $\mathcal{A}_{\varphi,\mathfrak{V}}$ as in the forementioned proof. But now we set

$$\mathcal{T}'_{\varphi,\mathfrak{V}} := \bigcup_{\psi \in \mathsf{csub}} \mathcal{T}_\psi \cup \{A_\varphi \sqsubseteq \bot\} \cup \{\bigsqcap_{x \in W} A_x \sqsubseteq B \mid \mathcal{W} \in \mathfrak{V}\},$$

where B is a fresh concept name. Then a is a cautious instance of B w.r.t. $\mathcal{K}_\varphi := (\mathcal{T}'_{\varphi,\mathfrak{V}}, \mathcal{A}_{\varphi,\mathfrak{V}})$ under ABox repairs iff every maximal valuation falsifying φ contains some $\mathcal{W} \in \mathfrak{V}$. Notice that $(\mathcal{T}'_{\varphi,\mathfrak{V}}, \mathcal{A}_{\varphi,\mathfrak{V}})$ has as many ABox repairs as φ has maximal valuations falsifying it.

Suppose now that brave instance checking was repair-polynomial. Then, there would be an algorithm for solving it that would run in time bounded by $p(\mathcal{K}, |\mathsf{Rep}_\mathcal{K}|)$, where p is a polynomial. Then, we can decide whether there is a new maximal valuation falsifying φ by running this algorithm for time $p(\mathcal{K}_\varphi, |\mathsf{Rep}_{\mathcal{K}_\varphi}|)$. If it answers *no* or does not finish in that time bound, then a new valuation exists. Otherwise, the no new valuation exists. □

A similar method can be used to prove that brave instance checking is not repair-polynomial either.

Theorem 12. *Brave instance checking w.r.t. ABox repairs is not repair-polynomial, unless* P = NP.

Proof. We use an idea similar to the proof of Theorem 11, but using a reduction from the following NP-complete problem [5,10,11]: given a monotone Boolean formula φ and a set $\mathfrak{V}$ of valuations, decide whether there exists a minimal valuation $\mathcal{V}$ that *satisfies* φ and does not contain any valuation in $\mathfrak{V}$.[4]

Given an instance $\varphi, \mathfrak{V}$ of this problem, we construct the TBoxes $\mathcal{T}_\psi, \psi \in \mathsf{csub}$ and the ABox $\mathcal{A}_{\varphi,\mathfrak{V}}$ as in the proof of Theorem 9. We define

$$\mathcal{T}''_{\varphi,\mathfrak{V}} := \bigcup_{\psi \in \mathsf{csub}} \mathcal{T}_\psi \cup \{ \textstyle\bigsqcap_{x \in W} A_x \sqsubseteq \bot \mid W \in \mathfrak{V} \}.$$

Then, a is a brave instance of A_φ iff there exists a valuation satisfying φ that does not contain any $W \in \mathfrak{V}$. Using the same argument from the proof of Theorem 11, this shows that brave instance checking is not repair-polynomial. □

To the best of our efforts, we have not been able to find a similar hardness result for IR instance checking. However, it is possible to show that the any-time method described in the previous section cannot work when dealing with ABox repairs. The reason behind this negative result is that ABox MinAs cannot be enumerated with polynomial delay. In fact, they cannot be enumerated in output polynomial time.

Theorem 13. *Given an inconsistent KB $\mathcal{K}$ and a set $\mathfrak{M}$ of ABox MinAs of $\mathcal{K}$, deciding whether $\mathfrak{M} = \mathsf{Min}_\mathcal{K}$ is coNP-complete.*

Proof. We show hardness through a reduction from the same NP-complete problem used in the proof of Theorem 12.

Given an instance $\varphi, \mathfrak{V}$ of this problem, we construct $\mathcal{T}_{\varphi,\mathfrak{V}}$ and $\mathcal{A}_{\varphi,\mathfrak{V}}$ as in the proof of Theorem 9. Then, $\mathfrak{M} := \{(\mathcal{T}_{\varphi,\mathfrak{V}}, \{A_x(a) \mid x \in W\}) \mid W \in \mathfrak{V}\}$ is the set of all ABox MinA of $(\mathcal{T}_{\varphi,\mathfrak{V}}, \mathcal{A}_{\varphi,\mathfrak{V}})$ iff every minimal valuation satisfying φ contains some $W \in \mathfrak{V}$. □

Using standard techniques from enumeration complexity (see e.g. [19]), it is easy to show that Theorem 13 implies the impossibility of enumerating in output polynomial time.

---

[4] One can think of this problem as the dual of the one considered in the proof of Theorem 9.

Corollary 14. *All ABox MinAs of an inconsistent DL-Lite$_{Horn}$ KB cannot be enumerated in output polynomial time (unless* P = NP*).*

5   Conclusions

We have studied the complexity of answering inconsistency-tolerant instance queries under different semantics considered in the literature for the description logic *DL-Lite$_{Horn}$*. To the best of our knowledge, we are the first to consider any case of inconsistent-tolerant query answering problems under KB repairs. In the literature, the TBox is typically considered to be correct and fixed [20,21,23,24, 32,35].

We have shown that considering KB repairs reduces the complexity of inconsistency-tolerant instance checking. Indeed, although cautious and IR instance checking is shown to be intractable, the brave semantics can be verified in polynomial time in this case. Moreover, we provided an any-time algorithm for verifying IR instances. The algorithm is based on enumerating all MinAs with polynomial delay, and verifying that the complement of their union (which increasingly approximates the intersection of all repairs) still entails the desired instance query. A simple consequence of this algorithm is that IR instance checking is *MinA-polynomial*; that is, it can be solved in time polynomial on the size of the KB and the number of MinAs.

For the cautious semantics, it remains open whether instance checking w.r.t. KB repairs is repair-polynomial or MinA-polynomial. Given recent work on the enumeration of maximal consistent subformulae of a Horn formula [26], it is likely that repairs in *DL-Lite$_{Horn}$* can be enumerated with polynomial delay, which would suggest a repair-polynomial algorithm for cautious instance checking. In practical terms, however, a MinA-polynomial algorithm would be more interesting. Indeed, empirical analyses have shown that realistic ontologies typically contain very few MinAs, but a very large number of repairs [2,3,22].

When restricting to ABox repairs, we have shown that the causes for hardness for the inconsistent-tolerant semantics go beyond the sheer number of repairs available, as suggested in previous work. We have shown that brave and cautious instance checking are not repair-polynomial. This means that these problems may take super-polynomial time, even for KBs that have a polynomial number of repairs. In addition, the any-time algorithm proposed for IR instance checking under KB repairs cannot work for ABox repairs, since ABox MinAs cannot be enumerated in output polynomial time, much less with a polynomial delay.

The study of repair-polynomial and MinA-polynomial algorithms is much in the spirit of parameterized complexity theory [9]. In this context, *repair-polynomial* is analogous to *fixed-parameter tractability* where the number of repairs is the fixed parameter. It thus makes sense to try to understand the precise parameterized complexity class to which these problems belong. Dually, it would be interesting to find other meaningful parameters under which tractability can be regained.

Another important open question is the effect on the complexity when more complex queries, such as conjunctive queries, are considered instead of the simple instance queries that were the scope of this paper. We conjecture that brave and cautious conjunctive query answering is not repair-polynomial even under KB repairs. A thorough analysis of this case will be the focus of future work.

We conclude by highlighting that there exist other inconsistency-tolerant semantics beyond the three studied in this paper; see [8] for some examples. These differ mainly on the properties of the repairs that are considered for making an inference. If our conjecture is correct and all KB repairs from a $DL\text{-}Lite_{Horn}$ KB can be enumerated with polynomial delay, then most of these semantics will be repair-polynomial under KB repairs. However, this result is unlikely to be helpful in practice. Thus, in future work we will focus on developing specialized techniques and finding special cases for which inconsistency-tolerant instance checking—and conjunctive query answering in general—remains feasible.

References

1. Arenas, M., Bertossi, L.E., Chomicki, J.: Consistent query answers in inconsistent databases. In: Vianu, V., Papadimitriou, C.H. (eds.) Proceedings of the Eighteenth ACM SIGACT-SIGMOD-SIGART Symposium on Principles of Database Systems (PODS 1999), pp. 68–79. ACM Press (1999). http://doi.acm.org/10.1145/303976. 303983

2. Arif, M.F., Mencía, C., Ignatiev, A., Manthey, N., Peñaloza, R., Marques-Silva, J.: BEACON: an efficient SAT-based tool for debugging $\mathcal{EL}^+$ ontologies. In: Creignou, N., Le Berre, D. (eds.) SAT 2016. LNCS, vol. 9710, pp. 521–530. Springer, Cham (2016). doi:10.1007/978-3-319-40970-2_32

3. Arif, M.F., Mencía, C., Marques-Silva, J.: Efficient axiom pinpointing with EL2MCS. In: Hölldobler, S., Krötzsch, M., Peñaloza, R., Rudolph, S. (eds.) KI 2015. LNCS, vol. 9324, pp. 225–233. Springer, Cham (2015). doi:10.1007/ 978-3-319-24489-1_17

4. Artale, A., Calvanese, D., Kontchakov, R., Zakharyaschev, M.: The DL-Lite family and relations. J. Artif. Intell. Res. **36**, 1–69 (2009)

5. Baader, F., Peñaloza, R., Suntisrivaraporn, B.: Pinpointing in the description logic $\mathcal{EL}^+$. In: Hertzberg, J., Beetz, M., Englert, R. (eds.) KI 2007. LNAI, vol. 4667, pp. 52–67. Springer, Heidelberg (2007)

6. Bienvenu, M.: On the complexity of consistent query answering in the presence of simple ontologies. In: Hoffmann, J., Selman, B. (eds.) Proceedings of the Twenty-Sixth AAAI Conference on Artificial Intelligence (AAAI-12). AAAI Press (2012). http://www.aaai.org/ocs/index.php/AAAI/AAAI12/paper/view/4928

7. Bienvenu, M., Bourgaux, C., Goasdoué, F.: Querying inconsistent description logic knowledge bases under preferred repair semantics. In: Brodley, C.E., Stone, P. (eds.) Proceedings of the Twenty-Eighth AAAI Conference on Artificial Intelligence (AAAI-14), pp. 996–1002. AAAI Press (2014). http://www.aaai.org/ocs/ index.php/AAAI/AAAI14/paper/view/8231

8. Bienvenu, M., Rosati, R.: Tractable approximations of consistent query answering for robust ontology-based data access. In: Rossi, F. (ed.) Proceedings of the 23rd International Joint Conference on Artificial Intelligence (IJCAI-13), pp. 775–781. AAAI Press (2013). http://www.aaai.org/ocs/index.php/IJCAI/IJCAI13/paper/ view/6904

9. Downey, R.G., Fellows, M.: Parameterized Complexity. Monographs in Computer Science. Springer, New York (1999)
10. Eiter, T., Gottlob, G.: Identifying the minimal transversals of a hypergraph and related problems. Technical report. CD-TR 91/16, Christian Doppler Laboratory for Expert Systems, TU Vienna (1991)
11. Eiter, T., Gottlob, G.: Identifying the minimal transversals of a hypergraph and related problems. SIAM J. Comput. **24**(6), 1278–1304 (1995)
12. Eiter, T., Lukasiewicz, T., Predoiu, L.: Generalized consistent query answering under existential rules. In: Baral, C., Delgrande, J.P., Wolter, F. (eds.) Proceedings of the 15th International Conference on Principles of Knowledge Representation and Reasoning (KR 2016), pp. 359–368. AAAI Press (2016)
13. Fredman, M.L., Khachiyan, L.: On the complexity of dualization of monotone disjunctive normal forms. J. Algorithms **21**(3), 618–628 (1996)
14. Gottlob, G., Malizia, E.: Achieving new upper bounds for the hypergraph duality problem through logic. The Computing Research Repository (CoRR) abs/1407.2912 (2014). http://arxiv.org/abs/1407.2912
15. Hagen, M.: Algorithmic and Computational Complexity Issues of MONET. Ph.D. dissertation, Institut für Informatik, Friedrich-Schiller-Universität Jena (2008)
16. Horridge, M., Parsia, B., Sattler, U.: Explaining inconsistencies in OWL ontologies. In: Godo, L., Pugliese, A. (eds.) SUM 2009. LNCS, vol. 5785, pp. 124–137. Springer, Heidelberg (2009). doi:10.1007/978-3-642-04388-8_11
17. Johnson, D.S., Yannakakis, M., Papadimitriou, C.H.: On generating all maximal independent sets. Inform. Process. Lett. **27**(3), 119–123 (1988)
18. Kalyanpur, A., Parsia, B., Sirin, E., Cuenca-Grau, B.: Repairing unsatisfiable concepts in OWL ontologies. In: Sure, Y., Domingue, J. (eds.) ESWC 2006. LNCS, vol. 4011, pp. 170–184. Springer, Heidelberg (2006). doi:10.1007/11762256_15
19. Kavvadias, D.J., Sideri, M., Stavropoulos, E.C.: Generating all maximal models of a boolean expression. Inform. Process. Lett. **74**(3–4), 157–162 (2000). http://dx.doi.org/10.1016/S0020-0190(00)00023-5
20. Lembo, D., Lenzerini, M., Rosati, R., Ruzzi, M., Savo, D.F.: Inconsistency-tolerant semantics for description logics. In: Hitzler, P., Lukasiewicz, T. (eds.) RR 2010. LNCS, vol. 6333, pp. 103–117. Springer, Heidelberg (2010). doi:10.1007/978-3-642-15918-3_9
21. Lembo, D., Lenzerini, M., Rosati, R., Ruzzi, M., Savo, D.F.: Inconsistency-tolerant query answering in ontology-based data access. J. Web Semant. **33**, 3–29 (2015). http://dx.doi.org/10.1016/j.websem.2015.04.002
22. Ludwig, M., Peñaloza, R.: Error-tolerant reasoning in the description logic $\mathcal{EL}$. In: Fermé, E., Leite, J. (eds.) JELIA 2014. LNCS, vol. 8761, pp. 107–121. Springer, Cham (2014). doi:10.1007/978-3-319-11558-0_8
23. Lukasiewicz, T., Martinez, M.V., Pieris, A., Simari, G.I.: From classical to consistent query answering under existential rules. In: Bonet, B., Koenig, S. (eds.) Proceedings of the Twenty-Ninth AAAI Conference on Artificial Intelligence (AAAI-15), pp. 1546–1552. AAAI Press (2015). http://www.aaai.org/ocs/index.php/AAAI/AAAI15/paper/view/9817
24. Lukasiewicz, T., Martinez, M.V., Simari, G.I.: Inconsistency handling in datalog +/- ontologies. In: Raedt, L.D., Bessière, C., Dubois, D., Doherty, P., Frasconi, P., Heintz, F., Lucas, P.J.F. (eds.) Proceedings of the 20th European Conference on Artificial Intelligence (ECAI-2012). Frontiers in Artificial Intelligence and Applications, vol. 242, pp. 558–563. IOS Press (2012). http://dx.doi.org/10.3233/978-1-61499-098-7-558

25. Marino, A.: Analysis and Enumeration: Algorithms for Biological Graphs. Springer, New York (2015)
26. Marques-Silva, J., Ignatiev, A., Mencía, C., Peñaloza, R.: Efficient reasoning for inconsistent horn formulae. In: Michael, L., Kakas, A. (eds.) JELIA 2016. LNCS, vol. 10021, pp. 336–352. Springer, Cham (2016). doi:10.1007/978-3-319-48758-8_22
27. Nielsen, L.R., Andersen, K.A., Pretolani, D.: Finding the K shortest hyperpaths. Comput. Oper. Res. **32**(6), 1477–1497 (2005)
28. Parsia, B., Sirin, E., Kalyanpur, A.: Debugging OWL ontologies. In: Ellis, A., Hagino, T. (eds.) Proceedings of the 14th International Conference on World Wide Web (WWW 2005), pp. 633–640. ACM (2005)
29. Peñaloza, R., Sertkaya, B.: Complexity of axiom pinpointing in the dl-lite family of description logics. In: Coelho, H., Studer, R., Wooldridge, M. (eds.) Proceedings of the 19th European Conference on Artificial Intelligence (ECAI-2010). Frontiers in Artificial Intelligence and Applications, vol. 215, pp. 29–34. IOS Press (2010)
30. Peñaloza, R., Sertkaya, B.: Understanding the complexity of axiom pinpointing in lightweight description logics. Artificial Intelligence (2017, to appear)
31. Peñaloza, R.: Axiom pinpointing in description logics and beyond. Ph.D. thesis, Technische Universität Dresden (2009). http://nbn-resolving.de/urn:nbn:de:bsz:14-qucosa-24743
32. Rosati, R.: On the complexity of dealing with inconsistency in description logic ontologies, pp. 1057–1062. AAAI Press (2011). http://dx.doi.org/10.5591/978-1-57735-516-8/IJCAI11-181
33. Schlobach, S., Cornet, R.: Non-standard reasoning services for the debugging of description logic terminologies. In: Gottlob, G., Walsh, T. (eds.) Proceedings of the 18th International Joint Conference on Artificial Intelligence (IJCAI-03), pp. 355–362. Morgan Kaufmann (2003)
34. Schlobach, S., Huang, Z., Cornet, R., Harmelen, F.: Debugging incoherent terminologies. J. Autom. Reasoning **39**(3), 317–349 (2007)
35. Tsalapati, E., Stoilos, G., Stamou, G.B., Koletsos, G.: Efficient query answering over expressive inconsistent description logics, pp. 1279–1285. AAAI Press (2016). http://www.ijcai.org/Abstract/16/185

ArgQL: A Declarative Language for Querying Argumentative Dialogues

Dimitra Zografistou$^{(\boxtimes)}$, Giorgos Flouris, and Dimitris Plexousakis

Foundation for Research and Technology, Heraklion, Greece
{dzograf,fgeo,dp}@ics.forth.gr

Abstract. We introduce ArgQL, a declarative query language, which performs on a data model designed according to the principles of argumentation. Its syntax is based on Cypher (language for graph databases) and SPARQL 1.1 and is adjusted for querying dialogues, composed by sets of arguments and their interrelations. We use formal semantics to show how queries in ArgQL match against data in the argumentation model. The execution is realized by translating both data and queries into standard models for storage and querying.

1 Introduction

The recent evolution of social media and debate forums has caused a reshaping of the Web, turning it into a worldwide podium, wherein humans accommodate their inherent need for socializing and expressing themselves. Due to the easiness with which users can upload digital content, as well as the ability for their involvement in public debates[1], online communities have become populated with opinions and beliefs about political or social topics, with criticisms or consultations and with reviews on products, services etc.

The process of human argumentation has been an object of longstanding theoretical studies, which have found their way into computational models [7,13] of the area of argumentation. Roughly, these models address the representation and reasoning requirements of drawing conclusions through the process of exchanging arguments [9], with part of them to also be taking into account relevant cognitive features like preferences [1], beliefs and intentions [2]. However, the process of identifying arguments according to certain criteria and allowing for navigation in a graph of interconnected arguments has been given less attention.

To cover this gap, we introduce *ArgQL* (Argumentation Query Language) a declarative language, designed on a data model for argumentation. ArgQL constitutes a first step to understand the informational and theoretical requirements of searching in debates. Yet, there are still miscellaneous obstacles until being able to query real debates on the web, with processing textual information to be the most difficult to overcome. The fact that there is a considerable amount of people involved in argumentation, amplifies the significance for a language with relevant terminology. ArgQL offers a simple and quite elegant way to express

---

[1] http://www.debate.org.

S. Costantini et al. (Eds.): RuleML+RR 2017, LNCS 10364, pp. 230–237, 2017.
DOI: 10.1007/978-3-319-61252-2_16

queries of the form: "How an argument with a given conclusion is attacked?". To the best of our knowledge, this is the first effort to approach argumentation from the scope of data models and query languages.

In this document, we show some initial results. The requirements we set for ArgQL, led us use a hybrid syntax, with features from both SQL-like and graph database query languages. The semantics of ArgQL are also presented. As for the execution, we currently deal with the technical as well as the theoretical issues lying in the translation of the data model and ArgQL, into RDF and SPARQL.

2   Related Work

There are no equivalent languages to directly compare the potentials of ArgQL. Nevertheless, considerable efforts have been invested, to make steps closer to the realization of the vision for a globally interconnected and computable web of opinions [3,8]. A wide number of tools have been developed, that facilitate the participation in online debates. A comprehensive review is found in [15]. Some of them offer better visualization and exploration, such as DebateGraph[2], others support reasoning like Parmenides [5], while others allow for user engagement, like Debatewise[3].

AIF (Argument Interchange Format) [6] is an RDF ontology for arguments and is considered to be the cornerstone to the realization of the opinion web. Accompanied with a set of mappings from the different argument representations [4,16,17] to its concepts, AIF became the interlingua, which bridges arguments among the various tools. These data are gathered into a public database AIFdb [11] and queried by several search engines, like ArgDF [14]. DiscourseDB[4], is another equally interesting platform for exploring dialogues, with the extra feature of dialogues summarization.

To sum up, there is a wide number of systems that offer visualization and semantic search in dialogues. For all of them, the process of querying dialogues, merely constitutes an application field for the traditional query languages like SQL or SPARQL. On the other hand, ArgQL highlights the different information needs of such a process and focuses on designing solutions, that cover these requirements. In the future, it could be integrated into the existing argumentation tools enriching them with extra semantics and capabilities.

3   A Formal Model for Arguments

Our argumentation model is defined by the tuple $\mathcal{L} = (\mathcal{P}, -, \simeq, \rightarrow)$. $\mathcal{P}$ is an infinite set of propositions and $\wp(\mathcal{P})$ its powerset.

The mapping $- : \mathcal{P} \rightarrow \mathcal{P}$, represents the notion of *contrariness*. We say that, two propositions $x, y \in \mathcal{P}$ are conflicting iff $x = \bar{y}$. Contrariness mapping is

---

[2] http://debategraph.org/.
[3] http://debatewise.org/.
[4] http://discoursedb.org/.

symmetric (if $x = \overline{y}$, then $y = \overline{x}$), anti-reflexive ($x \neq \overline{x}$) and non transitive (if $x = \overline{y}$ and $y = \overline{z}$, with $x \neq z$, then $x \neq \overline{z}$). Given a subset $P' \subset \mathcal{P}$, we say that P' is *inconsistent* if $\exists x, y \in P'$, s.t. $y = \overline{x}$, otherwise it is *consistent*.

The mapping $\simeq \subseteq \mathcal{P} \times \mathcal{P}$ captures the *equivalence* on the informational content between two propositions $x, y \in \mathcal{P}$ and we write it as $x \simeq y$. Equivalence retains the following properties: *(i) Reflexivity:* $x \simeq x$ *(ii) Symmetry:* if $x \simeq y$, then $y \simeq x$ *(iii) Transitivity:* if $x \simeq y$ and $y \simeq z$, then $x \simeq z$.

Mappings $-$ and $\simeq$ will be later used to define the relations between arguments. Given that they serve opposite representation needs, in order to resolve the ambiguities caused by their coexistence in the same model, we demand the satisfaction of the following constraints: $\forall (x, y, z) \in \mathcal{P}$ *(i)* if $x \simeq y$ then $y \neq \overline{x}$. *(ii)* if $x \simeq y$, then $\overline{x} \simeq \overline{y}$ and *(iii)* if $x \simeq y$ and $y = \overline{z}$, then $x = \overline{z}$

Finally, with $\rightarrow$ we denote the deduction from a set of propositions to a conclusion. For example, when we write "$a, b \rightarrow c$", we say that propositions a, b imply proposition c. Such expressions form *arguments*. In particular:

Definition 1 (Argument). *An argument is a tuple $a = \langle pr, c \rangle$, where $pr \in \wp(\mathcal{P})$ is a finite, consistent set, called premise set and $c \in \mathcal{P}$ is the main claim of an argument, called conclusion. It holds that $pr \rightarrow c$ and $c \notin pr$. With $\mathcal{A}$ we refer to the infinite set of arguments.*

The notions of contrariness and equivalence between propositions, allow us to define two types of relations between arguments, *attack* and *support*, respectively. The infinite set $\mathcal{R} \subseteq \mathcal{A} \times \mathcal{A}$ keeps any relation between two arguments. Given a relation $r = (a_1, a_2) \in R$, we denote by $src(r) = a_1$ the source argument of r and by $dst(r) = a_2$ its destination.

Definition 2 (Attack). *Attack relation is defined as: $R^a = \{(a_1, a_2) \mid a_1, a_2 \in \mathcal{A}, a_1 = \langle pr_1, c_1 \rangle, a_2 = \langle pr_2, c_2 \rangle$ and $c_1 = \overline{c_2}$ (rebut) or $\overline{c_1} \in pr_2$ (undercut)$\}$*

Definition 3 (Support). *Support relation is defined as: $R^s = \{(a_1, a_2) \mid a_1, a_2 \in \mathcal{A}, a_1 = \langle pr_1, c_1 \rangle, a_2 = \langle pr_2, c_2 \rangle$ and $c_1 \simeq c_2$ (endorse) or $\exists p \in pr_2$, s.t. $p \simeq c_1$ (backing)$\}$*

It holds that $R = R^a \cup R^s$. It is also provable that $R^a \cap R^s = \emptyset$, but for the sake of space, the proof is omitted. A knowledge base conformed to the current model has the form of a graph and we call it debate graph. In particular:

Definition 4 (Debate graph). *A debate graph is a tuple $D = (A', R')$, where $A' \subset \mathcal{A}$ is the set of argument nodes, while the set of edges R', holding the relations between arguments in A', is defined as $R' = \{(a_1, a_2) \mid a_1, a_2 \in A'$ and $(a_1, a_2) \in \mathcal{R}\}$.*

The infinite set of all possible debate graphs is denoted as $\mathcal{D}$. We define any *path* in a debate graph as follows:

Definition 5 (Path). *Given a debate graph $D = \langle A', R' \rangle$, and two arguments $a, b \in A'$, a path between a and b denoted as $P^D_{a \rightarrow b}$ is a sequence of relations $r_1, r_2 \ldots, r_n \in R'$, where $n \geq 1$, $src(r_1) = a$, $dst(r_n) = b$ and $\forall i \in \{1, .., n-1\}$ it holds that $dst(r_i) = src(r_{i+1})$. A path is written as $r_1/r_2/ \ldots /r_n$.*

4   ArgQL Specification

4.1   Syntax

The syntax of ArgQL is Cypher-like[5], a language for the Neo4j graph database. The main idea is that it supports pattern expressions matching against data in a knowledge base, designed according to the model described in Sect. 3. Like any query language, ArgQL uses variables to bind data and they are prefixed with ?. Let $\mathcal{V}$ be the infinite set of variables. We assume the set $PV = \mathcal{P} \cup \mathcal{V}$. Constant values for the propositions in $\mathcal{P}$ are represented as literals and they are given in quotes. Figure 1 shows the BNF grammar. Note that, at this stage of our work, we have not studied how the results of the query are returned, thus the syntax does not contain any *select*-like statement, yet. In the future, we intent to allow for returning more complex structures, such as complete parts of dialogues. Reserved keywords of the language are in bold. They are not case sensitive, but for the sake of space the respective rules have been omitted.

```
        query ::= 'MATCH' pattern(',' pattern) *
      pattern ::= argpattern (pathpattern argpattern)*
   argpattern ::= variable | '<' premisepattern ',' proposition '>'
premisepattern ::= variable ( premisefilter ) ?
 premisefilter ::= '[' ( '/' | '.' | '!' | '=' | '!=') propositionset ']'
 propositionset ::= '{' proposition (' . ' proposition)* '}'
  pathpattern ::= path ('/' path) *
         path ::= relsequence | '(' relsequence ')' length
  relsequence ::= relation ('/' relation )*
     relation ::= ('ATTACK'|'SUPPORT'|'REBUT'|'UNDERCUT'|'ENDORSE'|'BACK' )
       length ::= '+' | '*' num
  proposition ::= variable | string
     variable ::= '?' ('a'..'z'|'A'..'Z')('a'..'z'|'A'..'Z'|'_'|'o'..'9')*
       string ::= '"'.*?'"';
          num ::= 'o' .. '9' +;
```

Fig. 1. Extended BNF for ArgQL

The main body of the query is included inside the *match* clause. ArgQL allows to state multiple pattern expressions. A single pattern expression(rule *pattern*) consists either of one argument pattern, or it can be followed by a sequence of alternations between path patterns and another argument pattern. Next we will discuss separately about the role of argument patterns and path patterns.

Argument patterns. They constitute fundamental elements of ArgQL, used to match arguments. Generally, argument patterns represent expressions like: find arguments with conclusion "some text", written as $\langle ?pr,$ *"some text"*$\rangle$, or find arguments with the proposition "some text" in their premise set, that corresponds to the argument pattern $\langle ?pr[/\{$ *"some text"*$\}], ?c\rangle$.

---

[5] https://neo4j.com/developer/cypher-query-language/.

Typically an argument pattern ap can be either a single variable, which matches any argument in $\mathcal{A}$, or be of the form $ap = \langle pr([filter])?, c \rangle$, where $pr \in V$ and $c \in PV$. Variable pr matches the premise part of arguments and essentially it takes values from $\wp(\mathcal{P})$, whereas c matches the conclusion part and may be either a variable or a constant proposition value. The occurrence of the expression $[filter]$ is optional. When existed, it adds constraints on the premises. ArgQL supports a number of filters, that correspond to such constraints like the requirement for a premise set to include some given propositions, or the premise sets of two arguments to join etc. Later versions of the language will allow for multiple filters on a premise part, but for now, we consider only a single one. The following list presents the available filters. To formally describe them, we assume the set s included in the filter, with $s = \{p_1, \ldots p_n\}$, $p_i \in PV$ and $1 \leq i \leq n$.

Inclusion: $f_{incl} = \big[/s\big]$ Requirement for s to be included in pr.

Jointness: $f_{join} = \big[.s\big]$ The sets pr and s must have common elements.

Disjointness: $f_{disj} = \big[!s\big]$ The sets pr and s must be disjoint.

Equality: $f_{eq} = \big[=s\big]$ The sets pr and s must be exactly the same.

Inequality: $f_{ineq} = \big[!=s\big]$ The set pr must be different than s.

A matching instance of an argument pattern is an argument in $\mathcal{A}$. The cases where an argument pattern is a single variable, or it has the form $\langle ?pr, ?c \rangle$ are equal and they both match any argument in the knowledge base.

Path patterns. They are used to describe sequences of arguments that must be matched (and the relations that connect them). A match of such an expression is essentially a sub-graph from the debate graph. We exploit the syntax of SPARQL 1.1 [10] for property paths. In particular, a path pattern may indicate a path in two ways. The direct one represents a path pattern as a sequence of relations separated by the symbol '/' (e.g. *attack/undercut/support/...*). The indirect uses one of the '+', '*' numerical indicators to restrict the length of the path. Expression *path* '+' means one or more occurrences of *path* while the expression *path* '*'n, with $n \geq 1$, requires for exactly n repetitions of *path*. These two ways can be mixed in arbitrary ways to support many complex types of path patterns.

Next, we give some representative examples of the supported match expressions. The first captures a case from Dung semantics [7].

Q1. Find arguments which "defend" (attack their attackers) all arguments with conclusion "cloning is immoral".

    match ?arg (attack/attack)+ <?pr, "cloning is immoral">

Q2. Match argument paths which include two sequences of the path attack/support and one more attack and result to an argument, whose premise set includes the proposition "cloning contributes positively to the field of artificial insemination".

    match ?arg (attack/support)*2/attack

    <?pr[/{"cloning contributes positively to the field of artificial

    insemination"}], ?c>

Q3. Match pairs of arguments whose premise sets join each other.

    match <?pr₁, ?c₁>, <?pr₂[.{?pr₁}], ?c₂>

4.2   Semantics

In this section we describe the semantics of ArgQL. We define the set $\mathcal{S} = \mathcal{P} \cup \wp(\mathcal{P}) \cup \mathcal{A}$ and a *mapping function* $\mu : \mathcal{S} \cup V \mapsto \mathcal{S}$, such that $\mu(x) = x, \forall x \in \mathcal{S}$. For simplicity we will abuse notation and use μ also for argument patterns. For example, given an argument pattern $ap = \langle pr[filter], c \rangle$, we denote by $\mu(ap)$ the argument obtained by the substitution of pr with $\mu(pr)$ and c with $\mu(c)$, for which, $\mu(pr)$ satisfies its filter if existed.

For the satisfiability of the filter f by the premise set, we restrict ourselves to those mappings for pr, for which $\mu(pr) \subset \wp(\mathcal{P})$. We write $\mu(pr) \vDash f$ to describe that the matching set of propositions satisfies f. In order to describe the semantics for $\vDash$, we will need the set s, as was defined before. In accordance with the argument pattern, we abuse notation also for s and write that $\mu(s) = \{\mu(p_1), \dots, \mu(p_n)\}$. The following list sets the conditions for each filter to be satisfied:

- for $f = f_{incl}$, $\mu(pr) \vDash f$ iff $\mu(s) \subseteq \mu(pr)$
- for $f = f_{eq}$, $\mu(pr) \vDash f$ iff $\mu(s) = \mu(pr)$
- for $f = f_{ineq}$, $\mu(pr) \vDash f$ iff $\mu(s) \neq \mu(pr)$
- for $f = f_{join}$, $\mu(pr) \vDash f$ iff $\mu(s) \cap \mu(pr) \neq \emptyset$
- for $f = f_{disj}$, $\mu(pr) \vDash f$ iff $\mu(s) \cap \mu(pr) = \emptyset$

Each path pattern p determines a set of all possible paths that could match with it. That set is denoted as $\odot p$. Essentially, if p has no length indicators, $\odot p$ has a single element, otherwise its cardinality is defined by the indicator. The set $\odot p$ is formally defined as:

Definition 6. *Let p, p', p'' path expressions. $\odot p$ is defined inductively as follows:*

- *If $p \in \{attack, support, undercut, rebut, endorse, back\}$ then: $\odot p = \{p\}$*
- *If $p = p'/p''$, then: $\odot p = \{p_1/p_2 \mid p_1 \in \odot p', p_2 \in \odot p''\}$*
- *If $p = p' * 1$, then: $\odot p = \{p_1 \mid p_1 \in \odot p'\}$*
- *If $p = p' * n$ and $n > 1$, then $\odot p = \{p_1/p_2 \mid p_1 \in \odot(p' * 1), p_2 \in \odot(p' * (n-1))\}$*
- *If $p = p'+$, then: $\odot p = \{p_1 \mid p_1 \in \odot p' * k$, for some $k \geq 1\}$*

A pattern expression e may have one of the forms: $e = ap$ or $e = ap\ pe\ e'$, with e' another pattern expression. We denote as $init(e) = ap$ the initial argument pattern for both cases. Next, we define the evaluation of a complete pattern expression e against a debate graph D.

Definition 7 (Evaluation). *Let a pattern expression e and a debate graph $D = \langle A', R' \rangle$. The evaluation of e against D, written as $\mathcal{E}val_D(e)$ is defined:*

- *If $e = ap$, with $ap = < pr[f_{ap}], c >$, then:*
  $\mathcal{E}val_D(ap) = \{\mu \mid \mu(pr) \vDash f_{ap}$ and $\mu(ap) \in A'\}$
- *If $e = ap\ pe\ e'$, then: $\mathcal{E}val_D(e) = \{\mu \mid \mu \in \mathcal{E}val_D(ap) \cap \mathcal{E}val_D(e')$ and $\exists p' = P^D_{\mu(ap) \to \mu(init(e'))}$ s.t. $p' \in \odot pe\}$*

4.3   Query Execution

To implement our language, we chose to leverage existing and well-optimized storage schemes and languages, in particular RDF and its associated query language, SPARQL 1.1. The reasons for our choice is that, first of all, our target scenario concerns the web, where RDF/SPARQL are the standard languages. Furthermore, RDF represents a graph data model and SPARQL 1.1 provides useful property paths. Finally, SPARQL is accompanied with well-defined semantics [12], which makes the transition from ArgQL to be straightforward.

Our implementation is ongoing work, so we just present the general idea here. First of all, concepts of the data model must be translated into an RDF scheme. In order to be compatible with the state of the art and the recent tendency of the argumentation community, we turn to the RDF representation of the AIF ontology [6]. AIF defines classes equivalent with the basic concepts of the argumentation model presented in Sect. 3. Each element in the tuple $\mathcal{L}$, is mapped to a particular set of triples in AIF. Next, ArgQL queries are translated into SPARQL and are executed against the translated data, which are now instances of AIF scheme. Each expression in the "match" clause in Fig. 1, corresponds to a different graph pattern in SPARQL. After the execution of SPARQL, RDF results are translated back into the expected form for the answers of ArgQL. The equivalence between the expected results and the results received by SPARQL has to be theoretically proved. To test the whole process of the execution in practice, we aim to perform it on the AIFdb corpora [11], an RDF knowledge base in AIF scheme, consisting of over 2,000 argument maps with over 30,000 individual nodes.

5   Research Plans and Conclusions

In this work we presented ArgQL, a query language for argumentation. The first version supports a core subset of queries and it refers to a minimal data model which consists only of arguments and their interrelations. We have shown the syntax, its semantics and we briefly described the idea of its implementation.

Our future plans include the completion of both theoretic and technical issues of translation, as well as the experimentation on real datasets. Next, we intent to enrich our data model with more complicated concepts, e.g. topics of discussion and adjust the language specification to the new features. In subsequent time, ArgQL will be integrated with reasoning mechanisms, to allow for dynamic queries, which e.g. will capture well-known argumentation semantics [7], compute acceptability etc. with simpler (in terms of syntax) queries.

In order to tackle more practical, from the web perspective issues, we are going to incorporate facilities that allow "smart" searching within the textual content of argument, such as advanced keyword-searching and content-based searching, imprecise textual mappings (e.g., taking into account synonyms, or typos in the text), exploratory/navigational capabilities etc. Finally, we plan to determine formally the expressive power and complexity of ArgQL.

Aknowledgements. This work is funded by the Institute of Computer Science (ICS) of the Foundation for Research and Technology - Hellas (FO.R.T.H.). We also thank Dr. Theodore Patkos for the insightful discussions about the topic.

References

1. Bench-capon, T.J.M., Doutre, S., Dunne, P.E.: Value-based argumentation frameworks. In:Artificial Intelligence, pp. 444–453 (2002)
2. Tudor Berariu. An argumentation framework for BDI agents. In: Zavoral, F., Jung, J., Badica, C. (eds.) Intelligent Distributed Computing VII. SCI, vol 511, pp. 343–354. Springer, Cham (2014). doi:10.1007/978-3-319-01571-2_40
3. Bex, F., Lawrence, J., Snaith, M., Reed, C.: Implementing the argument web. Commun. ACM **56**(10), 66–73 (2013)
4. Bex, F., Prakken, J., Reed, C.: A formal analysis of the AIF in terms of the aspic framework. In: Proceedings of the 2010 Conference on Computational Models of Argument: Proceedings of COMMA 2010, Amsterdam, The Netherlands, pp. 99–110. IOS Press (2010)
5. Cartwright, D., Atkinson, K., Bench-capon, T.: Supporting argument in edemocracy. In: Proceedings of the Third Conference on Electronic Democracy (EDEM 2009), pp. 15–160 (2009)
6. Chesñevar, C., McGinnis, J., Modgil, S., Rahwan, I., Reed, C., Simari, G., South, M., Vreeswijk, G., Willmott, S.: Towards an argument interchange format. Knowl. Eng. Rev. **21**(4), 293–316 (2006)
7. Dung, P.M.: On the acceptability of arguments and its fundamental role in nonmonotonic reasoning, logic programming and n-person games. Artif. Intell. **77**(2), 321–357 (1995)
8. Flouris, G., Bikakis, A., Theodore, P., Plexousakis, D.: Globally interconnecting persuasive arguments: The vision of the persuasive web. Technical report, FORTH-ICS/TR-438 (2013)
9. García, A.J., Simari, G.R.: Defeasible logic programming: an argumentative approach. Theory Pract. Log. Program. **4**(2), 95–138 (2004)
10. Garlik, S.H., Seaborne, A., Prud'hommeaux, E.: SPARQL 1.1 Query Language. http://www.w3.org/TR/sparql11-query/
11. Lawrence, J., Reed, C.: AIFdb Corpora. Frontiers in Artificial Intelligence and Applications, pp. 465–466. IOS Press (2014)
12. Pérez, J., Arenas, M., Gutierrez, C.: Semantics and complexity of sparql. ACM Trans. Database Syst. **34**(3), 16:1–16:45 (2009)
13. Rahwan, I., Simari, G.R.: Argumentation in Artificial Intelligence, 1st edn. Springer Publishing Company, Incorporated (2009)
14. Rahwan, I., Zablith, F., Reed, C.: Laying the foundations for a world wide argument web. Artif. Intell. **171**(10–15), 897–921 (2007)
15. Schneider, J., Groza, T., Passant, A.: A review of argumentation for the social semantic web. Semant. web **4**(2), 159–218 (2013)
16. Toulmin, S.E.: The Uses of Argument. Cambridge University Press, July 2003
17. Walton, D.N.: Argumentation Schemes for Presumptive Reasoning. L, Erlbaum Associates (1996)

Author Index

Alberti, Marco 7
Alfonso, Enrique Matos 151
Arndt, Dörthe 22

Binnewies, Sebastian 37
Bisquert, Pierre 135
Briola, Daniela 53

Calvanese, Diego 70
Cantone, Domenico 87
Croitoru, Madalina 135

De Angelis, Emanuele 103
Dimou, Anastasia 22
Dumas, Marlon 70

Fioravanti, Fabio 103
Flouris, Giorgos 230
Frühwirth, Thom 119

Gall, Daniel 119
Gavanelli, Marco 7

Hecham, Abdelraouf 135

Lamma, Evelina 7

Maggi, Fabrizio M. 70
Mannens, Erik 22
Mascardi, Viviana 53
Meester, Ben De 22
Meilicke, Christian 168

Meo, Maria Chiara 103
Miettinen, Pauli 199
Montali, Marco 70
Moreno, Ginés 184
Muggleton, Stephen H. 1

Nicolosi-Asmundo, Marianna 87
Nolle, Andreas 168

Paramonov, Sergey 199
Paulheim, Heiko 168
Peñaloza, Rafael 215
Pettorossi, Alberto 103
Plexousakis, Dimitris 230
Proietti, Maurizio 103

Riaza, José A. 184
Riguzzi, Fabrizio 7
Ruffinelli, Daniel 168

Santamaria, Daniele Francesco 87
Stamou, Giorgos 151
Stepanova, Daria 199
Stuckenschmidt, Heiner 168

Verborgh, Ruben 22

Wang, Kewen 37

Zese, Riccardo 7
Zhuang, Zhiqiang 37
Zografistou, Dimitra 230

Printed in the United States
By Bookmasters